Spring 85

ON HOME AND THE WANDERER

A Journal of
Archetype
and
Culture

Spring 2011

SPRING JOURNAL
New Orleans, Louisiana

CONTENTS

ON HOME AND THE WANDERER

In Memoriam: Rafael López-Pedraza (1920-2011)
Axel Capriles M. .... *i*

Rediscovering Home: A Myth for Our Time
Hendrika de Vries 1

Home as Self, Home as Soul: The Wisdom and Narrative of Place
Robin van Löben Sels 17

In the Footsteps of Scheherazade, An Inspiring Image of Feminine Development and Creativity: Aisha's Story in Jungian and Transcultural Perspective
Valentina Lucia Zampieri 37

On Home and Identity: Following the Way of the Roma
Alexandra Fidyk 75

The Hope of Finding Home: Exploring the Wandering Complex
Elena Pourtova 103

Remain True to the Earth: Home and Wandering in Nietzsche
Paul Bishop 125

The Wonder of Wandering: Archetype, Myth, and Metaphor in William Faulkner's "The Bear"
Dennis Patrick Slattery 165

Cultural Tourism and Soul Care: Traveling to Recover the *Anima Mundi*
Kaj Noschis 187

Who Am I? India, Jung, and Me
Jörg Rasche 199

Sacred Travel, Divine Traveler
Julie A. Sgarzi 227

JUNGIANA

The Baynes Film of Jung's 1925-26 Expedition to East Africa
(with a Foreword by Diana Baynes Jansen)
Blake Burleson 247

THE GIEGERICH/ROMANYSHYN DEBATE:
CONTINUING RESPONSES

Wolfgang Giegerich: The Search for Psychological "Soul"
John Hoedl 305

The Giegerich/Romanyshyn Debate about Depth Psychology and Climate Change: No Soul in Nature?
Linda Buzzell 309

Giegerich, Romanyshyn, and the Eco-Apocalypse Witnesses-Only Club
Craig Chalquist 313

BOOK REVIEWS

The House of C. G. Jung: The History and Restoration of the Residence of Emma and Carl Gustav Jung-Rauschenbach by Andreas Jung, Regula Michel, Arthur Rüegg, Judith Rohrer, and Daniel Ganz and *At Home in the World: Sounds and Symmetries of Belonging* by John Hill
Leonard Cruz 317

Healing Pandora: The Restoration of Hope and Abundance by Gail Thomas
Dennis Patrick Slattery 325

C. G. Jung and Nikolai Berdyaev: Individuation and the Person: A Critical Comparison by Georg Nicolaus
Gert Sauer 333

FILM REVIEWS

Black Swan, directed by Darren Aronofsky
Terrie Waddell 339

The King's Speech, directed by Helena Bassil-Morozow
Glen Slater 347

In Memoriam
RAFAEL LÓPEZ-PEDRAZA (1920-2011)

BY AXEL CAPRILES M.

If anything can be said about Rafael López-Pedraza, it is that he was an original man, a man who knew how to respond to the instinct of creativity that demands a personal answer. Rafael died on 9 January 2011, and we lost not only an analyst who made psychotherapy his passion but a man who helped us to "take breath, stimuli, images, far beyond where air normally reaches the lungs."[1] I remember clearly the beginnings of my analysis with him, toward the end of 1975. Overwhelmed by vocational conflicts, I consulted him about one of my banal troubles. Rafael, who was unashamedly counting coins at his desk, stood up, took an alchemy book, showed me an image, closed the book, sat down, and changed the topic of conversation without responding to my concerns. With his powerful body language he told me: "Let's not talk nonsense anymore. Let us now go to important issues (*"Dejémonos de tonterías y vamos, ahora, a asuntos importantes"*). He had, in every sense, an unconventional and heterodox psychotherapeutic style.

López-Pedraza was born in Santa Clara, Cuba, but moved to Caracas, Venezuela in adulthood for business reasons. He was an autodidact who had learned mainly from suffering and life. In 1962, he traveled to Europe, where for the next eleven years he studied analytical psychology at the C. G. Jung Institute in Zürich. He also worked in one of the most innovative psychiatric clinics of the time,

---

1. Rafael López-Pedraza, "Reflections on the Duende (An Examination of *The Theory and Play of the Duende,* by Federico García Lorca)," in López-Pedraza, *Cultural Anxiety* (Einsiedeln, Switzerland: Daimon Verlag, 1990), p. 56.

the Klinik am Zürichberg, founded in 1964 by C. A. Meier. During that time, he became acquainted with his wife, Valerie Heron, and established enriching friendships with James Hillman and Adolf Guggenbühl-Craig. In 1969, Hillman and López-Pedraza traveled to London and visited the Warburg Institute and the Wellcome Library, where they learned of the Hermetic tradition. There they found *The Hieroglyphics of Horapollo*[2] and the *Picatrix,*[3] a book of talismanic medicine. Then followed the readings and meetings at the Spring House in Untere Zaune, in Zürich, which produced great and powerful emotional experiences and gave birth to much of what today is known as archetypal psychology, what Rafael always referred to as the psychology of archetypes. The ways López and Hillman saw the image—the insistence of Rafael on the importance of *sticking to the image* and of James on *saving the phenomena*—enhanced an understanding of a polytheistic psychology that was miles apart from the traditional Jungian psychology that revolved around balances and the self. Fairy tales did not always prove the transcendent Self.

In 1977, López-Pedraza, who had by then returned to Caracas, surprised the scholarly audience with a tremendously original book, *Hermes and His Children.*[4] In it, Rafael developed a psychology of the image with a style and feeling for the undignified and what is at the borderlines. Remembering the Cuban poet Lezama Lima, who said "the image, what makes possible the impossible,"[5] Rafael connected the psychotherapeutic relationship with the elaboration of an emotional image, the "impossible image that produces psychic transformation."[6] Psychotherapy is a psychic mover based on a subtle appreciation of values and the reading of images. For López-Pedraza, the image is what works psychically. Relating to the emotions, valuing them, or allowing the spontaneous appearance of a metaphor is what moves the reflective

---

2. *The Hieroglyphics of Horapollo Nilous,* translated by A. J. Cory (London: W. Pickering, 1840).

3. Recently published as *Picatrix: Un traité de magie médiéval,* translation, introduction, and notes by Béatrice Bakhouche, Frédéric Fauquier, and Brigitte Pérez-Jean (Turnhout: Brepols, 2003).

4. Rafael López-Pedraza, *Hermes and His Children* (Zürich: Spring Publications, 1977).

5. Rafael López-Pedraza, "Moon Madness—Titanic Love: A Meeting of Pathology and Poetry," in López-Pedraza, *Cultural Anxiety,* p. 13.

6. *Ibid.*

instinct. The main teaching of Rafael was that work with images takes place through indirection and slowness. The work implies a depressed flow of the libido, rebounds and leaps of which we get with the passing of time, consciousness through repercussions, through curious emotional impacts, the growth of a different type of awareness, an experience rooted in the body.

For López-Pedraza, as he wrote in his book of essays, *Cultural Anxiety*, our times are a consequence of a psyche that resists the slow pace that allows it to get in contact with the emotions, the result of the absence of symmetry between soul and body. Acceleration, slowness, emptiness, mimetics, failure, the "inability to form an image" were thus the theme of this collection.[7] For a reflection to take place, we need a particular *tempo*. And three elements of human nature work against the slowness necessary for psychic reflection to take place: the acceleration of the Puer Aeternus (the Eternal Boy), the histrionics and the superficiality of Hysteria, and the psychopathic mimeticism and immoderation of Titanism. Each of these inhibits the development of a consciousness of failure. López wrote, "Psyche does not learn from Titanic excess. . . . We need to make a clear distinction between the suffering, humiliation and pain of Psyche—from which psychological learning, knowledge and soul-making, or soul-initiation can come—and the repetitive suffering of the Titans—the daily nauseating boredom of the existential level of life."[8] The experience of failure refers to what the classics called *Anima media natura,* a median state of the soul where the individual is not wildly craving success. On the other end of the spectrum of human experience, there is the animated slowness that the Spanish call *temple,* a time-space where the psyche prepares itself adequately, the "slowness of movement that may appear in some bullfighting *suertes,* in singing or dancing flamenco and—why not say it?—in life itself," moments when the Dionysian appearance of what the Andaluz and the Spanish poet Federico García Lorca called *duende* is experienced, the *daimon* of the present.[9]

Rafael López-Pedraza was one of the pioneers in the study of art and psychology. He was always interested in the possibility of learning

---

7. López-Pedraza, "Moon Madness—Titanic Love," *Cultural Anxiety*, p. 17.
8. *Ibid.,* p. 18.
9. López-Pedraza, "Reflections on the Duende," *Cultural Anxiety*, p. 65.

psychology from art if the spectator could stick to the image instead of projecting interpretations onto a work of art. In addition to several articles, López-Pedraza's legacy for the study of psychology and art consists of two books, one published—*Anselm Kiefer: The Psychology of "After the Catastrophe—*"[10] and one unpublished—*Dionysus in the Work of the Great Masters*. In *Anselm Kiefer*, our Caribbean psychologist shows an extraordinary ability to move swiftly at middle height, from the images of a painter to the collective psychology of his times, to show the juxtaposition of art, history, mythology, and psychology, the construction that becomes a presence in ourselves that is capable of moving our imagination and making psyche. For López-Pedraza, Kiefer's works are an opportunity to study the shadow of power as one of the most threatening of all shadows and the infinite capacity of humankind for stupidity, the kind of amnesia connected with the psychopathic inferiority existing in all of us. It is also an imaginative lecture about the hysterical states whereby specific segments of a nation are fused with a mad inflation, where the redeemer, the hero, and magic coincide. Art gives us the possibility of reconstructing the underground movement through which the fantasies of a man unfold the cultural complexity of his times: not just art as psychology but psychology as the art of differentiating and making consciousness, of creating forms capable of preserving individual experience, of containing the horror and madness of a mimetic collective. Art can be an expression of the archetypal forms that allow for a cultivated life, for a space suitable for the epiphany of soul. The emphasis on individual experience is important. The reading of art is a ritual act, a metaphoric movement that allows us to come into contact with the productions of the unconscious and to work with our historic complexities and complications and destiny.

López-Pedraza was an unapologetic defender of individuality. For him, collective consciousness was no consciousness at all. And in this sense he was a passionate analyst of all types of collective madness, as expressed, first and foremost, in different expressions of ideological monotheism, sectarianism, totalitarianism, and obscurantism. Identification with the hero is another of the dominant manifestations

---

10. Rafael López-Pedraza, *Anselm Kiefer: The Psychology of "After the Catastrophe"* (New York: George Braziller, 1996).

of historical madness. It is a state of possession, a monopoly of psychic energy taken by the charisma of the hero and an identification with the historic complexes and spirits of the dead.

In his works on the myths of Dionysus, Artemis, and Amor and Psyche, Rafael López-Pedraza developed the heart of his psychology: that is, the study and understanding of emotions by themselves as psychic realities belonging to a totally different world from the world we usually apprehend through ego consciousness. The only way to approach the emotions is through the feeling function, a function that unavoidably moves us to individual valorizations. For Rafael, what psychoanalysts have called the unconscious for years is, in fact, the affective psyche, the realm of the emotions. "The soul is what I call the emotional field and Psychotherapy, the office to which I devote myself, is my field from which to observe and live them."[11] The emotions are the roads toward our interiority and our instinctive apparatus.

I cannot end this remembrance of Rafael López-Pedraza without mentioning the man and the friend. He was a person with an extraordinary capacity for making personal connections and for addressing the individuality of each person. The many private conversations and warm interchanges of emotions and ideas that took place over bottles of wine after seminars and lectures are probably the most fruitful legacy of his teachings. More than an author of nine books, Rafael López-Pedraza was a lover and performer of the art of living, a researcher of the forms capable of preserving the individual experience, a cultivator of the intimate spaces suitable for the epiphany of soul.

—Axel Capriles M., Caracas, Venezuela

Axel Capriles M., D.Ec., is professor of psychology at the Catholic University of Caracas. He has a degree in psychology, a diploma from the C. G. Jung Institut Zürich, and a doctorate in economics. He is a past president of the Venezuelan Society of Jungian Analysts, director of the C. G. Jung Foundation of Venezuela, and the current editor of the Venezuelan journal *Revista Venezolana de Psicología de los Arquetipos y Estudios Junguianos*. He is a columnist for the main daily journal of Caracas, *El Universal*. His published books include *El complejo del dinero* (*The Money Complex*; Consorcio de Ediciones Capriles, 2004) and *La picardía del venezolano o el triunfo de Tío Conejo* (*The Success of Uncle Rabbit*; Taurus, 2008). Another book, *The Fantasies of Juan Bimba*, is forthcoming.

---

11. Rafael López-Pedraza, *Emociones: una lista* (Caracas: Festina Lente, 2008), p. 9.

Rediscovering Home:
A Myth for Our Time

HENDRIKA DE VRIES

> He is beginning to feel alone and to hear nothing but echoes reverberating back.
> —Loren Eiseley, *The Firmament of Time*

Pablo Neruda, the South American poet, called the twentieth century "The Sadder Century" and immortalized it in verse as "the century of émigrés, the book of homelessness."[1] Today, a decade into the twenty-first century, this pervasive feeling of homelessness has become the normal state for many. We are a transient global society of people suffering from what psychologist Henry M. Seiden calls a "non-pathological longing for home."[2] As the natural world shrinks and our distance from the mythic wisdom of the dreaming earth widens, our naturally relational body grieves a loss it cannot name.

Hendrika de Vries, M.T.S.,M.F.T, is a licensed depth-oriented Marriage and Family Therapist in private practice in Santa Barbara, California. She has served as adjunct faculty in the Mythological Studies and Counseling Psychology programs at Pacifica Graduate Institute. Her recent publications include "The Chrysalis Experience: A Mythology for Times of Transition," in *Depth Psychology: Meditations in the Field*, edited Dennis P. Slattery and Lionel Corbett (Daimon Verlag and Pacifica Graduate Institute, 2000); and "Beyond Forgiveness: Re-Weaving the Remains of War," *Spring: A Journal of Archetype and Culture* 81 (2009). Her current research interest is the archetypal theme of interdependence.

Disconnected from nature and increasingly uprooted from the habitats of our childhoods, we are millions of fast-paced urbanized bodies deafened to the homing call of our ancient soul. How can a flesh-and-blood body that is disconnected from its own nature grieve and move through the experiences of personal loss and global upheavals? How can a human spirit that cannot hear the mythic tales and stories that are rooted in its natural flesh find its way home?

It has been argued that rather than the myth of Oedipus it is the epic of the Greek warrior-hero Odysseus trying to find his way home that most represents the "universal psychological experience of our species."[3] However, the theme of the victorious warrior-hero finding his way home does not adequately speak to the imagination of the twenty-first century, in which many war veterans find themselves psychologically and sometimes even physically homeless. The ones without homes share their plight with the women and children who constitute a large percentage of the homeless people in our urban streets. In our rushed global culture, the loss of home may in fact be more realistically symbolized by the distress of the urban child growing up in our transient and broken homes, estranged from the healing powers of the natural world.

Not surprisingly, one of the most frequently quoted movie sayings in recent cinema history was "E.T. phone home," the comment made by the little alien trapped on earth in Steven Spielberg's 1982 science fiction movie *E.T.: The Extra-Terrestrial*. Jungian analyst John Hill, who has been writing and lecturing on the issue of home for over twenty years, describes E.T. as a "Christ-like hero" who "descends from heaven; teaches children about love; is persecuted, dies, and is resurrected; to finally ascend to a home among the stars." The little extraterrestrial pointing his long finger "upward to his lost home, awakens thoughts of a final dwelling place beyond the horizon of human understanding, a home not of this world."[4]

As an archetypal theme, the loss of home and the longing to return, both actually and symbolically, has always had an important place in Western mythology, history, religion, and literature and more recently in film. But instead of safety and belonging, the background stories that inform Western consciousness frequently depict our relationship to home in terms of exile and punishment, of obedience and disobedience to a higher authority, whether earthly or divine. These archetypal and historical patterns have a profound impact on the way we address the loss of home and the desire to belong. The biblical story of exile from the Garden of Eden for disobedience lives deep in our Western religious psyche and has had a powerful influence on our cultural attitudes toward pain, suffering, and loss.

Refugees and immigrants forced to leave the hardships of their homelands; slaves unable to protect themselves; workers, whether legal or illegal, seeking a new homeland with a better life for themselves and their families; or the homeless pushing their belongings in shopping carts in our affluent cities all tend to trigger emotional responses conditioned by cultural attitudes and religious morals that can prevent us from hearing the deeply human condition in the immediacy of their experience.

Our mythic stories of home have become infused with religious and cultural concepts of property and authority; of colonization, dominance, and victimization; and of reward and punishment. No wonder we yearn for a regressive return to the original Garden of Eden before the conflict with authority and the whole snake incident with its problematic issue of personal choice reared its ugly head. Or if not the past, then we fantasize about a place in the future, our heavenly reward for good behavior, preferably far away from the troublesome flesh of the body and its connection to earth.

But while a vision of a home in a disembodied spiritual future, "a home not of this world," may bring hope, a regressive longing for a lost paradise, or temporary respite from sorrow, the flesh-and-blood relational body needs to experience the touch of the Sacred within this present world of here and now. It needs the soulful imagination of Presence to help it grieve and move through the losses experienced within the context and meaning of this current world. It needs access to the deeply healing myths rooted in its natural flesh and to hear the world's multicultural, multiethnic narratives of grief, loss, and adaptation in a global culture struggling to find its way home.

As an immigrant, I have my own story of adaptation that began with my parents' decision to leave Amsterdam, the city of my birth and my formative years in The Netherlands, to immigrate to Australia. Two years of being interned in a German POW camp and his subsequent struggle to find peace in the upheavals of postwar Europe had left my father emotionally depleted and longing for the natural wide open spaces of the land down under. The move did indeed heal his troubled soul, and I would discover years later that my psyche was also deeply enriched and my mind expanded by this experience—but at the time I was a very unhappy young teenager.

To this day I remember the wintry dampness on my skin as the dock slowly disappeared into the gray distance. Through tear-filled eyes I could see my friends waving their hands in a final gesture of departure as they held up the banner of the swim club I had belonged to since I was seven years old. My body pressed hard into the ship's iron railing in an attempt to fight the widening gap between the disappearing land and MS *Johan Van Oldenbarnevelt,* the Dutch emigrant ocean liner that was dragging me away from my home. It was the winter between my thirteenth and fourteenth birthdays and I was leaving the home, language, culture, and landscape that my senses had known since birth.

The next time my feet would touch land it would be to feel a hot midsummer sun burn my pale skin, to hear words and phrases in a language with which I had no emotional connection, and to look up at night at an unfamiliar celestial sky over an alien landscape. Our new home was on the edge of the Australian bush surrounded by vast stretches of sheep ranches with the lone sound of a single train passing through the night. Here even the greatest treasure my parents had nurtured in me, my imagination, lost its way and could not reach into the total otherness of the new land and its people.

For many weeks after our arrival I dreamed each night of flying myself like a bird across the ocean back to Amsterdam. The dreams felt so real to me that I would experience an intense fatigue in my body, especially my arms, as I woke up each morning.

> *In these dreams I fly over my beloved Amsterdam, check out the old canal district where I lived, and, without my feet ever touching the ground, I fly back to Australia.*

The dreams could be interpreted as an expression of homesickness. John Hill writes that "homesickness and homelessness differ from early abandonment in that they presuppose ego development and the capacity to form enduring attachments with others."[5] And I was indeed desperately in need of forming new attachments.

While my mother had passed on to me the gift of dreaming, including telepathic and sometimes prognostic dreams, and I had been raised to share and talk about my dreams as she and my grandmother had, my father was close to the earth. And it was my father who took our new Australian sheepdog, Loki, and me for a long walk one hot and dusty afternoon. I remember that the flies were buzzing around my head and I was irritated with my dad's talk about the amazing adaptations of flora and fauna. But then he began to tell me a story about the ancient spirit of nature that was trying to express itself through the trees and creatures of this dusty land. As his story unfolded, his intense love and respect for nature gently made its way into my heart and I understood why he had always had such a special way with animals and plants. His story gave me a glimpse of a creative shape-shifting magic in the living earth's capacity for adaptation. By the time we reached home I had begun to get a visceral sense of the alien landscape as nature's way of speaking a sensuous language that I had not quite gotten used to yet.

> *That night I dream that I am standing in the center of a dusty patch of large stones, bush shrub, and tall ancient Eucalyptus trees shedding their bark. It is dusk but the air is still warm. I have the strange sensation of hearing the trees address me. The words are unclear but the energy is undeniable. I am very still. I know that I am in the presence of an ancient power, that its source is the earth, and I understand that it has greeted me.*

This dream marked the end of my flying-to-Amsterdam dreams. It would be many years before I would read about the Australian aboriginal mythology of "Dreamtime" and the shamanic practice of flying in soul retrieval. The dream could be interpreted as an expression of the compensatory function of the psyche of a homesick teenager, of course, or even as the symbolic expression of a positive father complex. However, we could also imagine that the spirit of the land, of Earth, was truly speaking to a girl whose soul was somewhat lost between continents. Might it not be possible that my father, seeing the malaise in my soul, had taken me on a walk in nature to open up my shut-down senses and help me rediscover my connection to the living earth? It was from within this interconnectedness of the alien trees, the hot dusty road, and my father's storytelling attunement to the spirit of the land that my body was able to surrender to the kinship that would touch my soul in the dream.

I believe that healing imagination is conceived when we meet the Other as subject to subject. Many years later, after having just moved to Denver, Colorado, as a young wife and mother I had a similar experience. Having lived at sea level all of my life, I was not sure how my body and psyche would adapt to the rugged heights of the Colorado Rockies. The cultural mythology of gold miners and gun-toting cowboys did not speak to my soul, and on our weekend mountain explorations, I would sit on the rocks, gaze at the majestic beauty of the snowy peaks, and feel the disconnect as a deep physical ache in my stomach. In those moments my "I" would greet the majestic landscape as the "Thou," and once again it was a dream that connected my body to the earth and landed my soul.

> *In the dream I am sitting on a jagged granite ledge overlooking vast mountain ranges. I have taken off my cowboy boots as if I had entered holy ground. At that moment, a Native American Indian chief in full headdress steps in front of me. I stand up and we face each other on that steep outcropping at the timberline in what I take to be the Colorado Rocky Mountains. We keep a respectful distance between us and I know in the dream that he is a spirit and not a physical being. He welcomes me to his land in a language that is not English but that I can somehow understand, and he tells me he will be my guide. I feel that I can be at home in this rugged land as his guest and am curious to discover what I will be shown. I wake up relaxed.*

As a newcomer to the United States, I had never before dreamed of Native Americans. From a Jungian depth-psychological perspective, the powerful Indian chief could be interpreted as a positive animus figure, an archetype. But I preferred to let him be who he claimed to be, a guide to this new country in which he was after all a native, a spirit from the land that was to become our family home for the next eleven years. In that mountainous landscape, the living earth had touched my soul and opened my imagination to the image that resonated in my body and enabled me to relax.

In the vein of poets and mystics and the traditions of indigenous people around the world, an increasing number of contemporary writers, especially in the field of ecopsychology, are bearing witness to an evolution in Western consciousness that challenges the "convenient belief in a lifeless, soulless Earth."[6] Drawing on the phenomenology of the French philosopher Maurice Merleau-Ponty to elucidate their vision of an organic physically alive world that has a psychic correspondence with our sensing body, they call us back into experiencing the world as an inherence of "wild Being."[7] Merleau-Ponty's work, which was unfortunately interrupted by sudden death, explores the oneness of our being with both nature and culture as a oneness of flesh, a complex interconnectedness in which our body is made of the same flesh as the world and the world shares in the flesh of our bodies. In his unfinished notes he actually wrote himself a reminder to "do a psychoanalysis of Nature: it is the flesh, the Mother."[8]

Ecopsychologist Andy Fisher explains that Merleau-Ponty's concept of flesh is a concept of being, an elemental power or medium that is "more primary than mind and matter, which are differentiations within the flesh. In this case, language, too, is a kind of flesh; one that is 'less heavy,' or 'more transparent,' than other kinds."[9] Language itself can be understood as a complex interconnected and reciprocal conversation of the body with the multidimensional voices of the environment. Not just limited to the speech of the human language, we find ourselves in a living landscape of language rich with the voices of the nonhuman world of other creatures, of trees, rocks, rivers, and oceans. With this wider perception of language we discover that the natural world opens itself up as home and sustenance to the lived experience of the body.

Unfortunately, language that is uprooted from its natural soil and disconnected from embodied experience can block access to this inclusive way of being in the world. In his comprehensive book on home, *At Home in the World: Sounds and Symmetries of Belonging,* John Hill explores the complex psychological relationship between language and our experience of home. He presents case studies to demonstrate that our use of language is integral to our sense of belonging and draws the reader's attention to the way we have split the language of our intellect from the emotional intelligence of the body and the language of the heart.

Hill explores the split with the metaphors of "father-tongued language" and "mother-tongued language." He writes that a "'father-tongued' language—developed in school, specialized in university, and perfected in a profession—has become a powerful instrument that has enabled us to organize, control and promote the vast complexity of contemporary civilization."[10] But while it "may lead to success in the outer world, we risk forgetting our first language our 'mother tongue.'" The "mother tongue" is the language of instinct and emotion, of mother and baby, of lovers and close friends, of music, myth, and poetry and the sensuous body. It is a relational language, "the language of depth and connectedness between self and other."[11]

In our rapidly changing world, the "father tongue" has become increasingly disconnected from its roots and has split itself off from the symbol-creating mind and emotional intelligence of the physical body. For many generations of immigrants and transient citizens in our fast-moving culture, the "mother tongue" was left behind in another place on the planet and the "father tongue" became the adaptive language, the one that secured a belonging in the new homeland. The "father tongue" landed the corporate job or simply made one more valued in a culture that places little value on the soft body, the earth, or the deep stories and interdependence of all flesh. Hill stresses the necessity of incorporating both tongues but notes that "the process of integrating both father and mother tongues can extend over generations."[12]

We need to be careful, of course, not to perpetuate such splits through our use of gender-biased language. As I shared earlier, in my personal experience of finding my way home in a new country it was my father who helped reconnect my soul to the earth. Today many of us hold within us a number of languages with their own cultural nuances and mythic roots in different landscapes. Our images and stories of home are often spread out over several states, countries, and even continents. But no matter what our gender or place of origin, in our technological culture we all carry within us the experience of both "father" and "mother" tongues, if not always in equal balance or well integrated.

For men and women alike, the early language of touch and fundamental relatedness takes us deep into the sensory memory, emotional intelligence, and mythic imagination of the lived experience of the body. And as David Abram has observed, "At the most primordial level of sensuous, bodily experience, we find ourselves in an expressive, gesturing landscape, in a world that *speaks*."[13] Through this felt language of depth and interconnectedness the primal body can begin to "hear" the homing signal that brings us closer to rediscovering home in the changing landscape and upheavals of our complex world.

"The body is your only home in the universe. It is your house of belonging here in the world."[14] So wrote the wise and gentle Irish poet and philosopher John O'Donohue. But what do we really mean by our body as home? Do we recognize that the body extends beyond the boundaries of our skin, that the body is inherently wildly imaginative and relational? From the earliest experience in the womb, the living body is in relationship with another being. As we differentiate and individuate, we move into ever-widening spheres of relationship and interconnectedness that ensure a sense of belonging and being at home in the world. In this open-ended ongoing conversation with the physical and cultural world around us, the body as lived experience is always engaged in a reciprocal process of creating home. And ecopsychologists assert that "this process wishes to continue beyond the human realm, that our humanity is incomplete until we have established our kinship of social relations with the larger natural world and so satisfied our longing to feel at home in or at peace with the cosmos as a whole."[15]

But for the body to engage in this open-ended ongoing conversation with the world presupposes a certain kind of embodiment that is free from restrictions and polarities, a body that is free to experience and express its instinctual deep knowing. It presupposes, in other words, a body that is allowed to know and express its own mind. Merleau-Ponty, who devoted his life to the phenomenology of the body as lived experience, used the term "*lived* body" in an attempt to describe and understand "the fundamental interrelatedness of consciousness and embodiment, and thus to bypass the dualisms mind/body, interior/exterior, and consciousness/nature."[16] In *Feminist Interpretations of Maurice Merleau-Ponty,* writers examine the body's capacity for intertwining itself with the natural world from the perspective of the female body. And we are reminded that the *lived* body's movements and actions are always mediated through cultural laws and customs.

What happens to the concept of the body as home when the body is prevented (for whatever reason) from connecting with its own wild flesh, its source of being and unfolding inspiration? What happens when the *lived* body cannot or is forbidden to remember that it is inextricably woven into the elemental "flesh" of the natural world? How can a body that is disconnected from the "mother language" of the encompassing earth find its way home?

The dis-ease of a culture that is disconnected from Nature and the instinctual life has certainly been the topic of many current writers, especially in the field of depth psychology. Carl Jung himself observed the dangers of our urban culture and saw the loss of our connection with the world of instinct and the archetypal functions that give them form and meaning as "largely responsible for the pathological condition of our contemporary culture."[17] In the book *The Earth Has a Soul*, which is based on an edited collection of Jung's personal writings, lectures, and interviews, Meredith Sabini reminds the reader of Jung's deep concern for the loss of our emotional and mythic connection with Nature. Sabini refers to his concept of synchronicity, the meaningful correspondence between internal and external realities, to reiterate Jung's emphasis on the interconnectedness of matter and spirit and the potentially devastating effects of our attempts to take soul out of Nature. She embraces Jung's work as a contribution to the connectedness theory to draw her own parallels between the contamination of the earth's air, water, and soil and "similar diseases of blood and tissue in people."[18]

However, Carl Jung and others also remind us that we do not have to be helpless victims of our cultural pathologies. While the destructive splits we have created do exist, we also live within an amazing natural world of organic coherence and evolutionary possibilities that has given us the tools of consciousness and the mythic imagination to dial in and reconnect with the "voices" of home.

Throughout human existence the imagination has responded to our endless questions and concerns about life and meaning by providing dreams and archetypal stories that can be heard as messages from Home—if we have the ears to hear. One such particular mythic story is the ancient Celtic tale of the "Selkie" or the "Sealskin" that is told in many countries in the northern regions of the world and was popularized in the film *The Secret of Roan Inish* (1994). The story of this mythological sea creature was told and analyzed by Jungian analyst and *cantadora* (storyteller) Clarissa Pinkola Estés in her deeply wise and widely read book *Women Who Run with the Wolves*. Estés calls it a story about "the return to home, the wild home, the soul-home," and entitles her own performance version "Sealskin, Soulskin."[19]

Selkies are mythical creatures, seals that can become human by taking off their animal skins. We are told that in their human form the females are slender and graceful and the handsome males have the power of seduction. But if a human man steals a female Selkie's skin, she is in his power and must become his wife. In most versions of the tale a very lonely man stumbles upon a group of beautiful naked women dancing on the shore. As he watches their graceful bodies dance and listens to the women's sensual laughter he spies the pile of sealskins and stealthily takes and hides one of them. Unable to find her animal skin, one of the Selkies must now become the captor's wife. They usually have one child or several. But after some years the seal woman's body begins to sicken and wither as she mourns for the recuperative powers of her home in the sea. The tale comes to an end when the Selkie mother's child discovers the hidden sealskin and sets her free.

In some accounts the child is taken back into the sea by the mother, in others the child stays on land with the father. But in some, as in Estés' version, the mother breaths her own breath into the child's lungs and takes him with her to visit his grandfather, the old bull seal of the depths, before returning him back to the shore.[20]

Much has been said and written about the mythic mystery and meaning of the shape-shifting Selkies. Clarissa Pinkola Estés' exquisite psychological interpretation of the story has reminded her countless readers to nurture their wild souls and remember the source of their true nature. But what can we learn from the mythic child that is born of this strange marriage? In some versions it is a boy, in others it is a girl. In a strange way he or she closely resembles a twenty-first-century child. His or her parents are from different parts of the earth. One parent is ego driven, lonely, and controlling, the other is deeply depressed and suffering from what might once have been called homesickness. Predictably, the child becomes what many psychotherapists now call a parentified child. The parentified child is not unusual in immigrant homes, where the child is often the first in the family to speak the language of the new land and becomes the translator of this adaptive language for one or both parents. Frequently, an immigrant child will continue to speak the "mother tongue," or the emotional language of the old country, with the mother and communicate in the language of the new land with the father. From a family-systems perspective, it is not at all surprising that the Selkie child embodies the role of the rescuer, the one who helps the depressed parent find her way home. And ultimately, with the separation of the parents, this mythic child becomes the child of what we of the twenty-first century now call a child from a "broken home."

Whether we look at this child as an external child or as an internal structure within the individual human psyche, it is uniquely an initiated child. By taking the child down into the deep waters of the earth to meet the old seal grandfather, the mother has initiated him or her into the "mother tongue" of the world, into the soul language of the ancient mysteries of flesh, myth, and ancestors. Baptized in the primal waters of the earth, this human child carries within him or herself both a felt animal kinship with the earth soul and the desperate loneliness of the disconnected "father tongue," the wandering human spirit without a home. By embodying both, the child bridges the split and now "represents a new order in the psyche."[21]

Psychologist Robert Jay Lifton, whose award-winning books addressed the horrific challenges survivors of Hiroshima and the Holocaust faced in the last century, might have described this child as symbolic of the emerging "Protean self." Lifton observed that in an effort to overcome our global spiritual homelessness, "we have been evolving a sense of self appropriate to the restlessness and flux of our time."[22] Drawing on the mythic image of the shape-shifting Greek sea god Proteus, he described this emerging self in terms of a shape-shifting resilience supported by a more fluid mythic imagination to help us find our way home in the immense changes and upheavals of our global age. Like the grandfather seal in the Selkie story, Proteus was an old bull seal. He was in charge of all of Poseidon's seals and could change his shape at will. According to Homer in the *Odyssey*, his range was so prolific that he could take "on a whiskered lion's shape, / a serpent then; a leopard; a great boar; / then sousing water; then a tall green tree."[23]

For Lifton, "myths reveal psychological and historical possibilities as bequeathed by human evolution."[24] Having looked into the dark horrors of our age of fragmentation, he saw the evolution of a capacity for a less rigid, more fluid imagination and flexible action in the face of change and destruction as a "path of hope" through which individuals were reaching toward a global connectedness and belonging. The fluidity and the flexibility of Proteanism, he wrote, "enables men and women alike to call forth that potential for weblike connectedness and empathic sensitivity generally associated, for whatever combination of cultural and psychobiological reasons, with women."[25] In this Protean pattern, as in the mythic child of the Selkie, the "father tongue" and "mother tongue" come together to form a new potential, the child of a new psychic order.

In our quest and longing for home we are challenged to look beyond our differences of gender, nationality, and ethnicity to examine what it means to be deeply human. Like the child of the lonely man and the homesick shape-shifting Selkie, many of us are adult children of a fast-paced, exciting, and exhausting ego-driven culture who also hear the homing call of the earth's soul. Depth psychologists remind us that "the process of bridge building can take place within the individual human psyche"[26] and that we have the fluidity to dive into the depths of our oceanic oneness and the mythic imagination to create new links across differences and divisions of culture and nature. Given these tools, we still have a chance to transform the twenty-first century into a century of global belonging rather than the century of rootless wandering and spiritual homelessness. If we heed the Homing signals, we have the capacity and resilience to respond and change our relationship to the natural Home we all share. Perhaps we will even realize that it is not so much the Earth that needs our healing but we who need Hers.

The twenty-first-century child is phoning home on a mobile; he or she is not an E.T., an extraterrestrial who is not of this world, but an earth child from an endangered planet that is his or her only home. Earth children, who carry both the mother tongue and the father tongue intertwined within their experience, are longing to hear our response. The question is whether we can let our hearts and minds be touched and moved by their plight before it is too late.

We no longer have the luxury of our regressive longing for a home without conflict in a paradisiacal past or fantasizing about a future home away from our much-maligned earth. The world soul is pressing in on us and is sounding its homing signal to the children in the world who will inherit whatever home we bequeath them. Recently my eleven-year-old granddaughter watched the movie *Food, Inc.* and decided to become a vegetarian overnight. She has since started recruiting her classmates also. While her decision was influenced by not wanting animals in the world to suffer, she has also reclaimed her own body and its connection with the natural world. In her own young way she is feeling her way home.

There is a warning in Norse mythology. When the old established order went up in flames, the god Wotan, after much wandering, returned to seek counsel from Erda, the ancient goddess of deep Earth wisdom. However, Erda's thoughts had become so "beclouded by the deeds of men" that she no longer had the clarity to respond.[27]

As a grandparent I am excruciatingly aware of the short time we all have to pass on our lived experiences of this dreaming earth to our grandchildren and to the other children of this world. We have such a brief opportunity to share with them the majestic beauty, the mysterious language, and the healing capacity and deep wisdom of our Natural Home.

I want my grandchildren and their children to hear the Earth speak through their dreams and be touched by its sensuous delights and awesome beauty through their sensory bodies and animal kinship. I want them to inherit the mythic stories that can connect them to the depths of the Earth's healing baptismal waters and the shape-shifting adaptations and mysteries of the living mind in Nature. I want them to feel free to discover from within the lived experience of their own relational being that this amazing earth right now is their Sacred Habitat. I want them to put on their animal skins and dive deep. There may be other homes in the universe in the future, but right now this is the one that is sounding its Homing call. This Sacred Earth, this ground, these oceans, these rivers, mountains and trees, this is Home for all the children of the world.

NOTES

1. Pablo Neruda, "The Sadder Country," in *Blooming through the Ashes: An International Anthology on Violence and the Human Spirit*, edited by Clifford Chanin and Aili McConnon (New Brunswick, N.J.: Rutgers University Press, 2008), p. 280.

2. Henry M. Seiden, "On the Longing for Home," *Psychoanalytic Psychology* 26, no. 2 (2009): 197.

3. *Ibid.*

4. John Hill, *At Home in the World: Sounds and Symmetries of Belonging* (New Orleans, La.: Spring Journal Books, 2010), 165.

5. *Ibid.*, p. 90.

6. Craig Chalquist, "Terrapsychology: Reengaging the Soul of Place—An Introduction," *Spring: A Journal of Archetype and Culture* 76 (Fall 2006): 230.

7. Maurice Merleau-Ponty, *The Visible and the Invisible*, edited by Claude Lefort, translated by Alphonso Lingis (Evanston, Ill.: Northwestern University Press, 1968), p. 253.

8. *Ibid.*, p. 267.

9. Andy Fisher, *Radical Ecopsychology: Psychology in the Service of Life* (Albany: State University of New York Press, 2002), p. 133.

10. Hill, *At Home in the World*, pp. 72–73.

11. *Ibid.*, p. 73.

12. *Ibid.*, p. 74.

13. David Abram, *The Spell of the Sensuous: Perception and Language in a More-Than-Human World* (New York: Random House, 1996), p. 81.

14. John O'Donohue, *Anam Cara: A Book of Celtic Wisdom* (New York: HarperPerennial, 2004), p. 48.

15. Fisher, *Radical Ecopsychology*, p. 122.

16. Johanna Oksala, "Female Freedom: Can the Lived Body Be Emancipated?" in *Feminist Interpretations of Maurice Merleau-Ponty*, edited by Dorothea Olkowski and Gail Weiss (University Park: The Pennsylvania State University Press, 2006), p. 213.

17. C. G. Jung, "Foreword to Allenby," in *The Symbolic Life: Miscellaneous Writings*, vol. 18 of *The Collected Works of C. G. Jung*, edited and translated by G. Adler and R. F. C. Hull (Princeton, N.J.: Princeton University Press, 1977), § 1494. Also quoted and discussed in detail in *The Earth Has a Soul: C. G. Jung on Nature, Technology & Modern Life*, edited by Meredith Sabini (Berkeley, Calif.: North Atlantic Books, 2008).

18. Meredith Sabini, "Introduction," in Sabini, *The Earth Has a Soul*, p. 15.

19. Clarissa Pinkola Estés, *Women Who Run with the Wolves: Myths and Stories of the Wild Woman Archetype* (New York: Ballantine Books, 1992), p. 257.

20. *Ibid.*, p. 261.

21. *Ibid.*, p. 289.

22. Robert Jay Lifton, *The Protean Self: Human Resilience in an Age of Fragmentation* (New York: Basic Books, 1993), p. 1.

23. *Ibid.*, p. 5.
24. *Ibid.*, p. 13.
25. *Ibid.*, p. 215.
26. Hill, *At Home in the World*, p. 76.
27. Jean Shinoda Bolen, *Ring of Power: The Abandoned Child, The Authoritarian Father, and the Disempowered Feminine—A Jungian Understanding of Wagner's Ring Cycle* (San Francisco: HarperSanFrancisco, 1992), p. e 213.

HOME AS SELF, HOME AS SOUL:
THE WISDOM AND NARRATIVE OF PLACE

ROBIN VAN LÖBEN SELS

Throughout his work Carl Jung implies that coming home suggests "homing in" on ourselves or coming into our own. Individuation is a perpetual leaving and return to a sense of personal identity or ego consciousness. For analogy, think of the simple rhythms of waking and sleep. Still, even in individuation, the word "home" means different things to different people, just as experiences of coming home feel different to different people and feel different at different times of life.

"Coming home" to soul or experiencing homecoming to the depths of our instinctual life may be no less individuating than "coming home" to self, yet I would like to suggest that "coming home to soul" differs from our usual concepts of individuation in interesting ways.[1] Some writers, including Jung, use ideas of self and soul interchangeably, but

---

Robin van Löben Sels, Ph.D., received her doctorate in Psychiatry and Religion from Union Theological Seminary in New York City. She attended the Jung Institute in Zurich and graduated from the C. G. Jung Institute of New York. Her professional affiliations include the Inter-Regional Society of Jungian Analysts and the International Association of Analytical Psychology. She is the author of *A Dream in the World* (Routledge, 2003), *Dreamwork(ing): A Primer* (Trout & Mountain Press, 2010), several articles, and a book of poetry.

I find it helpful to differentiate between these two, so in this essay I will interweave ideas of "home as self" and "home as soul" as personal or human experience. But I believe that the idea of the wisdom and narrative of place anchors both perspectives.

Jung's idea of the self, even "Self" with a capital "S," is primarily a concept that is related to yang, or masculine, principles of ego development and ego consciousness. And it is rooted in spirit. For most of his life, Jung had a fairly high center of gravity, meaning that he thought of himself as a thinker and that he highly valued thoughts and ideas. Others also perceived Jung as a heady, scholarly sort of person, and the idea of the self remains a cherished concept throughout Jung's work, even as he spoke of the Self deconstructing itself or undoing its own symbolism, as in *The Visions Seminars*.[2] So using the lens of Jung's idea of the self to look at the archetype of home means paying attention to ideas and concepts of home as well as images of home. This is a kind of yang attention to the archetype of Home as we imagine home and as the image of home appears in dreams, memories, ideas, and activities out in the actual world.

My sense of soul experience is more akin to a yin quality of attention that is more concerned with the feminine energy of body and instinct than with images or ideas. After all, soul relates us to the mysteries of flesh and the depths of affect, to nature in Jung's "just-so" sense and to the earth, meaning to our actual planet. So seeing the archetype of home through the lens of soul means that we are privileging the emotional matrix in which images are embedded more than the images themselves. Emotional energy is the very energy that draws dreams into our lives to begin with, from beyond the dark and beyond the pale, as it were, as if dreams themselves emerge from the heart of our planet to seep into the frail surface skin of our human consciousness, as invisible as the air we breathe and perhaps as limited; we simply do not know.[3] What we *do* realize is that whether it is a grace note or a passion, the emotion carried through a dream is what carries and blends the *human* voice (as opposed to a spiritual or meaningful voice) if we can hear it.

Naturally, emotions need images to embody them, just as the soul needs the self and the self needs the soul in order to *feel* embodied. For better or for worse, we are creatures who dream as well as wake, think as well as feel, and sense as well as imagine, even as we lack full awareness of our experiences. So if for the sake of discussion we speak of self and soul in different breaths or choose between them to look at myth or fairytale (or dream or poem or work of art), let us remember that self and soul are in no way exclusive of one another. In reality (and myth and fairytale and dream), self and soul emerge in counterpoint, if not simultaneously. Some writers easily include both. Clarissa Pinkola Estés, for example, gives a wonderful example in her piece called "Homing: Returning to Oneself," which is her version of the Celtic legend of the Selkie, or Seal Woman.[4]

There is homecoming after great travail and there is homecoming of deep welcome and rejoicing, as in the biblical story of the Prodigal Son. And sometimes we realize that the biggest reason we leave home is in order to return. There is also leaving home as a compelling psychological need that is as necessary and inevitable as growing up. A friend once said that the difference between a boy child and a girl child (or masculine energy and feminine energy) is that a girl child seldom stops to think about where she might end up, whereas the young boy tends to follow a dream. A little boy runs away from home in order to go somewhere—he heads off into the woods to make his way, to join a buddy, to join the circus, to ride the rails—whereas a girl child leaves home or runs away in order to leave something behind her—her anger or hurt or fear propelling her goodness knows where. I wonder if that is true. And if it is, what does that mean for us?

When we leave home (or grow up), usually we take along with us a great deal of unconscious baggage. Whatever we think we left behind (back "there," wherever "there" is) arrives where and when we arrive, as if it had been waiting for us all along. Deeply engraved images and memories of parents, siblings, and ancestors line the winding walls of psyche, for all the world like portraits along a soulish stair. These images (among others) reiterate, over time, conscious and unconscious experiences of relatedness with parts of our selves and with the psyche as well as relationships with others who have been important to us, version after version, memory after memory, until all imaginable iterations seem to jostle each other into consciousness. Many of us have our first embodied experience of the psyche's reality as we traipse up and down, up and down these winding inner stairs in our dreams.

In addition to coming home and leaving home, what about "being at home" and "being homeless"? There are public homes and shelters, there are temporary homes and bomb shelters. There is the "family home," meaning the "house where I grew up" (though as an army brat I lived in dozens of temporary homes before I even began school), and there are "family homes," meaning generational homes, the home "where my grandparents lived," the homes of cousins and aunts and uncles. And there are orphanages and homes for the unwed, the aged, and the dying: Home as sanctuary, Home as prison. Such creatures of imagination we are! Yet I think our original intelligence is place-based. Our imaginations are first stimulated and infused by our earthly surroundings and the earthly terrain where we dwell, and when we can realize (and feel) how all our metaphors are rooted in the nonsymbolic, we can understand how the earth houses us all.

And graveyards: how we wander, as children and adults, reading names and dates, running our fingers over fading images on headstones. A headstone is one of those metaphors, a stony metaphor for life and death dug from the earth, carved with a message from ourselves to ourselves and *placed* in the earth. Headstones, fashioned from the very bones of the earth itself, can mark our memories and intimations of immortality. Sometimes we read with recognition and sometimes we simply imagine lives—our own, as well as the lives and deaths of others—from these fading words and dates and weatherworn designs. I remember the five modest headstones I saw clustering near the much larger headstone of Thomas Smith, buried in the early 1800s at age forty-eight in a graveyard on Maggie Bean Road in Massachusetts. I remember reading about and imagining his five young wives, each one dead in childbirth. Several tiny unengraved headstones cluster nearby. Instead of five marriages and five separations, as we hear of in our consulting rooms today, Thomas Smith was the *survivor* of five marriages, one after the other, with few remaining children to survive *him*. In the early nineteenth century, families and homes could be broken just as they are now, but for different reasons. Death came early for Thomas and his many wives, as it did for others in his time.

Image (and the self) held primary sway with Carl Jung for many years. Only near the end of his life could Jung more soulfully record the values and personal emotions in which those images had been embedded. This happened as he began to *feel* more kin to all the life around him. He ended his autobiography (*Memories, Dreams, Reflections*) with a moving description of an experienced release from earlier feelings of alienation: "There is so much that fills me," he wrote, "plants, animals, clouds, day and night, and the eternal in man. The more uncertain I have felt about myself, the more there has grown up in me a feeling of kinship with all things. In fact it seems to me as if *that alienation which so long separated me from the world* has become transferred into my own inner world, and has revealed to me an unexpected unfamiliarity with myself."[5] No longer as at home with himself as he thought he was as he opened himself to the uncertain depths of an inner life, Jung could finally open himself to the world at large.

Longing seems to be the most common feeling associated with the archetype of Home: longing and nostalgia, both of which imply feelings and images touched upon with an intensity that we hesitate to feel, at depths we can barely comprehend. Wanderers all, longing pulls us back and down, but also it points us toward some thing? some time? somewhere? someone? Longing points the way but never promises to get us there. Yet the *depths* of longing carry some kind of hope of some fulfillment we cannot imagine, except to feel convinced that what can *answer* our longing exists somewhere. "When the Guest is being searched for," sings the poet Kabir, "it is the *intensity of the longing* for the Guest that does all the work."[6]

Many writers imagine longing on a grand scale. John O'Donohue reminds us of how the longing of a whole people can be *felt* as it is captured in the web of their language, for the native language of each of us is another kind of home, an inner landscape to which we belong from birth.[7] In *Lost in Translation,* Eva Hoffman describes what it was like to lose her sense of identity when as a very young immigrant she was moved from one country to another and one language to another. Eva articulates (in her new language) with great courage and heartbreaking accuracy what it was like for her as a youngster to lose her mother tongue and have to find her way in a new country in a language she could neither speak nor understand.[8]

The dreams and memories, the thoughts and whispers and voices of "our" people, whoever we are, are stored in "our" language. Words *form* our minds and form *in* our minds, and we see our selves and the world and find our selves *in* the world through the lenses of the words and images inherent in our native tongue. Throughout our lives, no power can awaken and open our minds so deeply.

O'Donohue tells us that in the Irish language, for example, there are no specific substantive nouns of longing and belonging. Perhaps the Irish mind never saw longing and belonging as fixed, closed realities or separate things, or perhaps the early Celtic people held the experience of longing constantly in mind. But where the meaning of belonging and longing come together in a wider, implicit sense of life and living, they form a larger embrace of human experience that the Irish call *dúcas*.[9] *Dúcas* captures the *inner sense and content of belonging* in that it means one's essential birthright and heritage; it also means one's native place.[10] In the Irish language, the act of birth brings possibility and limitation, but it also confers rights.

Of the many deep layers to the way we belong to ourselves and the world, there is none more dense and difficult to penetrate than the time and place of our first awakening as children.[11] In the Irish tradition, says O'Donohue, there is a deep sense of the way a place and its soul-atmosphere penetrate during that time of childhood, so the phrase "*ag fillead ar do dúcas*" means both returning to your native place and rediscovering who you are. The return home in this language is also the retrieval and reawakening of a hidden and forgotten treasury of identity and soul. "To come home to where you belong is to come into your own, to become what you are, to awaken and develop your latent spiritual heritage," he writes.[12] Remember Jung's idea of individuation as "coming into one's own," and certainly the process and experience of individuation implies an ongoing development of one's spiritual heritage.

For the Irish mind, soul-searching is the excavation of the *dúcas* in and around us in order to belong more fully to ourselves and to participate in our inner heritage in a critical and creative way. When we fail to engage in soul-searching, our unconscious anxiety and fear prescribe the styles of belonging that characterize our sense of homelessness in modern life: styles of belonging that have no self-criticism or self-reflection corral our deepest longings into fixed, empirical frames, as they do with any lack of psychological development. Then we—or the people of any language—have fundamentalism—the polar opposite of *dúcas*.[13] I must say that the gifted Irish language puts other languages to shame, including my own; I know of no single word in my native tongue that can embrace such depth of meaning.

HOME AS SELF, HOME AS SOUL

I mentioned nostalgia earlier, in connection with the word "longing." Nostalgia's Greek origins also speak of our painful longing for home. To be lost in collective nostalgia, however, is to feel like exiles in our time. To be lost in collective nostalgia is to feel lost "between the wars," as T. S. Eliot put it, to feel we are of a "lost generation," as Gertrude Stein added, and now this includes the Baby Boomers whose overwhelming consumerism and booming expansion cannot hide a sense of fruitless activity. Longing and nostalgia can be described as homesickness not only for the people we have left behind but also for places that have been dear and familiar to us: real, concrete places, where once we felt "at home." If only we could find that place again, that tree with that mountain behind it, that hidden space by the river, that cave or that building or that community! If only we might feel we could be *all* of ourselves again.

Have you ever "gone home" to the place where you grew up, only to find that it literally does not exist anymore? A shopping mall stands where the playground stood; a record store stands where your best friend used to live. Other families have moved into your house and changed it beyond recognition and the neighborhood does not look the same. Your grade school (if it still stands) looks impossibly small, although in memory the corridors were so big that once, you remember, you lost your way to your homeroom. Signs on nearby freeways (roads that were not there before) are in a language you can neither read nor pronounce (Hmong, in the small southern California town where once I lived) as well as in English.

For a long time I experienced memories of place as a kind of skeleton on which I felt I could hang my memories of home. In the inner landscape of my memory, recollections of place made up a stony floor of the canyon that my personal experience seemed to etch into my memories of the countries where I had lived. It was as if places where I grew up were in me, echoing into my present while they provided backgrounds, contexts, a stage—for what? I now wonder. For my personal life and development? But come to think of it, what *was* the color of the soil, the shape of the hills, the regular weather? I can remember only bits and pieces. But the pieces I can remember are important. If I were back there now, I suspect I could find my way almost anywhere by body memory. When we look at memories of place through the context of soul, "place" is all over the place, buried in our neural pathways. The wisdom and narrative of place is much more than a skeleton. Now I realize that places themselves have generated the images with which I think. Memories of places I've known and places I've been have constructed my imagination, as now they measure my daily reconstructions of my view of the world.

I suspect that on its own (sans ego), the body expects place to stay unchanged. Once I have walked over a hill past that certain rock and tree, it is my body that remembers how to get there again, even as my mind forgets. Once I have driven somewhere I can usually get there again, but when I am only a passenger, neither mind nor body pay attention to the route and I seldom remember a thing. This not only reiterates the importance of the body that underlies all of our experience of heart and mind, it also tells us that our bodies relate to place as something that will stay put and remain unchanged (or ought to). When actual terrestrial change happens, the body is thrown off. This is because the body itself is a *place,* a kind of portable place.

If I pay close attention to myself while watching clips of old war movies, I find that I am cringing not only at scenes of mindless human destruction but also at scenes (and sounds) of horrible, senseless destruction and pollution of the land, of the earth, that is far more toxic to the water, the air, and the earth itself than any earthquake or tornado. Our bodily stability cannot help but resonate with the stability of place, the stability of the earth, and similarly, it rocks and shakes with anxiety and instability and earthly trauma. This makes profound sense because the only real place each of us inhabits throughout our lives is the place where our body is, and our bodies hold memories of life that consciousness can never access.

In analytical psychology we often talk of the mystery within us. What about the mystery out there, outside our skin, outside and everywhere? We wake up on this planet, each of us formulating a tiny bit of space as all together we rocket through immense space. Though we know that time is a concept, a human construct (and different peoples have very different ideas of and about time),[14] space somehow doesn't seem to be our idea. The space where our body is is the only space we can really call our own, and it is woven of elements and rhythms and materials that we will never actually see, touch, or fathom. These essences form the memories that our bodies contain. We also talk in analytical psychology about the value and desirability of psychological "wholeness," if only because we intuit that it may take a "whole" person to be able to perceive a whole world. We intuit that we need round lives to live on this round earth, round lives to perceive the promise that the earth we live on is the same earth whose life-giving breath we all inhabit and the same earth whose mystery we each experience from our own unique and individual place within its depths.

Yet lest we always take the idea of home and place so literally, let us remember Basho, the Japanese haiku master, who begins his *The Narrow Road to the Deep Interior* with these words: "The moon and the sun travel night and day. The years trail on without interruption. Whether steering a ship at sea or leading a horse on land, each person's life is a journey and the journey itself is home."[15] For Basho, each person's journey is their place of belonging and journeying is our natural condition.

I find that I use something like Basho's perspective often in my psychoanalytic work: therapy or analysis is often experienced as a period of voluntary exile from life (and self) as previously known, and the end of analysis can be experienced as a homecoming (though one is often alarmingly free). In that way, psychoanalytic work makes wanderers of us all and we consult the unconscious background of home and exile with every dream. Over time we unearth memories of losing that place or leaving that place: we feel again how it is to be torn between vows of return someday, of course, and swearing that we will never, ever go back. So speaking psychoanalytically, there is "building home" and there is "destroying home," literally and figuratively, in mind and in heart, in psyche and soul, otherwise known as growing up—at least enough to evolve a capacity for exchange and understanding. There is home as place and home as feeling; there is home as sensation and even home as thought, just as there is "home at last" and home as finding something, someone, or someplace that feels "just right."

Because dream images so frequently contradict both conscious and unconsciously fixed frames and ideals and help dissolve these, dreams help us guard against conscious literalism and fundamentalist thinking. I once had a telephone session with a patient who was grieving the loss of a relationship of twenty-five years, the dissolution of which she realized was already under way when she discovered that her former partner hadn't told her of the death of his dog, which had happened several months earlier. Having no animals of her own, she had enjoyed driving with her partner and the dog to the beach, sharing in the dog's care as if the dog belonged to them together. She told me her dream of the night before she called: Someone gave her a dog that arrived in the back of a New York taxi, an old beagle that was either hung over, exhausted, or ill. She had wanted a puppy and didn't like beagles, but she took the dog in her arms. End of dream.

I hazarded something to the effect that now she had her own animal and no longer needed the animal body of her life to be translated through someone else's animal (or life.)

"But I don't like beagles," came the far small voice over Skype, and the session ended.

That afternoon I received an e-mail telling me that sleeping on her couch on a large pale yellow towel was an old, fat, sweet beagle. As it lay on its side, its visible ear twitched from time to time and its eye opened, clear, and she and the dog gazed long at one another. She said to it with love, "Just rest."

And to me, "Thank you."

Presenting the dreamer with an old-soul dog instead of a spirited puppy, her dream offered her a *solutio* that helped the dreamer open her heart to another even when that other—in this case, her animal, instinctual, bodily self—wore the temporary guise of a tired old beagle. And as the dream found a home in our work and our relationship, a bit of her disowned life energy also found a home in her psyche.

In other dreams, images of home picture where such-and-such might have happened, sometimes something that is consciously remembered, sometimes something that is not. Looking through the lens of self, dreams bring us news, urging on our imaginative energy and psychological integration. Other examples: I'm in my home, but it isn't the one I really live in, and I'm surprised to find a whole hidden wing. Or I'm back where I grew up and people are demanding that I look behind the house where I was afraid to go alone: something is happening there now. Or I'm playing in the basement of my old family home with my friend and my children. When I take my children upstairs to bed, my friend stays below. I hear a scream. The cellar door is closed; I know something terrible is happening to her. I wake up. Or my dream home that looks like the one I really live in has many new rooms I didn't know about. Or I'm the hostess of a grand old home where I serve afternoon tea; I stable my horses out back (while in reality

I live in a walk-up studio on 94th Street). Or I'm living in a castle, gazing out the windows. I rarely look down, but when I do, I see someone who yesterday made me feel small, so ashamed. Or my house is full of junk. Dirt coats the floor and the doors won't close. Or I can't find home; I've forgotten how to get there.

In dreams, images of home are endlessly elastic and varied. Creative people, especially poets, have dream images of a certain kind: almost always there are structures with three walls but not four or the roof is missing. For such people, an experience of home often includes a dimension of being that is wide open to the elements. In life this openness may be felt as a lack of security or proper boundaries or it may be recognized as the gift of psychological mediumship (a psychologically "medial" personality) with highly sensitive unconscious connections to the outer world. Such a psychic structure *is* a real gift, but the openness and sensitivity it necessarily entails often cost dearly in real life. This inherent capacity unrolls before the emerging person large tasks of ego strengthening and integration if a personal life is to be lived with any self-integrity at all.

I always ask about a dream home in detail. Does it have windows? What does it look like inside as well as outside? Who lives there? Does it connect to the outdoors? How? How does it feel to be wherever you are? How does it feel to come upon much more space than you thought you had where you live? How does it feel to come upon someone else living in the home you thought you dwelled in alone? Who else is there? Where you are? *Who* are you when you are there?

Dreams of the many literal homes I've lived in since I was young have been few, even of the home where I grew up: the clearest image I can now remember is before the new room was added (after my baby sister arrived), when I had "a room of my own." That's the important phrase here: "a room of my own." Those words trail memories of struggling to maintain my self, my small eight-year old standpoint, and memories throughout my life of struggling to regain—let alone maintain—"a room of one's own" (thank you, Virginia Woolf). I only glimpse in brief all those temporary homes and trailer courts, apartments and rented rooms and rooms let out to us by unfamiliar relatives where my mother and I stayed briefly during the army years before my father was unexpectedly shipped overseas to the Pacific Theater.

"Homes," like the memories of these experiences, return as semi-conscious images: a tiny green forest with a footpath where I found a little snake, a pencil drawing of a ship and clouds on a piece of plywood that hung on a wall that someone who had lived in a trailer before I did had drawn (I made clouds like that for years); curtains blowing over my bed at night in southern California, the white fabric sooty-black within a week with smog from orange-grove smudge pots right outside my window; soft brown dust between my bare toes as I walked to the Safeway with two dimes for an 18¢ loaf of bread clutched in my hand along roads yet unpaved (in rural southern California, believe it or not). Note how sensual these memories are. Associations like these reconnect my consciousness to a dreaming body. Like night dreams and myths, daydreams are in-between kinds of things, sometimes no more than a cloud based upon shadow, lingering on the movement of the wind.

So—we have coming home, leaving home, feeling at home, and homelessness. What about mythic imaginings? What about the biblical story of Mary and Joseph fleeing, finding no room at the inn except in a stable? They huddled together, the two of them, and placed their newborn in a manger to be warmed by animals. Images of home and homelessness underlie the whole of our Western religious sensibility. What does it mean, that biblical passage where a scribe tells Jesus that he will follow him wherever he goes and Jesus replies that "the foxes have holes and the birds of the air have nests; but the Son of man hath no where to lay his head"?[16] What can these questions and images tell us about the archetype of Home and the archetype of the Wanderer in the Western psyche, then and now? We hear stories as history (Jesus' birth under the reign of Herod), and mythic stories, spirit and soul, are told and retold every winter solstice throughout Christendom. Most of us know these images beyond memory: they have seeped into the bones of the collective psyche from the culture we are born into, whether we belong to any kind of church or not.

America's collective psyche is full of images of home—home is where the heart is, a man's castle is his home, woman as homemaker—and our children attend high school classes in home economics (or used to) or they have homecoming parties. Someone is a homebody and makes home brew. Gardens are homegrown, bread is homemade, and children's games still include the uplifting call of "Home free!" What

HOME AS SELF, HOME AS SOUL

do we mean when we say (usually of ravenous teenagers or guests who overstay their welcome) "They are eating us out of house and home?" Remember the movie *E.T.*? "E.T. phone hooooooome!" Few of us were untouched by that scene. Home, home on the range; our collective heartstrings resonate with such scenes and sayings, and yes, usually it is the heart that responds, rather than the head.

What do we feel about the "problem of the homeless"? What do we feel (not think) about homeless persons who feel quite at home remaining homeless, thank you? Lately in America, issues of Homeland Security have burgeoned, justifying actions and behavior that is at variance with our collective ideal (image) of America as the home of the free. Our country is a country populated by immigrants from all over the world, yet now we build walls and craft laws to keep foreigners out. Go home (meaning away). Go back to where you came from. No asylum here.

Asylum. Shelter. Abode. Habitat. Infirmary. Native land. Grave. These are Roget's synonyms for the word "home." When we "home in" on something we pinpoint it or use radar to locate it. Meanings for the word "homeless"? Alone. Destitute. Displaced. Forlorn. Jung frequently referred to our isolation from nature as a source of our psychological distress: "No voices now speak to man from stones, plants and animals," Jung writes, "nor does he speak to them believing they can hear. . . . This enormous loss is compensated for by the symbols in our dreams."[17] But dream symbols hardly compensate for such a devastating loss of connection to the outer world. Perhaps Jung was remembering his years of feeling trapped in a perpetually expanding inner self when he wrote those words. Perhaps to the particular person Jung was at that particular time, the idea of psychological compensation felt like compensation enough.

What do we mean when we say a place is "homelike" or when a feeling of home shines through a place that formerly seemed strange and alien? Can the earth itself feel homelike? Comfortable. Habitable. Homey. Sometimes, as in Irish fairy tales, we feel we have been abducted from home, yet we end up finding something for which we have been unconsciously longing all our days, something that we've been unable to see through eyes glazed over with the everyday. Perhaps our eyes, our vision, needs to become "homely." "Homely," meaning primarily comfortable and homelike, has additional connotations of something common and humble, something informal or in plain style. Meanings of "homely" shade off into the words "stark" and "simple" and, today, "ugly" and "vulgar." Perhaps we need to develop eyes that can see through what we impulsively (and collectively) judge as homely, ugly, and plain.

All living languages are homely in their own ways. Surely the Romans spoke Latin with no difficulty, finding it expressive and capacious. But when languages die (when languages lose their homeland?) they become rigid and homely. Hierarchies and divisions occur. In the Middle Ages, Vulgar Latin (popular Latin) was distinguished from literary or standard Latin: commoners spoke the vernacular, while Latin was the language of scholar, court, and law. The Vulgate Bible was the Latin version of the Bible deliberately prepared for commoners by St. Jerome at the end of the fourth century, so even Vulgar Latin was once a Roman "mother tongue." One of Jung's goals was to learn to both speak and write aristocratic Latin, but while the male alchemists may have spoken this language, their *sorores mysticae* probably did not.

In the Middle Ages, educated men (most women were not educated) wrote and spoke High Latin. Women were the first to actually write (compose poetry, song, narrative) in "vulgar" or informal language. Women wrote in the living language of their mother tongue, the simple language, the language of home. They found it natural to express poetry and religious experience in words that could speak to many rather than a few. Plain speech was woman speech. Among these women were gifted souls, troubadours and Beguines who complained that it was hard enough to describe mystical experience with plain speech, let alone try to translate it into head or church or logo-speech. The Beguines got around High Latin and a great deal else by living a communal religious life of service outside the Church, although the Church subsumed them within a hundred years.

Perhaps we can say that we start from home and we end up at home, somehow, our final resting place in terms of self *and* soul, but that wandering lies inevitably between. In between, we are on the path, on the journey, between homes, between acts, between countries, between relationships, between ourselves, between parts of ourselves, and between each other. The wisdom of place, outer and inner, actually narrates this journey. As a category of understanding, then, the image of the Wanderer is relating the psyche to itself, in both aspect and essence. The image of the Wanderer underlies the psychological hero-heroine journey as well as the evolution of ego consciousness. The image of the Wanderer underlies as well the evolution of the psyche into soul, and it is central to the depths of mystical experience.

I think of Jung's use of the image of the orphan here. Gerhard Dorn, one of Jung's alchemists, connects the orphan, the widow, and the moon—solitary sojourners and wanderers all. And the Philosopher's Stone is called "orphan" because of its uniqueness. As the word that describes a gem, "orphan" means something like our modern word "solitaire"—an apt name for the unique *lapis Philosophorum*. Jung tells us that the stone refers to the homeless orphan who is slain at the beginning of the work for purposes of transformation from unconsciousness into consciousness by way of the immemorial "passion play" of death and rebirth. Through the lens of the Self, the orphan, the alienated one, the boy child whose heroic goals long ago carried him far from home, is a necessary sacrifice, for an archetypal drama of death and rebirth lies hidden in the *coniunctio*, where profound human emotions clash together in every problem of the opposites.[18]

Jung's personal story both evokes and refers to what I call the wisdom and narrative of place when he tells us how he built his stone tower by the lake. At Bollingen, Jung hand-carved a four-sided stone as a kind of monument to express what his tower meant to him. The third side (facing the lake) is covered with Latin quotations from alchemy and translates as follows:

> I am an orphan, alone; nevertheless I am found everywhere. I am one, but opposed to myself. I am youth and old man at one and the same time. I have known neither father nor mother, because I have had to be fetched out of the deep like a fish, or fell like a white stone from heaven. In woods and mountains I roam, but I am hidden in the innermost soul of man. I am mortal for everyone, yet I am not touched by the cycle of aeons.[19]

On the fourth side of the stone Jung carved (in Latin) "In remembrance of his seventy-fifth birthday C. G. Jung made and placed this here as a thank-offering, in the year 1950." Because it stands outside the tower, the stone is an explanation of the tower and a manifestation of the occupant, incomprehensible to others.[20]

I suspect that Jung's words and actions at Bollingen express aspects of the archetype of home that he forged into expressions of his gratitude for an experience of soul: an experience of home lost, homelessness, and home regained (and *embodied*) in both inner and outer worlds. According to Jung's memoirs, his personal experience and embodied activities at Bollingen were fully earthed in body from beginning to end. *The Visions Seminars* records Jung saying, "When the great swing has taken an individual into the world of symbolic mysteries nothing comes from it, nothing can come from it, unless it has been *associated with the earth,* unless it has happened when that individual was *in the body.*"[21]

If by "swing" Jung means an experience of *enantiodromia,* where inner world becomes outer world and vice versa (as I think he does), how else *could* it happen? Without body, not only is there is no ego "home" to receive human experience but there is no "home" there to *register* embodied experience for the ego to receive. A "great swing" cannot happen in the mind alone. Jung knew this, and he knew this through personal experience. Despite the extraordinary perceptive ability that grounded Jung in his inner world and despite his great personal integrity (Jung's idea of the subjective equation), by the end of his life, "the dividing walls" between inner and outer worlds had become wonderfully transparent. His own experience of the "great swing" is what enabled Jung to find himself as a "son of the earth," no longer *trapped* by an inner world but at home there, as at home as he was in the natural world.[22] It was as an *earth creature* that Jung discovered in himself the fullness (roundness) of his human nature, as can we all.

The poet Mary Oliver seems to have taken for granted the reality of the outer world. Was she once a girl child venturing away from home in order to leave something behind? Perhaps. But if so, we do not need to know exactly what she left in order to know what she found. Mary Oliver writes through a lens of soul. She tells us that she recognizes in her experience of home the relationship of her own mind to landscape, especially to places with which she has become intimate. Her poetry is filled with landscape as a rich companion, a steady ballast against what she describes as "lesser moods"—flightiness, indifference—and absences of heart and mind. Something in her, says Oliver, longs for whatever supersedes (even if it cannot pass through) understanding: faith, grace, rest, peace—she calls it by many names. Oliver says that she could call this something unsatisfied at the center of her life *a longing for home* that makes her "shaky, fickle, inquisitive, and hungry."[23] What a graphic depiction of how archetypal energies affect us!

Oliver tells us that her most familiar landscapes steady her and quiet this longing. She finds her landscapes "fun, and familiar, and healthful, and unbelievably refreshing, and lovely. And they are "the theatre [*soul-space*] of the spiritual; it is the multiform utterly obedient to a mystery."[24]

> And here I build a platform and live upon it, and think my thoughts, and aim high. To rise, I must have a field to rise from. To deepen, I must have a bedrock from which to descend. The constancy of the physical world, under its green and blue dyes, draws me toward a better, richer self, call it elevation (there is hardly an adequate word), where I might ascend a little—where a gloss of spirit would mirror itself in worldly action. . . . Nature, all around us, is our manifest exemplar. Not from the fox, or the leaf, or the drop of rain will you ever hear doubt or argument. . . . One of the perils of our so-called civilized age [is] that we do not yet acknowledge enough, or cherish enough, this connection between soul and landscape—between our own best possibilities, and the view from our own windows. We need the world as much as it needs us and we need it in privacy, intimacy, and surety.[25]

I'm with Oliver. And I, like Mary Oliver, experience a "better, richer self" here on earth as the earth itself infuses us with soul.

NOTES

1. Every archetype is multifaceted and is a vehicle for more than one pair of opposites or opposing valences of energy. As a collection of symbolic energy patterns, an archetype such as Home gives rise to multiple and multiply-opposing affect-images, whether we find them in dreams, behavior, ritual, mythology, or in manifest clinical situations.

2. C. G. Jung, *The Visions Seminars: From the Complete Notes of Mary Foote,* vol. 2 (Zürich: Spring Publications, 1976), p. 473.

3. Certainly the air we breathe is limited: if our fragile, livable envelope of atmosphere were laid out before our feet rather than extending above our heads, we would come to the end of it in the brief space of an early morning walk, assuming that it takes two and a half

hours to cover ten miles. We cannot imagine limits to consciousness, though surely we recognize limited limitation when we designate all that is not conscious as "unconscious."

4. Clarissa Pinkola Estés, *Women Who Run with the Wolves: Myths and Stories of the Wild Woman Archetype* (New York: Ballantine Books, 1992), pp. 255–296.

5. C. G. Jung, *Memories, Dreams, Reflections,* edited by Aniela Jaffé, translated by Richard and Clara Winston (New York: Vintage Books, 1989), p. 359, my italics.

6. Kabir, "Friend, Hope for the Guest While You Are Alive," in *Essential Sufism,* edited by James Fadiman and Robert Frager (New York: HarperCollins, 1997), p. 256, my italics.

7. John O'Donohue, *Eternal Echoes: Celtic Reflections on Our Yearning to Belong* (New York: HarperCollins, 1999).

8. Eva Hoffman, *Lost in Translation: A Life in a New Language* (New York: Penguin Books, 1989).

9. *Dúcas* becomes an adjective when it describes the nature of the relationship we have with someone when there is real affinity of soul, a flow of spirit and vitality between two people. It refers to a person's deepest nature, to a whole intuitive quickness of longing in us that tells us how to think and act that we would call instinct. An old Irish proverb believes that instinct is a powerful force within us: "*Briseann an dúcas amac tri suile an cait*" (*Dúcas* will break forth even through the eyes of a cat).

Dúcas is also used to interpret, explain, or excuse something in a person: "He cannot help it—he has the *dúcas* for that." In some sense, says O'Donohue, *dúcas* seems to be a deeper force than history. We belong to our *dúcas*; our *dúcas* is our belonging. *Dúcas* suggests the wildness of uninhibited Nature, and a proverb says that *dúcas* is impervious to outside training: "*Is treise an dúcas na an oilluint*" (*Dúcas* is stronger than education or upbringing). O'Donohue, *Eternal Echoes,* p. 254.

10. *Ibid.*

11. Thus the importance in analytic work of one's first memories and first dreams, the first story one remembers, and so forth. These give us a glimpse into the times and places that personal ego consciousness begins to accrue, forming a little archipelago of islands of emerging awareness in an otherwise featureless ocean of existence.

12. O'Donohue, *Eternal Echoes*, p. 254.
13. *Ibid.*, p. 255.
14. Pema Chödrön tells us that the Navajo teach their children that every morning the sun is born new, lives for the day, and passes on, never to return. As soon as the children are old enough, adults take them out at dawn and say "The sun has only one day. You must live this day in a good way, so that the sun won't have wasted precious time." Pema Chödrön, *The Wisdom of No Escape and the Path of Loving-Kindness* (Boston: Shambhala Publications, 2010), p. 33.
15. Basho, quoted in Richard R. Powell, *Wabi Sabi for Writers* (Avon, Mass.: Adams Media, 2006), p. 55.
16. Matthew 8:19–20, King James Version.
17. C. G. Jung, "Approaching the Unconscious," in *Man and His Symbols*, edited by C. G. Jung (New York: Doubleday, 1964), p. 95.
18. C. G. Jung, *Mysterium Coniunctionis*, vol. 14 of *The Collected Works of C. G. Jung*, edited and translated by G. Adler and R. F. C. Hull (Princeton, N.J.: Princeton University Press, 1970), pp. 13, 35.
19. Jung, *Memories, Dreams, Reflections*, p. 227.
20. *Ibid.*, p. 228.
21. Jung, *The Visions Seminars*, p. 473, my italics.
22. Jung, *Memories, Dreams, Reflections*, p. 354.
23. Mary Oliver, "Home," in *Long Life: Essays and Other Writings* (Cambridge, Mass.: Da Capo Press, 2004), pp. 89–91, my italics.
24. *Ibid.*, p. 90.
25. *Ibid.*, pp. 90–91.

In the Footsteps of Scheherazade, an Inspiring Image of Feminine Development and Creativity:

Aisha's Story in Jungian and Transcultural Perspective

VALENTINA LUCIA ZAMPIERI

INTRODUCTION

Why Scheherazade? Why reconsider today from a psychological perspective the heroine of *The Thousand and One Nights*, so popular in both "Oriental"[1] and Western culture and so often the object of collective projections? Scheherazade is indeed not only one of the most famous feminine characters of world literature, but she has also become, especially since

---

Valentina Lucia Zampieri is a Jungian analyst and psychotherapist in private practice in Zurich. With an academic background in architecture, psychology, and philosophy, she trained at the C. G. Jung Institute in Zurich and studied ethnopsychoanalysis in Paris. She has worked as an interior designer in Milan and New York and as a psychotherapist in Venice and Cairo. She is particularly interested in exploring cross-cultural issues in analysis.

Author's Note: The following article was written some months before the recent revolutionary events in Egypt so that no reference to them appears in it. Yet, in many respects, Aisha, the young Egyptian woman whose case is described in this article, could very well represent many of the young people in Midan Tahrir who, thanks in part to the clever use of social media, played a pivotal role in bringing about such a momentous change in Egyptian history.

the 19th century, a real "myth" that has grown beyond the borders of the literary scene. Her name immediately evokes a multitude of differing images, ranging from Oriental femininity and beauty to perfumes, fashion labels, and kitsch nightclubs. Beyond sublimations and stereotypes, I believe that Scheherazade embodies an uncommon and complex combination of characteristics and archetypal traits that can make her an inspiring, symbolic image of feminine development and creativity. Contacting such energy may have an impact on the psychic growth of many women still struggling nowadays to make their way in societies permeated by the shadow of patriarchy.

This is indeed a general issue that applies to both Oriental and Western women,[2] given the fact that patriarchal aspects—different forms of male dominance and gender subordination—can be traced, with some variations, in both cultures. In this article, I will focus on Oriental women, but only after clarifying some necessary, preliminary remarks about the risks and limits of every statement pronounced on this subject from a Western position. As the anthropologist Lila Abu-Lughod has effectively demonstrated, the stereotypical images of Muslim women circulating in the Western world confine them to a very limited set of tropes and themes: the veiled woman, the oppressed woman, the woman deprived of freedom and civil rights, the woman ruled by her religion, the woman submitted to men, etc. But these do not mirror at all the complexity and diversity of their lives, nor their reality as human beings. The particularities of individual lives and narratives always render questionable generalizations, both scientific and popular, about the patterns of Arab social life and culture that impact women's experiences. Moreover, every time a Western woman feels the need or entitled to speak about and on behalf of Oriental women, she should be wary not only of her projections but also of any form of patronizing arrogance that might depend on or even reinforce Westerners' sense of superiority, embarrassingly resonating with the rhetoric of colonial feminism.[3] On the basis of my personal experience in the Middle East, I share these ideas and hope to avoid, as much as possible, such clichés; nevertheless, I remain aware of the inevitable biases of my perspective, deriving from my cultural background.

A digression about my personal and professional path might help to comprehend better the relevance of the figure of Scheherazade as a feminine way. My encounter with her was first inspired by a mysterious dream I had in 2003, in which she was mentioned in connection with a beautiful ring I found in Khan El Khalili, the souk of Cairo. Her appearance in the dream immediately brought me back to my first readings as a child, when I deeply enjoyed the magical atmosphere surrounding many of the tales of *The Thousand and One Nights*,[4] and I was particularly fascinated by Scheherazade, the charming heroine of the frame-story, who was capable of the most inventive story-telling in order to save her own life. Later, at the time of the dream, I was training as an analyst at the C.G. Jung Institute in Zurich and travelling extensively in the Middle East, driven by a strong interest in the culture of this area. I felt that Scheherazade had not emerged by chance from my unconscious, and I decided to put myself in her footsteps, sure that she was somehow indicating a message for me to integrate or a way to follow on my personal journey. I extended my trips to almost all the countries that gave birth to the tales of the *Nights*, from Morocco to Iran, and started a series of readings and research about Scheherazade herself that finally found a form in my diploma thesis for the Jung Institute in 2006.[5]

Soon after that, I moved to Cairo, where I lived and worked for two years as a psychotherapist at the Counselling Center of the American University in Cairo (AUC)[6] and as a Jungian analyst in private practice. Once again, it was my fascination with the Middle East that fostered in me not only an animating wish to plunge myself entirely into this culture, but also a willingness to lose my usual points of reference, to question my conscious and unconscious apriorisms, to ultimately confront an experience of "disorientation," voluntarily chosen in search of new perspectives. Briefly speaking, it was a quest for a full immersion in the experience of otherness—both outside and inside myself. Cairo proved the ideal location for such an experience, sometimes challenging but on the whole extremely rewarding. Professionally, it also meant the challenge of "decentering" (see section 3 of this text) myself and my usual system of reference to overcome my ethnocentric biases while becoming more flexible in meeting the specific cultural and symbolic realities of the persons with whom I worked (mostly Egyptians and Middle Easterners). Born and brought up in Italy, I have mostly lived in Western countries (Italy, the United States, Switzerland, and France). Also my academic background in architecture, philosophy, and psychology was deeply rooted in and informed by Western culture. The exposure to the Middle Eastern tradition, first through my trips, then during the years spent in Cairo, meant to me not only broadening my cultural perspective but also opening to a new symbolic dimension and an inner trajectory in which Scheherazade became a sort of psychopomp.

In fact, she accompanied me during my stay in Egypt not only as an inner figure—her strategy with the king often helped me find the right approach to various patterns of Arabic society—but also as a topic I brought up in my conversations with friends and colleagues. To my surprise, she also entered the analytical setting during sessions with some female analysands. This happened after I gave a seminar at AUC to present my work and share my views about her. The participants—both women and men—provided me with very stimulating feedback, but I was struck most by the comments I received during the analyses of some of the women who attended the seminar: Scheherazade proved to be still very alive in their psyche, as a strong affective, inspiring presence, and a sort of feminine reference point, although not always perceived in her entire multifaceted complexity. My presentation activated in them the energy related to this figure, so loved and deep-rooted in their culture, and fostered a series of spontaneous amplifications and associations to their own personal history and psychic process. This also led to acute insights about how to uncover in themselves and integrate some of Scheherazade's features in their conscious attitude. Realizing the impact that the evocation of Scheherazade had made on them, I was encouraged to continue my work on the inspiring role this figure might play in various phases of the individuation process of women not only in the Middle East but from other cultural backgrounds as well.

On my return to Zurich from Cairo in 2009, I felt the need to acquire some additional theoretical and clinical tools which were specifically conceived for cross-cultural psychology and which focused on the role culture can play in psychotherapy. I had the opportunity to do this by participating in a programme about Transcultural Psychiatry[7] at the University of Paris in 2009-10. This program provided me with stimulating perspectives on these issues, including an introduction to the principles of ethnopsychoanalysis (or ethnopsychiatry), while exposing me to a fascinating clinical approach and to specific psychotherapeutic techniques that will reverberate more and more in contemporary times characterized by massive migrations and the mixing (*métissage*) of different cultures.

In this article, I begin an integration of the principles of ethnopsychoanalysis with those of Jungian psychology by exploring how the character of Scheherazade informed the analysis of one of my analysands while I was practicing in Cairo. After describing the main points of Scheherazade's significance from a psychological standpoint (section 1), I will, in sections 2 and 3, describe those aspects of ethnopsychoanalysis that, in my view, are the most interesting contributions to consider integrating into a purely analytical perspective. Sections 4 and 5 concern some facets of my clinical work with Aisha, a woman in Cairo for whom Scheherazade came to represent a particularly meaningful symbolic image. In presenting Aisha's case, my purpose is to focus on its cultural aspects and to integrate the Jungian analytical approach with the transcultural clinical perspective, which combines psychoanalysis and anthropology as the main theoretical fundamentals of ethnopsychiatry (see sections 2 and 3). In fact, given its specific focus on the role of culture in psychic processes and psychotherapeutic theory and practice (section 2), this approach has proven to be particularly useful in all psychotherapies in which therapist and patient do not share the same cultural background.

1. Scheherazade's way

Scheherazade's key role in the frame story of *The Thousand and One Nights* (a summary of which is provided at the end of this article) conveys an image of feminine power, not only of seduction but also of intelligence, cunning, and creativity in facing the king and saving her own life. This may represent a paradox for a collection of tales that were mainly conceived in the Middle Ages and stem from a set of cultures where women were (and often still are) marginalized from the social and political scene and where a deep ambivalence toward the feminine is apparent in many of their essential cultural expressions (from religion to social and legal systems).[8] This paradox supports the intriguing hypothesis of some authors that see in *The Thousand and One Nights* the survival, despite unfavorable social and collective conditions, of the voice of the feminine principle in the dimension of imagination and storytelling.[9] The real authors of the *Nights* might then be the women secluded in the harems, whose imaginations triumphed over the patriarchal devices of segregation and legal discrimination by creating, through storytelling, another world where the feminine could express itself in all its quintessential facets.[10]

The tension between the sexes, that still nowadays underlies so many gender-related dynamics in Arab-Muslim culture (and that, in a more concealed way, is present in Western culture as well), is hyperbolically portrayed in the prologue of the *Nights* in the relationship between the king and his first wife. Despite being locked up in the harem, she easily succeeds in cheating on him with a male slave, enacting a vicious circle of abuse and betrayal that is built into the very structure of this basic division between private and public space in the traditional Muslim society.[11] The result is a harsh struggle between masculine power as the need to control and dominate and feminine power as *fitna*, the uncontrollable and disruptive capacity to destabilize through sex the male social order and to create chaos.[12]

Within this context, Scheherazade and the king represent, first of all, the archetypal tension between the feminine and the masculine that has its roots in the biological realm and whose dialectic is present in every psychological process, like the one portrayed in the tale itself. On the objective level, king Shahrayar may symbolically represent the state of inflated isolation, lack of eros, and one-sidedness of a sick masculine consciousness, a hypertrophied ego totally identified with his position and power. In Jungian terms, he could be defined as a man whose one-sided consciousness has become totally identified with his persona while losing contact with his anima: split from his feminine side, he no longer has access to the depths of his unconscious and to the Self as the leading and regulating center of the whole psyche. Moreover, as the king, he symbolizes the dominant attitude and central content of collective consciousness, which in this case is the fear, repression, and marginalization of the feminine principle as a leitmotiv of the strictly patriarchal society he rules. His murderous resolution is to kill first his wife; later, absolutely convinced of all women's evil nature, deceitfulness, and uncontrollable lust, he slays all the virgins he marries after he sleeps with each for a single night only: once again, this is a hyperbolic, symbolic image of masculine violence, acted out to its extreme consequences.

If we look at the tale from the perspective of feminine psychology, the corresponding intrapsychic configuration would be that of a woman suffering from a severe negative animus problem. Shahrayar, with his compulsion to kill young women, dramatically represents the particularly cruel, despotic, sadistic traits of an animus that has introjected the culturally induced patriarchal values still infiltrating or dominating so many societies: such an animus has the power to alienate a woman from her innermost feminine nature by repeatedly violating her feelings and intuitions, suppressing over and over again her creative potentialities of development, and sabotaging her choices and undertakings at any level. Only a reconnection to the instinctual and spiritual roots of the feminine self can restore a healthy ego-self axis and redeem the negative animus, thus transforming it into an effective supporter of feminine development and creating a harmonious cooperation between the feminine and masculine factors in the psyche, which is symbolically portrayed by the *coniunctio* at the end of the tale. Given the universalism of the issues at stake, here lies the transcultural symbolic meaning of Scheherazade's story, which is capable of speaking to women from any cultural background.

Scheherazade appears in the tale when the tension is at the apex and the risk of a "gendercide"[13] is becoming apparent. The reasons she gives to her reluctant father, the vizier, to let her become the king's next bride have mainly a collective—social and political—significance: with her initiative, she hopes to stop the slaying of the young women and to free them and all her people from the huge tragedy that has engulfed the kingdom for three years. In this perspective, Scheherazade can be seen as a political heroine and her pertinence as a role model becomes clear: she saves not only herself but also the whole kingdom by slowly changing the mind of the highest authority, the king.[14] The political relevance of the character of Scheherazade has been stressed by Mernissi as well as several other authors of Arab-Muslim culture, who see in her not only a symbol of the eternal feminine but also a civilizing agent,[15] introducing new values in the kingdom and promoting the triumph of words and dialogue (as *dia-logos*) over insane violence.[16] Given her active, determined attitude and her concern for women's condition, other interpreters have found in her a sort of feminist *ante-litteram*.[17]

I personally came to realize that beyond the everlasting popularity of the *Nights*' heroine in the Middle East, the political dimension of her role is not so obvious for many women; yet, once correctly enhanced and clarified, the complexity of the character and her potential as an inspiring model become evident. I think in fact that, even on a collective scale, Scheherazade can convey a message of hope for the feminine condition that still nowadays can prove helpful for all women, maybe to an even greater extent for those living in the Arab-Muslim world who belong to her same cultural tradition. She is not only a powerful image of the resilience and creativity of the feminine spirit under the worst circumstances; she also shows women how to step out of the victim role and actively struggle to change their situation, using methods and means that do not comply with the patriarchal status quo and dominant mentality but that are instead deeply ingrained in the innermost nature and wisdom of the feminine principle. Scheherazade opposes violence and hatred with eros and imagination and struggles not to repress and destroy but to relate, heal, and transform. Ultimately, she opposes the king's culture of terror, repression, and death and promotes a culture of dialogue, life, and relatedness, which is deeply rooted in feminine values.

The first evidence of Scheherazade's capacity to overcome the victim position is the very fact that she volunteers to be the king's next bride. Unlike the other virgins of the kingdom, and most of the feminine protagonists of myths and fairy tales with a similar pattern,[18] she is neither abducted nor forced to marry Shahrayar. She chooses to do so out of her own free will. Such a courageous, proactive gesture reveals a deep strength and an enterprising attitude. This is evident from the beginning of the relationship with Shahrayar and could be at the root of his transformation, for he is himself at first bewildered by the initiative of his vizier's daughter.

In addition to the sociopolitical implications, the psychological reading of the *Nights*' frame-story offers many other thought-provoking ideas relevant to feminine development—including in a broader sense the growth of the feminine side in men's psyche. In my view, one of the most intriguing elements in the tale is the way Scheherazade is presented when she first appears in the story. Despite some differences in the details of the description, all editions and translations of the *Nights* emphasize particularly the heroine's intelligence, culture, and wisdom. Beauty is of course mentioned and present, but it is not the paramount feature of Scheherazade's being. Instead, it is the combination of attractiveness with her acute mind, charm, and sensitivity that makes her such a special character. Should she rely only on her physical beauty and sex appeal in her encounter with the king, she would probably die like all the previous girls. The birth of three children during the "thousand and one nights" clearly indicates that sex is also a component in the alchemy between her and Shahrayar, but what seems more decisive is her capacity to relate to him through both senses and mind, to arouse his curiosity both sexually and intellectually, and ultimately to engage him in a many-sided relationship that finally turns out to be transformative and healing.

In her gift for relatedness, Scheherazade incarnates the quintessence of the feminine principle. Her eros is evident throughout the tale. It shows in the empathy, patience, and nurturing attitude she is able to develop toward the king with whom she remains constantly attuned, despite his initial tyrannical behavior; but it is also apparent in the authentic compassion she experiences for the other young women of the kingdom, which was a primary motivation in her offering to marry the king.

On the other hand, her strategy in facing Shahrayar is so precise and clever, so carefully elaborated and organized in every detail, that it clearly denotes a lucid mind, able to think, discriminate, anticipate, and judge in a very differentiated way. It is the rational side of her character, the strong logos function supporting her ego and clearly at work in her storytelling as well as in the acquisition and purposeful use of her erudition. Actually, intelligence and culture alone would not be enough to face a dramatic challenge like the one that Scheherazade chooses for herself. In addition, a positive animus, boosting her strength and creativity, is needed as well as uncommon courage and unswerving determination. These, together with a solid self-confidence, derived from trust in her own resources and creative talents, join with a strong connection to the Self in order to remain centered and inspired by her own inner vision and goal.

Cunning is of course another essential ingredient in Scheherazade's recipe. This trickster aspect turns out to be crucial for the happy end of the story and, beyond many ungenerous readings that tend to reduce the heroine to her shrewdness, it can also be seen as a sign of cleverness and inventiveness,[19] a non-violent, non-aggressive, mostly feminine way of proceeding, used since time immemorial by women to make their way in patriarchal societies. Myths and fairy tales abound with examples of how women can rescue themselves and others, realize their plans, unblock and transform situations through tricks. With the fundamental help of her younger sister Dinarzad, a sort of positive shadow or supporting alter-ego, Shaharazad succeeds in carrying out her plan in every detail. Considering the life–threatening situation in which she interacts with the king and exercises her narrative talent, her sang-froid, self-confidence, and presence of mind prove even more impressive.

Since their very first meeting, night is the privileged time for Scheherazade's and Shahrayar's encounters. In fact, it is late every night, after lovemaking, that Shaharazad initiates telling a story to the king. Her feminine voice becomes a poetic metaphor for the voice of the unconscious as it is mostly at night-time, after the light of consciousness dims and the rational, objective order is suspended, that the soul is finally allowed to speak its own language, made of images and symbols. Dreams are like stories told by the unconscious every night and, just like dreams, Scheherazade's tales have a healing effect on Shahrayar's psyche, promoting a process of maturation and transformation[20] that finally succeeds in liberating him from his compulsion to kill. As an experienced "psychotherapist", Scheherazade handles with care what could be defined as the transference / countertransference dynamics between herself and the king; more than that, she acts as a "rescuing anima",[21] bringing him awareness of his feelings, filtering the contents of the collective unconscious—wisely distributed in the archetypal images of the fairy tales—through to his consciousness, restoring the connection of his ego to the Self. The positive *lysis* of the tale is more than a conventional "happy end". It implies the realization of an authentic *coniunctio* of the feminine and the masculine as the result of a deep process of transformation, involving not only the protagonists but the whole kingdom. New personal and collective values are established, as life prevails over death, love and compassion over hate and violence. The seeds of a new attitude toward the feminine are finally planted.

Scheherazade succeeds in promoting such a process thanks to the rare combination of features that she embodies. These reveal a deep balance and integration of the feminine and masculine energies within herself. Because of this inner harmony and complexity, which results in a yin-yang balanced personality, a refined *intelligence du coeur*, an eros-centered relatedness, and a deeply rooted wisdom, she represents a composite pattern of the feminine and a multifaceted, symbolic image of the feminine Self. And it is this image that is still capable of inspiring and empowering contemporary women in both the personal and the collective dimension of their individuation journey.

2. The role of cultural material in psychotherapy
a. Ethnopsychoanalysis, or ethnopsychiatry

The experience of the effectiveness of Scheherazade as a facilitator of insights and as a stimulus to psychic elaboration in my analytical work in Cairo leads to the consideration of a very interesting theme, that is, the use of cultural material in psychotherapy, and more generally the role of culture in psychic processes.

Ethnopsychoanalysis, or ethnopsychiatry (since the beginning the discipline has admitted a double designation), has from its outset dealt with these issues in its epistemological reflections on psychiatry as well as in its psychotherapeutic theory and practice, effectually deconstructing the ethnocentrism of western psychiatry and psychology.[22] Ethnopsychoanalysis developed in France in the wake of the work of Georges Devereux,[23] who was both an ethnologist and a Freudian analyst. In his transcultural therapy work, Devereux used his anthropological knowledge not only as a fundamental approach to clinical material, according to his complementarist method, but also with the specific purpose of adapting his psychoanalytic interpretations to the cultural background of his patients. Cultural representations peculiar to the patients' culture were introduced by him to translate his analytical interventions into a language and a symbolic world with which his patients were familiar.[24] He called such interventions "cultural levers"(*leviers culturels*) and repeatedly insisted that they were not ends in themselves but just means to facilitate insights and their elaboration. In other words, cultural levers were used by Devereux as psychotherapeutic tools in the service of a purely psychoanalytic technique. Ultimately, in his view, psychoanalysis was the only perspective capable of promoting self-awareness and psychic transformation, and the patient's specific culture, with its peculiar representations, remained subordinated to it.

After Devereux, the fundamentals of ethnopsychiatry were theoretically developed and translated into original methods of therapeutic interventions mainly by Tobie Nathan and Marie Rose Moro. In their work, both these psychiatrists focused on migrant populations and minorities of the outer suburbs of Paris and explored in depth the cultural dimension in therapy, giving cultural representations a different and far more relevant role than Devereux did.

For Nathan, a person's psyche develops within a cultural frame that becomes a sort of containing envelope, providing a sense of safety, stability, and a system of reference in terms of categories to interpret the world. Approaching the cultural dimension of the patients' psyche is therefore an essential step in psychotherapy: it gives a key to access their world-view and activate their psychic, symbolic, and social resources, thus reorganizing their psychic structure.[25] Therefore, in Nathan's method, cultural representations were never subordinated to the psychoanalytic perspective; on the contrary, he took more and more distance from psychoanalysis and radicalized the importance of the cultural approach.

The goal of psychotherapy is for Nathan mostly that of reconstructing a specific cultural frame. In order to facilitate such a process, he created a highly innovative therapeutic setting that is still today widely adopted in ethnopsychiatry and has become a sort of badge of the movement: it consists of a multicultural group of therapists, involving several mental health care professionals of different cultural and linguistic backgrounds that work together with interpreters and cultural brokers. In this setting, patients, often accompanied by their families, are invited to discuss their problems and life stories, which are explored with frequent and precise references to their original cultural background.

In the last twenty years, the most interesting developments in the field of ethnopsychoanalysis are found in the work of Marie Rose Moro, a child psychiatrist and Freudian psychoanalyst whose practice at the Avicenne Hospital in the suburbs of Paris has particularly focused on children and families with a migration background. Moro's position is aligned with Nathan's regarding the importance of investigating the cultural dimension and in adopting the multicultural group setting in psychotherapy.²⁶ She differs from him on two main points: she advocates a more dynamic conception of culture and psychoanalysis—that includes regular dream-work—to approach intrapsychic conflicts and family dynamics.

Moro, based upon M. Serres' definition of culture²⁷ and her own constant experience of hybrid cultural identities in her work with migrants, has developed a vision of culture metaphorically expressed through the image of the bridge that is able to connect other cultures and representation systems, even dramatically different ones. Culture is thus conceived as the creation of intermediate spaces, within which individuals can actively choose collective symbols and transform cultural representations through their own personal interpretations.

According to Moro, the therapist's task in psychotherapy is that of understanding the patients' individual investment of collective representations, the function they fulfil within their psyche, and the possibilities of elaboration they open up. The goal of transcultural therapies with migrant persons is not so much the reconstruction and reinforcement of the original, "traditional" cultural frame, as in Nathan's system, but rather the elaboration of a narrative able to interlink multiple cultural references and to connect the different life-worlds they find themselves in-between. The individual's investment and creative reinterpretation of collective symbols can play a decisive role in the therapeutic process and mobilize symbolic resources with healing effects.

On these bases, Moro has developed the concept of *métissage* (mixing and crossing) that has become today a key notion in the field of ethnopsychoanalysis. In her theory, this concept assumes an eminently positive connotation, aimed at enhancing the creative potential of the mixing of cultures and the value of cultural diversity. She actually implements a *métissage* of persons, thoughts, and techniques in her own theoretic and psychotherapeutic work, which is rooted in psychoanalysis but also deliberately eclectic and open to multiple contributions from different fields of research. The therapist becomes then a sort of weaver able to interlace several threads.²⁸

Another fundamental concept in Moro's thought is that of *décentrage* (decentering), developed from Piaget's work and intertwined with the notion of cultural countertransference. The ability to decenter is an essential requirement for the therapist working in a transcultural setting: it implies, first of all, the willingness to open up to and learn about different cultures by expatriating oneself or working with multicultural teams in one's own country. Such an experience necessarily facilitates an awareness of the ethnocentrism of one's own theoretic and methodological approach and fosters a general repositioning of the whole clinical and personal perspective.[29] Beyond that, the decentering process also entails an introspective attitude, in terms of working out the unconscious images, both personal and collective, evoked by the confrontation with cultural otherness in the therapeutic encounter. Freud associated such defensive projections with the experience of the "unheimlich" (uncanny), whereas Jung associated them with the archetype of the shadow. Ethnopsychoanalysis, too, underlines how becoming aware of these unconscious fantasies and collective representations of the "other" is an inescapable task for any professional working with clients from different cultural backgrounds.

b. The role of culture in Jungian psychology

The importance of culture in psychic processes was of course clear to Jung, too, who included the cultural level in his schema of the psyche[30] as a constitutive layer of its collective dimension. He was extremely interested in exploring different cultures and their symbols and dug deeply into them in his research, clinical work, and travels.[31] Yet, there is no doubt that in the Jungian system, most of the emphasis is put on the collective unconscious, the deepest layer of the psyche. Its contents, the archetypes, are primordial images, common to all times and cultures,[32] that function both as structuring patterns of psychic functioning and as patterns of behavior, linked to instincts. The archetype is therefore a psychosomatic concept, linking body and psyche, instinct and image, drives and symbolic function. Late in his life, Jung distinguished between the archetype *per se*, which is "irrepresentable" and cannot be directly observed or experienced, and the archetypal representations (images and ideas),[33] which are instead realizable by man's consciousness and culturally influenced, being filtered by the cultural layers of the collective unconscious.

Consistent with his model, to understand collective psychology and the impact of culture on psychic processes (and vice versa), Jung mostly referred to the archetypal level of the psyche, often not engaging in more careful analyses of the historical and cultural aspects of the contexts he was describing.[34] While he alluded to the cultural unconscious, he never expanded significantly on it. As a consequence, Jungian theory and psychotherapy have traditionally focussed either on the personal or on the archetypal levels of the psyche, not emphasizing cultural context and its components.[35]

However, an archetypal image or experience is mostly embedded in and filtered through historical and cultural matrices. In 1962 the Jungian analyst Joseph Henderson was the first to formally introduce the concept of "cultural unconscious"[36] to postulate a layer of the psyche existing between the personal and the archetypal. Along these lines, in the last decade, interest in the role of culture in psychic processes has increased: Thomas Singer and Samuel Kimbles have coined the term "cultural complex" to elaborate on the cultural level of psychological experience (both collective and individual) and describe it through the application of Jung's theory of complexes.[37] A cultural complex consists of unquestioned assumptions, underlying prejudices, and long-lasting beliefs held to be true by most of the members of the same group. The influence of culture is so strong that the individual internalizes its schemes, principles, and expectations often without being aware of it. Entrenched in the cultural unconscious, cultural complexes have a pervasive influence in everyday life, shaping our identity, categories, and behavior;[38] often dormant, once triggered, they can unleash a tremendous amount of energy, with particularly dramatic consequences when such dynamics occur on a wide collective scale.

Beyond their effectiveness in describing the psychological nature of conflicts between groups and cultures, such conceptual additions to classical Jungian theory are particularly helpful in clinical work, especially in transcultural psychotherapies. Since both the therapist and the patient are carriers of a specific cultural code[39] they are also affected by the shadow of the group to which they belong. It is, therefore, particularly important for the therapist to be aware of the impact of cultural complexes, especially when it comes to working out their role in transference-countertransference dynamics.

It is clear that, moving from quite different theoretical premises and focuses of interest, contemporary developments in Jungian psychology and ethnopsychoanalysis converge on essential points in their theory and therapeutic practice, particularly when it comes to the need for a thorough elaboration of the countertransference. Convergence points are apparent between the two founders of these fields, too: Devereux repeatedly stressed that the universal element in human nature is psyche itself, whose basic structure and functioning remains the same for everybody; this is similar to Jung's concept of the archetypes, common to all human beings, despite their cultural and personal differences.

3. The Intergration of Two Concepts from Ethnopsychoanalysis, *Décentrage* and Cultural Countertransference, into a Jungian Approach

Two basic principles of ethnopsychoanalysis may be easily integrated into the Jungian approach. The concept of *décentrage* implies a methodological and introspective process that can foster a general reassessment of the analyst's stance particularly fruitful when working with an analysand from a different cultural background. It encourages self-reflexivity both in terms of awareness of the cultural biases of the method and as inner work on one's personal and cultural shadow. This is why decentering overlaps in several ways with the parallel process of elaboration of the countertransference, more particularly its cultural aspects.

Jung was one of the pioneers of the therapeutic use of the countertransference, and considered it to be an indispensable tool of psychotherapy and a highly important organ of transformation for the analyst.[40] It must be accepted and carefully examined: it is a mark of that mutual transformation brought about by multiple analytical dynamics, where the communication between the unconscious of the analyst and that of the patient represents the most authentic analytical element.

In the framework of ethnopychoanalysis, Devereux emphasized, as Jung did, the importance of the analyst's unconscious processes, emotions (first of all anxiety), and defensive strategies in the interaction with the patient, as a source of knowledge.[41] He widened the notion of countertransference by demonstrating the cultural dimension of countertransferential reactions and invited the therapist to observe and analyze the latent cultural pressures, implicit categories, and unconscious models affecting his/her perceptions, thoughts, and behavior in the relationship with the patient.

Later, Nathan introduced the definition of "cultural countertransference" and Moro thoroughly explored its clinical aspects. She described the cultural countertransference as the inner position assumed by the therapist in relation to the patient's cultural otherness, that is to say, all the culturally coded elements defining him/her as a cultural being: his/her way of speaking, of doing, of thinking his/her story and suffering, etc.[42] The cultural countertransference is therefore linked not only to the therapist's personal history, age, sex, professional identity but also to his/her cultural, social, political identity. Moro underlines the peculiarity of this concept, standing at the crossroad of the singular and the universal, the individual and the collective.[43]

In conclusion, to synthesize the perspectives of contemporary ethnopsychoanalysis and post-Jungian theory concerning the elaboration of the countertransference, the analyst's reactions reflect not only his/her individual responses to the patient but also include responses that are based upon the associations and values that arise from the collective with which the analyst identifies. Such reactions are triggered by the perception of the other as "different" —from the most apparent phenotypic differences to the language, the accent, the gestures etc.—and are influenced by the group's collective representations of the "foreigner" as "stranger", which inevitably include stereotypes, prejudices, fixed images, and fantasies.[44] The complexes in the analyst's cultural unconscious can play a decisive role in his/her countertransferential responses: it is therefore of paramount importance for him/her to be aware of the shadow of the group with all its cultural complexes[45] and of its effect on his/her own personality. Work on one's personal shadow, so emphasized in Jungian psychology as a fundamental stage in every analysis, implies also the consideration of the cultural shadow as one of its fundamental facets.

4. "The wind through my hair": Aisha's story

The relevance of the cultural dimensions in psychotherapy became more and more apparent to me throughout my work as a psychoanalyst in Cairo, particularly with Aisha, an analysand whose story and suffering were so abundantly infused with the influences of the social, religious, and all-encompassing cultural scene in which she lived. Thirty years old, married, and mother of two little girls, Aisha was working full time in a bank while continuing her studies in a master's degree program. She came to see me because of an increasing state of stress and anxiety alternating with moments of deep sadness and psychophysical exhaustion; she also had relationship problems causing frequent tension with her husband. Tall, thin, dressed with sober elegance, and wearing a *hijab*,[46] big dark eyes and a shining smile, she immediately struck me with her lively mind, remarkable talkativeness, and deep interest in psychology.

The eldest of three siblings, she was born in an Egyptian, Muslim, middle-class family in Alexandria and described her parents (both high-school teachers) as loving, supportive, stimulating, "religious but not fanatical", open-minded, and liberal. Education was extremely valued in her family, and the gifted Aisha was since her early school years a very brilliant student, the best in her class throughout her academic career. It was for her the surest way to win her parents' love (especially her father's) and to be positively mirrored by them. But the internalization of this need to perform and achieve in order to be seen, loved and recognized, together with some lack of attunement in her early relationship with her mother, created a deep narcissistic wound in her. Never satisfied with her good grades, constantly compelled to get better ones, and afraid not to be up to the next challenge, she could never build a realistic sense of self-worth and her self-esteem constantly fluctuated, being totally dependent on others' feedback and appreciation. She complained of forever feeling anxious and under pressure because of her parents' expectations and quickly recognized in her adult life the projective component of this pattern as the trigger of her exhausting compulsion to overload herself with too many activities, to succeed, and to "be special". Aisha was extremely quick in understanding these psychic mechanisms on the cognitive level, but it took us a long time to approach her deeper woundedness and to start empowering her sense of self-worth.

The analytic sessions were for Aisha the only time she could really devote to herself by tearing herself away from her full weekly schedule. During the first phase of the analysis, we worked not only on the complexes and deep patterns implied in her overactivity but also on the psychological meaning of her commitments and the concrete possibility of dropping some of them. At the beginning, cutting back on her activities was totally inconceivable because of Aisha's demanding animus, which was fuelled by her strong father complex. Practically speaking, she needed to work, due to financial reasons, but she could enjoy neither her job nor her studies in finance, since they allowed no space for creativity. The scarce time spent with her daughters was also a burden: she was tired and stressed at the end of the day and often felt guilty for her lack of patience and joy with them. As the analysis progressed, Aisha questioned more deeply the sense of continuing in a master's program that she had chosen with no regard for her intellectual interests but only to comply with her ego ideal and to please her parents' expectations. Her true passion had in fact always been writing—poems, short stories, journals—and it still represented her "secret garden", the place where she could withdraw, experience, and cultivate her creative side, even if in an erratic and discontinuous way.

But at the end of high school Aisha could not trust her writing talent enough to choose literature or journalism for her undergraduate studies. Thanks to a grant offered to the best students, she left Alexandria and moved to Cairo to attend the most prestigious university in the city, where she chose finance as her major to have more job opportunities in the future. This move represented a dramatic change in her life: once she overcame the initial phase of disorientation and homesickness, she began to enjoy independence, academic life, and social activities with the other students. Exposed to both Western values implemented at the university, which were consistent with her upbringing, and to more conservative values supported by religious movements she intermittently joined, she started to swing between these polarities and to experience an increasing inner conflict about her moral standards. This is a typical inner struggle for many young people of her milieu in Egypt, who are often raised in westernized families and later embrace much stricter principles supported by several Islamist movements spreading in Egyptian society.

Her tension intensified when she started to date a fellow European student; and, once this relationship was over, she immediately entered into a second one with an Egyptian boy. These relationships caused a sense of guilt, which revolved round her physical contact with them and the harsh judgement she cast on her behavior from a moral and religious perspective. All this was still tormenting her several years after these events took place; actually, it was rekindled by the fact that she was at that time maintaining a virtual, but passionate, romantic relationship with a man she had met only once at work but with whom she had daily exchanges by e-mail and on Facebook. Despite—in fact, paradoxically, also because of—the total lack of real contacts, Aisha was quite obsessed by the presence/absence of this "ghost lover" in her life. She was tormented with the dilemma of whether to meet him again or not, and she dedicated a considerable amount of time and energy to their correspondence.

We often discussed the meaning of this Facebook love-story, which can also be seen as a contemporary, cultural strategy of circumventing confinement and gender-related guidelines through the use of new technologies,[47] such as social networks, and whose outcome was a successful compromise between personal needs and social rules. For Aisha, this virtual romance clearly represented the best possible escape from her daily "cage" (as she used to define her present life condition) and served the precious purpose of keeping her psychically alive and animated; she was energized not only by the strong intimacy of this secret relationship but also by the possibility of testing new forms of self-expression. But the side effects often included a creeping sense of guilt toward her husband. She had met him six years before and portrayed him as a good-looking, intelligent, affectionate man, loyal to her and committed to their children, willing to take care of them and mostly present at home (the last are rather unusual traits in an Egyptian man). As he was an extremely religious, fervent practising Muslim, politically involved in a fundamentalist movement, she had projected on him at their first meeting the image of a savior who could rescue her from the immoral inclinations she had indulged in during her previous relationships.

It was during her engagement that Aisha had decided to wear the veil. She explained to me that it had been her own autonomous, heart-felt decision, motivated by her faith, her will "to be a good Muslim", and her desire "to be closer to God." But, from the very beginning, it had been a struggle. She felt ambivalent, torn apart, and disliked veiling for aesthetic and practical reasons; as a result, she soon started to regret her decision. But, once married, taking the *hijab* off was no longer an option. The only time she had tried, a family drama ensued and her husband threatened her with divorce. Despite his positive qualities and the undeniably strong aspects of their marriage, the tension between them because of religious issues kept increasing. It was indeed a concrete interpersonal conflict, but it was also a replica of Aisha's long-lasting inner conflict between her tough, harshly critical, judgemental animus—to which her husband represented an ideal magnet for projections—and her rebellious, unconventional side looking for more freedom.

The veil became a central issue in Aisha's analysis. I must add this was the case with most of my Muslim female analysands in Egypt, who were mainly educated women from middle and upper class backgrounds, capable of assuming a critical and self-reflective stance toward the veiling practice. Whether or not they chose to wear the veil, in agreement with or in opposition to their families, influenced in either sense by the current mainstream mentality in Egypt or by religious considerations, the *hijab* topic always emerged. Ultimately, it has deep significance and represents an identity, a spiritual and social statement in a Muslim woman's life, and a major step in her individuation process. As a consequence, most women devoted significant time in their analysis to explore and work out the reasons and consequences of their choice, as well as connected feelings and deeper spiritual implications.

Yet, in this article, I will not expand further on this crucial topic, so often the object of misunderstandings, superficial judgements, political manipulations, and paroxystic media coverage in the Western world. Nevertheless, I would like to refer to the thorough analyses of the complex practice of veiling made by gender studies scholars, like Leila Ahmed and Lila Abu-Lughod, who have approached it from anthropological and historical perspectives.[48] On the same topic, the anthropologist Saba Mahmood, in her ethnography of the women's mosque movement, addresses the meaning that this phenomenon assumes more specifically in Egyptian society, where it has increased dramatically in the last decades. She explains that many women who deliberately choose the new form of Islamic modest dress, including the *hijab*, adopt it for very similar reasons to those expressed by Aisha. They perceive it as a bodily means to cultivate virtue and faith, the outcome of their professed desire to be close to God and engage in a religious path of spiritual development.[49]

For Aisha it was particularly difficult to stay emotionally in tune and connected to the reasons that had originally motivated her choice. Thus, the veil progressively became for her not only the main object of confrontation with her husband but also the symbol of her ambivalent bond to Islam. She was, in fact, a genuine believer, respectful of most of the main norms of her religion, including the five daily prayers; but she had a hard time complying with the specific Islamic rules concerning women. One day she arrived for analysis literally furious and determined to divorce since her husband had harshly blamed her for standing unveiled close to their open balcony at home. As usual, she had reacted in a very aggressive way and a big argument had followed. Aisha was often enraged at what she considered to be men's privileges in Islam—from polygamy to their freer dress code. In her dreams she was mostly without the *hijab* and often swimming in the ocean, something she in reality could do only on the beaches reserved to women on the North coast. The feeling of "the wind through my hair" was present in several dreams and became in her analysis a touching, powerful metaphor of a growing wish for freedom.

There were phases of deep questioning and crisis in her process, when Aisha seriously considered taking the *hijab* off, separating from her husband, and even leaving home and her whole family to move abroad and continue her life alone. Yet, she could never find the determination to live out her fantasies of total liberation, so that for some time she kept swinging back and forth and feeling torn between two opposite ways of life—one grounded in her daily reality and reinforced by her sense of duty and responsibility, the other depicted in her inner images and nourished by her nostalgia for freedom. Despite the torment as the analysis progressed, the intense inner work started to bear some fruits: an increased sense of self-worth, a more realistic awareness of her talents as a hidden treasure rooted in herself, and less dependence on others' feedback.

At the end of the first year of analysis, two factors represented a sort of turning points in Aisha's story. First, she decided to take a year's sabbatical from her university program to consider whether she should drop it entirely or start a new program in a field of study closer to her real interests. The practical result was a positive slowing down of her schedule to a better rhythm with more time to devote to her daughters and to herself. She started to write more consistently and we often discussed during our sessions the inner dialogues accompanying her writing process, namely a tense conflict between her critical animus and the "inner artist" trying to find her own voice.

Second, she attended my seminar on Scheherazade. Something clicked in her, to the extent that she felt the need to bring the subject to analysis in order to explore the reasons why the character had impressed her so deeply. The aspect that emerged at first was her strong identification with Scheherazade as the cultural representation of a woman who belongs to her same culture and to a patriarchal system that is highly detrimental to women. These features resonated with Aisha's feeling of being trapped in a fixed life structure whose rules, mostly established by men, were hindering her personal development. The confinement of women in the harem in Scheherazade's story somehow evoked Aisha's ambivalent feelings about the veil, which she experienced positively as a protection and as the outcome of her own deliberate religious choice but also negatively as a sort of extension of the harem walls, a control device conceived by men to defend themselves from women's seductiveness and ultimately to tarnish their femininity.

What puzzled Aisha was Scheherazade's strategy to fight the system by remaining inside it, instead of making her escape. She was intrigued by the heroine's courage, inventiveness, and active attitude in facing the king and transforming her role from victim to creative artist by using her most precious human resources and narrative talent. The double achievement was that of promoting changes from within the system and empowering herself through the expression of her creativity. Aisha felt provoked, challenged, and inspired by these elements.

Seeds of hope and transformation were finally planted in her process through her exposure to and investment in Scheherazade as a powerful collective symbol that embodied traits that resonated with her own story and mirrored aspects of her own inner conflicts; moreover, beyond the symbolization of her psychodynamics, this archetypal image constellated Aisha's inner potentialities, revealing new possible forms of development. As a result, Aisha experienced a feeling of hope different from that elicited by the Facebook and e-mail exchanges with her virtual lover. It was somehow stronger and more grounded as it originated from an inner process and took root in what had always been her secret inner garden, that is, her passion for writing.

Scheherazade served as a symbol constellated by the transcendent function and pointing to a third path in-between the two opposite life-trajectories Aisha had long contemplated and been torn between. The transferential aspect was of course present, too, as it was not a trivial detail that I was the one who conveyed the message, the intermediary and the link between her and Scheherazade's wisdom. It was the beginning of a new phase in the analysis: hypotheses already long considered were suddenly invested with new energy. Aisha started to sense a possible way out of her cage through the search for a creative form of expression that was not incompatible with her concrete life circumstances but made a new sense out of them. Creativity was possible despite, and even because of, a difficult environment and unfavorable conditions; being a writer could coexist with her role of mother and wife. She was fascinated by Scheherazade's erudition and eloquence and found in them a symbolic encouragement to cultivate her intellectual side and make the best use of her verbal resources.

After a series of autobiographical short stories, Aisha started to write some tales about contemporary women in Cairo, focusing on their struggles and difficulties in present Egyptian society; these ranged from problems within the family, particularly in relationships with men, to social issues and patriarchal interpretations of Islam. Later she created a blog under a pseudonym in which she combined vignettes from her journal and a selection of her stories. Her wish was to share some of her experiences and reflections with other women in similar conditions and hopefully to induce more awareness in them. Her larger goal, following in the footsteps of Scheherazade, would be to promote from within the system, through words and narratives, changes in culture and mentality.

In writing Aisha found not only a creative expression for her feelings and thoughts but also a positive outlet for her narcissistic need to be special and appreciated. This was nurtured by the positive feed-back she received from her readers and led to a substantial improvement of her fragile self-confidence. It brought about also the sublimation of the energy invested in the Facebook love-story that gradually had less and less space in her life. This stage represented a meaningful facet of her self-empowerment process as it presaged the shift from virtual love as a sort of hetero-induced validation to the integration of an inner force fostering her self-expression.

As a complex, multifaceted archetypal image, Scheherazade also succeeded in evoking totally unexplored and undeveloped parts of Aisha's personality, disclosing new ways of inner search and growth. For example, we thoroughly discussed integrating Scheherazade's message in intra- and interpersonal dynamics with the masculine to find a more peaceful and eros-centered way for Aisha to relate to her animus and, in outer life, to her husband. It was of course a tortuous process that implied several ups and downs; but, once Scheherazade was integrated as a sort of inner psychopomp, Aisha could face with new strength and inspiration various obstacles and develop effective strategies to circumvent patriarchal aspects of her culture. Practically speaking, she neither divorced nor took off the *hijab*; nevertheless, she succeeded in finding her way within her culture, by creating spaces of inner and outer freedom from where she could make her voice heard and develop a sort of counter-narrative capable of giving a new sense to her individual experience.

In conclusion, we could say that the cultural representation of this literary heroine functioned in Aisha's process as an inspiring symbol and model for the feminine Self, capable of constellating deep resources in order to move forward, beyond inner and outer conflicts, and to transform suffering into a larger quest for meaning.

In one of the last dreams she brought to analysis, Aisha was sitting alone in a garden, close to a fountain, the soothing sound of the water in the background. Her long hair falling loose on her shoulders, she was writing, feeling free and at peace.

5. Case discussion
a. *Décentrage* (Decentering)

Working on these specific issues intertwined with Egyptian culture, social pressure, and religion meant to me the constant necessity of a cultural decentering (cf. section 2). My initial choice of moving to and working in Egypt was only the first, albeit fundamental, step in this direction, and I had later to consciously renew and implement decentering as a methodological stance in each psychotherapy, by decentering myself, my perceptions, my clinical method, and practice and by acknowledging their specific cultural nature.[50] I also learned to see beyond my initial, spontaneous fascination for Arabic/Egyptian culture and to face the ambivalence that the confrontation with cultural otherness in my daily life and work activated in me as an unavoidable consequence of the continuous questioning and repositioning of my own cultural identity.

Analysands like Aisha presented to me, through their life experiences, shadow aspects of the Arab Muslim collective that often resonated with some negative judgements and prejudices of mine. I had to make a constant effort, on the one hand, to remain conscious of the cultural biases of my personal and professional perspective and to limit their effect on the therapy; on the other hand, I had to avoid falling into the trap of "culturalism", that is, the tendency to excessively focus on the cultural features of the analysands' stories, reducing them to what is instead always the result of a multifactorial web of components.[51] Beside the impact of the collective, in its cultural and archetypal dimensions, there is always the subjectivity and the personal story in the foreground: such threads interweave to form that unique fabric that is an individual's existence, expressed through a narrative in analysis.

That is why it is highly recommended to adopt a multidimensional approach, which combines an anthropological perspective for an accurate assessment of the cultural elements, together with a psychoanalytical method to address the individual dimension of the psychodynamics and which always includes, as an essential therapeutic tool, the therapist's self-reflective work on his/her countertransferential feelings. This seems indeed to be the most balanced and correct key to access, in its many nuances, such a complex mesh of components as an analysand's story in a transcultural setting.

b. Analysis of the cultural transference and countertransference

The analysis of the transference/countertransference dynamics was of course a central element of my work in Egypt, with specific attention to the elaboration of its cultural facets. Besides my individual self-examination, I often discussed the topic during intervision sessions with colleagues and started researching and reading about it in transcultural psychiatry literature.

With Aisha we discussed the meaning it had for her to analyze with a western, European, non-Muslim analyst. She explained that, among different options, she had intentionally chosen me as an analyst on the basis, in part, of my cultural background. She felt safer about confidentiality, and freer, less prone to judgement and more comfortable in tackling specific culture-related, sensitive issues with a professional who did not belong to her same culture and who might therefore have a more neutral and detached perspective, less influenced by Islam and an Arabic mindset. My outsider position seemed in fact to play a decisive role with several other patients in Egypt, including the students I saw for counselling consultations at AUC. When their main difficulties had to do with cultural alienation, gender, and sexuality (particularly homosexuality, which remains a big taboo in Egypt and is still regarded as a major sin in Islam[52]), they preferred seeing a western therapist, like me, for the same reasons Aisha had shared with me.

Also because of my being a European, Aisha saw me as a free, emancipated, independent woman, able to travel and move at will while doing a fascinating, creative job which deeply intrigued her. I tried to handle with care the projective side of her transferential idealization and to give it back to her as inspiring elements that, despite the objective differences of culture and life condition, might still be important to integrate in her psychic process. I think Aisha's heterogeneous cultural references, that is to say her previous, significant exposure to Western values while remaining deeply rooted in her original culture, contributed to reinforce her positive transference. As a beneficial consequence, this was also conducive to her attempts at finding her own way through a mixed logic, relying on the integration (*métissage*) of multiple cultural perspectives.

As mentioned before, Aisha's response to Scheherazade as a symbol could also be seen in the frame of her positive transference. In this respect, I played the roles of both analyst and teacher who conveyed a particularly precious knowledge, enabling her to envisage her situation by the light of a new wisdom. As a matter of fact, I did not invite Aisha to my seminar about Scheherazade, since, as a rule, I avoid creating double relational links with my analysands; but she heard about it at AUC and showed up without notice. We discussed all these aspects during our sessions, and I must admit this is one of the rare cases when the breach of a sensible analytical rule bore positive fruits.

As for the analysis of the cultural aspects of my countertransference reactions, it meant observing, behind our strong alliance and my prevalent feelings of deep empathy with Aisha, my ambivalence not only toward her culture but sometimes also toward her as a particular cultural being, who was often porous to the influence of the collective despite her deep ambivalence toward it. At some stage, to my great and unpleasant surprise, I even had to deal with some racist judgements and attitudes in myself, which were totally antithetical to my general conscious principles. When she was, for example, considering complying with her husband's wish to have a third child, in the hope it would be a boy—despite her being constantly exhausted and complaining of not having enough time for her two daughters—I found myself strongly irritated with the Arab-Muslim "must" of the large family and with the different value and status attributed to male children. I also indulged in condescending considerations of the limitations of Egyptian women when it comes to defending their rights and promoting real changes within the family and in the social arena and the contrasting "superiority", as it were, of Western women in protecting and emancipating themselves from the grip of the patriarchal collective. Similar prejudices, typical expressions of the abovementioned shadow of the cultural group, were activated in me also with respect to religion—for example by Aisha's recurring sense of guilt for not respecting the whole Muslim daily praying schedule, namely for not being able to get up for *fajr*, the first prayer before dawn.

I felt uncomfortable, even ashamed of myself when these countertransference reactions surfaced to my consciousness; yet, facing and working them out helped me not only to protect the analysand and our relationship from the acting out of my cultural shadow, but also to remain aware of the risk of imposing my own cultural values and views in the analysis.

c. Awareness of the ethnocentric biases of analytical psychology

This issue became particularly critical when, thanks to increased self-awareness and self-empowerment due to the analysis, Aisha began questioning more drastically her choices and life situation: how might she reconcile her increasing wish for independence and her duties as a mother? Was "becoming herself" possible within her family? Was creativity compatible with her present job and studies? Was divorce an option for her and the necessary condition for being with her Facebook beloved, taking off the *hijab*, and finally feeling free? Could she take off the *hijab* and still be a good Muslim? I often wondered which role Aisha's cultural transference was playing in triggering such questions and doubts which anyhow seemed to me quite consequent in her psychic process. My position remained the same throughout the analysis, that is, one of empathy, encouragement, and support. I tried to accompany her in her psychic journey by helping her to analyze both the constellated intrapsychic dynamics with related feelings (psychoanalytic reading) as well as the objective consequences and practical implications on the social scene (social anthropological reading) for all the possibilities she considered for her future. Yet, I always abstained from joining her in overtly criticizing Egyptian society or her husband's behavior and opinions; likewise, I refrained from taking any definite stand or formulating any open advice about her decisions in progress, not only to preserve the canonical analytical neutrality, but also to avoid conditioning her process with my ethnocentric perspective.

I was in fact quite aware of the cultural, that is, western bias of my theoretical and clinical approach. Case discussions with Egyptian colleagues brought my attention even more to this matter: Jungian analysis, as well as most psychological and psychiatric theories, are widely based on notions and principles that are imbued with western values and constantly refer to a western model of mental health that is far from being neutral and universal.[53] Therapeutic goals such as autonomy and independence are, for example, strictly linked to the individualistic structure of western societies and implicitly refer to the separation between individual and society upon which western liberal thinking rests.[54] Within this framework, there is mostly a dialectical tension between the individual's real desires and obligatory social conventions and norms, and individual choice is always the prime value. Subsumed and unquestioned in western psychology, such conceptions are nevertheless quite extraneous to the Arab-Muslim tradition. That is why the psychological approach needs to be reframed when working with patients like Aisha who, despite her westernized education and upbringing, still lives in a collectivistic society revolving round the central values of the family, social interconnectedness, and Islamic principles.[55]

Individuation, the key concept and goal in Jungian analysis, needs to be redefined in psychotherapy with non-westerners. Although it may remain the main existential aspiration, it must in most cases inevitably involve a series of adjustments and compromises with the collective (in terms of family, society, and religion) that exceed by far those already envisaged by Jung when he underlined the necessity of including collective relationships as a constitutive facet of the individuation process.[56] It is quite hard for a western therapist to conceive, encourage, and integrate such compromises into a psychotherapeutic process, but it is often the only way to protect the patient from the isolation and social alienation he/she would necessarily experience when pursuing a too individualistic path incompatible with his/her culture.

Moreover, it is always essential to remain aware of differences, both cultural and individual, and respectful of every possible path toward individuation. To quote and reframe Abu-Lughod's provocative question: are liberation, emancipation, and equality part of a universal language and goals for which all women and people strive?[57] Writing about the young Egyptian women seeking to become pious Muslims, Saba Mahmood argues that the drive for freedom and liberation is a historically situated desire whose motivational force cannot be assumed a priori.[58] Other desires and goals might be more meaningful for other groups of people in a culturally different environment. Muslim women who deliberately choose to follow socially-prescribed religious conventions, taking on the veil in their process, consider them to be "the scaffolding" through which the self is realized, not as signs of their subordination as individuals.[59]

In conclusion, it is apparent how a sensitive appreciation of cultural complexity and a clear awareness of the biases and limits of western psychology theories and methods are basic requirement for any professional engaging in transcultural therapies.

I would like to express my sincere and warm thanks to Dr. Gesine Sturm, clinical psychologist and anthropologist, Ph.D., Service de Psychopathologie de l'enfant et de l'adolescent et Psychiatrie Générale, Hôpital Avicenne, Université Paris 13, for her careful and sensitive reading of my article, her several stimulating remarks and her invaluable bibliographical suggestions in ethnopsychoanalysis and anthropology. — Valentina Lucia Zampieri

The Thousand and One Nights : A Summary of the frame story

Two very powerful kings, the king of Samarkand and the king of India and China, are brothers. They find out that they are both cheated on by their wives. After putting them to death, they set out on a journey during which they happen to witness still another clear example of infidelity by the wife of a powerful djinn.

Confirmed in their notion of women's evil nature, treachery, and ungovernable lust, they return to their kingdoms. Shahrayar, the more powerful and cruel of the two, starts to act out a very perverse form of revenge: he marries each night a young, virgin girl, sleeps with her and has her slain the following morning. This criminal "gendercide" continues for three years, until Scheherazade, the daughter of Shahrayar's vizier, volunteers to be the king's next wife. With the help of her younger sister Dinarzad, she implements a very smart plan: every night she tells the king a very fascinating story that she interrupts at its climax at sunrise, leaving Shahrayar burning with curiosity to hear the rest. Every day the king decides therefore to delay Scheherazade's execution in order to hear the conclusion of the tale...

This continues for one thousand and one nights, at the end of which Shahrayar is finally cured through Scheherazade's presence and storytelling, and in love with her. He decides to spare her life and they live happily, with their three sons, for the rest of their days.

NOTES

1. I use with much reluctance this vague, inaccurate category, being mindful of what Edward Said explained in his famous book *Orientalism*, where he examined thoroughly the relationship between the Western conception and study of the Middle East and the effective reality of this region. By deconstructing the scholarly discourse on Orientalism and the notion of "Orient", Said successfully showed how this discourse is the result of Western projections and relationships in terms of power (in the economic, political, military and cultural spheres) between the Middle East and the Western world. E. Said, *Orientalism* (New York: Pantheon, 1978). Nevertheless, I use this category for lack of a better all-embracing adjective to define a culture that is mainly Arab and influenced by Islam but includes—within my own perspective and present context—also peoples who speak languages

other than Arabic and are Muslim (such as Persians and Turks) or speak Arabic but are not Muslim (such as the Christian minorities in the Middle East). The "myth" of Scheherazade can also be seen as a product of Orientalism, as her image was heavily influenced by Western interpretations of *The Thousands and One Nights*, starting from the very first translation into French by Antoine Galland (1704).

2. I am aware of how too rigid a binary opposition between women "of the West" and women "of the East" might fix differences in a way that they might be considered in too essentialist terms, as if they were innate. This is neither my opinion nor my experience, but I use and juxtapose these abstract typifications for the sake of clarity in the economy of my present text.

3. For a synthetic exposition of these themes, central in Lila Abu-Lughod's work, see her two articles "The Muslim Woman: The Power of Images and the Danger of Pity," www.eurozine.com/articles/2006-09-01-abulughod-en.html, 2006, and "Do Muslim Women Really Need Saving? Anthropological Reflections on Cultural Relativism and Its Others," *American Anthropologist* 104(vol. 3, 2002), pp. 783-790, also available at www.smi.uib.no/seminars/Pensum/Abu-Lughod.pdf. See also the interview, "Lila Abu-Lughod on Attitudes Toward Muslim Women in the West" at www.asiasociety.org. For a deeper and more extensive treatment of these topics, see Lila Abu-Lughod, *Writing Women's Worlds* (Berkeley/Los Angeles/London: University of California Press, [1993], 2008).

4. The complex genesis and history of *The Thousands and One Nights*, with the debate about its oral origins, the first manuscripts, and its several versions and translations, is widely illustrated in the introduction to *The Arabian Nights*, translated by H. Haddawy (New York: Norton & Co, 1990), pp. xii-xxxiv.

5. V. L. Zampieri, *The Way of Scheherazade. The Redemption of the Wounded Masculine Principle through Feminine Wisdom and Storytelling*, Diploma Thesis (Zürich: C. G. Jung Institut-Zürich, 2006).

6. See www.aucegypt.edu.

7. See www.clinique-transculturelle.org.

8. F. Mernissi, *Scheherazade Goes West: Different Cultures, Different Harems* (New York: Washington Square Press, 2001), pp. 20-21.

9. F. O. Dubosc, *Così parlò Shahrazad: Trasgressione e conoscenza nelle Mille e una notte* (Milano: Vivarium, 2003), pp. 19-21.

10. M. Chebel, *La féminisation du monde: Essai sur Les Mille et Une Nuits* (Paris: Payot, 1996), pp. 270, 274, 278.
11. F. Mernissi, *Scheherazade Goes West*, pp. 45-46.
12. F. Mernissi, *Beyond the Veil: Male-Female Dynamics in Modern Muslim Society* (Bloomington and Indianapolis: Indiana University Press, 1987), pp. 31, 43-44.
13. M. Jurich, *Scheherazade's Sisters: Trickster Heroines and their Stories in World Literature* (Westport-London: Greenwood Press, 1995), p xvi.
14. F. Mernissi, *Scheherazade Goes West*, p. 49.
15. Taha Hussein, *Ahlam Shaharazad*, Engl.tr. *The Dreams of Shahrazad* (1943) and Tewfik El Hakim, *The Devil's Pact* (1938) as quoted in H. Aboul-Hussein, Ch. Pellat, *Chéhérazade personnage littéraire* (Algers: Société Nationale d'Edition et de Diffusion, 1976), p. 114.
16. A. Kilito, *L'oeil et l'aiguille: Essai sur les Mille et Une Nuits* (Paris: Edition de la Découverte, 1991), p. 15.
17. M. Lahy-Hollebecque, *Schéhérazade ou l'éducation d'un roi* (1927), new edition *Le féminisme de Schéhérazade* (Paris: Pardès, 1987), p. 193.
18. I am referring here to fairy tales like *Bluebeard* (C. Perrault) or *Fitcher's Bird* and *The Robber's Bridegroom* (J. and W. Grimm) and to myths like Demeter and Persephone.
19. V. Kast, *Fairy Tales for the Psyche* (New York: Continuum, 1996), p. 34.
20. M.L. von Franz, *Individuation in Fairy Tales* (Boston and London: Shambala, 1990), pp. 84, 87 and H. Dieckmann, *Märchen und Symbole: Tiefenpsychologische Deutung orientalischer Märchen* (Fellbach-Oeffingen: Bonz Verlag, 1977), pp. 12-17.
21. A. and B. Ulanov, *The Witch and the Clown: Two Archetypes of Human Sexuality* (Wilmette, Illinois: Chiron Publications, 1987), pp. 250-251.
22. For a deeper analysis of the origins, main positions, cultural debates, and recent developments in the field of ethnopsychoanalysis, see G. Sturm, "Current developments in French Ethnopsychoanalysis," *Transcultural Psychiatry*, 2010 (in press); "Le racisme et l'exclusion," in M. R. Moro, Q. De La Noë, Y. Mouchenik, eds., *Manuel de psychiatrie transculturelle* (Grénoble: La pensée sauvage Editions, 2006), pp. 265-

278; and *Les therapies transculturelles en groupe 'multiculturel. Une ethnographie de l'espace thérapeutique*, doctoral dissertation in psychology (Paris: Université Paris XIII et Brême: Université de Brême, 2005), pp. 304-318.

23. G. Devereux, *Essais d'ethnopsychiatrie générale* (Paris: Gallimard, 1970); *Ethnopsychanalyse complémentariste* (Paris: Flammarion, [1972], new ed. 1985); and *Basic Problems in Ethnopsychiatry* (Chicago/London: University of Chicago Press, 1980).

24. G. Devereux, *Psychothérapie d'un Indien des plaines* (Paris: Jean-Cyrille Godefroy, 1982).

25. T. Nathan, *La folie des autres: Traité d'ethnopsychiatrie générale* (Paris: Dunod, 2001).

26. I. Réal, M.R. Moro, "La consultation transculturelle d'Avicenne (Bobigny, France). Un dispositif métissé à géométrie variable," in Moro, De La Noë, Mouchenik, eds., *Manuel de psychiatrie transculturelle*, pp. 217-237.

27. M. Serres, "Discours et parcours," in C. Lévi-Strauss, *L'identité* (Paris: Grasset, 1977), p. 40, as quoted in M. R. Moro, *Psychothérapie transculturelle des enfants de migrants* (Paris: Dunoud, 1998), p. 12.

28. M. R. Moro, "Bases de la clinique transculturelle," in Moro, De La Noë, Mouchenik eds., *Manuel de psychiatrie transculturelle*, pp. 167-168.

29. *Ibid.*, p. 169 and M. R. Moro, *Parents en exil: Psychopathologie et migrations* (Paris: PUF, 2001), pp. 60-61.

30. See the diagram of the psyche formulated by Jung in W. McGuire, *Bollingen: An Adventure in Collecting the Past* (Princeton: Princeton University Press, 1989), reproduced in T. Singer and S. L. Kimbles, eds., *The Cultural Complex: Contemporary Jungian Perspectives on Psyche and Society* (London and New York: Routledge, [2004], repr. 2008), p. 3.

31. C. G. Jung, *Memories, Dreams, Reflections* (London: Collins and Routledge & Kegan Paul, 1963). On the influence that Jung's trips and cross-cultural encounters had on his thinking and on the possibility of applying Jungian ideas to contemporary intercultural work, see H. Abramovitch and L. Kirmayer, "The Relevance of Jungian Psychology for Cultural Psychiatry," *Transcultural Psychiatry* 2003, vol. 40 (2), pp. 155-163.

32. C. G. Jung, *Psychological Types,* CW 6, § 747.
33. C. G. Jung, "On the Nature of the Psyche," in *The Structure and Dynamics of the Psyche,* CW 8, § 417.
34. Singer and Kimbles, eds., *The Cultural Complex,* p. 3.
35. T. Kirsch, "Cultural complexes in the History of Jung, Freud and their Followers," in Singer and Kimbles, eds., *The Cultural Complex,* p. 185.
36. J. Henderson, "The Archetype of Culture," in A. Guggenbühl-Craig ed., *Der Archetyp. Proceedings of the 2nd International Congress of Analytical Psychology* (Basel and New York: S. Karger, 1962).
37. T. Singer and S. L. Kimbles, "Introduction" in Singer and Kimbles, eds., *The Cultural Complex,* p. 2; T. Singer with C. Kaplinsky, "Cultural Complexes in Analysis," in M. Stein, ed., *Jungian Psychoanalysis: Working in the Spirit of C.G. Jung* (Chicago: Open Court, 2010), pp. 22-37.
38. B. Meador, "Light the Seven Fires—Seize the Seven Desires," in Singer and Kimbles, eds., *The Cultural Complex,* p. 172.
39. For Moro, the cultural code (*codage culturel*) represents the particular element in the human nature which is determined by the specific culture an individual refers to, the language and the categories he uses to make sense of reality. See M. R. Moro, "Les débats autour de la question culturelle en clinique," in T. Baubet, M. R. Moro, *Psychopathologie transculturelle* (Paris: Masson, 2009), pp. 32-33.
40. C. G. Jung, "Problems of Modern Psychotherapy," in *The Practice of Psyhotherapy,* CW 16, § 163.
41. G. Devereux, *From Anxiety to Method in the Behavioural Sciences* (The Hague: Mouton & Co, 1967), Fr. tr. *De l'angoisse à la méthode dans les sciences du comportement* (Paris: Flammarion, 1980), pp. 75-85.
42. M. R. Moro, *Psychothérapie transculturelle de l'enfant et de l'adolescent* (Paris: Dunod, 2004); *Parents en exil: Psychopathologie et migrations,* pp. 51-53.
43. *Ibid.*
44. J-F. Rouchon, A. Reyre, O. Taïeb, M. R. Moro, *L'utilisation de la notion de contre-transfert culturel en clinique,* L'Autre: cliniques, cultures et sociétés, vol. 10, n.1 (Grenoble: La pensée sauvage Editions, 2009), pp. 80-89.

45. Singer and Kimbles, "Introduction", in Singer and Kimbles, eds., *The Cultural Complex*, p. 4.

46. *Hijab* is the headscarf worn by Muslim women to cover their hair and neck. Unlike the *niqab*, it leaves the face uncovered and is the most remarkable marker of a modern version of Islamic modest dress that also includes other features, such as long skirts or loose pants, long sleeves, etc. Since the late 1970s, it has been adopted by more and more women, from varied socioeconomic and cultural backgrounds, throughout the Muslim world.

47. Interesting reflections on the impact that the internet and new technologies are having on the Muslim world, and particularly on women, can be found in several articles on Fatema Mernissi's website, www.mernissi.net, and in F. Mernissi, "L'amour au temps d'internet," in *L'amour dans les pays musulmans* (Paris: Editions Albin Michel, 2009), pp. 169-189.

48. Abu-Lughod has effectively argued that veiling today should not be reductively confused with lack of agency or even a symbol of regression but is instead to be considered in continuity with the socially shared standards, religious beliefs, and moral ideals found within the Muslim culture and tradition, whose historical roots Leila Ahmed has exhaustively explored in her work. See: Lila Abu-Lughod, *The Muslim Woman: The power of images and the danger of pity*; *Do Muslim Women Really Need Saving? Anthropological Reflections on Cultural Relativism and Its Others*, pp. 785-786; see also L. Ahmed, *Women and Gender in Islam: Historical Roots of a Modern Debate* (Cairo: The American University in Cairo Press, [1993], repr. 1998).

49. S. Mahmood, *Politics of Piety: The Islamic Revival and the Feminist Subject* (Princeton: Princeton University Press, 2005).

50. M. R. Moro, "Les débats autour de la question culturelle en clinique", in T. Baubet, M.R. Moro, *Psychopathologie transculturelle*, p. 40 and M. R. Moro, T. Baubet, "Les soins en situation transculturelle," *ibid.*, p. 155.

51. M. R. Moro, "Les débats autour de la question culturelle en clinique," in T. Baubet, M. R. Moro, *Psychopathologie transculturelle*, p. 40-42.

52. B. Whitaker, *Unspeakable Love: Gay and Lesbian Life in the Middle East* (London: Saqi Books, 2006).

53. G. Sturm, "Le racisme et l'exclusion," in Moro, De La Noë, Mouchenik eds., *Manuel de psychiatrie transculturelle*, p. 268.

54. L. Abu-Lughod, *The Muslim Woman* and S. Mahmood, *Politics of Piety*, pp. 148-155.

55. The specific topic of psychotherapy with Arab and Muslim clients is thoroughly analyzed in two very helpful books by M. Dwairy: *Counseling and Psychotherapy with Arabs and Muslims: A Culturally Sensitive Approach* (New York and London: Teachers College Press, Columbia University, 2006) and *Cross-Cultural Counseling: The Arab-Palestinian Case* (New York, London: The Havorth Press, 1998). See also www.marwandwairy.com.

56. C. G. Jung, *Psychological Types*, § 758.

57. Abu-Lughod, *Do Muslim Women Really Need Saving?*, p. 788.

58. S. Mahmood, "Feminist Theory, Embodiment, and the Docile Agent: Some Reflections on the Egyptian Islamic Revival," *Cultural Anthropology*, vol.16 (2, 2001), p. 223.

59. S. Mahmood, *Politics of Piety: The Islamic Revival and the Feminist Subject*, p. 148.

ON HOME AND IDENTITY: FOLLOWING THE WAY OF THE ROMA

ALEXANDRA FIDYK

> This need for home lies deep within all of us. It's hard to be resilient if there is no safe base from which to journey forth. But home doesn't have to be brick walls and a picket fence. I comfort myself with this thought. Nomadic people carry their homes with them. Aid workers make themselves at home in some of the most remote or dangerous places in the world simply by pinning up photographs, bringing along pieces of cloth, musical instruments, toys, favourite drinking mugs—anything that will help ground and nurture them.
>
> —Anne Deveson, *Resilience*[1]

In "Ecopsychology and the Sacred: The Psychological Basis of the Environmental Crisis," David Tacey calls for a new concept of identity, "an alternative vision as to how to live in a different way."[2] He explains: "What we require is nothing less than a new state of

---

Alexandra Fidyk, Ph.D., is an Assistant Professor in the Department of Secondary Education, University of Alberta, Canada, and Adjunct Faculty at Pacifica Graduate Institute, California. Her work draws from the fields of process philosophy, depth psychology, Buddhist thought, curriculum theory, and poetic inquiry. She has published poetry, chapters, articles, edited collections, and has forthcoming books in education and analytical psychology. She is an associate editor for the *International Journal of Jungian Studies* and an editor of the current issue of the *Jungian Journal of Scholarly Studies*. She is a certified Jungian psychotherapist.

consciousness, one that collapses the old distinction between self and world, which has become for us a hardened dualism preventing the self from participating fully in the world."³

This new concept of identity would include all that resides "outside" our selves—the lakes, rocks, birds, oil spills, and ancestors—as part of our experience of subjectivity. South African Jungian analyst Ian McCallum asks, "How long is it going to take to acknowledge that there is indeed a menagerie within each of us . . . a wolf, a hyena, a lion . . . a wild man and a wild woman?"⁴ To become aware of our ecological kinship is to come home to a more inclusive definition of self that is always already united with animals, elements, and wild places. The term ecological, derived from the Greek *oikos,* meaning home, includes the sacred, for this planet is not only our physical home but also our spiritual home.

Conceptions of identity, self, and subjectivity are connected to constructs of home, house, and security, and all inform reconceptualizations of being and knowing, most particularly a non-dual consciousness. Home, for many, is not only a physical place; rather, home dwells at the crossroads of the inner and outer. In the West, "home" is regularly associated with "house," but the concept is also linked to spaces of familiarity, *familias,* family—loci of organization. "While home is located," notes Mary Douglas, "it is not necessarily fixed in space—rather, home starts by bringing space under control."⁵ Since medieval Europe, "home" has evolved from venues for public affairs—less bounded spaces that were open to the comings and goings of diverse persons who were involved in various activities (imagine a vibrant market square)—into our current conception of "home" as enclosed physical spaces with rooms allotted for specific functions of a "family" that is separate from the "outside" world. Over nearly 300 years, home in the West has increasingly come to connote an inside/outside and private/public distinction, an ordering and control of space. Witold Rybczynski attributes this shift from public to private to an accompanying transformation in human consciousness that marked the emergence of something new: "the appearance of the internal world of the individual, of the self, and of the family."⁶ This movement reflects the evolution of self and individual from a premodern conception of self as intertwined with the wolf, tree, and other to a modern conception of the self as bounded, separate, and increasingly isolated and further to a postmodern conception of self as contradictory and multivalent.[7] For some, a post-postmodern view has arisen. Rather than insist on the duality of modernity and postmodernity, it has unfolded from and embodies both paradigms, one nested within the other, whereby the emergence of self connotes paradox, part steady core and part fluctuating layers.

While the terms identity, self, and subjectivity are related, they are not synonymous. Self, a term closely equated with the term individual, implies a sense of indivisibility and connectedness and yet has also come to imply a sense of uniqueness and personal choice. Identity and subjectivity are interrelated. Subjectivity refers to different subject positions to which we subject ourselves and to which we are subjected. A poststructuralist subjectivity refers to "the conscious and unconscious thoughts and emotions of the individual, her sense of herself and her ways of understanding her relation to the world"—a "subjectivity which is precarious, contradictory and in process, constantly being reconstituted in discourse each time we think or speak."[8] Identity involves membership in groups, often considered common categories of being. Identity within modernity implies something that is fixed, stable, separate, and coherent—and often identity cannot or will not be questioned because one is deeply invested in it. Where individualism is highly regarded, firm psychological, political, cultural, and geographical boundaries become prized and protected. Taken to extremes, one might even see his separate self as independent from his body and nature to the extent that his capacity to distance and differentiate from others is seen as a success of psychological development. Any realization of a kinship with the more-than-human world is far from his concept of identity. This process of increasing autonomy and independence lends an aura of authority to the separative tendencies of Western culture.

A more relational point of view values greater complexity in relationships that empower the individual and foster development and creativity. Hyper-individuality, which is increasingly common in the West, is a kind of relationship that denies and often destroys the larger context, whether that context be a friendship, a family, or an ecosystem. The valuing of relationships among people could easily be extended beyond the human realm to include relationships with land, water, and wolf—an ecopsychological perspective. As Catherine Keller explains, by defining "relationship" more inclusively, one can create "places of inner and outer freedom in which new forms of connection can take place. Liberated from relational bondage, we range through an unlimited array of relations—not just to other persons, but to ideas and feelings, to the earth, the body, and the untold contents of the present moment."[9]

Home is closely associated with identity. In *At Home in the World*, John Hill intimately explores the philosophical and psychological significance of home. He writes:

> For some, home is an expanse—the body, an inner life, planet Earth, or a space in which to create. There are those who need an empty space in order to connect with something that they can call their own. Other home narratives are about being on the move. A woman once told me she had never stayed for more than a few years in one place. Already as a child, her encounters with the new, the foreign, or the alien were like a second home for her. She could not bear to stay too long in one place, and always felt curious to explore homes beyond the horizon.... Home may take on the significance of a place of exile, a pilgrimage, or being a nomad—a frame of mind so aptly expressed in the words of a Native American: "I can place my tepee anywhere in the world because my soul is at one with the earth."[10]

Regardless of the structure of home, few narratives are untouched by memories of it. Increasingly, there are fewer people who have never moved or changed their abode, yet there are still some who cannot see beyond their location. When confronted by what is considered alien, they become insecure and cannot open to the richness that lies beyond the familiar. Home—often understood as nation or homeland—can become an ideology where stranger, migrant, and nomad are perceived as a threat and "everything is done to keep *such people*, especially if they are from another race or culture, out of their home and out of their heart."[11]

As an archetypal theme, home touches all rooms of human life—geography, culture, nationality, ethnicity, relations, art, and values. Home, for Hill, "represents the way we contain our life and define our relationship to the outside world."[12] Where he couples home with homelessness as twin themes, I wed "settled" and "nomadic" as the two complementary points of flux within the archetype of home. Rather than considering whether one has or does not have a situated home, I consider home at the margins, "on the move," within a narrative of the European Roma.[13] ("Roma" is the term many peripatetic communities who speak Indian languages and reside in Europe choose rather than the name "Gypsies."[14])

This position of marginality and movement speaks readily to my own narrative and orientation to home. While others may not initially see me as an outsider, a subversive or mercurial nature can quickly locate me on the periphery, transgressing cultural constructs, and often moving sideways to the mainstream. I grew up on a sustaining farm in northern Saskatchewan (Canada), following seasonal patterns and nature's rhythms. I was the middle child in a large family with my Ukrainian Orthodox grandparents living in the same yard. As my mother's family was Scottish-Irish Protestant, no formal religion was followed in our home. Our house was located on the main route between the Saulteaux First Nations Reserve (Ojibwa Nation) and a small ethnically diverse farming town. My elementary school for "farm kids" was segregated from the three urban schools. This split was my first experience of institutional discrimination. During high school I went to Finland as a Rotary Exchange student, and thereafter acquired several foreign student and work visas (China, India, Egypt, South Africa, Kosovo, and the United States), a legal alien (*gaigin*) identification card to teach in Japan, and a misnamed "*gringa*" identity on a work visa for Colombia. It was in Finland where I first met elaborately dressed Romani people and experienced the ways they were perceived and mistreated by non-Roma (*gadje*) people.

From an early age my orientation to life has had the tendency to set me apart from my own family and others more than a life of travel. While it may be said that my movement was not entirely forced by external factors, certainly it was beckoned by psychological ones. An image of Hermes symbolizes poignantly this way of life—a "journeyer [who] is at home while underway, at home on the road itself, the road being understood not as a connection between two definite points on the earth's surface, but as a particular world."[15] Hermes is the god of "the margins, the boundaries, the *limins* of many things,"[16] bridging spaces between psychological and physical realms, between divine and human being, between the invisible and the visible. A settled life was one that I have never consciously considered, although a fixed home was certainly a meaningful part of my earlier lived experience and opened a door for me to move across diverse cultural and geographical borders. At this point in my life, however, it is nomadic narratives, experience, and consciousness that resonate within, that speak to me, and that permit me to journey in this "world-of-the-road."[17]

Many in depth psychology feel called upon to question, undo, and revise the single, homogeneous point of view, that sense of perspective and critical distance that was born of the Enlightenment and that triumphed in colonialism, imperialism, and the rational version of modernity—elements of which still live as "a hardened dualism preventing the self from participating fully in the world." This world view, as well as that of any paradigm, frames one's sense of being in the world, and one's sense of home and identity cannot simply be erased from these narratives, including those narratives located on the peripheries. What one has inherited as culture, as language, as history, is not to be forgotten or denied, but it can be rerouted and rewritten. More than ever, one's sense of being, identity, and culture is experienced through movement. As Iain Chambers notes, "The 'I' does not pre-exist this movement and then go out into the world, the 'I' is constantly being formed and reformed in such movement in the world."[18] Awareness of the complex and constructed nature of one's identity opens her up to other possibilities—to recognize in "my" narrative "other" narratives, to uncover amid the apparent completeness of the modern individual the incoherence, the estrangement, the gap rendered accessible by the foreigner, who subverts it and forces each of us to acknowledge the question of him or her in oneself.

The new state of consciousness that Tacey and others—Gary Snyder, David Abram, Annie Dillard, Barry Lopez, Thomas Berry, and Joanna Macy—call for, whereby the "old distinction between self and world" collapses, would defuse not only the antagonism between self and the world but also that which dwells between identity and otherness and the ever-present danger of exclusion. Fixed, singular identities constellate perceptions of self and other that reduce the complexity of others into what either resembles the self or denotes only difference. Often those deemed different are denigrated as inferior and thus worthy of ill treatment, exclusion, and exploitation. Gypsy, Traveller, and Rom cultures have historically been among these excluded groups. A series of stereotypes, images, and racial biases have been combined to negate Roma and to render them hugely problematic: criminals by nature, dishonest, immoral, amoral, and, most important, nomadic.

II

In what follows I offer a brief and partial telling of a collective Roma identity that has been constructed through elements drawn from their relationship to home, movement, and a nomadic way of being—qualities that consistently appear in literature, folktales, and academic writing. I have chosen the Roma as one of many marginalized people who have managed to maintain an arm's-length relationship with the project of modernity—a project that seeks to order and border home, space, and knowledge—and as a people who have been forbidden a place within pluralist democracies. In the current political climate, many have become exiles or refugees from their traditional routes and patterns of life, often forced to continue traveling or to demonstrate their worth before they are permitted to join communities. For members of a community caught in perpetual movement, a sort of wandering, any discussion of home questions the norms and controls of dominant society that determine or permit a home's position within a particular location. The efforts of Romani groups to create a "homeplace"[19] can be read not as a site of deviance but as a site of resistance to the sanctioned efforts of nation-states to destroy, contain, assimilate, or control them. Modernist thinking attempts to make notions of home, place, and culture static and rigid in order to clearly define who is in and who is out. It closes the door on a nomadic lifestyle, excludes all those who lead a mobile way of life. In many ways, this marginal position demands a redress of relationship in the form of ethics among humans and with nature. It, too, challenges the Western notion of citizenship that has traditionally been based on people's sense of belonging to a spatial territory, the rights extending from this belonging, and their claims to land ownership and the use or exploitation of land. Indeed, the affinity of settled peoples to particular places and localities contrasts sharply with the general relationship to land and ecology that exists among nomads. Citizenship is in need of reframing as "good relations," governed by relatedness, hospitality, and reciprocity with an ecological place and all its inhabitants, not just between people or in the context of political rights. In welcoming other constructs of home and identity, we might well be hosting both a new sense of consciousness and relationship. As Hill reminds, "Home is created between people. . . . Our narrative identity emerges into consciousness in and through relationships with others. . . . Home also emerges into consciousness in the reciprocal interaction between the human and nonhuman environment."[20]

III

Despite different accounts, there is an agreement that Roma migrated to Europe from the Punjab region in northwest India during the ninth to fourteenth centuries.[21] They traveled toward the Caucasus and China and through the Middle East toward the Balkans. By the end of the sixteenth century, Roma covered all the territory of the Central and Western Europe of today without ever forming or claiming a homeland. Roma were initially welcome in Western Europe, where they were seen as noble pilgrims and were offered gifts. Playfully and wittily, they presented themselves as "Little Egyptians" who had been sentenced by the pope to seven years of wandering as punishment for betraying Christianity. This story ensured both safe passage through non-Christian territory and money and shelter. However, with the rise of Protestantism in Europe and its accompanying work ethic, this sentiment began to change, and Roma were increasingly viewed from the confines of the new ethic as parasitic nomads and thieves who were incapable of work.[22]

From the early nineteenth century, Roma became associated with those who worked with rubbish, excrement, and sex. They figured as the symbol of stench and infection in many parts of Western Europe. Thus, "the disease-carrying capacity of Gypsies and other vagrants" was associated with "the stench of the poor" and one became symbolic of the other.[23] This "historical geography of disgust" illustrates how the Roma came to occupy the opposite of what was acceptable and valued by settled society.[24] The common denominator in the historically diverse forms of the collective Romani identity is their alleged strangeness. Through resistance to heteronormative ways of living, Roma have and continue to be seen as "deviants" in the dominant social and political order, as a group who cannot conform. Joined by the "diachronic stereotypes of primitivism,"[25] the assertion that the common denominator across the collective identities of Romanies is "strangeness" has remained practically unchanged from the early stages of capitalism to the era of late-stage socialism and the contemporary "new democracies" of Eastern Europe. Gypsies did not fit on either side of the Iron Curtain: on the "Western side," they were politically invisible and had no useful place in the eyes of the public. On the "Eastern side," socialist state authorities, who viewed nomadism as a backward and unhealthy lifestyle associated with criminal behavior, enforced various forms of punishment. Socialism contributed to strengthening the demeaning stereotypes about Roma that saw them as incapable of living according to the norms of "socialist coexistence."[26] In a society where presumably "everyone is given a chance of thriving," the image of Roma as unworthy of participating in that dream was "hammered into the public mind."[27] The nomadism of Romani people was dangerous for the totalitarian political system and "offensive to its workerist ideology," as Anne Bancroft notes.[28] John MacLauglin calls this telling of history "not [a] history in any evolutionary or purposeful sense. It was instead an endless repetition of hardship and poverty. As such it lacked its own narrators and even an audience, and still awaited a wider sympathetic narrative representation."[29]

Today the greatest number of Roma live in Central and Eastern Europe. Eastern Europe is home to between six and eight million Roma. Accurate population estimations are difficult to obtain because of infrequent data collection, Roma mobility, and the reluctance of community members to register as "Roma" in censuses for fear of being stigmatized.[30] In Western Europe, the largest population of Roma lives in Spain, followed by France and Italy.[31]

European Roma continue to carry a deeply polarized narrative: no other people have been so persistently discriminated against and yet so excessively romanticized.[32] Romani scholar Ian Hancock writes, "The history of the Romani people can hardly be matched in terms of oppression and injustice."[33] They have endured slavery and genocide, sterilization and expulsion, and yet they have survived. Roma are mostly confined to shantytowns, are often denied formal education, have almost no prospect for social mobility, and are subjected to extremely demeaning stereotypes. They are viewed as dirty, lazy, and contaminated. Margaret Brearley calls Roma the "near-universal scapegoat for the ills of postcommunist society."[34] At the same time they are admired as musicians, dancers, and free spirits. Roma are often viewed as "the very *epitome* of freedom,"[35] a popular sentiment expressed in novels, poems, and songs and in the public imagination. They are Europe's untouchables, but they are also a romantic dark self of European whites, one that carries a "secret allure of the peripheral."[36]

Most contemporary constructions of nomads draw on a long history of fear about the dispossessed traveler and the assumed "threat they pose to moral and political order."[37] Because nomads travel in groups or communities, they are seen as more dangerous than individual vagrants and thus pose a greater physical danger to individuals and their property. The idea of a "traveling underworld" has been a source of concern to European states for centuries.[38] Historically, this underworld included a wide range of social categories and occupations: "the young . . . beggars . . . peddlers and tinkers, soldiers and mariners, many entertainers, students, unlicensed healers and even fortune-tellers."[39] And of course this list includes Roma.

Today, New Travellers,[40] digital kids, sex-trade workers, migrants, refugees, and exiles can be added to this growing list. The efforts of state infrastructures to "deal with" this supposed threat have constituted "a brutal and undemocratic project."[41] Yet the continued attempt to control this "dangerous" group continues to be one of the least challenged aspects of legally enforced and legitimized repression and needs to be interpreted as a threat to every group that resists the heteronormative position on home, place, and identity as well as those who do not.

Nomadic groups such as the Roma, who appear to devalue settled identity and transgress the concept of place to which identity and home have been closely tied, are often reviled and rejected. Historically, laws were passed soon after they arrived in Europe that forbade them to settle; thus, their means of livelihood had to be portable. Although forms of economic activity such as receiving alms and telling fortunes were respected in Egypt and India, they were no longer culturally acceptable in the European context and were either criticized or forbidden. Roma were persecuted everywhere they went, by massacre, systematic deportation, and enslavement.[42] Although they have been officially freed from slavery since the mid-nineteenth century, Roma have endured programs of forced assimilation in many countries, pressure to abandon their culture, and rules forbidding any temporary encampment. Moving in groups, the Romani "were seen as physically threatening and ideologically disruptive. Their very existence constituted dissidence."[43]

Claiming membership in an ethnic group ensures liberties and entitlements that membership in a society or culture does not.[44] Many Roma do not claim an ethnic identity in the sense of an "inherited past," because "for them, identity is constructed and constantly made in the present in relations with significant others."[45] Nor do they claim a national identity, which makes them increasingly vulnerable to the loss of rights and protection under the law of the nation where they currently reside. The tendency for Roma in Europe to not have an attachment to a nation or land is often read negatively from the point of view of settled people, but it can also be read as contributing positively to alternative ways of conceptualizing identity, home, and relationship along the continuum within the archetype of home.

IV

A settled existence dwells firmly in the dualism that separates humans from the world. The sedentary, single fixed perspective is the point of view from which history was written, from which the state and all of its apparatus has grown and in most cases continues to be maintained. Provocative work has been done on the nomadic/sedentary interface by Gilles Deleuze and Félix Guattari around the notion of nomadology.[46] They see nomadology as an alternative approach to understanding history as told from multiple narratives that thus creates an uninterrupted flow of deterritorialization that establishes a line of flight[47] away from territories, grand designs, and monolithic institutions. Traveller researcher Robbie McVeigh characterizes sedentarism "as that system of ideas and practices which serves to normalize and reproduce sedentary modes of existence and pathologies and repress nomadic modes of existence."[48] This notion includes the "active and intentional incitement of fear and hatred of nomads"[49] seen in campaigns both historically and currently across Europe. Sedentarism includes "a host of other less tangible ideas, actions and structures which construct being sedentary as the only acceptable mode of existence within contemporary society."[50]

Post-Enlightenment, in the wave of social evolutionist thought, it was assumed that societies shifted from traveling to sedentary modes of existence, that the progress of "civilization" was a one-way shift that each group of people must follow, beginning with nomadic groups and terminating in sedentary communities. This shift was regarded as a "good thing"—as a move away from wild places and upward toward security, success, and modernity. In the context of colonization and the securing of borders, those acting on behalf of nation-states used brutal and inhumane tactics to force First Nations, Native Americans, and Aboriginal peoples around the world into settled life with predetermined locations. The shift to sedentary life generally was assumed to be total, irreversible, and inevitable. One late "triumph" of sedentarism was the formation of the nation-state in Europe, Canada, the United States, and Australia with fixed borders that prevented people from readily moving across designated lines.[51] Those fixed borders eradicated territories or frontiers that were the peripheral areas of a state. Here political authority of the center was thin, less controlled, and enabled people to move across these lines in any direction. A border, conversely, is known and geographically drawn, a divide that is strongly guarded.[52] With the arrival of the nation-state and the notion of the border, space began to be "occupied in a totalized way"—there were fewer places for nomads to traverse. This shift to occupying and policing land parallels the transition of home from a public to private space.

The contemporary distrust of and overt violence directed at Roma, in particular, draws upon this history of geopolitical development that is rooted in the very existence of nomads who challenge hegemonic ideas about the success, superiority, and victory of a settled way of life. New Travellers and migrants symbolize the survival and resilience of a nomadic way of life, and their numbers are increasing. They represent something more than the survival of cultural and ethnic nomads; they demonstrate the birth of a new type of nomadic existence and a new consciousness that embraces alternative modes of being/becoming, modes that renew our ties with nature and bring the suppressed side of home into view. The fact that nomads continue to exist is evidence that the project of modernity is incomplete, flawed. Nomads are living evidence of the survival of unwanted elements from the premodern world, in particular a more intimate relationship with nature. For contemporary societies steeped in the sedentary mode, the resilience and reemergence of nomadic life is a disturbing prospect. Yet it signals a profound potential for living with the world.[53]

V

"Travelling," writes Hancock, "is part of [Romani] history. Our ancestors trekked for thousands of miles from India to Europe and out into the world, so there is certainly some truth to the stereotype of the 'travelling gypsy.'"[54] He argues that a distinction must be made between traveling with a purpose and traveling because local law forbids one to stop and therefore leaves no choice. Even for settled people, a fixed connection between geography, home, and culture is increasingly under question. For peoples without a permanent national territory that can be called a homeland, the delinking of these concepts is a central fact of existence.

Gypsy, Traveller, and Rom cultures are identified both negatively and positively with the nomad image. Negative images include phrases such as "parasitic nomads,"[55] "inborn wanderers,"[56] and "thieving gypsy bastards."[57] Romani peoples carry the dark projections of many settled people and are deemed to be at odds with and, thus, a threat to settled society. Some see them as a group that is "*incapable* of social conformity."[58] The Roma offer an embodiment of nomadic consciousness that is essential to the development of an ethic of hospitality and a more complete understanding of home that includes both nomadic and settled aspects of being. While many Roma have become settled or partially settled, voluntarily or by force, the collective identities of Roma peoples have been constructed through movement, intimate relations with their environments, and knowledge of how to burrow under or go around fixed perimeters to explore in-between spaces.

How might being engaged with the narratives of nomadic peoples contribute to a more inclusive and complex construction of home, identity, and human subjectivity? How does one develop a sense of self as a dynamic, developing entity, situated in changing contexts that house narratives of both the mobile and settled? Borrowing from nomads, one can conceive of such transformation by favoring a decentered vision of the subject. "Nomadic subjectivity," argues Rosi Braidotti, "is about the simultaneity of complex and multi-layered identities."[59] This identity is constructed around the belief in the "potency and relevance of the imagination . . . as a way to step out of the political and intellectual crisis of these postmodern times."[60] For Braidotti and others, attending the nomadic subject is a move against the "settled and conventional nature of theoretical and especially philosophical thinking" rooted firmly in the rationality of modernity.[61]

As an image or a symbol, the nomad represents the relinquishing and deconstruction of any sense of fixed identity. It is a way of resisting assimilation into dominant ways of representing the self.[62] Nomadic subjects have a peripheral consciousness; "they forgot to forget injustice and symbolic poverty: their memory is activated against the stream; they enact a rebellion of subjugated knowledges."[63] Their way of being/becoming is about "transitions and passages without pre-determined destinations of lost homelands."[64]

"Nomadism" in this context—as used by feminists (Donna Haraway, Luce Irigaray, bell hooks, Judith Butler), liberation psychologists (Gloria Anzaldua, Mary Watkins, Helene Shulman), postcolonial thinkers (Gayatri Spivak, Stuart Hall, Paul Gilroy), and philosophers (Gilles Deleuze, Felix Guattari, Jacques Derrida)—"refers to the kind of critical consciousness that resists settling into socially coded modes of thought and behaviour. It is the subversion of set conventions that defines the nomadic state, not the literal act of travelling."[65] Thus, Nomadism "is not fluidity without borders but rather an acute awareness of the nonfixity of boundaries. It is the intense desire to go on trespassing, transgressing."[66] Political images other than the classical ones such as Travellers, Gypsies, and Romani come to mind that portray the complex interaction of levels of subjectivity: the itinerant worker, the illegal alien, the cross-border sex worker, the foreign student, and various other forms of displacement, diaspora, and hybridity.

Braidotti continues:

> Nomadism is a form of intransitive becoming: it marks a set of transformations without end product. Nomadic subjects create politically informed maps for their own survival. Nomadic travelers are oral geniuses, relying on memory and knowing places by heart. Hence the importance of "visiting" not in the bourgeois mode, but rather as the attempt at sharing the same embedded location. This kind of "visiting" is the opposite of the consumeristic mode of apprehension of the "other" in the tourist subject position. The "visit" is an exchange that calls for both accountability and care.[67]

The importance of the embedded, embodied, and organic subject is its ethical and political accountability. Such becoming is not topologically bound; it takes place in the transitions between potentially contradictory positions. To be in process or in transition does not locate the subject outside history or time. To be in process invites the subject to come home in new ways. The politics of situated knowledge rests on process ontology, becoming through experience and complex and fluid dynamics that position the primacy of relations over the permanence of substances.[68] Identity then becomes imagined more as process and less as product, "a practice marked by its gestures toward otherness in oneself and others."[69]

VI

> *"[I]t ain't where you're from, it's where you're at[.]" [This perspective] grants a priority to the present, emphasizing a view of identity as an ongoing process of self-making at a time when myths of origins are so appealing.*
>
> —Paul Gilroy[70]

While there is no uniform nomadic identity, the term "Romanes" has been used to "refer both to Romani, the Gypsy language[,] and to the 'gypsy way of doing things.'"[71] "Gypsy culture"[72] inhabits and constructs its internal coherence alongside or in opposition to other dominating cultures that occupy the same geographical and political space. Roma have created semi-autonomous cultural spaces instead of legally, politically defined territory. By taking things from surrounding systems and inverting their meaning for their own use, the Roma have turned the dominant culture sideways to serve their own needs, thus becoming "brilliant *bricoleurs*."[73] According to social anthropologist Judith Okely, such "overlaps [between Roma and non-Roma groups] are not simplistic copying nor the influence of the majority systems on a seemingly passive and receptive minority."[74] Rather, Roma have illustrated ingenuity and inventiveness by selecting and rejecting elements of culture.[75] She argues that for centuries they have offered a "pioneering example of cultural coherence and identity" and have simultaneously been open to "being dismissed as hybrid"[76]—an identity that does not count legitimately.[77] Roma have continuously created and recreated their cultural autonomy, which has diversified through the centuries in the midst of others' spaces and cultures. Roma are not archaic remnants awaiting the presumed higher evolution of the dominant sedentary systems that confront them.

The Romanes way is characterized not by a mythical homeland of Indian origin but by "a created alternative and imagined autonomous space in song, horse dealing activities, demarcated residence, communality, commensuality and speech."[78] Given such innovation while living in the midst of other, typically more powerful and repressive social formations, it is important to note the tension within Romani culture between individualism and group solidarity at both the social and organizational levels. Such tension points to the need to reconsider the notion of creativity. In painting, dance, music, song, and art, Roma do not subscribe to the Western notions of individual genius or the invention of new things; rather, they understand creativity to be a collective midwifery of something that is birthed for the current situation. This brilliance of mimetic artistry transferred to the "where you're at" is representative of the subversion and transgression that characterizes nomadic consciousness.

The Romanes way resembles Braidotti's image of the nomad as the type of subject "who has relinquished all idea, desire, or nostalgia for fixity" and expresses "the desire for an identity made of transitions, successive shifts, and coordinated changes, without and against essential unity."[79] Yet unity unfolds through seasonal patterns of movement and rather fixed routes: "it is a cohesion engendered by repetitions, cyclical moves, rhythmical displacement."[80] This concept of identity reflects affective bonds with place as well as intersubjective and trans-species connection to homeplaces and landscapes. It "includes the natural world in a broadened definition of self."[81]

VII

Addressing the question of identity from within modernity and postmodernity begins with an understanding that the condition governing such formation is the affirmation of a difference: nomadic and settled, Roma and non-Roma, center and periphery. While every identity is relational, difference is a precondition for the existence of any identity. In the process of creating a collective identity—creating an "us" by demarcating a "them"—there will always be the possibility of antagonism.[82] This happens when the "other" who has been considered different becomes perceived as rejecting "our" identity and so threatens "our" existence. At such moments, any form of us/them relationship—whether cultural, ethnic, linguistic, or other—becomes political.

In "For a Politics of Nomadic Identity," Chantal Mouffe suggests that the future of democracy points toward the recognition that politics is a dimension inherent in all human social relations and is not just contained in society's institutions. She argues that politics needs to tame hostility and defuse the potential antagonism inherent in human relations.[83] The crucial question for democratic politics is not how to arrive at a consensus without exclusion or how to create an "us" that would not have a corresponding "them," but how to establish an "us" and "them" discrimination in a way that is compatible with pluralist democracies as positioned within a new paradigm.[84] Certainly democracy needs some consensus, but it also needs collective identities around positions that are clearly differentiated and are maintained through a new understanding of ethics and citizenship.

As cultural, social, and psychological dimensions interpenetrate, the movement, then, is to see through one's own cultural locations, to leave the comfort and familiarity of what one knows, and to move beyond such borders. It is to see one's own culture as someone else's culture. It is to bring the nomad, stranger, or other into relations with the "settled" so each can enter into and create dialogic spaces where individuals can share their cultural experiences with one another. It is to acquire a plurality of vantage points from which one can view oneself and other in order to "participat[e more] fully in the world." It is to position the nomadic/sedentary split as an interrelational process of becoming rather than an either-or divide of dominance. It is to collectively create new homeplaces that welcome diverse communities, including animals, elements, and wildness. It is to open the doors to one's home, to host difference by reimagining and experiencing the other's identity. To do so enacts an ethic of hospitality that accommodates otherness and renders borders permeable. As Hill notes, "Reviving hospitality furthers the process of translating one home in terms of another."[85] "By accepting that hybridity creates us as separate entities, it affirms and upholds the nomadic character of every identity."[86] For Hill, "Cultural pluralism invites each person to adjust in his or her own way to a world of different cultures, now located in ever-increasing proximity."[87]

By resisting the ongoing temptation to construct identity and home in terms of exclusion, terms that are fortified by dominance, and by recognizing that identities include multiple dependent and independent elements, one can defuse the potential for violence that exists in every dualistic construction of "us and them." However, it is precisely the tension that exists between identity and difference that makes it possible to protect against any attempt to annihilate an other through complete fusion or total separation. Thus, it is in locating this tension in a new consciousness that values its emergent potentiality and the liquidity of its paradoxical nature. The articulation of and engagement with such tension is necessary to newly emerging identities and their accompanying structures of home and invites each person to be at home while underway.

"On Home and Identity"

i

The Settled and the Nomadic
live very different lives.

The Settled,
in his habits,
throws his net,
just so far.
His catch
is heavy:
his house – its goods and chattels –
his favourite haunts and streets,
the buildings and parks of
his beloved city.

The Nomadic
throws her net
much farther
over new rooms,
new cities – mosques, temples, cathedrals –
across deserts, plains, and atop mountains.
Her catch

is light:
little more than what she can carry.

It is the same:
Each is content.

The Settled,
and the Nomadic
understand Home,
in similar ways.

To answer the question
What is Home?
is to answer the question of identity.

ii

The fetus is both Settled and Nomadic.
It can travel without leaving home.

Initially, Home is a body,
the mother's body.
Her hands are doors,
open and closed.

As infant,
with closed eyes
then first steps –
the mother disappears.
These movements
mark the beginning
of the Nomadic.

With eyes open,
and steps back,
there is delight in seeing
the mother again,
in being Settled.
As child
Home expands.
Walls, windows, doors
here or there,
it does not matter.

Home is still circumscribed
around
her body.

In time, the child realizes
the material world
is independent of the mother,
even of itself,
and it can – must –
be explored.

The question becomes vital,
because it is one of identity:
will he settle or
will she travel?

iii

No longer a body,
but a place,
a house, a town, a land.

No longer a place,
not even an elusive place:
Elsewhere.

No longer an idea, desire or nostalgia
for fixity.
Life becomes transitions,
successive shifts,
coordinated changes,
without and against
essential unity.
Life becomes one movement –
seasonal patterns through
fixed routes.
Cohesion engendered
by repetitions,
cyclical moves,
rhythmical displacement.

Life becomes
coherence with mobility.

iv

To answer the question
What is Home?

is to answer the question of identity.

Home is a feeling of pregnancy –
psychologically and topographically –
of interrelations,
of thrown-togetherness,
of growing-togetherness. . . .

The Settled and the Nomadic
will tell you this.*

---

*This suite of found poems draws from the short story, "Philadelphia Green Blue – Musings on the Meaning of Home" by Yann Martel, located in *Writing Home: A PEN Canada Anthology*, edited by Constance Rooke (1997). Found poetry is a type of poetry created by using words, phrases, and sometimes whole passages from other sources and reframing them as poetry. This recasting makes changes in spacing, lines, or through additions and deletions and consequently meaning.

NOTES

1. Anne Deveson, *Resilience* (Crows Nest, New South Wales: Allen & Unwin, 2003), p. 200.

2. David Tacey, "Ecopsychology and the Sacred: The Psychological Basis of the Environmental Crisis," *Spring: A Journal of Archetype and Culture* 83 (Spring 2010): 331.

3. *Ibid.,* p. 330.

4. Ian McCallum, *Ecological Intelligence: Rediscovering Ourselves in Nature* (Cape Town: Africa Geographic, 2006), p. 165.

5. Douglas, quoted in David Morley, *Home Territories: Media, Mobility and Identity* (New York: Routledge, 2000), p. 16.

6. Witold Rybczynski, *Home: A Short History of an Idea* (New York: Penguin, 1986), p. 18.

7. Susan Casey Walsh, "Being Homeless: Female Subjectivity and Difference," *Journal of the Canadian Association for Curriculum Studies* 2, no. 1 (2004): 113–143.

8. Chris Weedon, *Feminist Practice and Poststructuralist Theory,* 2nd ed. (Malden, Mass.: Blackwell, 1997), quoted in Walsh, "Being Homeless," p. 137.

9. Catherine Keller, *From a Broken Web: Separation, Sexism, and Self* (Boston: Beacon, 1986), p. 3.

10. John Hill, *At Home in the World: Sounds and Symmetries of Belonging* (New Orleans: Spring Journal and Books, 2010), p. 7.

11. *Ibid.,* p. 8, my italics.

12. *Ibid.,* p. 9.

13. This telling of a Romani narrative is woven of fact and fiction from Romani voices and non-Romani studies. Narrative yields a form of understanding of human experience that is not directly amenable to other forms of exposition or analysis. So what is offered here is one interpretation of a Romani narrative that is not only descriptive of self but, more important, is also fundamental to the emergence and reality of that subject. Here, a narrative of self is both a receptive and a creative activity. Borrowing language from the literary sphere, narrator, character and spectator are always already caught up in narratives that we enact and continue to construct; in this narrative, the same holds true.

14. *Romani* and *Romanes,* sometimes spelled *"Romany,"* are the general names for the language of the Roma, the Sinti, and the Calé.

Romani is the only Indo-Aryan language that has been spoken exclusively in Europe since the Middle Ages. It is part of the phenomenon of Indic diaspora languages spoken by traveling communities of Indian origin outside of India. The term Roma has gained increasing currency as a cover term for all populations that speak (or at some time spoke), the Romani language, and while its use in this way is sanctioned by different Romani organizations (Nordic Roma Council, Sa-Roma, Inc., and the Roma National Congress), not all groups accept it by any means; see Ian Hancock, *We Are the Romani People* (Hertfordshire, UK: University of Hertfordshire Press, 2005), p. xix. The name Rom or Rrom, which is the self-designation of the speakers, also surfaces in other traveling (peripatetic) communities that speak Indian languages or use an Indic-derived special vocabulary: Lom (Caucasus and Anatolia) and Dom (Near East). In India itself, groups known as Dom are castes of commercial nomads: service providers such as metalworkers and entertainers. Roma refers to all groups residing in Central and Eastern Europe, or respectively, those who in the nineteenth and twentieth centuries emigrated from Central and Eastern Europe to Western Europe and overseas. See "Romani, Romanes, Romany: The Language of the Roma, the Sinti, and the Calé," *Romlex* website, http://romani.uni-graz.at/romlex/whatisromani.xml, accessed 7 April 2011.

15. Karl Kerényi, *Hermes: Guide of Souls* (1976; repr., Putnam, Conn.: Spring Publications, 2003), p. 46.

16. Richard E. Palmer, "The Relevance of Gadamer's 'Philosophical Hermeneutics' to Thirty-Six Topics or Fields of Human Activity," lecture delivered at the Department of Philosophy, Southern Illinois University at Carbondale, Illinois, April 1, 1999, available at http://www.mac.edu/faculty/richardpalmer/relevance.html.

17. Kerényi, *Hermes: Guide of Souls,* p. 46.

18. Iain Chambers, *Migrancy, Culture, Identity* (London: Routledge, 1994), p. 24.

19. "Homeplace" is a term used by bell hooks to signify a home's position within a particular location. See hooks, *Yearning: Race, Gender, and Cultural Politics* (Boston: South End Press, 1990), pp. 41–50.

20. Hill, *At Home in the World,* pp. 259–260.

21. See Zoltan D. Barany, *The East European Gypsies: Regime Change, Marginality, and Ethnopolitics* (Cambridge: Cambridge

University Press, 2002); Julio Vargas Clavería and Jesús Gómez Alonso, "Why Romà Do Not Like Mainstream School: Voices of a People without a Territory," *Harvard Educational Review* 73 (Winter 2003): 559–590; and Dina Ringold, Mitchell Alexander Orenstein, and Erika Wilkens, *Roma in an Expanding Europe: Breaking the Poverty Cycle* (Washington, D.C.: The World Bank, 2003).

22. Dimitrina Petrova, "The Roma: Between the Myth and a Future," *Social Research* 70 (Spring 2003): 111–161.

23. Jim Mac Laughlin, "European Gypsies and the Historical Geography of Loathing," *Review: A Journal of the Fernand Braudel Center* 22, no. 1 (1999): 39–40.

24. *Ibid.*, p. 39.

25. Sevasti Trubeta, "'Gypsiness,' Racial Discourse and Persecution: Balkan Roma during the Second World War," *Nationalities Papers* 31, no. 4 (2003): 503.

26. Ágnes Kende, "The Hungary of Otherness: The (Roma) Gypsies of Hungary," *Journal of European Area Studies* 8, no. 2 (2000): 187–201.

27. *Ibid.*, p. 194.

28. Anne Bancroft, "Closed Spaces, Restricted Places: Marginalisation of Roma in Europe," *Space and Polity* 5, no. 2 (2001): 148.

29. Mac Laughlin, "European Gypsies and the Historical Geography of Loathing," p. 38.

30. Barany, *The East European Gypsies*; Arno Tanner, "The Roma of Eastern Europe: Still Searching for Inclusion," *Migration Information Source,* May 2005, http://www.migrationinformation.org/Feature/display.cfm?id=308, accessed 7 April 2011.

31. Clavería and Alonso, "Why Romà Do Not Like Mainstream School."

32. Belinda Cooper, "'We Have No Martin Luther King': Eastern Europe's Roma Minority," *World Policy Journal* 18, no. 4 (Winter 2001/2002): 69–78.

33. Ian Hancock, "The Roma: Myth and Reality," *Patrin Web Journal,* 5 September 1999, § 4, http://www.reocities.com/paris/5121/mythandreality.htm, accessed 7 April 2011. Hancock's work is used extensively, for he is a Romani, a professor of linguistics, and the

director of the Romani Archives and Documentation Center at the University of Texas at Austin.

34. Margaret Brearley, "The Persecution of Gypsies in Europe," *American Behavioral Scientist* 45, no. 4 (2001): 591. I interpret a European Romani narrative through the lens of the scapegoat complex in "'Gypsy Fate': Carriers of Our Collective Shadow," *Jungian Journal for Scholarly Studies* 4, no. 1 (2008), http://www.thejungiansociety.org/Jung%20Society/e-journal/Volume-4/Fidyk-2008.pdf.

35. Hancock, "The Roma: Myth and Reality," § 6, italics in original.

36. Mac Laughlin, "European Gypsies and the Historical Geography of Loathing," p. 38. See also Fidyk, "'Gypsy Fate': Carriers of Our Collective Shadow"; and Maja Miskovic, "Roma Education in Europe: In Support of the Discourse of Race," *Pedagogy, Culture, & Society* 17, no. 2 (2009): 201–220.

37. Robbie McVeigh, "Theorizing Sedentarism: The Roots of Anti-Nomadism," in *Gypsy Politics and Traveller Identity*, edited by Thomas Acton (Hatfield, Hertfordshire: University of Hertfordshire Press, 1999), p. 8.

38. *Ibid.*

39. A. L. Beier quoted in *ibid.*

40. Since the 1960s, people have turned to living on the road in caravans, buses, vans, and trucks, choosing a less materialistic and greener way of life. Some are forced onto the road through economic circumstances, substance abuse, or mental health issues; some have opted to escape unhealthy home situations; and others have chosen an alternative lifestyle. Among these are the highly mobile, tech-savvy individuals who use wired public spaces and retired "snowbirds" (residents of Canada and the northern United States who winter in the southern states and return to their northern homes in the spring and summer).

41. McVeigh, "Theorizing Sedentarism," p. 8.

42. The Ottoman court in 1818 incorporated new edicts into the penal code, among them: "Gypsies are born slaves," and "Any Gypsy without an owner is the property of the Prince"; Hancock, *We Are the Romani People*, p. 21. In England during the sixteenth century, King Edward VI passed a law stating that Romanies be "branded with a *V* on their breast, and then enslaved for two years." If they escaped and

were recaptured, they were then to be branded with an *S* and made slaves for life; *ibid.,* p. 27. Spain shipped Romanies as slaves to the Americas; others were transported by Columbus to the Caribbean. Portugal shipped Romanies to its colonies in Maranhão (now part of Brazil), Angola, and even India—the Romanies' country of origin. Russia, Scotland, England, and Virginia followed suit; *ibid.,* p. 2.

43. Sociologist Jean-Pierre Liegeois, quoted in Diane Tong, *Gypsy Folktales* (San Diego: Harcourt Brace Jovanovich, 1989), p. 3.

44. Ewa Steiger-Kruczek and Cyril Simmons, "The Rroma: Their History and Education in Poland and the UK," *Educational Studies* 27, no. 3 (2001): 281–290.

45. Michael Stewart, *The Time of the Gypsies* (Boulder, Colo.: Westview Press, 1997), p. 28.

46. Gilles Deleuze and Félix Guattari, *A Thousand Plateaus: Capitalism and Schizophrenia,* translated by Brian Massumi (London: Athlone Press, 1988).

47. A line of flight is a moment when one briefly escapes territorialization. Often the de-territorialization is brief and inconsequential, but with just a slight move a new pattern can unfold. In this moment, the individual enters unimagined realms of potentiality and becoming-other.

48. McVeigh, "Theorizing Sedentarism," p. 9.

49. *Ibid.*

50. *Ibid.*

51. *Ibid.,* p. 17. Here McVeigh draws upon Anthony Giddens, *The Nation-State and Violence,* vol. 2 of *A Contemporary Critique of Historical Materialism* (London: Polity, 1985), pp. 49-50.

52. *Ibid.*

53. *Ibid.,* p. 10.

54. Hancock, *We Are the Romani People,* p. 101.

55. Petrova, "The Roma: Between the Myth and a Future."

56. Trubeta, "'Gypsiness,' Racial Discourse and Persecution," p. 503.

57. British comic strip reprinted in Hancock, *We Are the Romani People,* p. 103.

58. Trubeta, "'Gypsiness,' Racial Discourse and Persecution," p. 503, Trubeta's italics.

59. Rosi Braidotti, "Difference, Diversity and Nomadic Subjectivity," p. 10, unpublished paper in author's possession.
60. *Ibid.*
61. *Ibid.*
62. *Ibid.*, p. 11.
63. *Ibid..*
64. *Ibid.*
65. *Ibid.*
66. Braidotti, *Nomadic Subjects: Embodiment and Sexual Difference in Contemporary Feminist Theory* (New York: Columbia University Press, 1994), p. 36.
67. Rosi Braidotti, "Difference, Diversity and Nomadic Subjectivity," p. 15.
68. Rosi Braidotti, "Posthuman, All Too Human: Towards a New Process Ontology," *Theory, Culture & Society* 23, nos. 7–8 (2006): 197–208.
69. Mary Watkins and Helene Shulman, *Toward Psychologies of Liberation* (New York: Palgrave Macmillan, 2008), p. 160.
70. Paul Gilroy, *Small Acts* (London: Serpent's Tail, 1993), pp. 201–202.
71. Michael Stewart, "The Puzzle of Roma Persistence: Group Identity without a Nation," in *Romani Culture and Gypsy Identity*, edited by Thomas Acton and Gary Mundy (Hatfield, Hertfordshire: University of Hertfordshire Press, 1997), p. 89.
72. Stewart, *The Time of the Gypsies.*
73. Judith Okely, "Cultural Ingenuity and Travelling Autonomy: Not Copying, Just Choosing," in *Romani Culture and Gypsy Identity*, edited by Thomas Acton and Gary Mundy (Hatfield, Hertfordshire: University of Hertfordshire Press, 1997), p. 191.
74. *Ibid.*
75. *Ibid.*
76. *Ibid.*, p. 192.
77. This suggestion of Roma being open to "being dismissed as hybrid" signals their internalized collective sense of self, which has been co-constructed in relation to the dominant society where they live. This identity is reflected, for example, in the Romani language: the word "Roma" means "people" in the plural masculine gender, with an inherent connotation of "us" as opposed to "them." Outsiders are

referred to by the general term "*gadje*" (also a masculine noun in the plural). Petrova and others note that calling all "others" by one name, "*gadje*," is a strikingly frequent conversational practice when Roma speak with Roma. This frequent reference to a generalized "other" is usually not found in any other insider ethnic discourse. This denotation reflects a high degree of "us/them" opposition that has been historically reinforced by centuries of internalized oppression and isolation. Petrova, "The Roma: Between the Myth and a Future."

78. *Ibid.*, p. 195.
79. Braidotti, *Nomadic Subjects,* p. 22.
80. *Ibid.*
81. Tacey, "Ecopsychology and the Sacred," p. 332.
82. Chantal Mouffe, "For a Politics of Nomadic Identity," in *Travellers' Tales: Narratives of Home and Displacement,* edited by George Robertson, Melinda Mash, Lisa Tickner, Jon Bird, Barry Curtis, and Tim Putnam (London: Routledge, 1994), pp. 107–108.
83. *Ibid.*, p. 108.
84. *Ibid.*
85. Hill, *At Home in the World,* p. 224.
86. Mouffe, "For a Politics of Nomadic Identity," p. 111.
87. Hill, *At Home in the World,* p. 224.

The Hope of Finding Home: Exploring the Wandering Complex

ELENA POURTOVA

Introduction

I have a recurring dream about wandering. In the dream, I have no house. It is night already, and I am getting ready to sleep in a university lecture hall, high up in the back rows. I don't want anyone to see me so I can stay in the hall until people return in the morning.

I fear these dreams. They are difficult to interpret symbolically, perhaps because they are so close to reality for me. The image of a university lecture hall brings back two memories. In my student years, one of my friends who had no place to live used to come to the faculty zoological museum before it closed, hide himself in a high built-in closet, and stay there for the night. The amphitheatre with the tall

---

Elena Pourtova is a Jungian analyst and a member of the International Association of Analytical Psychology and the Russian Society of Analytical Psychology. She is an Assistant Professor and Chair of Consulting Psychology at the High Psychology School in Moscow. She lectures at the Moscow Association of Analytical Psychology and is a teacher of Jungian analysis in Moscow and other Russian cities. She is the author of the chapter, "Moscow is Like a Sweet Berry", in *Psyche & and the City: A Soul's Guide to the Modern Metropolis*, Tom Singer, ed. (Spring Journal Books, 2010).

staircase in my dream reminds me of another friend from later days who used to spend the night on the steps of a doorway when he had no home to go to.

Why do I take this to heart? I have never spent a night in a doorway, but I have very often been close to it in my life! By the time of this dream series, I had already lived a rootless existence for twenty years; I had left my parents' home but had not yet set up my own home. I rented apartments and lived in hostels. I often moved from one place to another. In one of the cities where I did university studies, I lived in eight places in six years. I was expelled from hostels several times. And the time when my landlady called in the evening and angrily told me to get out the next morning with all my things, including my furniture, was the culmination of these eviction stories! During such moments, I imagined that I might spend a night not only in doorways but also freezing under a fence or wandering around, becoming a beggar.

Beggars in Russia are entirely different from those in the West. Beggars in France or Canada sleep in the streets, stretching themselves out without hiding as if demonstrating their dignity. They also feel within their rights to ask for money. Beggars, homeless people, and tramps in Russia are shy and hide themselves in cellars or attics, trying to stay out of sight and avoid censure and arrest. They seldom ask for money; it is easier for them to rummage around in dumpsters. They are deprived of their civil rights and are extremely humiliated. During the twenty years while I was getting a good education, working at respectable jobs, and doing my postgraduate course, I felt deep inside myself that I was like one of those homeless tramps.

A lot of water has passed under the bridge since then. I have undergone two courses of psychoanalysis. Now I come across similar characters among my clients, and my image of the tramp embodies many features of different persons. However, the tramp is still my guide in the space of wanderings.

In this article, I explore the inner space of wandering, beginning from the place of intolerable feelings that the experience of homelessness creates. I then move on to an exploration of what I call the wandering complex, which is characterized by an attachment to wandering, to always being on the road and never at home, the inclination to perceive any relationship as temporary. I explore how Soviet culture influenced the formation of this complex, and then go on to give examples of the wandering complex, in its negative and positive aspects, in the book and film *Chocolat*, and in the story of Exodus from the Bible.

Joanne Harris's *Chocolat* and a Wandering Complex

When I read *Chocolat*, a novel by Joanne Harris, I find myself at once in the state of homelessness that I know very well.[1] Its main characters are tramps, Vianne Rocher and her six-year-old daughter Anouk, and Anouk's imaginary rabbit, Pantoufle. In the background of this story is another mother-daughter pair, Vianne's mother and Vianne herself as a little girl. Vianne explains her mother's influence on her life:

> From my mother I learned what shaped me. The art of turning bad luck into good. The forking of the fingers to divert the path of malchance. The sewing of a sachet, brewing of a draught, the conviction that a spider brings good luck before midnight and bad luck after. Most of all she gave me her love of new places, the gypsy wanderlust which took us all over Europe and further.... By my eighteenth year I had lost count of the cities in which we had lived, the languages we had spoken. Jobs were as varied; waitressing, interpreting, car repair. Sometimes we escaped from the windows of cheap overnight hotels without paying the bill. We rode trains without tickets, forged work permits, crossed borders illicitly. We were deported countless times. Twice my mother was arrested, but released without charge. Our names changed as we moved, drifting from one regional variant to another; Yanne, Jeanne, Johanne, Anne, Anouchka. Like thieves we were perpetually on the run, converting the unwieldy ballast of life into francs, pounds, kroner, dollars, as we fled where the wind took us.[2]

How familiar this description is to me! I could also tell stories about moving from one place to another and about changing jobs or relationships with people. And the lawlessness and the absence of rules that Vianne describes, the feelings of guilt and being blamed by others, of being able to play any role and use different names, thus easily losing one's own identity, are well known to me.

Just as Vianne and her mother moved constantly from one place to another, Vianne continues to live this same kind of vagabond lifestyle with her daughter, Anouk. The story of *Chocolat* is about Vianne's emerging attempts to change this kind of wandering existence, stay in one place, and form meaningful relationships.

Investigating this wandering complex, we see that Vianne at first does not question the way she was brought up by her mother:

> Don't think I suffered; life was a fine adventure for those years. We had each other, my mother and I. I never felt the need for a father. My friends were countless. And yet it must have preyed upon her sometimes, the lack of permanence, the need always to contrive. Still we raced faster as the years wore on, staying a month, two at the most, then moving on like fugitives racing the sunset.[3]

But eventually Vianne begins to recognize the frenetic tempo at which she lives, and that her behavior and resistance to forming attachments to places or to people are becoming compulsive. She starts to acknowledge the opposite, more negative side of the wandering complex.

The quote above activates my clinical thinking about wandering, which whispers terms that are only too familiar to me: narcissism, resistance to the Oedipal complex, the *puer* archetype, the withdrawal from everyday life, and so forth. Even if this is so, these words protect me from stress and the deep feelings such stress cause. Or perhaps I am becoming like the character of the Black Man in *Chocolat*, taking on a critical and judging position. I shall try to put my clinical perspective aside and follow the image of wandering developed in the book.

The following fragment of text reveals how Vianne's inner conflict becomes more and more obvious as her identification with her daughter allows her to come emotionally closer to her own experience as a child and to sense what remains in the shadow of the picture she presents of "life as wonderful adventure":

> Hasn't there been . . . a kind of regret? I think there has. Twenty-five years, and at last the spring has begun to grow tired, just as my mother grew tired in the final years. I find myself looking at the sun and wondering what it would be like to see it rise above the same horizon for five—maybe ten, maybe twenty—years. The thought fills me with strange dizziness, a feeling of fear and

> longing. And Anouk, my little stranger? I see the brave adventure we lived so long in a different light now that I am the mother.[4]

The dizziness she experiences is important; for Vianne, stopping her endless wandering from town to town with Anouk means losing a foothold. Does her wandering actually provide her psyche with some sort of stability? Does her lifestyle protect her from some of her feelings? Later, when Vianne starts developing relationships with the inhabitants of a small town, she begins to experience her own vulnerability. As a result, we learn what her dizziness means:

> Is this what my mother feared? . . . Was this what she fled? Not her own death, but thousands of tiny intersections of her life with others, the broken connections, the links in spite of themselves, the responsibilities? Did we spend all those years running away from our loves, our friendships, the casual words uttered in passing that can alter the course of life?[5]

To have permanent relationships, to stop moving around and being elusive, to belong to somebody and to own something—this is what, to Vianne, is terrible, frightening. Though at this point in the story she is not yet able to establish relationships with people, she begins to form attachments to objects by allowing herself to own things, something she has never done before:

> This is the first time we have really owned such things. . . . The novelty of possession is still an exotic thing to us, a precious thing, intoxicating. I envy the table its scars, the scorch marks caused by the hot bread tins. I envy its calm sense of time and I wish I could say: I did this five years ago. I made this mark, this ring caused by a wet coffee cup, this cigarette burn, this ladder of cuts against the wood's course grain. This is where Anouk cut her initials, the year she was six years old, this secret place behind the table leg. I did this on a warm day seven summers ago with the carving knife. Do you remember? Do you remember the river ran dry? Do you remember?[6]

As Vianne experiences a pang of envy toward others for what they have accomplished, what they have lived through and remembered together, she begins to long for the reality of existence where what is routine has value and weight. Only then can she allow her desire to establish relationships with others enter her consciousness.

> At first one feels a kind of superiority. We are a race apart, we the travelers. We have seen, experienced, so much more than they. Content to run out their sad lives in an endless round of sleep-work-sleep, to tend their neat gardens, their identical suburban houses, their small dreams; we hold them in a little contempt. Then, after a while, comes envy. The first time it is almost funny; a sharp sudden sting which subsides nearly straight away. A woman in a park, bending over a child in a pushchair, both faces lit by something which is the sun. Then comes the second time, the third; two young people on the seafront, arms intertwined; a group of office girls on their lunch break, giggling over coffee and croissants . . . before long it is an almost constant ache. . . . The names on the hotel registers change as we pass. We leave no trace as we pass on. Ghostlike, we cast no shadow.[7]

Unlived life seems to be a price of wandering.

The Wandering Complex in Analytical Practice

In my analytical practice, I come across numerous illustrations of different aspects of the wandering complex described in the novel. I remember the story of a woman who had a candidate's degree in two sciences (the equivalent of two master's degrees) by the time she was thirty. She preferred to study at two universities simultaneously. She managed to complete her work in each program on schedule, but did not see any point in wasting her free time on the usual "student's stupid things." In the course of analytical training, she became aware that she had never been to a graduation party and had no girlfriends from any of her places of study. The fact that she studied at more than one university at the same time freed her from social obligations at any of them and from establishing close relations with other people, interactions that would have provided "intersections of her life with others." At the age of thirty, she had no close relationships, neither girlfriends nor boyfriends. It is worth adding that the father of this woman was a military man who constantly moved the family from one garrison to another in her childhood and that she had to change schools many times.

Here is another story. A woman, one of my clients, told her girlfriend about how she had lived in a series of rented flats. The girlfriend expressed her sympathy about my client's wanderings. My client felt humiliated and irritated by her friend's sympathy. Gradually she realized that in telling her friend about her misfortunes, she had expected her friend to admire her. My client believed that living in rented flats was a heroic act in her efforts to overcome the difficulties she faced at that time. For her, each new difficult situation served as an excuse to confirm her heroic Ego. Her girlfriend's sympathy destroyed my client's picture of herself as a heroine, pointing out instead how needless this kind of life is and perhaps even suggesting that my client had a right to a life filled with more ease.

Lyn Cowan introduces an interesting distinction between martyrs and genuine sufferers.[8] The martyr's suffering is demonstrable and external; its source is projected onto the outside. It is a strategy of the Ego in which one is proud of the sufferings one has lived through on the outside as a way to avoid real immersion in sufferings and being transformed by them. Rimma Kazakova, a Soviet poet, describes a pattern of heroic self-overcoming and the aspiration for endless self-improvement that was very popular in the mid-1980s in the Soviet Union:

> Like a tumbleweed,
> My fate is rolling and making haste . . .
> My norm of pain is full of bitter taste,
> And I improve myself indeed.
>
> As if asleep, I keep myself aloof,
> And want my heart to be pretty sure
> I'll have some moments of light relief.
> What else shall I endure?
>
> As if cursed and buried
> For being in somebody's debt,
> I'll do my best not to be bad,
> If I am able to do all that.[9]

Another client had a burning dream about her grandmother's inheritance. At first, she regretted that her grandmother was not rich enough to leave family jewels to her. But then generational bonds came to the forefront, replacing the focus on valuable objects. In her imagination, anything that her mother or grandmother had once possessed embodied generational bonds. In Russia, objects associated with different times inevitably accumulate in a house where several generations of a family have lived. The objects become material carriers of layers of the collective unconscious, and the house itself turns into a multilevel symbol of psyche, just as the house in Jung's well-known house dream did, a house set upon a Gothic foundation with a modern facade. But my client's family had no patrimonial house in which to store its history and memory. The Revolution, the Civil War, the extermination of well-to-do farmers, and other events in Russia forced many families to flee in search of safety, thus inevitably losing their houses.[10]

Such absence of things, the carriers of the patrimonial soul, is very typical in Russia. For a long time in our country, ties with the past were looked at as narrow-mindedness or even as presenting a dangerous risk. Emphasizing the collective and condemning anything private or individual depreciated the material carriers of individuality and often led to the loss of individual soul.

What follows is a fragment from the book by a Russian colleague who conducts seminars in reconstructing family history:[11]

> Sometimes at the beginning of group work, I ask members of the group to recall and describe a thing that has existed in their families for a long time. These objects may not have an official status of "a family relic," but they carry the soul and memory of the family. The objects group members describe clearly show a soul and memory these things possess. Here are a few descriptions taken from my records almost at random:
>
> —The silver earrings that I wear. My great-grandfather brought identical silver earrings from the fair as gifts to his three daughters to treat them equally. My grandmother got the same cheap earrings as her sisters right before the collectivization. Afterwards there could be no fairs. We were sent into exile to Kazakhstan.
>
> —A portrait of my grandmother in watercolors. When she was missing during the war, one of her relatives pasted a mourning border over her portrait. When my grandfather saw this, he got furious and began to tear that border off. He managed to tear it off only from two sides of the portrait, then he gave up doing that and began to run around shouting angrily and trying to find out who had done that, thus having buried her alive. My grandmother did return home alive. However, her portrait still has that mourning border on its two other sides.

—A special small knife with a hook and a nacreous handle for peeling oranges. It is blunt. I tried to use it when I was a grownup. It seemed to be inconvenient or unusual. It belongs to a different life where everything is in order and each trivial move needs its own tool.

—A photo of my grandparents at a resort when they were young. All women are in crepe de chine dresses, looking so pretty and laughing, as if they were in Hollywood. And it has an oblique inscription below: "In memory of Yalta. 1939."

—It is a cactus in my family, a darling of my grandfather. It grows slowly; I am not sure how old it is. It has become covered with some bark and looks bald below. My grandmother called it "Gosha's fright," constantly grumbling that it bothered her. But the cactus blossomed very beautifully, a day or two, and I heard how she was telling it that it was not enough. When my grandfather passed away, the cactus, believe it or not, stopped blossoming and my grandmother even liked it.

—A Singer sewing machine. It is suitable for every material, from chiffon to canvas. It is a simple and reliable mechanism that works like a devil; it is next to impossible to break. Its serious mechanical beauty is so attractive. It supported the entire family in evacuation and nobody dared to get rid it. So it still exists.[12]

Ekaterina Mikhailova recalls the words of Osip Mandelstam, a Russian poet, who said that as soon as materialism prevailed, material things began to disappear.[13]

Homelessness was an essential attribute of the Soviet system that was closely connected with public values of anti-individualism. Apartments belonged to the state, and this eliminated the individual's right to have a personal space. Angela Connelly, who was an analyst in Moscow in the 1990s, described brilliantly the consequences for the psyche of developing in the context of the Kommunalka, or communal flats that allotted each person only 4.3 square meters of space at the height of Stalinism.[14]

Broken borders and the loss of one's inner self are inevitable components of the lack of personal space for development. I remember an aphoristic expression of Vardges Petrosyan, a Soviet writer who describes this Soviet attitude of moving the inner psyche space outside very accurately: "The soul also has a house and this house is the soul of the other."[15] One of the popular theories in Soviet-era psychology was Vadim Petrovsky's Theory of Reflected Subjectivity. According to Petrovsky, the most important manifestation of personality is the ability of an individual to penetrate the soul of another person and continue to exist there as an internalized image in the other person. The more people the personality penetrates as an introject, the more significant this personality becomes. Its other name is the Theory of Being in Others.[16] It describes a pattern of feeling from the reality of one's own life and places a high value on existing within others.

At the end of Joanne Harris's *Chocolat,* the secret that the heroine was abducted in her childhood is revealed. This secret explains her mother's fear of prosecution and her need to always be on the run. Lawlessness was a basic value that defined the wandering life of the mother and her daughter. Because the mother was not aware that she had the right to have her child, her life with the child became illegal and the child was not able to have *her* right to live properly.

In my practice, I come across the wandering complex in people whose birth was surrounded by uncertainty, including those whose mothers planned to abort them but did not follow through. Deep inside, these individuals remain in doubt about their birth and do not feel they have the right to live. Here is a dream a client had when he was five years old. This client had an older brother and sister, but his mother had had five abortions between her second child and him, her third child:

> I am running away from a huge bull, with my brother and sister ahead of me. They are running faster and I am lagging behind, and the bull is just about to catch up with me. Suddenly, someone's hands pick me up; it is a nurse. She carries me away to the house where a fireplace burns and little children are sitting on a bench along the wall. At first, I think I have been rescued and then I understand that it is a house of a cannibal; the children on the bench are waiting for their turn to be thrown into the fireplace, and I am waiting for my turn too.

My client unequivocally interpreted the children sitting on the bench as aborted siblings, and his waiting for his turn to be killed was something that he had felt all his life. This dreadful state of expectation undermined all his undertakings; each successful stage of his life ended in failure; nothing from his achievements from one stage transferred to the next stage. Each time, all his positive accomplishments were annulled and he had to start anew. As a result, at the age of forty he described his life as a series of short bright periods, each characterized by certain achievements; however, they were poorly connected with each other and failed to define his identity.

In such cases, it is impossible to establish close relationships because they bring about great anxiety and an unbearable fear of dependency. This pattern is beautifully described by the poet Vera Pavlova:

> Don't run up on the porch
> of my burnt-out house so swiftly.
> Don't look at my face so closely,
> You do see—it's uncovered.
> Don't touch my hands—
> It looks like Akhmatova's rhyme.
> You'd better go home. All right?
> Get out of here,
> Disappear.[17]

Undercut roots inevitably lead to undercut ties with the following generation and to doubts about pregnancy—to keep or not to keep? Poet Andrei Voznesenski describes a mother explaining her dilemma:

> When you were an embryo
> (Your father showed his insistence),
> We all became embroiled
> Whether or not
> To keep your very existence?
> Your beautiful hair
> Your brilliant mind
> And your question today:
> "Not to keep it or bear it,
> What's one of a kind?"[18]

The question of "to keep or not to keep" is about the reality of existence and the decision of whether of not to give life, and these remain in the shadow of consciousness. At one session, I was impressed with a client's story about how she was a twin who had not been identified during her mother's pregnancy. After her mother gave birth to her sister, the mother's birth pangs continued and the doctors tried to stop them. The client believes that she remembers this moment. She was rushing somewhere, trying to get through, and then after a sudden flash everything came abruptly to an end. In her words, she has followed this pattern all her life. She rushes somewhere, trying to arrive at her destination, and suddenly all comes to an end. I was amazed at how well she was aware of what had *not* happened in her life! But she ignored the full story. She did not focus on the fact that despite the doctor's faulty actions, she was born after all! Someone guessed that the delivery was not finished and managed to correct the situation, thus helping her to be born. This is also a part of her story, but it does not seem to define her life.

Collecting fragments of reality is a very important part of the process of restoring the integrity of the psyche. In this process, one realizes that the pieces of the picture of one's existence are inconsistent with each other, but they are alive. Jung writes:

> We see [the self] entering into manifestation, freeing itself from unconscious projection, and, as it grips us, entering into our lives and so passing unconsciousness into consciousness, from potentiality into actuality. What it is in the diffuse unconscious state we don't know; we only know that in becoming ourselves it has become man.
>
> This process of becoming human is represented in dreams and inner images as the putting together of many scattered units, and sometimes as the gradual emergence and clarification of something that was always there.[19]

"The clarification of something that was always there" is a part of the process of psychotherapy. My client who expected her friend to admire her for her "heroic" wanderings entered a sham marriage to solve her housing problems. This episode in her biography appeared twice. At a final stage of therapy, the theme of her fictitious marriage began to appear in her dreams. The key dream that changed the contents of this series is as follows:

> I fictitiously marry my colleague I work with. I have known him for a long time. Our wedding is taking place and there are many guests. One of them makes a joke about me and it hurts me. I do not show that I am hurt and continue to smile. My fictitious bridegroom flares up at this carelessly tossed-off remark and challenges my offender to clear up the situation. Here I understand that my bridegroom is deeply offended for me

because he has really loved me for a long time and our wedding was not fictitious for him at all. I feel extremely grateful to him.

It was in this dream that my client experienced "the clarification of something that was always there." She had had other dreams about the development of her relationship with her bridegroom, who initially seemed to be merely her opposite in a marriage of convenience. In the final dream of this series, she saw herself as the wife of the president of the country. She understood this dream as an accurate depiction of the real status of her inner bridegroom/husband—the governor of her inner space and the state of her psyche. And it was important for her that she was no longer a bride but a mature married woman who had strong ties with this inner man.

Finally, there is the topic of being orphaned. At a certain stage of the therapy, one of my clients had a strong feeling that he had been orphaned for a long time despite the fact that his parents were still alive. In his imagination, he saw himself as a wanderer deprived of home and family in a world where nobody cared for him. He perceived his contacts with others to be unsuccessful knockings at closed doors. Hungry and frozen, he was not allowed to set foot across a threshold and was sometimes scolded for his efforts. He perceived some events in his life as a sudden permission to warm himself at someone's home hearth, but only for a short time. He did not have the right to stay longer and enjoy another's favor. From time to time, he would come across evidence of someone else's well-being, which caused pangs of envy. At other times, though, he felt gratitude and saw a possibility that he could keep this warmth, which he was not entitled to in his outer life, inside himself.

It was curious to me to watch the internal route he pursued. At first, he moved farther and farther away from identification with his parents. In his living through the "experience" of being orphaned, he was losing his last ties with his parents. And after an especially acute period of despair, he, like Gerda from Andersen's fairy tale "The Snow Queen," began to gather from each contact with individuals who were important to him parts that his "internal child" and "internal parent" lacked; in this way, he began to complete himself. His attitude toward being orphaned gradually changed. He understood that only in this way could he get rid of the ties that bound him to his parents, especially aspects of such ties that symbolized dependence on authority and the passive expectation of well-being granted by authorities "for good behavior." This issue also comes to the fore regarding questions of housing during the Soviet era. Then, the state distributed apartments like a kind parent who knows the needs of his children. Having lost his former ties with his parents, my client could create his inner house, feel his new identity, and thus be able to build up his external relations and solve vital problems in a different way.

The topic of the orphan is also touched upon in the film version of *Chocolat*. There is an episode in which the heroine Vianne unintentionally breaks an urn that contains the ashes of her mother, who had indoctrinated her into the wandering lifestyle. It is a very beautiful image of how the loss of former ties with the dead define the life of a living person. Only after the loss of the ashes does Vianne have a chance to stop wandering, to root herself in life, and create her own home.

Forty Years in the Wilderness[20]

In Jung's view, images and figures in the Bible represent independent products of the unconscious psyche arising, like crystals, from an archetypical matrix. For Jung, the experiences and stories recorded in the Bible were about those whose consciousnesses underwent archetypical experiences but were not overwhelmed by them.

The biblical story of a forty-year march in the wilderness until the last generation remembering slavery dies is a remarkable image whose details reveal the steps necessary for solving the internal problem of acquiring a home, the Promised Land. In this story, the prophet Moses, who received messages directly from God, led the Jewish people to the Promised Land, assisted by Aaron and Miriam, who were also prophets but heard the voice of God in dreams and visions, not directly, as Moses did. During the people's journey, God took care of them, providing them with food (manna), protection (clouds), and the law (the Torah). But from time to time, the people lost touch with God and began to have doubts and complain about the hardships of their journey.

If we consider these events as analogous to the internal analytical journey, this brings to mind a conscious process of individuation (or psychotherapy) in which from time to time the Ego loses its sense of direction and its ties with the Self. What happens at such moments of disjuncture in the biblical story and how are these ties are restored?

The first episode of disjuncture is called "the disobedience of the people that lusted." The people, tired of eating manna, demand meat and remember the advantages of slavery: "We remember the fish which we did eat in Egypt freely; the cucumbers, and the melons, and the leeks, and the onions, and the garlick: But now our soul is dried away, there is nothing at all, beside this manna, before our eyes."[21]

This is similar to how revolutionary changes of the 1980s in Russia at first generated a general enthusiasm and readiness to move on to a capitalist society, but as people began to realize what they had lost of the former system, they began to feel quite nostalgic for the socialist times when they got many things for free.

The same thing happens in psychotherapy; the client may undervalue a person they used to depend on for care, seeing him or her as a convenience of life until they are gone, when the client experiences loss and grief. Losing an object and the resulting depressiveness are the main events that change the structure of the psyche such that the reality principle replaces the pleasure principle:

> If the previous disorders in the relations between a mother and a child complicate both the experience of losing an object and overcoming a depressive position, then the absence of such disorders and the mother's high quality care cannot relieve the child of the necessity of experiencing and overcoming this period that plays a structuring role for his psyche.[22]

In the process of grieving, the advantages of the former way of life may be exaggerated. (It is hard to believe that the Jews ate fresh fruit and fish in slavery.) These "craving" parts are responsible for maintaining illusions when the entire inner journey is experienced as a journey to a richer life instead of as a journey to develop the personality. These parts are manifested in the client's attempts to use psychotherapy to return to a former state of well-being and lack of awareness of what has been lost because of suffering. In Jung's view, these are attempts to regressively restore the Persona.[23] James Wyly calls it the search for lost phallicism.[24]

During the episodes of "the disobedience," Moses fulfills a maternal function for the Jewish people and convinces God not to destroy what has not yet come to maturity. This maternal aspect of Moses' attitude toward the people is clearly expressed: "Have I conceived all this people? Have I begotten them, that thou shouldest say unto me, Carry them in thy bosom, as a nursing father beareth the sucking child, unto the land which thou swarest unto their fathers?"[25] The value of a maternal aspect in analytic work with those who feel abandoned by God is excellently shown in Kathrin Asper's *The Abandoned Child Within*.[26] She compares the maternal and paternal approaches in psychotherapy and shows the importance of a maternal strategy of carrying the child in one's arms, contrasting it with a paternal strategy of leading the child by the hand. The function of the analyst as mediator is to give meaning to the client's strong motives that may threaten integrity and teach them how to resist the pressure arising from different aspects of the unconscious. This episode from the Bible comes to an end with God's decision to distribute Moses' responsibilities among seventy elders and with the death of "the people that lusted." This place was named Kibroth-hattaavah (the graves of craving).[27]

Each of these three things (a redistribution of responsibility, the graves of craving, a new name for a place) may also take place intrapsychically and through analysis. In analysis, distributing responsibility among the parts of psyche is in effect a process of finding internal allies for the Ego that understand the sense of loss and are ready to support the Ego during episodes of despair that occur from time to time. For example, a client who integrates the function of Miriam, who provided the people with a source of water, may be able to rely on his or her own dreams during these periods. And the seventy elders may be interpreted to mean the ability to use mature and skilled parts of the psyche to work toward the conscious goal of therapy (individuation). That "the people that lusted" died and that their deaths were commemorated with the name of a particular place may be understood as the client's conscious acceptance of the loss of illusions about a former way of life. This experience in therapy becomes a significant turning point, radically changing the direction of internal movement.

In the second episode of disjuncture with God, it is Miriam and Aaron who disagree with God. They become Moses' rivals, asking "Hath the Lord indeed spoken only by Moses? Hath he not spoken also by us?"²⁸ If in the first episode the people want too much from Moses, then in the second, Moses is devalued and his ability to adequately reflect the voice of God is doubted.

In inner development, this situation is similar to an interruption caused by the loss of one's bearings when it is necessary to restore a correct balance. In my work with my clients, I often find them at a crossroads when they decide to get training as psychotherapists in order "to achieve better results in the analysis." In other words, they want to become Aaron-like; they want to serve as priests themselves in someone else's analytical wandering. On the other hand, a client who invests energy in his or her Miriam-function runs the risk of turning the task of listening to his or her dreams into a hobby or indulgent bursts of self-expression without reflecting about the analytical value of the artistic products created. I recall an episode from Jung's story when his Anima tempted him to treat everything he did as art.²⁹

As a result of Miriam and Aaron's challenge to Moses' leadership, Miriam became leprous and was expelled from the camp for seven days. But the people waited for her return before they journeyed on. This suggests a recognition of the true value of Miriam (the journey is impossible without her) and stresses that her position is subordinate to that of Moses and is touched by the shame of leprosy.

The last episode of disobedience is the main one in this story because it dooms the Jewish people to a forty-year wandering in the wilderness in order to lose their servile position. This story takes place near the Promised Land; it is found and some scouts are sent there. After forty days of exploration, they bring back the fruit of this land and tell the people that the land "flowed with milk and honey." But then the scouts describe this land as inaccessible and dangerous:

> The people be strong that dwell in the land, and the cities are walled and very great.... It is a land that eateth up the inhabitants thereof; and all the people we saw in it are men of a great stature. And there we saw the giants... and we were in our own sight as grasshoppers, and so we were in their sight.³⁰

The scouts' survey of the Promised Land represents the maturation of some internal parts that have the ability to come out of a crisis and use the fruits of the completed work. These parts may live as if everything has already been overcome and accomplished in psychotherapy. But their adjustment to a new reality frightens the Ego, which is not ready to enter this reality or to bear the responsibility of assuming the new role of the owner of the long-desired and suddenly located land. The disintegration of the psyche takes place when its less mature parts project their hostility onto the external environment so that the mature aspects cannot prevail against this danger and face the risk of destruction; that is, the less mature parts feel that they are grasshoppers compared to giants in the land. The psyche becomes "a land that eateth up the inhabitants thereof" in this process.

I see this state of mind often in my dealings with my clients. As soon as they feel that have experienced positive gains in psychotherapy, and I think that the exhausting process is coming to an end, regression ensues, taking different forms. The client who has developed good contact with his or her dreams and through them can access deeper parts of his or her psyche decides that he or she wants me to interpret the dreams for them instead (preferring to have manna but not honey). Or the client's great expectations of therapy suddenly spoil positive results that are achieved by small steps (becoming a grasshopper in the giants' sight). Or the success of analysis becomes perceived as threatening because it may come to an end, and the contact with the psychotherapist may be lost.

In the story, God's angry reaction has become a real source of danger: "How long will this people provoke me? And how long will it be ere they believe me, for all the signs which I have shewed among them? I will smite them with pestilence, and disinherit them, and will make of thee a greater nation and mightier than they."[31] Moses tries to calm God down:

> Then the Egyptians shall hear it . . . and they will tell it to the inhabitants of this land. . . . Now if you shalt kill all this people as one man, then the nations which have heard the fame of thee will speak, saying, Because the Lord was not able to bring this people into the land which he sware them, therefore he hath slain them in the wilderness. And now . . . let the power of my Lord be great, according as thou hast spoken. . . . The Lord is longsuffering, and of great mercy, forgiving iniquity and transgression. . . . Pardon . . . the iniquity of this people according unto the greatness of thy mercy, and as thou hast forgiven this people, from Egypt even until now.[32]

In both life and in psychotherapy, forgiveness is an important experience at the end of wandering. It is necessary to admit one's fear of defeat, forgive oneself for imperfection, and allow oneself time to acknowledge that a way out of a situation tied up with the loss will inevitably be found.

In the Biblical story, God makes the people wander for forty years in the wilderness, one year for each day the scouts spent in the Promised Land, until the last person who remembers slavery has died. For me, this is a story about psychotherapy. As soon as one important stage comes to an end (finding the space for an internal future), another stage begins (building self-esteem and understanding that one has a right to a proper life). This story also reminds me of the history of my country, which had a long period of slavery. After the abolition of serfdom in Russia in 1861, Anton Chekhov wrote about the need "to squeeze the slave out of oneself drop by drop."[33] This phrase became aphoristic and one of its modern versions is as follows: "If we squeeze the slave out of ourselves drop by drop, then eventually it will amount to the whole of Russia."[34]

In exploring these issues, it seems that the bigger the changes the soul needs, the longer may be the road of wanderings. It is this that suggests the purpose and value of this road.

NOTES

1. Joanne Harris, *Chocolat* (London: Black Swan, 2007).
2. *Ibid.*, p. 44.
3. *Ibid.*, p. 45.
4. *Ibid.*, p. 46.
5. *Ibid.*, p. 156.
6. *Ibid.*, p. 190.
7. *Ibid.*, p. 192.
8. Lyn Cowan, *Masochism: A Jungian View* (Dallas, Tex.: Spring Publications, 1982).
9. Римма Казакова, «Сойти с холма». Журнал «Юность» 3 (1984), страница 37 [Rimma Kazakova, "Like a Tumbleweed," in

Come Down the Hill, a collection published in *Yunost* 3 (1984): 37], translated by Sklyanin Yuri Nikolayevich.

10. Houses are being lost even now. Recently, I watched a TV report about how the last Muscovite to live in the pre-Revolutionary house of his forefathers was evicted and offered a flat on the outskirts of the city because his house was needed by investors for housing for the elite in the city's center.

11. Екатерина Михайлова, "Я у себя одна," или Веретено Василисы (Москва: Класс, 2003) [Ekaterina Mikhailova, *"I Have Only Myself,"* or *Vasilisa's Spindle* (Moscow: Class, 2003)].

12. *Ibid.*, p. 191.

13. *Ibid.*, p. 188.

14. Angela Connolly, "Through the Iron Curtain: Analytical Space in Post-Soviet Russia," *Journal of Analytical Psychology* 51, no. 2 (2006): 173–189.

15. Вардгес Петросян, Армянские эскизы (Москва: Советский писатель, 1978) [Vardges Petrosyan, *Armenian Sketches* (Moscow: The Soviet Writer, 1978)], translated by Sklyanin Yuri Nikolayevich.

16. В. А. Петровский, Личность в психологии: парадигма субъектности (Ростов на/Д: Феникс, 1996) [V. A. Petrovsky, *Personality in Psychology: A Paradigm of Subjectivity* (Rostov-on-Don: Phoenix, 1996)].

17. Вера Павлова, Небесное животное: стихи (Москва, Журнал «Золотой Век», 1997), стр. 178 [Vera Pavlova, *Celestial Animal: Poems* (Moscow: Journal "The Golden Age," 1997), p. 178].

18. Андрей Вознесенский, «Говорит мама», сборник «Не отрекусь» Избранная (лирика, БелАДИ, 1996), стр. 115 [Andrei Voznesenski, "Mother Speaks," in *I Do Not Renounce: Poems* (Minsk: BelADY, 1996), p. 115], translated by Sklyanin Yuri Nikolayevich.

19. Carl Jung, "Transformation Symbolism in the Mass," in *Psychology and Religion: East and West*, vol. 11 of *The Collected Works of C. G. Jung*, edited and translated by G. Adler and R. F. C. Hull (Princeton, N.J.: Princeton University Press, 1970), §§ 398–399.

20. This section contains material from "Images of Individuation in Biblical Stories," a paper Julia Kazakevich and I presented at a conference of the Moscow Association of Analytical Psychology on 10–12 June 2007.

21. Numbers 11:5–6. All quotations from the Bible are from the King James Version.
22. Андре Грин, «Мертвая мать», Антология современного психоанализа, Французская психоаналитическая школа, под редакцией А. Жибо, А. В. Россохина (Санкт-Петербург: Питер, 2005), стр. 334, Russian translation of Andrй Green, "La Mere Marte," in *Narcissisme de Vie, Narcissisme de Mort* (Paris, Les Editions de Minuit, 1983), pp. 222–253. [Editor's note: Translated into English as *Life Narcissism, Death Narcissism*, translated by Andrew Weller (New York: Free Association Books, 2001).]
23. *Ibid.*
24. Джеймс Уайли, В поисках фаллоса. Приап и инфляция мужского (St. Petersburg: В. S. К., 1996), Russian translation of James Wyly, *The Phallic Quest: Priapus and Masculine Inflation* (Toronto: Inner City Books, 1989).
25. Numbers 11:12.
26. Катрин Аспер, Психология нарциссической личности. Внутренний ребенок и самооценка (Москва: Добросвет, 2008), Russian translation of Kathrin Asper, *The Abandoned Child Within: On Losing and Regaining Self-Worth* (New York: Fromm International Publishing Corporation, 1993).
27. Numbers 11:34–35.
28. Numbers 12:2.
29. К. Г. Юнг, Воспоминания. Сновидения. Размышления. (Киев: AirLand, 1994), Russian translation of Carl Jung, *Memories, Dreams, Reflections*, edited by Aniela Jaffe, translated by Richard and Clara Winston (New York: Pantheon Books, 1963), p. 185.
30. Numbers 13:28, 32–33.
31. Numbers 14:11–12.
32. Numbers 14:13–19.
33. Anton Chekhov to A. S. Suvorin, 7 January 1889, quoted in Geoffrey Borny, *Interpreting Chekhov* (Canberra: Australian National University Press, 2006), p. 149.
34. Journalist Alexander Morozov, quoted at "Quotations about Being Forced Slaves," Aforism website (in Russian), //aforism.chat.ru/IZBR/izbr-slaves.htm.

REMAIN TRUE TO THE EARTH:
HOME AND WANDERING IN NIETZSCHE

PAUL BISHOP

Shall I ever reach it? Doubt upon doubt. The goal is too far, and if one manages to reach it, one has usually also consumed one's energies in the long searching and struggle: one attains one's freedom and is weary like a mayfly in the evening.
   —Nietzsche to Carl von Gersdorff, 1 April 1874

My soul, where are you? Do you hear me? I speak, I call you—are you there? I have returned, I am here again. I have shaken the dust of all the lands from my feet, and I have come to you, I am with you. After long years of wandering, I have come to you again. Should I tell you everything I have seen, experienced, and drunk in? Or do you not want to hear about all the noise of life and the world? But one thing you must know: the one thing I have learned is that one must live this life.
   —Jung, *The Red Book*

Paul Bishop, D. Phil., is professor of German at the University of Glasgow. In a series of books and articles he has tried to situate Jung within a tradition of German thought linking the classical aesthetics of Goethe and Schiller with the philosophy of Nietzsche and, ultimately, depth psychology. He is currently editing a collection of papers on the subject of the archaic. Among his most recent publications are *Reading Goethe at Midlife: Ancient Wisdom, German Classicism, and Jung* (Spring Journal Books, 2011); and *Analytical Psychology and German Classical Aesthetics,* vol. 1, *The Development of the Personality* (Routledge, 2007) and vol. 2, *The Constellation of the Self* (Routledge, 2008). His other research interests include Stefan George, Ludwig Klages, Thomas Mann, Rainer Maria Rilke, and Arthur Schopenhauer.

The theme of the wanderer is a major one in German Romanticism (as well as in its stylistic predecessor, the *Sturm und Drang*). As far as Romanticism is concerned, one might think in particular of the poetry of Eichendorff; of Schubert's 1822 piano sonata in C major, Op. 15 (known as the "Wanderer Fantasy"); or of Schumann's 1827 setting of Wilhelm Müller's cycle of poems, *Die Winterreise* (1823).[1] Travel is an important topos in the German novel, for example in Goethe's *Wilhelm Meisters Lehrjahre* (1796) and *Wilhelm Meisters Wanderjahre* (1821/1829) or Ludwig Tieck's *Franz Sternbalds Wanderungen* (1798). In painting, one thinks of works by Caspar David Friedrich, such as his iconic *The Wanderer above the Sea of Mist* (1818) or his depictions of sublime landscapes that place the viewer in the perspective of a traveler or works by Carl Gustav Carus, such as his *Pilgrim in a Rocky Valley* (ca. 1820). In terms of the *Sturm und Drang*, one thinks of such poems as Goethe's "Wanderer's Stormsong" ("Wanderers Sturmlied");[2] of Werther's cry, "Yes, I am only a wanderer, a pilgrim, on the earth! Are you anything more than this?" (*Ja, wohl bin ich nur ein Wanderer, ein Waller, auf der Erde! Seid Ihr denn mehr?*); and of Faust's portrayal of himself as someone whose demise—because of (the consequences of) his own actions—he prophetically foretells in the scene "Forest and Cave" ("Wald und Höhle"):

> Am I not fugitive, the homeless rover,
> The man-beast void of goal or bliss,
> Who roars in cataracts from cliff to boulder
> In avid frenzy for the precipice?[3]
>
> *Bin ich der Flüchtling nicht? der Unbehauste?*
> *Der Unmensch ohne Zweck und Ruh,*
> *Der wie ein Wassersturz von Fels zu Felsen brauste,*
> *Begierig wütend nach dem Abgrund zu?*

As two commentators on German literature and culture have observed, the Romantic conception of the Germans as a nation of wanderers, for all its inevitable one-sidedness as a national image, contains "enough truth to give the impression of a striking likeness," inasmuch as it derives from "the historical fact of the migration of peoples of the fourth and fifth centuries" and found "mythological support in the cognomen of 'Wanderer' which was attached to the god Wodan,"[4] before being confirmed by "the constant surge of the German emperors over the

Alps in the Middle Ages," by "the 'Sehnsucht nach Italien' of the eighteenth and nineteenth centuries," and finally by "the 'Drang nach Osten'" of German foreign policy in the 1930s and 1940s.[5] Of the elements listed by Elizabeth M. Wilkinson and L. A. Willoughby, the German fascination—one might almost say obsession—with Italy is of particular relevance, since it forms a link between such key figures of the German intellectual tradition as Goethe (the author of the *Italian Journey*), Nietzsche (who captures the spirit of Venice in his "Gondellied"), Freud (who frequently visited the Dolomites and Rome), and Jung (who developed something of "Rome complex"[6] but succeeded in visiting Pompeii and, notably, Ravenna).[7] As one commentator on the significance of Italy for the German literary imagination has remarked, the genre of travel literature is "particularly well suited" to the interpretative tools of psychoanalytic theory,[8] and just such a psychoanalytically informed investigation has been undertaken, with reference to Hölderlin, Goethe, Freud, and several others, by Jens Clausen.[9]

Dialectically, the motif of wandering brings with it the opposite (or, rather, co-implicate) notion of homeland, or *Heimat,* another huge topic in German artistic and intellectual culture.[10] Thus, even as Freud evoked the idea of "the-uncanny-as-the-unhomely" (*das Unheimliche*),[11] Georg Lukács evoked the sense of "transcendental homelessness" (*transzendentale Obdachlosigkeit*) in the modern world,[12] and Heidegger wondered whether the homelessness (*Heimatlosigkeit*) of modern human beings resided in our inability "even to think of the *proper* plight of dwelling as *the* plight,"[13] the idea of *Heimat* had been emerging in the twentieth century, not least through a powerful sense of its very lack, as a major theme of German literature and thought.

And this theme is not just German; it is global as well: Michel Onfray has described Neil Armstrong's moon landing on 21 July 1969 as "function[ing] in the psyche of the industrialized nations as a radical, metaphysical fracture."[14] At the moment of the moon landing, which surpasses the desires of Daedalus and the arrogance of Icarus, Onfray asks (as the earth becomes "something radically other, something worryingly strange, a suspended particle, a speck of dust amid the thousands of galaxies") who does not hear the laugh of the partridge, the bird that "claps its wings and crows for joy" when the ambitious son of the ingenious inventor, who "to unimagined arts / Sets his mind and alters nature's laws," flies too close to the sun and melts his waxen wings?[15]

I

As modern human beings, we all have to travel a lot because of our spiritual health: and one will travel more and more, the more one works. It is to the travellers that those who work for a change in general views will have to turn.
—Nietzsche, *KSA*, 8, 23[196], 473

Nietzsche's relationship to these twin themes of wandering and homelessness is complex, inasmuch as his relationship to Romanticism is highly ambivalent. In *The Gay Science,* Nietzsche distinguishes between "two kinds of sufferers": on the one hand, "those who suffer from the *over-fullness of life*" and who want "a Dionysian art and likewise a tragic view of life, a tragic insight," and, on the other, "those who suffer from the *impoverishment of life*" and "seek rest, stillness, calm seas, redemption from themselves through art and knowledge, or intoxication, convulsions, anaesthesia, and madness."[16] Nietzsche identifies the latter group, to which Schopenhauer and Wagner are said to have belonged, with Romanticism, whereas he associates the former group with the "Dionysian pessimism," or the "pessimism of strength," the "tragic sense of life" that he seeks to usher in.[17] Nietzsche equates Romanticism with *décadence,* and in *Ecce Homo* he describes himself as both a *décadent* and its antithesis, the very opposite of a *décadent*.[18]

Correspondingly, Nietzsche himself (following his retirement from the university in Basel in 1879) literally became a wanderer (or, more precisely, a nomad),[19] staying in various locations in Italy, Switzerland, France, and Germany, traveling between Graubünden and Nice, the Engadine and Turin, Genua and Geneva, Venice, Berlin, Naumburg, and Basel—journeys documented with beautiful photographs and autobiographical texts in David Farrell Krell's and Donald L. Bates's *The Good European* and evoked by Michel Onfray in the opening and closing pages of his *La Sculpture de soi*.[20] And Nietzsche's work constantly thematizes the motif of wandering in numerous ways, both explicit and implicit. For instance, he frequently uses the image of embarkation on a journey, describing (in the preface to the first volume of *Human, All Too Human*) the "great liberation" experienced by the "free spirit" as a moment when "a drive and impulse rules and masters it like a command; a will and desire awakens to go off, anywhere, at any cost; a vehement dangerous curiosity for an undiscovered world flames and flickers in all its senses";[21] or, in the preface to the second edition of *The Gay Science,* describing that work as "the rejoicing of strength that is returning, of a reawakened faith in a tomorrow and the day after tomorrow, of a sudden sense and anticipation of a future, of impending adventures, of seas that are open again, of goals that are permitted again, believed again."[22] Elsewhere in *The Gay Science* Nietzsche urges his readers to "send your ships into uncharted seas!"[23] "There is yet another world to be discovered—and more than one. Embark, philosophers!"[24] "At long last the horizon appears free to us again, even if it should not be bright; at long last our ships may venture out again, venture out to face any danger; all the daring of the lover of knowledge is permitted again; the sea, *our* sea, lies open again; perhaps there has never yet been such an 'open sea.'"[25]

Yet for us to be, as Nietzsche says that he is (and many Europeans today are), "homeless"[26] presupposes that there was, or will be, or might be, or could have been, something called home. In *The Birth of Tragedy,* Nietzsche describes "the loss of myth" as "the loss of the mythical home, of the mythical maternal womb" (*den Verlust der mythischen Heimat, des mythischen Mutterschoßes*),[27] to the restoration of which—of "the gods of his house, or his mythical home"—the German should turn to "a leader who might bring him back again into his long lost home whose ways and paths he scarcely knows anymore": *incipit* Richard Wagner.[28] Equally—*incipit tragœdia, incipit* Zarathustra—[29] in order for the Persian prophet, whose return Nietzsche in *Thus Spoke Zarathustra* so dramatically and lyrically effects, to leave "his home and Lake Urmi" and "go into the mountains,"[30] he has to have a home to begin with. In his very first discourse, delivered to the people in the marketplace, Zarathustra urges us to regard the earth as our home: "*Remain true to the earth,* and do not believe those who speak to you of supraterrestrial hopes!"[31] For (as we later learn) "*the heart of the earth is of gold,*"[32] and gold has "the highest value" (because, being "uncommon and useless and shining and mellow in lustre," it "always bestows itself").[33] And in his final sequence of discourses at the end of Part One, Zarathustra restates this theme:

> Stay loyal to the earth, my brothers, with the power of your virtue! May your bestowing love and your knowledge serve towards the meaning meaning of the earth!

> Do not let it fly away from the things of earth and beat with its wings against the eternal walls! Alas, there has always been much virtue that has flown away!
> Lead, as I do, the flown-away virtue back to earth—yes, back to body and life: that it may give the earth its meaning, a human meaning!³⁴

Far removed from the sense of "transcendental homelessness" of which Lukács speaks, Nietzsche's Zarathustra tells us that our true home is (like "paradise," according to Laurie Anderson) *exactly like where you are right now,* only not *much much better* but precisely as it is at the moment. Yet in Nietzsche's poetic texts, which are often not given the attention they deserve,³⁵ the themes of wandering and homelessness are frequently present, across the early, middle, and late periods of Nietzsche's intellectual creativity.

In 1860, while he was a student at Schulpforta (and perhaps for this reason), Nietzsche wrote a sequence of poems entitled "In the Distance" ("In der Ferne"), the second of which moves from a Wertherian sense of constriction, via a nostalgic recollection of domestic harmony, to a melancholy realization of loss:

> And this homeland where you were born,
> Where you have richly enjoyed life's bliss,
> This you have lost.
>
> *Und diese Heimath, wo du bist geboren*
> *Wo du des Lebens Wonne reich genossen,*
> *Hast du verloren!*—³⁶

Around the same time he wrote "Without a Homeland" ("Ohne Heimat"), a text that depicts, as Philip Grundlehner puts it, "a passionate self-emancipation from all restrictive boundaries."³⁷ Other poems bear the titles "Longing for Home" ("Heimweh"), "Departure" ("Abschied"), and "Despair" ("Verzweiflung").³⁸ True, many of these texts lack sophistication, much in the way that Nietzsche's musical compositions are said to do, yet they possess a certain naive vigor. Nevertheless, some later texts—such as a famous poem from 1884, known under various titles, including "Isolated" ("Vereinsamt")— restate this theme of abandonment with considerable power; its final verse reads:

> The crows cry,
> And fly in flocks towards the town:
> Soon it will snow,—
> Alas for him, who has no home!
>
> *Die Krähen schrei'n*
> *und ziehen schwirren Flugs zur Stadt:*
> *bald wird es schnei'n,—*
> *weh dem, der keine Heimat hat!*[39]

—the last phrase one that is echoed in a later poem, first sung by Zarathustra's shadow, itself a wanderer figure,[40] in "Among the Daughters of the Desert" ("Unter Töchtern der Wüste") in the Part Four of *Thus Spoke Zarathustra*, a poem which is also included in the *Dionysos-Dithyramben*.[41] And from the same year we find a poem called "The Wanderer" ("Der Wanderer"),[42] which, while echoing the mixture of escapist fantasy and nostalgic love of home in his earlier lyric ("Yet there is a feeling that quells the raging, / Wild urgency of the heart" [*Doch ein Gefühl ist's, das den ungestümen, / Den wilden Drang des Herzens hemmt*]),[43] combines wandering as a literary, even philosophical,[44] motif with painful biographical experience,[45] to the point where Nietzsche's pain seems inexpressible without sheer pathos:

> The good bird was quiet and pondered:
> "What did my piping do to him?
> Why is he still standing now?—
> The poor, poor wandering man!"
>
> *Der gute Vogel schweig und sann:*
> *"Was tat mein Flötenlied ihm an?*
> *Was steht er noch?—*
> *Der arme, arme Wandersmann!"*[46]

And a short, four-line poem, also entitled "The Wanderer" ("Der Wanderer"), features among the sixty or so poems that constitute "'Joke, Cunning, and Revenge,'" the "Prelude in German Rhymes" that opens *The Gay Science*,[47] the second edition of which bore on its title page a four-line motto entitled "Over the Door to My House."[48]

In a variety of texts, Nietzsche explores wandering as a metaphor for philosophy and indeed philosophy as a form of wandering. In the collection of his *Nachlass* writings known as *The Will to Power*, Nietzsche defines "philosophy, as I have hitherto understood and lived it," as "a voluntary quest for even the most detested and notorious sides of existence"—a quest that takes Nietzsche on "a wandering through ice and wilderness."⁴⁹ In *Ecce Homo,* Nietzsche offers a pragmatics of wandering as a propaedeutic to philosophical activity: "*Sit* as little as possible; credit no thought not born in the open air and while moving freely about—in which the muscles too do not hold a festival. All prejudices come from the intestines.—Assiduity—I have said it once before—the actual *sin* against the holy spirit."⁵⁰ In the work that he (rightly) described as "the actual book of the air of the heights" (*das eigentliche Höhenluft-Buch*),⁵¹ that is, *Thus Spoke Zarathustra,* a link is made between walking, wandering, and dancing. Speaking to Life itself in "The Second Dance Song," Zarathustra says: "My heels raised themselves, my toes listened for what you should propose: for the dancer wears his ears—in his toes!"⁵² And addressing the sky in "Before Sunrise" (the sky that bears "the sister-soul of [his] insight"), Zarathustra asks: "And when I wandered alone, *what* did my soul hunger after by night and on treacherous paths? And when I climbed mountains, *whom* did I always seek, if not you, upon mountains? / And all my wandering and mountain-climbing: it was merely a necessity and an expedient of clumsiness: my whole will desires only to *fly*, to fly into *you*!"⁵³

In order, then, to find a path through the problematics and thematics of wandering and home in Nietzsche's philosophy, which have received a good deal of critical attention in recent years,⁵⁴ I shall, in what follows, examine the motif of the wanderer and his shadow and relate these passages to two sections in Part Three of *Thus Spoke Zarathustra* entitled "The Wanderer" and "The Home-Coming" ("Die Heimkehr"), respectively.

II

> *He who has attained to only some degree of freedom of mind cannot feel other than a wanderer on the earth—though not as a traveller to a final destination: for this destination does not exist. But he will watch and observe and keep his eyes open to see what is really going on in the world; for this reason he may not let his heart adhere too firmly to any individual thing; within him there must be something wandering that takes pleasure in change and transience.*
> —Nietzsche, "The Wanderer"⁵⁵

Nietzsche brings the first volume of *Human, All Too Human* to a close with a lengthy aphorism entitled "The Wanderer," the opening lines of which have just been quoted. The passage goes on to address itself extensively to the perils of wandering—exhaustion, weariness, fear, and dread—only to turn to their "recompense," to those "joyful mornings" when "the Muses come dancing by him in the midst of the mountains" and when, "if he relaxes quietly beneath the trees in the equanimity of his soul at morning," as Nietzsche puts it, "good and bright things will be thrown down" to the wanderer from "their tops and leafy hiding-places"—"the gifts of all those free spirits who are at home in mountain, wood and solitude and who, like him, are, in their now joyful, now thoughtful way, wanderers and philosophers."[56]

"Born out of the mysteries of dawn," such wanderers "ponder on how, between the tenth and twelfth stroke of the clock, the day could present a face so pure, so light-filled, so cheerful and transfigured:— they seek the *philosophy of the morning*," thereby anticipating the motifs of the clock striking midnight and/or midday in *Thus Spoke Zarathustra*;[57] the title of Nietzsche's next book, *Daybreak* (1881); the topos of the morning (along with sunshine, forests, and springs) as a teacher of "the philosophy of psychical health and recovery";[58] the demand at the end of the fifth book of *The Gay Science* of "the spirits of my own book" (with their "most malicious, cheerful, and koboldish laughter"), "surrounded" as they are "by bright morning," for "more agreeable, more joyous tones" (a demand satisfied by the "Songs of Prince Vogelfrei" that immediately follow);[59] and the advent— proclaimed in *On the Genealogy of Morals* and triumphantly reasserted in the "History of an Error" in *Twilight of the Idols*—of "this man of the future . . . this bell-stroke of noon and of the great decision that liberates the will again and restores its goal to the earth and his hope to man" in the form of "Zarathustra the godless."[60]

But if the perils and recompenses of the wanderer's solitude bring to an end "Man Alone with Himself" (as the sixth and final book of volume 1 of *Human, All Too Human* is called), the second part of volume 2, entitled "The Wanderer and His Shadow," in its turn opens and closes with a dialogue between none other than the Wanderer and, of course, his Shadow. In a playful, even bantering tone, the dialogues enact a moment of psychic fission, akin to the moment when, in the words of Nietzsche's famous poem "Sils-Maria," "one becomes two"

(*Eins wird zu Zwei*).⁶¹ It is precisely the sense of Otherness that, according to Jung in *The Psychology of the Transference* (1946), marks, in alchemy as in analysis, the beginning of the next stage of development. For analysis, he writes, commences only when "the conflict begins and one becomes two" (*Eins wird zu Zwei*)—when the individual realizes that (s)he "has a shadow" (*einen Schatten*) and that her or his "enemy 'lies within.'"⁶²

In the opening dialogue, the Wanderer reassures the Shadow that he "love[s] shadow as much as [he loves] light," since "for there to be beauty of face, clarity of speech, benevolence and firmness of character, shadow is as needful as light." As such, light and shadow are "not opponents: they stand, rather, lovingly hand in hand, and when light disappears, shadow slips away after it."⁶³ In so speaking, the wanderer affirms the essential complementarity of light and dark, good and bad, even good and evil: a point that Goethe had made when, in his tribute to Shakespeare (1771), he suggested that "what we call evil is only the other side of good; evil is necessary for good to exist and is part of the whole, just as the tropics must be torrid and Lapland frigid for there to be a temperate zone,"⁶⁴ or when, in his review of Sulzer's *The Fine Arts* in 1772, he stated that, in nature, "beautiful and ugly, good and evil, all exist side by side with equal rights."⁶⁵ Jung reformulated this idea as a form of complementarism between consciousness and the unconscious in his model of the psyche as a closed system⁶⁶ or as a system of self-regulation⁶⁷ or, in *The Relations between the Ego and the Unconscious,* as a kind of equilibrium between good and evil.⁶⁸ Indeed, Jung appears to be almost directly echoing Nietzsche's words when, in that work, he writes that "the 'living form' needs deep shadows if it is to appear solid" (*die "lebende Gestalt" bedarf tiefer Schatten, um plastisch zu erscheinen*).⁶⁹

In their closing dialogue, the Shadow once again initiates the conversation, congratulating the Wanderer on his commitment to become "a good neighbour to the closest things."⁷⁰ The jokey banter between them about shadows being "better men" than humans, about shadows knowing how to "stay silent and wait" even better than the English(!), and about whether the Shadow could even be considered a "slave" of the Wanderer, conceals a deeply serious point. In his early lecture on "The Greek State" (1871/1872), Nietzsche had argued that "*slavery belongs to the essence of a culture,*" since "in order for there to be a broad, deep, fertile soil for the development of art, the overwhelming majority has to be slavishly subjected to life's necessity in the service of the minority, *beyond* the measure that is necessary for the individual."[71] Yet the true sense of this apparently shocking statement is that the individual must dedicate himself or herself to a higher (i.e., cultural) cause and in this way transcend the limitations of his or her individual self: a notion that, through the mouth of Zarathustra, Nietzsche calls *Selbst-Überwindung* and places under the sign of the *Übermensch*, the human-who-is-more-than-(just)-human. This becomes clear in *The Gay Science,* which talks about how "every strengthening and enhancement of the human type also involves a new kind of enslavement."[72]

Unlike those blessed Christians whose heavenly bliss, according to St. Thomas Aquinas, will be perfected by the sight of the torments of the damned,[73] the Wanderer maintains that "the sight of someone unfree would embitter for me all my joy," and hence he wishes no dog to follow him or even his shadow. Nor, as the day draws to its close, will his Shadow be following him for much longer. In imitation of that philosophical "dog" Diogenes the Cynic, who asked Alexander the Great to move out of his light,[74] the Shadow asks the Wanderer to "move a little out of the sunlight" and to "step under these trees and look out at the mountains"; but as "the sun is sinking," so, too, is the Shadow disappearing. The final words of the Wanderer—"Where are you? Where are you?" (*Wo bist du? Wo bist du?*)—recall, as Alan Cardew has pointed out, Schiller's lament in his poem "The Gods of Greece" ("Die Götter Griechenlands") for the passing of the classical world: "Whither art thou gone, fair world? . . . / Ah!—of yon bright picture, rapture-breathing, / Nought is left us but a shade" (*Schöne Welt, wo bist du? . . . / Ach, von jenem lebenwarmen Bilde / Blieb der Schatten nur zurück*).[75]

On later occasions Nietzsche referred back to this section of dialogue in *Human, All Too Human* between the Wanderer and his Shadow. For instance, he alluded to it in a section in Book Four of *The Gay Science* entitled "Delight in Blindness" where the Wanderer confesses to his Shadow his pleasure at his own "ignorance of the future" and his lack of desire to "perish of impatience and of tasting promised things ahead of time."[76] In Book Five, the Wanderer speaks again, although not so much to himself or to his Shadow as in order to comment more openly and generally, with scarcely veiled references to the subtitle of *Daybreak* and the title of *Beyond Good and Evil,* on the problem of the philosopher's "specific gravity," arguing that "the human being . . . who wants to behold the supreme measures of value of his time must first of all 'overcome' this time in himself," a test not only of "his strength" but also of "his prior aversion and contradiction *against* this time, his un-timeliness,"—or as Nietzsche puts it, "his *romanticism.*"[77] And in Part Two of *Thus Spoke Zarathustra,* the captain and crew of a ship land on an island with a volcano in order to shoot rabbits and see a shadow-like figure flying through the air.[78] On hearing about the sailors, the rabbits, and the flying man, Zarathustra tells his disciples that it must have been his shadow. "Surely you have heard," he asks, "something of the Wanderer and his Shadow?"[79] The motif of the wanderer thus reveals the complex network of correspondences that Nietzsche weaves across his individual texts.[80]

It is, however, in Part Three of *Zarathustra* that the themes of wandering and the home receive their most explicit treatment in this highly allusive and conceptually dense work. As it happens, they are also sections on which Jung commented in his seminar on *Zarathustra* (1934–1939), although by this stage—in 1938, several years into the project—Jung's enthusiasm for Nietzsche was beginning to show signs of flagging. In his first seminar on *Zarathustra,* on 2 May 1934, Jung warned his audience that the work they were about to study was no easy matter, even compared to the visions of Christiana Morgana that had been discussed in the previous seminar, begun in 1930.[81] *Zarathustra* is, Jung said, "a hell of a confusion and extraordinarily difficult."[82] And on 5 May 1937, Jung reminded his audience that he regarded *Zarathustra* as Nietzsche's "most significant work," inasmuch as in it he expresses "something which is really himself and his own peculiar problem" and that, while "in many ways he is the child of his time," Nietzsche was also "the forerunner of times that have come since and of times that are still to come."[83] Yet at his opening seminar in spring 1938, Jung began as follows: "Here we are again at our old *Zarathustra*! And when I looked through the chapters we have dealt with and those we have still to deal with, I must tell you frankly, I got bored stiff, chiefly by the style. The long interruption," he confessed to his audience, "has done no good to my enthusiasm apparently."[84]

Nevertheless, Jung's commentaries, like his impatience with the text, his omissions, or his silences, remain highly illuminating.

Furthermore, close attention to the passages Jung discussed (and did not discuss) will confirm the existence in Nietzsche of a dialectic that resolves the Heraclitean activity of wandering and the Parmenidean permanence of a home. For, paradoxically, it emerges that for the true wanderer, to be under way *is* in some sense to be at home: or in Zarathustra's terms, to be "a wanderer" is to celebrate the "homecoming" of the Self. (After all, just as wandering requires a home as a starting point, if not its ultimate destination, so Heraclitean *change* requires, logically, Parmenidean *permanence* to be thought, even if not actually enacted—hence, in response to Heraclitus's maxim that it is not possible to step into the same river twice, Cratylus's remark that is not possible to do so even once!)[85]

Part Three of *Zarathustra* and "The Wanderer" opens with a narrative segment that explains that Zarathustra intends to leave the Blissful Islands, on which he had been living during his discourses delivered in Part Two, so he makes his way over the ridge of the island to take a ship from the harbor and cross the sea back to land. As he climbs, then descends, the mountain (recalling the theme of ascent and descent found earlier in the text that returns to prominence in Part Three)[86] he delivers three discourses at various points on his journey. Just as Nietzsche defined philosophy as a wandering, so Zarathustra affirms his identity as "a wanderer and a mountain-climber,"[87] anticipating his later injunction that "one should live upon mountains."[88]

For Jung, the action of this chapter enacts "the night sea-journey," or "navigating on the sea of the unconscious to reach the new country."[89] Through such a journey one performs the *transitus,* or the transformation of the hero through the performance of difficult acts, represented in the cult of Attis through carrying the tree into the cave of the Mother, in the cult of Mithras through carrying the bull (and slaughtering the bull), or in Christianity through the iconography of the carrying of the Cross (and the crucifixion). Jung associated the *transitus* with the idea of *athla,* the "heavy work" undergone in the rite of initiations,[90] and identifies Zarathustra's crossing of the mountain with the *athla*.[91] (By the same token, there may be a personal component to this cross-mountain journey: Reinhart von Seydlitz recalls how, in the summer of 1877, Nietzsche had told him, laughing, of a dream in which he climbed up an endless mountain path.⁹² Today, one can still climb the *sentier Frédéric Nietzsche* at Èze outside Nice.)

Jung moves quickly through this chapter, but he would have found confirmation for his interpretation of it if he had paused on the sentence where Zarathustra equates "whatever may yet come . . . as fate and experience," his future "wandering" and "mountain-climbing," with his experience *of himself*, because "in the final analysis one experiences only oneself" (*man erlebt endlich nur noch sich selber*): Zarathustra's mountain-climbing might well be described as his ascent of the Self. For Zarathustra's wandering enacts a "return," a "coming-home," precisely of the Self: "It is returning, it is coming home to me [*Es kehrt nur zurück, es kommt mir endlich heim*]—my own Self [*mein eigen Selbst*] and those parts of it that have been long abroad and scattered among all things and accidents [*alle Dinge und Zufälle*]."⁹³ Standing now before his "last summit" and "before the deed that has been deferred the longest," Zarathustra contemplates his "most difficult path" and his "loneliest wandering," anticipating his vision in the next chapter, "Of the Vision and the Riddle," of "the most solitary man."⁹⁴

And so—if, again, we pause on lines over which Jung leapt—Zarathustra listens to the Hour,⁹⁵ which tells him that he is about to tread his "path of greatness" and that (in another echo of Heraclitus) "summit and abyss—they are now united in one!"⁹⁶ Yet the "path of greatness" Zarathustra traverses is a strange one: for the path he has trodden is erased by his steps, and over it there is now inscribed "Impossibility" (*Unmöglichkeit*). Stranger yet, when the footholds of the path disappear, Zarathustra is told he must climb upon his head, because how else could he ascend other than "upon your own head and beyond your own heart?" And for such a method of ascent, a degree of hardness is required, and here, as elsewhere,⁹⁷ Zarathustra (or, rather, his Hour) praises hardness: "Now the gentlest part of you must become the hardest. . . . All praise to what makes hard!"⁹⁸ In complete opposition to the Judaic (or Old Testament) ideal of "a land flowing with milk and honey" (Exodus 3:8), the Hour commends "this hardness" on the (psychological) grounds that "in order to see *much* one must learn to *look away* from oneself [*von sich absehn*]."⁹⁹ Because to understand the "ground" (*Grund*) and the "background" (*Hintergrund*) of all things, Zarathustra must transcend not the world but himself: "So you must climb above yourself—up and beyond, until you have even your stars *under* you!" [*So mußt du schon über sich selber steigen—hinan, hinauf, bist du auch deine Sterne noch* unter *dir hast!*].[100] Unlike the traditional iconography associated with Rosicrucian illumination, which posts a moment when the individual gazes out beyond the stars of the firmament into the marvels of the world beyond,[101] this lesson teaches the need for one to transcend one's *own* stars so that, as in the ancient *exercice spirituel* of the view from above,[102] Zarathustra may learn "to look down upon [him]self and even upon [his] stars."

Just as Zarathustra imagines to himself his "*ultimate* summit," he reaches the peak of the mountain: below, there is "the other sea spread out before him," and above, there is the night, "cold and clear and bright with stars."

At the top of the mountain, the only way forward is down—a fact Zarathustra realizes "with sadness" and to which he gives his assent: "My last solitude has begun." Recalling the moment of descent in his opening prologue[103] and anticipating his final descent at the end of Part Four, Zarathustra accepts that he must now descend again: "Ah, destiny and sea! Now I have to *go down* to you!" he cries.[104] Intriguingly, Jung reads these lines—

> I stand before my highest mountain and my longest wandering: therefore I must first descend deeper than I have ever descended[105]

—both biographically ("That is Nietzsche's feeling now; he knows he has to go down") and intertextually, referring—significantly—to a line from Goethe's *Faust,* Part II.

The significance of this references lies in the fact that the line Jung quoted—"In an ever-changed disguise / All men's lives I tyrannize" (*In verwandelter Gestalt / Üb ich grimmige Gewalt*)—[106] comes from the "Midnight" scene in Act 5 of Part II, when the mysterious Four Grey Women enter the palace. Of Want, Debt, Need, and Care, the most terrifying is the last—Care (*Sorge*).[107] Aside from the objective terror of the scene, which attracted the interest of Martin Heidegger (who devoted several sections of *Being and Time* to "care," or *Sorge,* as constitutive of the essential unity of Dasein's Being),[108] Jung himself had earlier commented in the scene in one of his early, foundational texts, "La Structure de l'inconscient." In his paper, Jung referred to this scene from *Faust* in connection with his insistence that there is no "theory" or "magical method"[109] by which one could "tear the libido away from the unconscious" and thus, in a manner of speaking, "get rid of" the unconscious.[110] For even if, through what he calls a regressive restoration of the persona, one "wants to continue to live rationally . . . trying to forget that one has an unconscious,"[111] such a strategy is bound to end in failure.

That this is the case Jung himself knew only too well from personal experience (as the *Red Book* amply testifies). And it is surely no coincidence that precisely the text from *Faust* that, in Jung's earlier article, had served to illustrate the power of the psyche, resurfaces in his seminar on *Zarathustra* when he wishes to discuss how Nietzsche "held onto his consciousness, which was entirely rational, and made nothing of the volcano" (i.e., the unconscious)—"but now it comes again."[112] According to Jung, Nietzsche had to give way to "something which he belittled and made very light of before"[113]—he had, in the words of "La Structure de l'inconscient," repudiated the unconscious as "something useless, infantile, and devoid of sense, impossible and obsolete."[114] But now, through *Zarathustra*, he realizes that he "has to go down," just as Jung, in the words of *Memories, Dreams, Reflections*, took the decision when embarking on his own "encounter with the unconscious" to let himself "drop."[115] We recall that the fear of being in some sense similar to Nietzsche was one of the things that had worried Jung as a student, and *Memories, Dreams, Reflections* speaks of Jung's need for reassurance that he was not like Nietzsche, who "had lost the ground under his feet because he possessed nothing more than the inner world of his thoughts (which incidentally possessed him more than he it)," had become "uprooted and hovered above the earth," and "succumbed to exaggeration and irreality" in a way that was "the quintessence of horror" for Jung.[116] (After all, as a good student of Zarathustra, Jung was preeminently concerned with *"this* world and *this* life.")[117]

Continuing with his commentary in his seminar on Zarathustra, Jung turns to the next sentences in "The Wanderer,"

> —deeper into pain that I have ever descended, down its blackest stream! So my destiny will have it. Well then! I am ready.

and observes that "Nietzsche promises the mountain will come afterwards . . . and we shall see how he constructs that high mountain which is not to be overcome,"[118] anticipating how Zarathustra's vision of a mountain provides the context to his intuition of the eternal recurrence in the following chapter, "Of the Vision and the Riddle."

In his seminar Jung skips over the lines where Zarathustra ponders the origin of the mountains from the depths of the sea, a geological restatement of the Heraclitean principle that "the highest must rise to its height from the deepest,"[119] and moves on to Zarathustra's third discourse, which he delivers during his descent of the mountain toward the sea. In what Jung (rightly) describes as a "remarkable passage," Zarathustra listens to the sound of the sea, comparing it to a "dark monster" that "dreams" and "groans with wicked memories," and he expresses the desire to "release" the sea from its "bad dreams." "The aspect of the unconscious," Jung explains in his equally remarkable commentary, "is like a dormant sea; one doesn't know what it will be when it wakes up," and so "for the time being it is mysterious, very still, like someone dreaming. But it breathes—it is alive with dreamlike life."[120] The fact that Zarathustra hears the sound of the surf as a groaning and believes that the sea is suffering from evil recollections constitutes, Jung remarks, a clear case of projection. Having made the projection, Zarathustra is liberated from the weight of his own evil, and in turn he considers curing the sea of *its* bad dreams and recollections. But to think in this way is to be anthropomorphic, as Jung shrewdly remarks, for "the unconscious has no bad recollections, as the sea has no bad recollections," and "how could one ever imagine being able to free nature from her world-creating dreams? Those dreams are divine, creative thoughts—the very life of nature."[121]

On the basis of his reading of this passage, Jung articulates a critique of Nietzsche as someone who "is always called the most honest philosopher, but he could not afford to be honest with himself." Because of what he sees as the "playful" tone of the lines toward the end of "The Wanderer,"—where Zarathustra chides himself for wanting to "caress every monster," "a touch of warm breath, a little soft fur on its paw"—thus (so Jung interpolates) "making light of it"—this critique of Nietzsche's person turns into a critique of what Jung calls the "aesthetical attitude."[122] Yet the description of the monster makes it sound distinctly lion-like, adumbrating the arrival of the lion in the final chapter of Part Four. Indeed, Zarathustra's statement that "*love* is the danger for the most solitary man, love of any thing *if only it is alive!*"¹²³ anticipates "the vision of the most solitary man" in the next chapter, "Of the Vision and the Riddle," which constitutes, according to Jung, an example of those stories in *Zarathustra* that "give an extraordinary insight into the real events, the real processes, of his [i.e., Nietzsche's] unconscious."¹²⁴

Understandably, given the complexities of this particular chapter (i.e., "Of the Vision and the Riddle"), Jung spent a number of seminars discussing it, and there followed lengthy discussions, prompted in part by the other participants, centering on "Of Involuntary Bliss" (in relation to Goethe, Marcus Manilius, and Hinduism), "Before Sunrise" (in relation to the *Tabula Smaragdina*), and—after a summer break—"Of the Virtue That Makes Small" (in relation to the idea of *apokatastasis*) and "Of Passing By" (in relation to alchemical symbolism).¹²⁵ So it was not until 30 November 1938 that Jung turned to "The Home-Coming," a chapter in which, it seems, he did not take much interest. Yet from the thematic perspective of the home-and-wandering dialectic, in light of Zarathustra's remarks in it about how "my own Self" (*mein eigen Selbst*) is "returning, it is coming home to me" (*kehrt nur zurück, es kommt mir endlich heim*), and because of its connections with this earlier chapter called "The Wanderer," it deserves much closer attention.

Jung is dismissive of this chapter because he reads its "critical remarks" purely as an expression of Nietzsche's "resentment." Unfortunately, this essentially biographical approach, while not entirely inappropriate to understanding Nietzsche, does not take into account the conceptual and rhetorical complexities of "The Home-Coming." For this chapter demonstrates how, for Nietzsche, the Self is the true Home and how the solitude of the Self is, far from being a *ressentiment*-laden sense of abandonment, rather a feeling of the most intense fulfillment. And it makes use of Nietzsche's play on *einsam* and *zweisam*, "single" (or "solitary") and "double" (or "twofold"), that his earlier works had elaborated.

III

Today one ponders one sentence, tomorrow another, and one thinks again from the depths of one's heart: for and against, into and beyond, as the spirit drives one, so that one becomes cheerful and one's head clears. Gradually there arises from reflection—genuine, because not

> *compelled—thus stimulated a certain general reorientation of views: and along with it that general feeling of spiritual recuperation, as if the bow has been equipped with a new string and pulled more tightly than ever before. It has been useful to travel.*
> —Nietzsche, *KSA,* 23[196], 474

Thus Spoke Zarathustra becomes more clear in the light of Nietzsche's other writings, especially the two prefaces he composed in 1886 (after completing *Zarathustra*) for the new edition of both volumes of *Human, All Too Human*. Following "Man Alone with Himself," the final (and, in this sense, solitary) section of the first volume of *Human, All Too Human,* the second volume of the 1886 edition opens with Nietzsche's description of his decision to enact steps he had outlined in the new preface to the first volume. He speaks of the "great liberation" of the "free spirit"[126] and affirms the moment when, as the earlier preface puts it, "solitude [*die Einsamkeit*] encircles and embraces him, ever more threatening, suffocating, heart-tightening, that terrible goddess and *mater saeva cupidinum.*"[127] It was, Nietzsche writes, "high time to say *farewell*" to Wagner,[128] and "henceforth alone [*einsam*] and sorely mistrustful of myself, I thus . . . took sides *against* myself and *for* everything painful and difficult precisely for *me*" and thus found "the way 'to myself' [*den Weg zu "mir" selbst*], to *my* task."[129] "It was only then," he adds, "that I learned that solitary's speech [*jenes einsiedlerische Reden*] that only the most silent and the most suffering understand," while "I, as physician and patient in one, compelled myself to an opposite and unexplored *clime of the soul,* and especially to a curative journey into strange parts, into *strangeness* itself, to an inquisitiveness regarding every kind of strange thing [*zu einer abziehenden Wanderung in die Fremde, in das Fremde, zu einer Neugierde nach aller Art von Fremdem*]."[130] In other words, the path to the Self leads to a strange wandering, and there is, by implication, nothing stranger than the Self. The theme of solitude or solitariness (*Einsamkeit*) occurs a number of times in the second volume of *Human, All Too Human,* such as in the beautiful aphorism in "The Wanderer and his Shadow" entitled "The Solitary speaks,"[131] and it recurs a number of times in *Daybreak* and in *The Gay Science* before it emerges as a central theme in *Thus Spoke Zarathustra.*

Just as Zarathustra's "ultimate solitude" (*letzte Einsamkeit*) begins in "The Wanderer" even as his "own Self" "comes home" to him, so in

"The Home-Coming" the reverse takes place: Zarathustra "comes home" to his "solitude." And just as, in "The Wanderer," Zarathustra's Hour speaks to him, so here he is addressed, as if by a mother (but this time not a cruel one), by Solitude herself.[132] Paradoxically, then, Zarathustra's solitude (*Einsamkeit*) is not solitary, inasmuch as it involves a duality, since Zarathustra is *with* his Solitude.[133] And it is Solitude who distinguishes between herself and "Loneliness" (*Verlassenheit*),[134] associating loneliness with the moment toward the end of the Prologue when Zarathustra, standing in the forest beside the corpse of the tightrope walker, heard above him—in an epic-heroic variation of the scenario presented in his 1884 poem called "The Wanderer"—the cry of a bird, espied an eagle with a serpent wrapped around his neck, and asked these animals to "lead" him as he wanders on his "dangerous paths," because it is "more dangerous among men than among animals."[135] *That* is solitude, *that* is *Verlassenheit*. By contrast, Solitude associates herself with an ecstatic and communicative plenitude:

> "But here you are at your own hearth and home [*bei dir zu Heim und Hause*]; here you can utter everything and pour out every reason, nothing is here ashamed of hidden, hardened feelings.
> Here all things come caressingly to your discourse and flatter you: for they want to ride upon your back. Upon every image [*Gleichnis*] you here ride to every truth. ..."[136]

And Zarathustra, too, confirms this aspect of linguistic expansion:

> Here, the words and word-chests of all existence spring open to me: all existence here wants to become words [*alles Sein will hier Wort werden*], all becoming here wants to learn speech from me [*alles Werden will hier von mir reden lernen*],[137]

thus both recalling his earlier affirmation in "The Child with the Mirror" ("I have become entirely speech and the tumbling of a brook from high rocks: I want to hurl my words down into the valleys. . . . I go new ways, a new speech has come to me")[138] and anticipating his later exclamation during his convalescence in the cave, when he tells his animals:

> How sweet it is, that words and sounds of music exist: are words and music not rainbows and seeming bridges between things eternally separated?
> ...
> Are things not given names and musical sounds, so that man may refresh himself with things? Speech is a beautiful foolery: with it man dances over all things.
> How sweet is all speech and all the falsehoods of music! With music does our love dance upon many-coloured rainbows.[139]

In "The Child with the Mirror," Zarathustra had admitted to his animals: "For too long I have belonged to Solitude; thus I have forgotten how to be silent," and Solitude repeats this phrase in "The Home-Coming," giving Zarathustra's words a slight variation: "'I have sat too long with Solitude, I have unlearned to be silent!'"[140] In this repetition and variation there is a strong implication that the silence of Solitude is the highest form of eloquence.[141]

As Zarathustra puts it in "The Home-Coming," the world "down there" (or, for us, down *here*) is a fundamentally noisy one, full of the ring of the cash register, constant cackling, and everything being talked down ("*alles wird verraten*"). There (or *here*), "passing by" is the best option, the "flies of the market-place" buzz and sting with their poison, "the stupidity of the good is unfathomable," and Zarathustra must learn to "hide" (*verbergen*) himself and his riches.[142] But here (or *there*), on his mountains (*Bergen*), now that his "greatest danger" (*größte Gefahr*)—described in "The Wanderer" as "love . . . for everything that lives"[143] and in this chapter as "indulging and pitying" (*Schonen und Mitleiden*)—is behind him,[144] everything is full of "blissful stillness," a stillness that anticipates the moment when, "enjoying and relishing his Solitude," Zarathustra will experience—in "At Noontide"—the perfection of the world.[145] In "The Home-Coming," there is an almost erotic quality to this "blissful silence," too ("O blissful silence around me! O pure odours around me! Oh, how this stillness draws pure breath from a deep breast! Oh, how it listens, this blissful stillness!"), a quality that is by no means undermined by the ironic recurrence of these words later in "The Song of Melancholy," when Zarathustra steps outside his cave for a breath of fresh air.[146]

In the concluding lines of "The Home-Coming," Zarathustra contrasts the fustiness of the scholarly world with the clear air of the mountains, but in his seminar Jung was not entirely convinced by Nietzsche's description of wise men and scholars as "gravediggers" who "dig diseases for themselves."[147] In flagrant contradiction of Zarathustra's discourse and in defiance of any Straussian reading of the text, Jung declared that "the lower regions are perfectly ordinary and normal; they are only bad because he [i.e., Nietzsche] makes them bad."[148] Even if Nietzsche has "certain thoughts which transcend the lower regions," this does not mean that he is "identical with those high thoughts," Jung argued. (Such an identification would, in Jungian terms, be an instance of "inflation," yet in fact it is Jung who is conflating the figure of Zarathustra and his author, Nietzsche.) One is tempted to apply to Jung's own reading what he says of Nietzsche: his "insight remains only half an insight; he doesn't draw the right conclusions."[149]

Jung's interpretation of the last two paragraphs is, however, truly ingenious (and an example of the extraordinary insightfulness of his commentaries). For he reads the episode when Zarathustra sneezes (his nostrils stimulated by the clear mountain air and his soul "tickled by sharp breezes as with sparkling wine") with reference to the primitive belief that when a child sneezes, its soul enters its body.[150] For Jung, Nietzsche understands "the moment when he leaves the lower regions" as "a sort of rebirth of his own soul, as if a new soul has entered him."[151] Yet the central thrust of "The Home-Coming," read in conjunction with the earlier chapter "The Wanderer," concerns not so much Zarathustra's soul as his Self.

And that conception of the Self is of something that "returns" to us, that "comes home" from its own wanderings, from "hav[ing] long been abroad and scattered among all things and accidents," just as Zarathustra returns from his many wanderings to *his* home and finds himself, so to speak, alone with Solitude. For with one's Self it can be said that one is never truly alone.[152] On this account of the Self, then, one's own Self is perhaps the strangest thing of all—and maybe this is the reason why, toward the end of his life, Jung is said to have felt as if the "alienation" that had "separated" him from "the world" had become "transferred into [his] own inner world," revealing to him "an unexpected unfamiliarity with [him]self."[153] Conversely, in the words of Jung's Eranos lecture of 1938, it is "only through an experience of symbolic reality that man . . . can find his way back to a world in which he is no longer a stranger."[154] Thus the resolution to the dialectic of home and wandering can ultimately be summed up in Zarathustra's injunction to *bleibt der Erde treu*—"remain true to the earth."

NOTES

1. For further discussion, see Andrew Cusack, *The Wanderer in Nineteenth-Century German Literature: Intellectual History and Cultural Criticism* (Rochester, N.Y.: Camden House, 2008).

2. For a detailed analysis of this text, see "*Wanderers Sturmlied*: A Study in Poetic Vagrancy" (1948), in Elizabeth M. Wilkinson and L. Willoughby, *Goethe: Poet and Thinker: Essays* (London: Arnold, 1962), pp. 35–54.

3. Johann Wolfgang von Goethe, *Faust: A Tragedy*, edited by Cyrus Hamlin, translated by Walter Arndt (New York: Norton, 2001), ll. 3348–3360, p. 93.

4. In his essay entitled "Wotan" (1936), Jung detected a reawakening and revival of "Wotan the wanderer" in the activities of the German Youth Movement ("armed with rucksack and lute, blond youths, and sometimes girls as well, were to be seen as restless wanderers on every road from the North Cape to Sicily, faithful votaries of the roving god"); in "the thousands of unemployed, who were to be met with everywhere on their aimless journeys" toward the end of the Weimar Republic; and in the way "the Hitler movement literally brought the whole of Germany to its feet . . . and produced the spectacle of a nation migrating from one place to another." C. G. Jung, *Civilization in Transition,* vol. 10 of *The Collected Works of C. G. Jung,* translated by R.F.C. Hull (London: Routledge and Kegan Paul, 1964), § 373.

5. Wilkinson and Willoughby, "*Wanderers Sturmlied*," p. 34.

6. See C. G. Jung, *Memories, Dreams, Reflections,* edited by Aniela Jaffé, translated by Richard and Clara Winston (London: Routledge and Kegan Paul, 1963), pp. 318–319.

7. See *ibid.*, pp. 314–318. For discussion of Jung's interest in Ravenna, see Daniel C. Noel, "A Viewpoint on Jung's Ravenna Vision," *Harvest: Journal for Jungian Studies* 39 (1993): 159–163; and Adrian Cunningham, "Jung in Ravenna: The Vision Fades," *Harvest: International Journal for Jungian Studies* 50 (2005): 164–179.

8. Gretchen L. Hachmeister, *Italy in the German Literary Imagination: Goethe's "Italian Journey" and Its Reception by Eichendorff, Platen, and Heine* (Rochester, N.Y.: Camden House, 2002), p. 6.

9. Jens Clausen, *Das Selbst und die Fremde: Über psychische Grenzerfahrungen auf Reisen* (Bonn: Edition Das Narrenschiff im Psychiatrie-Verlag, 2007). I am grateful to Christiana Ludwig for drawing my attention to this book.

10. For further discussion, see Peter Blickle, *"Heimat": A Critical Theory of the German Idea of Homeland* (Rochester, N.Y.: Camden House, 2002).

11. Sigmund Freud, "The Uncanny" (1919), in *The Standard Edition of the Complete Psychological Works of Sigmund Freud,* edited by James Strachey and Anna Freud, 24 vols. (London: Hogarth Press, 1953–1974), 17:217–255.

12. Georg Lukács, *Die Theorie des Romans: Ein geschichtsphilosophischer Versuch über die Formen der großen Epik,* 9th ed. (Berlin: Neuwied, 1984), p. 35; Lukács, *The Theory of the Novel: A Historico-Philosophical Essay on the Forms of Great Epic Literature,* translated by Anna Bostock (Cambridge, Mass.: MIT Press, 1974), p. 41.

13. Martin Heidegger, "Building Dwelling Thinking" (1951), in Heidegger, *Poetry, Language, Thought,* translated by Albert Hofstadter (New York: Harper and Row, 1954), p. 160; Heidegger, "Bauen Wohnen Denken," in *Vorträge und Aufsätze,* edited by F.-W. von Hermann, vol. 7 of *Gesamtausgabe* (Frankfurt am Main: Klostermann, 2000), p. 163.

14. Michel Onfray, "Les vengeances de la perdrix," in Onfray, *Les Vertus de la foudre: Journal hédoniste II* (Paris: Grasset, 1998), p. 50.

15. *Ibid.,* p. 49. Compare Ovid, *Metamorphoses,* translated by A. D. Melville (Oxford: Oxford University Press, 1987), book 8, ll. 218–249 and 187–217, pp. 178 and 177, respectively.

16. Friedrich Nietzsche, *The Gay Science,* § 370, Nietzsche's italics (*The Gay Science,* translated by Walter Kaufmann [New York: Vintage, 1974], p. 328). Page numbers given in subsequent citations to *The Gay Science* are to Kaufmann's translation.

17. Compare with Nietzsche's comments on his opposition to "Romantic pessimism"; Nietzsche, "Preface," § 7, in *Human, All Too Human,* vol. 2 (*Human, All Too Human,* translated by R. J. Hollingdale

[Cambridge: Cambridge University Press, 1986], p. 213. See also Nietzsche, *The Gay Science,* § 370 (pp. 328, 331); and Nietzsche, *The Will to Power,* § 1019 (*The Will to Power,* edited by Walter Kaufmann, translated by R. J. Hollingdale and Walter Kaufmann [New York: Vintage, 1968], pp. 526–527). For Nietzsche's understanding of "the tragic," see "What I Owe to the Ancients," § 5 (in *Twilight of the Idols; and The Anti-Christ,* translated by R. J. Hollingdale [Harmondsworth: Penguin, 1968], p. 110); and "Richard Wagner in Bayreuth," § 4 (in *Untimely Meditations,* translated by R. J. Hollingdale [Cambridge: Cambridge University Press, 1983], p. 213) Page numbers given in subsequent citations to *Human, All Too Human* and *Untimely Meditations* are to the Hollingdale translations.

18. Nietzsche, "Why I Am So Wise," § 2 (in *Ecce Homo,* translated by R. J. Hollingdale [Harmondsworth: Penguin, 1992], pp. 10–11).

19. Julian Young, *Friedrich Nietzsche: A Philosophical Biography* (Cambridge: Cambridge University Press, 2010), p. 291; see also Nietzsche, *Beyond Good and Evil,* § 242 (in *Basic Writings of Nietzsche,* edited and translated by Walter Kaufmann [New York: Modern Library, 1968], p. 366).

20. David Farrell Krell and Donald L. Bates, *The Good European: Nietzsche's Work Sites in Word and Image* (Chicago: University of Chicago Press, 1997); Michel Onfray, "Ouverture: Pérégrinations en quête d'une figure," in *La Sculpture de soi: La morale esthétique* (Paris: Grasset, 1993), pp. 11–21; and Onfray, "Coda: Les Rendez-vous bergamasque," in *La Sculpture de soi,* pp. 191–203.

21. Nietzsche, "Preface," § 3, in *Human, All Too Human,* vol. 1 (p. 7). Nietzsche continues: "'Better to die than to go on living *here*'— thus responds the imperious voice and temptation: and this 'here', this 'at home' is everything it had hitherto loved! A sudden terror and suspicion of what it loved, a lightning-bolt of contempt for what it called 'duty', a rebellious, arbitrary, volcanically erupting desire for travel, strange places, estrangements, coldnesses, soberness, frost, a hatred of love, perhaps a desecrating blow and glance *backwards* [*ein tempelschänderischer Griff und Blick* rückwärts] to where it formerly loved and worshipped" (*ibid.*). For Jung's interest in this final phrase, see *Transformations and Symbols of Libido* (1911–1912), part 2, chapter 4, in *Psychology of the Unconscious: A Study of the Transformations and*

Symbolisms of the Libido: A Contribution to the History of the Evolution of Thought, translated by Beatrice M. Hinkle (London: Routledge, 1991), §§ 284–285.

22. Nietzsche, "Preface," § 1, in *The Gay Science* (p. 32).
23. Nietzsche, *The Gay Science*, § 283 (p. 228).
24. *Ibid.*, § 289 (p. 232).
25. *Ibid.*, § 343 (p. 280).
26. *Ibid.*, § 377 (p. 377).
27. Nietzsche, *The Birth of Tragedy*, § 23 (in *Basic Writings*, p. 136).
28. *Ibid.*, p. 139.
29. Nietzsche, *The Gay Science*, § 342 (p. 274); Nietzsche, "How the 'Real World' at Last Became a Myth," in *Twilight of the Idols* (p. 41 in Hollingdale translation).
30. Nietzsche, *The Gay Science*, § 342 (p. 274); see also "Zarathustra's Prologue," § 1, in *Thus Spoke Zarathustra* (*Thus Spoke Zarathustra*, translated by R. J. Hollingdale [Harmondsworth: Penguin, 1969], p. 39). Lake Urmi is in northwestern Iran.
31. Nietzsche, "Zarathustra's Prologue," § 3 (p. 42). Page numbers given in this and subsequent citations to *Thus Spoke Zarathustra* are to Hollingdale's translation.
32. Nietzsche, "Of Great Events," in *Thus Spoke Zarathustra* (p. 155), Nietzsche's italics.
33. Nietzsche, "Of the Bestowing Virtue," § 1, in *Thus Spoke Zarathustra* (p. 100).
34. *Ibid.*, § 2 (p. 102).
35. For a discussion of the reasons for this neglect, and a defense of their significance, see Philip Grundlehner, "Introduction," in Grundlehner, *The Poetry of Friedrich Nietzsche* (Oxford: Oxford University Press, 1986), pp. xi–xxv. For further discussion, see Otto H. Olzien, *Nietzsche und das Problem der dichterischen Sprache* (Berlin: Junker und Dünnhaupt, 1941); Josef Nadler, "Friedrich Nietzsche: Dichterische Gestalt," in *Festschrift, Moriz Enzinger zum 60. Geburtstag, 30. Dezember 1951,* edited by Herbert Seidler (Innsbruck: Wagner, 1953), pp. 157–166; and Johannes Klein, "Der dionysische Realismus: Friedrich Nietzsche," *Geschichte der deutschen Lyrik von Luther bis zum Ausgang des zweiten Weltkrieges* (Wiesbaden: Steiner, 1957), pp. 643–665.
36. Translated in Grundlehner, *The Poetry of Friedrich Nietzsche*, p. 6; for the German text, see Nietzsche, *Jugendschriften 1854–1861*, vol.

1 of *Frühe Schriften,* edited by Hans Joachim Mette, Karl Schlechta, and Carl Koch (Munich: Beck, 1994), p. 192.

37. Translated in Grundlehner, *The Poetry of Friedrich Nietzsche,* p. 12. For the text, see Grundlehner, *The Poetry of Friedrich Nietzsche,* pp. 12–13; and Nietzsche, *Jugendschriften 1854–1861,* pp. 122, 228–229.

38. Nietzsche, *Jugendschriften 1854–1861,* pp. 223–225.

39. Friedrich Nietzsche, *Sämtliche Werke: Kritische Studienausgabe,* edited by Giorgio Colli and Mazzino Montinari, 15 vols. (Berlin/Munich: Walter de Gruyter/Deutscher Taschenbuch Verlag, 1967–1977 and 1988), vol. 11, 28[64], 329. Henceforth referred to as *KSA.* For further discussion, see Franz Norbert Mennemeier, "Friedrich Nietzsche: Vereinsamt," in *Von der Spätromantik bis zur Gegenwart,* vol. 2 of *Die deutsche Lyrik: Form und Geschichte: Interpretationen,* edited by Benno von Wiese (Düsseldorf: Bagel, 1964), pp. 245–254.

40. According to one of Nietzsche's most accomplished commentators, Laurence Lampert, Zarathustra's shadow is someone who, following Zarathustra's teaching, has become "a nihilist, but not a cheerful nihilist, for he fears that he will never find a home, and he has no desire to always wander"; Lampert, *Nietzsche's Teaching: An Interpretation of "Thus Spoke Zarathustra"* (New Haven, Conn.: Yale University Press, 1986), p. 298.

41. Nietzsche, "Among the Daughters of the Desert," § 2, in *Thus Spoke Zarathustra* (pp. 315–319). See also "The Desert Grows: Woe to Him Who Harbours Deserts . . ." ("Die Wüste wächst: weh dem, der Wüsten birgt . . ."), in Nietzsche, *Dithyrambs of Dionysus (Dionysos-Dithyramben),* translated by R. J. Hollingdale (London: Anvil Press Poetry, 1984), pp. 29–37.

42. Nietzsche, *KSA,* vol. 11, 28[58], pp. 322–323; translated (with extensive commentary) in Grundlehner, *The Poetry of Friedrich Nietzsche,* pp. 64–70.

43. Grundlehner, *The Poetry of Friedrich Nietzsche,* p. 68; Nietzsche, *Jugendschriften 1854–1861,* p. 192.

44. See Frédéric Gros, *Marcher, une philosophie* (Paris: Carnets Nord, 2009).

45. Especially relevant in this respect is the change in Nietzsche's relationship with his friend, the classicist Erwin Rohde, who had become engaged to Valentine Framm; Grundlehner, *The Poetry of*

Friedrich Nietzsche, p. 66. Grundlehner suggests there are strong parallels between the poem and attitude of the wanderer as described in an aphorism entitled "The Wanderer in the Mountains Addresses Himself," in the "Assorted Opinions and Maxims," § 237, in *Human, All Too Human,* vol. 2 (p. 273).

46. Grundlehner, *The Poetry of Friedrich Nietzsche,* pp. 66, 65; Nietzsche, *KSA,* vol. 11, 28[58], 322–323, translated (with extensive commentary) in Grundlehner, pp. 64–70.

47. Nietzsche, "Joke, Cunning, and Revenge," in *The Gay Science,* § 27 (p. 51).

48. "I live in my own place, / have never copied nobody even half, / and at any master who lacks the grace / to laugh at himself—I laugh" (*Ich wohne in meinem eignen Haus, / Hab Niemanden nie nichts nachgemacht / Und—lachte noch jeden Meister aus, / Der nicht sich selber ausgelacht*); Nietzsche, *The Gay Science* (p. 31).

49. Nietzsche, *The Will to Power,* § 1041 (p. 536 in Hollingdale and Kaufmann translation); see also "Preface," § 3, in *Ecce Homo* (p. 4). Page numbers in this and subsequent citations to *Ecce Homo* are to the Hollingdale translation.

50. Nietzsche, "Why I Am So Clever," § 1, in *Ecce Homo* (p. 24), Nietzsche's italics.

51. Nietzsche, "Preface," § 4, in *Ecce Homo* (p. 5).

52. Nietzsche, "The Second Dance Song," § 1, in *Thus Spoke Zarathustra* (p. 241).

53. Nietzsche, "Before Sunrise," in *Thus Spoke Zarathustra* (pp. 184–185), Nietzsche's italics.

54. See, for instance, Andreas Hüser, *Wo selbst die Wege nachdenklich werden: Friedrich Nietzsche und der Berg* (Zurich: Rotpunktverlag, 2003); Toyomi Iwawaki-Riebel, *Nietzsches Philosophie des Wanderers: Interkulturelles Verstehen mit der Interpretation des Leibes* (Würzburg: Königshausen & Neumann, 2004); and Lukas Labhart, *"Meine Art Natur": Individualität—Landschaft—Stil bei Friedrich Nietzsche* (Basel: Schwabe, 2006).

55. § 638 in *Human, All Too Human,* vol. 1 (p. 202).

56. *Ibid.,* § 638 (p. 203). Compare this passage with the distinctly chillier, darker moment for a wanderer high in the mountains in "Schopenhauer as Educator" (1874), § 4, in *Untimely Meditations* (p. 149).

57. "The Second Dance Song," in *Thus Spoke Zarathustra* (pp. 243–244), Nietzsche's italics. See also "The Intoxicated Song" § 10 ("midnight is also noonday") in *Thus Spoke Zarathustra* (p. 331); and "At Noontide," *ibid.* (pp. 286–289). In an aside found in the third essay of *On the Genealogy of Morals,* Nietzsche recalls, as an analogy to the courtyards and colonnades of the great temple of Artemis into which Heraclitus withdrew, his "most beautiful study—the Piazza di San Marco, in spring of course, and morning also, the time between ten and twelve"; *On the Genealogy of Morals,* III, § 8 (in *Basic Writings,* p. 545).

58. § 356 in *Human, All Too Human,* vol. 2 (p. 293).

59. § 383 in *The Gay Science* (pp. 347–348).

60. Nietzsche, *On the Genealogy of Morals,* II, §§ 24 and 25 (in *Basic Writings,* p. 532). See also "Mid-day; moment of the shortest shadow; end of the longest error; zenith of mankind; INCIPIT ZARATHUSTRA"; "How the 'Real World' at Last Became a Myth," in *Twilight of the Idols,* p. 41.

61. "Sils-Maria," in *The Gay Science,* p. 371; see also Grundlehner, *The Philosophy of Friedrich Nietzsche,* pp. 134–136. This poem is said to record the moment when, as Nietzsche puts it, Zarathustra "fell upon" him; "Thus Spoke Zarathustra," § 1, in *Ecce Homo* (p. 71). This moment finds a reprise in the poem "From High Mountains" ("Aus hohen Bergen"), which brings *Beyond Good and Evil* (1886) to its conclusion. In *Basic Writings,* p. 435.

62. Jung, "The Psychology of the Transference," in *Practice of Psychotherapy,* vol. 16 of *The Collected Works of C. G. Jung,* translated by R. F. C. Hull (London: Routledge and Kegan Paul, 1956), § 399.

63. Nietzsche, "The Wanderer and His Shadow," in *Human, All Too Human,* vol. 2 (p. 301).

64. Johann Wolfgang Goethe, *Essays on Art and Literature,* edited by John Gearey, translated by Ellen von Nardroff and Ernest H. von Nardroff (New York: Suhrkamp Publishers, 1986), p. 165.

65. Johann Wolfgang von Goethe, *Goethes Werke. Hamburger Ausgabe,* edited by Erich Trunz, 14 vols. (Hamburg: Christian Wegner, 1948–1960), 12:18.

66. C. G. Jung, "On Psychic Energy," in *Structure and Dynamics of the Psyche,* vol. 8 of *The Collected Works of C. G. Jung,* translated by R. F. C. Hull (London: Routledge & Kegan Paul, 1969), § 10.

67. For further discussion, see Gerhard Schmitt, *Zyklus und Kompensation: Zur Denkfigur bei Nietzsche und Jung* (Frankfurt am Main: Peter Lang, 1998), pp. 52–164.

68. C. G. Jung, *Two Essays in Analytical Psychology*, vol. 7 of *The Collected Works of C. G. Jung*, translated by R. F. C. Hull (London: Routledge and Kegan Paul, 1967), § 92. Compare *ibid.*, § 289, where consciousness asks: "Why is there this terrible conflict between good and evil?" and is told by the unconscious: "Look more closely—each needs the other; even in the best, precisely in the best, there is the seed of evil, and there is nothing so bad that something good could not proceed from it."

69 *Ibid.*, § 400.

70. Nietzsche, "The Wanderer and His Shadow," in *Human, All Too Human*, vol. 2 (p. 394). See also *ibid.*, §§ 5–6, 8, and 16 (pp. 303–305 and 308–309); "Preface," § 5, in *Human, All Too Human*, vol. 1 (p. 8); "Why I Am So Clever," § 10, in *Ecce Homo* (p. 36); and *The Will to Power*, § 696 (p. 370 in Hollingdale and Kaufmann translation).

71. Nietzsche, "The Greek State," in *On the Genealogy of Morality*, edited by Keith Ansell-Pearson, translated by Carol Diethe (Cambridge: Cambridge University Press, 2007), p. 166, Nietzsche's italics.

72. Nietzsche, "We Who Are Homeless," in *The Gay Science*, § 377 (p. 338). Compare with the principle enunciated in Friedrich Theodor Vischer's satirical novel *Auch Einer* (1879): "Service, sir, service! That's it! The moral principle should be: 'Thou shalt serve!' But who can understand that, if you only see individual beings and, behind them, Nothing? If you do not notice that the deeds and actions of the many have carved out something that stands over and above them—an upper storey, lasting ordinances, eternal laws, to serve which is pure pleasure, because this service elevates the servant into timelessness?" F. T. Vischer, *Auch Einer: Eine Reisebekanntschaft* (Stuttgart: Deutsche Verlags-Anstalt, 1900), pp. 32–33. As Jung remarked, "to serve a god" is "full of meaning" because "it is an act of submission to a higher, invisible, and spiritual being"; C. G. Jung, *Alchemical Studies*, vol. 13 of *The Collected Works of C. G. Jung*, translated by R. F. C. Hull (London: Routledge and Kegan Paul, 1968), § 55.

73. Thomas Aquinas, *Summa Theologiae*, III, *Supplementum*, q. 94, art. 1, quoted in Nietzsche, *On the Genealogy of Morals*, I, § 15 (in *Basic Writings*, p. 485).

74. See Diogenes Laertius, *Lives of the Great Philosophers*, book 6, chapter 2, § 38, in *Lives of Eminent Philosophers*, translated by R. D. Hicks (London: Heinemann; Cambridge, Mass.: Harvard University Press, 1972), 2:41.

75. Friedrich von Schiller, *The Minor Poems*, translated by John Herman Merivale (London: William Pickering, 1844), p. 20; Schiller, *Sämtliche Gedichte und Balladen*, edited by Georg Kurscheidt (Frankfurt am Main: Insel, 2004), p. 224. See Alan Cardew, "*The Dioscuri*: Nietzsche and Rohde," in *Nietzsche and Antiquity: His Reaction and Response to the Classical Tradition*, edited by Paul Bishop (Rochester, N.Y.: Camden House, 2004), pp. 458–473.

76. Nietzsche, *The Gay Science*, § 287 (pp. 230–231).

77. *Ibid.*, § 380 (p. 343), Nietzsche's italics.

78. Jung was struck by the curious imagery of this passage and discerned in its apparently unconscious use of Justinus Kerner's *The Seeress of Prevorst* an example of cryptomnesia. C. G. Jung, *Psychiatric Studies*, vol. 1 of *The Collected Works of C. G. Jung*, translated by R. F. C. Hull (London: Routledge and Kegan Paul, 1957), §§ 140–142. See also Jung, *Nietzsche's "Zarathustra": Notes of the Seminar Given in 1934–1939*, 2 vols., edited by James L. Jarrett (London: Routledge, 1989), 2:1218. For further discussion, see Paul Bishop, "The Descent of Zarathustra and the Rabbits: Jung's Correspondence with Elisabeth Förster-Nietzsche," *Harvest: Journal for Jungian Studies* 43 (1997): 108–123.

79. Nietzsche, "Of Great Events," in *Thus Spoke Zarathustra* (pp. 152–155).

80. In this way Nietzsche's writings are indeed—corresponding to the etymology of the word "text"—a "tissue," or something woven, as Jacques Derrida's conceit of the *texte* as *tissu* suggests. See, for example, "Plato's Pharmacy" in *Dissemination*, translated by Barbara Johnson (Chicago: University of Chicago Press, 1983), pp. 61–171; and "La pharmacie de Platon" in *La dissémination* (Paris: Seuil, 1972), pp. 69–196.

81. See C. G. Jung, *Visions: Notes of the Seminar Given in 1930–1934*, edited by Claire Douglas, 2 vols. (London: Routledge, 1998).
82. Jung, *Nietzsche's "Zarathustra,"* 1:3.
83. Ibid., 2:1037.
84. Ibid., p. 1209.
85. "For it is not possible to step twice into the same river"; Heraclitus, DK 22 B 91, in Jonathan Barnes, *Early Greek Philosophy* (Harmondsworth: Penguin, 1987), p. 117. Cf. "We step and do not step into the same rivers, we are and we are not"; DK 22 B 49a, in *Early Greek Philosophy*, p. 117. According to Aristotle, Cratylus went one step further and maintained that not only is it impossible to step twice into the same river but that "one could not do it even once"; *Metaphysics*, Book 4, chapter 5, 1010a 7, in Aristotle, *The Basic Works*, edited by Richard McKeon (New York: Random House, 1941), p. 746.
86. Lampert, *Nietzsche's Teaching*, p. 158.
87. Nietzsche, "The Wanderer," in *Thus Spoke Zarathustra* (p. 173). Indeed, *Zarathustra* itself is a kind of wandering, as Jung suggests when he describes the work as "a river of pictures, and it is difficult to make out the laws of the river, how it moves, or toward what goal it is meandering"; Jung, *Nietzsche's "Zarathustra,"* 2:1339.
88. Nietzsche, "The Home-Coming," in *Thus Spoke Zarathustra* (p. 205).
89. Jung, *Nietzsche's "Zarathustra,"* 2:1251. For the "night sea-journey," an idea Jung derived from Leo Frobenius, see Jung, *Psychology of the Unconscious*, §§ 324–325.
90. Jung refers to the Hypogaeum, or underground temple, at Hal Saflieni on Malta and discusses the idea of incubation, which C. A. Meier has discussed extensively; see Meier, *Healing Dream and Ritual: Ancient Incubation and Modern Psychotherapy*, translated by Monica Curtis (Evanston, Ill.: Northwestern University Press, 1967).
91. In "The Psychology of the Child Archetype," Jung associates the *athla* with the twelve labors of Hercules; see Jung, *The Archetypes and the Collective Unconscious*, vol. 9, part 1 of *The Collected Works of C. G. Jung*, translated by R. F. C. Hull (London: Routledge and Kegan Paul, 1969), § 289. In "The Phenomenology of the Spirit in Fairytales" he draws a link between, on the one hand, the number twelve and the "labours . . . that have to be performed for the unconscious before one

can get free," and, on the other, the ecclesiastical year, in which Christ's redemptive work is fulfilled, and the *longissima via* [*Rosarium philosophorum*, in *Artis Auriferae*, 1593, vol. 2, p. 150], the *diuturnitas immensae meditationis,* or the long duration of the alchemical work; "The Psychology of the Child Archetype," § 433 and note. In "Religious Ideas in Alchemy" (1937), Jung associates the motifs of the Anthropos, the four elements, the *lapis,* and the Cross with such "corresponding journeys" as those of Osiris, the labors of Hercules (Cretan bull—South; the mares of Diomedes in Thrace—North; Hippolytus in Scythia—East; and the oxen of Geryon in Spain—West; while the Garden of the Hesperides in the western land of the dead leads to the twelfth labor, the journey to Cerberus and Hades), the travels of Enoch (in the apocryphal *Book of Enoch,* chapters 17–36), and the symbolic *peregrinatio* to the four quarters of the world in Michael Maier's *Symbola aureae mensae duodecim nationum* (1617). Jung, *Psychology and Alchemy,* vol. 12 of *The Collected Works of C. G. Jung,* translated by R. F. C. Hull (London: Routledge and Kegan Paul, 1953), § 457.

92. Nietzsche, *Sämtliche Werke: Kritische Studienausgabe,* 14:306, citing Reinhart von Seydlitz, *Wann, warum und wie ich schrieb* (Gotha: Pethes, 1900), p. 36.

93. "The Wanderer," in *Thus Spoke Zarathustra* (p. 173). In "Of the Bestowing Virtue," § 2, Zarathustra tells his disciples that "we are still fighting with the giant Chance [*mit dem Riesen Zufall*], and hitherto the senseless, the meaningless, has still ruled over humankind" (p. 102); while in "Of Redemption" Zarathustra describes his "art and aim" (*Dichten und Trachten*) as being "to compose into one and bring together what is fragment and riddle and dreadful chance [*Bruchstück . . . und Rätsel und grauser Zufall*]" (p. 161). See also "Of Old and New Law-Tables," § 3 (p. 216).

94. "The Wanderer," in *Thus Spoke Zarathustra* (p. 173); see also "Of the Vision and the Riddle," § 1, in *Thus Spoke Zarathustra* (p. 176). The "vision" and the "riddle" relate to the idea of eternal recurrence, the means by which, as Zarathustra suggests in "Of Redemption," "all 'it was' is a fragment, a riddle, a dreadful chance [*ein Bruchstück, ein Rätsel, ein grauser Zufall*]—until the creative will says to it: 'But I willed it thus!'" (p. 163). Compare with Heidegger's reading of this passage in his 1953 lecture "Who Is Nietzsche's Zarathustra?" ("Wer ist

Nietzsches Zarathustra?"), in Heidegger, *Vorträge und Aufsätze* (Pfullingen: Neske, 1954), pp. 101–126; translated by Bernd Magnus in *The New Nietzsche*, edited by David B. Allison (Cambridge, Mass.: MIT Press, 1985), pp. 64–79. For further discussion, see Günter Wohlfart, "Wer ist Nietzsches Zarathustra?" *Nietzsche-Studien* 26 (1997): 319–330; and Laurence Paul Hemming, "Who Is Heidegger's Zarathustra?" *Literature and Theology* 12, no. 3 (1998): 268–293.

95. For another instance when Zarathustra is addressed directly by time, see "The Stillest Hour," which closes Part Two (p. 167 in Hollingdale translation).

96. "The Wanderer," in *Thus Spoke Zarathustra* (p. 173); compare "the path up and down is one and the same"; Heraclitus, DK 22 B 60, in Barnes, *Early Greek Philosophy*, p. 103.

97. Compare Zarathustra's injunction to "*Become hard!*" with his contention that "only the noblest is perfectly hard"; "Of Old and New Law-Tables," § 29 (p. 231). See also "Slowly, slowly to become hard like a precious stone—and at last to lie there, silent and a joy to eternity"; Nietzsche, *Daybreak*, § 541, translated by R. J. Hollingdale (Cambridge: Cambridge University Press, 1982), p. 214.

98. "The Wanderer," in *Thus Spoke Zarathustra* (p. 174).

99. Compare with "*Looking away* shall be my only negation" ("Wegsehen *sei meine einzige Verneinung!*"); (*The Gay Science*, § 276 [p. 141]); and "The psychologist has to look away from *himself* in order to see at all" ("Maxims and Arrows," § 35, in *Twilight of the Idols* [p. 26 in Hollingdale translation]).

100. "The Wanderer," in *Thus Spoke Zarathustra* (p. 174), Nietzsche's italics.

101. See the anonymous woodcut (now dated to the nineteenth century) entitled "The Spiritual Pilgrim Discovering Another World," which Jung discusses in "Flying Saucers: A Modern Myth of Thing Seen in the Skies" (1958), in *Civilization in Transition*, vol. 10 of *The Collected Works of C. G. Jung*, translated by R. F. C. Hull (London: Routledge and Kegan Paul, 1964), § 764. The woodcut is Plate VII in this volume.

102. See Pierre Hadot, *What Is Ancient Philosophy?* translated by Michael Chase (Cambridge, Mass.: Belknap Press, 2002), pp. 206–207. In *The Will to Power*, § 1004, Nietzsche explains that his goal is "to attain a height and a bird's eye view, so that one grasps how

everything actually happens as it ought to happen" (p. 520 in Hollingdale and Kaufmann translation).

103. "Like you," Zarathustra tells the sun, "I must *go down*—as men, to whom I want to descend, call it"; and "thus began Zarathustra's going-down"; Nietzsche, "Zarathustra's Prologue," § 1 (p. 39).

104. "The Wanderer," in *Thus Spoke Zarathustra* (p. 174).

105. *Ibid.* (pp. 174–175).

106. *Faust,* part II, ll. 11426–11427, in Johann Wolfgang von Goethe, *Faust: Part Two,* translated by David Luke (Oxford: Oxford University Press, 1994), p. 219.

107. See *Faust,* part II, ll. 11410–11427, in *ibid.,* p. 219. There is no better commentary on this scene than the article by Konrad Burdach, the source of Heidegger's interest in the link between Goethe and no. 220 of Hyginus's *Fables*; see Burdach, "Faust und die Sorge," *Deutsche Vierteljahrsschrift* 1 (1923): 1–60.

108. Martin Heidegger, *Being and Time,* translated by John Macquarrie and Edward Robinson (1927; repr., London: SCM Press, 1962), § 42, pp. 241–244.

109. See *Faust,* part II, l. 11404: "If I could clear magic from my path" ("*Könnt ich Magie von meinem Pfad entfernen*").

110. Jung, "La Structure de l'inconscient," in *Two Essays in Analytical Psychology,* § 476.

111. *Ibid.,* § 475.

112. Jung, *Nietzsche's "Zarathustra,"* 2:1253.

113. *Ibid.,* p. 1253.

114. Jung, *Two Essays in Analytical Psychology,* § 474.

115. Jung, *Memories, Dreams, Reflections,* p. 203.

116. *Ibid.,* p. 214.

117. *Ibid.*

118. Jung, *Nietzsche's "Zarathustra,"* 2:1253.

119. "The Wanderer," in *Thus Spoke Zarathustra* (p. 175).

120. Jung, *Nietzsche's "Zarathustra,"* 2:1254.

121. *Ibid.*

122. *Ibid.,* p. 1255. Jung's reference to Nietzsche's statement in *Untimely Meditations* that "after all, the world is an aesthetical problem" sounds not so much like a reference to the argument in the fourth essay in that collection, "Richard Wagner in Bayreuth" (as James L. Jarrett's editorial footnote suggests), as an allusion to *The Birth of Tragedy,* where

Nietzsche says "the existence of the world is *justified* only as an aesthetic phenomenon"; Nietzsche, "Attempt at a Self-Criticism," § 5. See also *The Birth of Tragedy*, § 5 and § 24 (in *Basic Writings*, pp. 22, 52, and 141).

123. Compare with Laurence Lampert's commentary: "At the beginning of part III, as at the beginnings of parts I and II, it is Zarathustra's love for mankind that moves him to action. Earlier that love had moved him downward to mankind and to disciples in order to give the gift of a teaching that would initiate the long ascent to the superman. Now, moved still by love of mankind, he descends to his own lot and destiny, to the depths necessary to achieve the ascent to the superman that the Hour requires"; Lampert, *Nietzsche's Teaching*, p. 160.

124. Jung, *Nietzsche's "Zarathustra,"* 2:1256.

125. Jung did not discuss the chapter "On the Mount of Olives," and he dispatched "Of the Apostates" in one sentence; *ibid.*, p. 1422. As mentioned, there is a palpable sense of *Zarathustra*-fatigue in the later seminars, and Jung began his autumn series on 19 October 1938 with the remark, "Ladies and Gentlemen: On the way of the 'eternal return' we come back to our old *Zarathustra* once more," injecting a whimsical tone into these meetings that were both serious and, it seems, good-humored.

126. Nietzsche, "Preface," § 3, in *Human, All Too Human*, vol. 1 (p. 6).

127. *Ibid.*, § 3 (p. 7). The allusion is to "the cruel mother of the Cupids" or "the cruel mother of sweet desires" in Horace, *Odes*, book 1, no. 19, and book 4, no. 1, in Horace, *Odes and Epodes*, edited and translated by Niall Rudd (Cambridge, Mass.: Harvard University Press, 2004), pp. 63 and 219, respectively.

128. Nietzsche, "Preface," § 3, in *Human, All Too Human*, vol. 2 (p. 210).

129. *Ibid.*, § 4 (p. 211).

130. *Ibid.*, § 5 (p. 212).

131. Nietzsche, "The Wanderer and His Shadow," § 200, in *Human, All Too Human*, vol. 2 (p. 359).

132. In "The Prophet," Zarathustra encounters Solitude personified in a negative guise, along with Brightness of Midnight and

Rasping Silence of Death (*Thus Spoke Zarathustra* [p. 157])—dismal female figures akin to the Four Grey Woman of *Faust*, Part Two.

133. Compare with the section of *The Gay Science* entitled "Multiplication Table": "One is always wrong, but with two, truth begins.—*One* cannot prove his case, but two are irrefutable" (*Ein Mal eins.—Einer hat immer Unrecht: aber mit Zweien beginnt die Wahrheit.—Einer kann sich nicht beweisen: aber Zweie kann man bereits nicht widerlegen*); *The Gay Science,* § 260 (p. 218). For further discussion, see Grundlehner, *The Poetry of Friedrich Nietzsche,* p. 136.

134. Compare with Annette von Droste-Hülshoff's poem "Farewell" ("Lebt wohl") and its line: "Abandoned, but not alone" ("*Verlassen, aber einsam nicht*"); see Annette von Droste-Hülshoff, *Poems,* edited by Margaret E. Atkinson (Oxford: Oxford University Press, 1964), p. 53.

135. "Do you remember, O Zarathustra? When once your bird cried above you as you stood in the forest undecided, ignorant where to go, besides a corpse. When you said: May my animals lead me! I found it more dangerous among men than among animals. *That* was loneliness [*Verlassenheit*]!"; "The Home-Coming," in *Thus Spoke Zarathustra* (pp. 202–203). See also "Zarathustra's Prologue," § 10 (pp. 52–53).

Loneliness is also associated with two subsequent moments in the middle and at the end of the Second Part, in "The Night Song" and "The Stillest Hour." "And do you remember, O Zarathustra? When you sat upon your island . . . And do you remember, O Zarathustra? When your stillest hour came and tore you forth from yourself"; "The Home-Coming," in *Thus Spoke Zarathustra* (p. 203). See also "The Night Song" (p. 129), and "The Stillest Hour" (p. 167).

136. "The Home-Coming," in *Thus Spoke Zarathustra* (p. 203).

137. *Ibid.* In his account the experience of the inspiration that led to *Zarathustra,* Nietzsche quotes from these passages; see "Thus Spoke Zarathustra," § 3, in *Ecce Homo* (p. 73). As Lampert notes, Zarathustra "has never before used philosophy's comprehensive word *being* except to ridicule its use" (see "Of the Afterworldsmen," in *Thus Spoke Zarathustra*), but "now . . . he claims for the first time that all 'being' wills to become word in his speech," although he "collapses philosophy's traditional distinction" (i.e., between *being* and *becoming*), for "not

simply being and becoming, but being as becoming comes to word in his speech"; Lampert, *Nietzsche's Teaching*, p. 190.

138. "The Child with the Mirror," in *Thus Spoke Zarathustra* (p. 108).

139. "The Convalescent," in *Thus Spoke Zarathustra* (p. 234).

140. "The Child with the Mirror" (p. 108); "The Home-Coming" (p. 202).

141. In his commentary, Laurence Lampert detects a Straussian thematics in this chapter: "Zarathustra and his solitude both take speech as their theme and contrast the openness possible in solitary speech with the guardedness and superficiality necessary in public speech"; Lampert, *Nietzsche's Teaching*, p. 189.

142. "The Homecoming," pp. 203–204. See also in Part Three, "Of Passing By"; and in Part One, "Of the Flies of the Market-Place," p. 80. As Lampert observes, "This chapter on the relation of speech and being twice contrasts the primary or authentic speech of Zarathustra, the speech of philosophy in which being itself comes to word, with common speech in which primary matters are veiled in idle talk"; Lampert, *Nietzsche's Teaching*, p. 190.

143. Lampert identifies Zarathustra's "greatest danger" as what he calls his "heart's twofold will"—the will that binds him to humankind and the will that draws him up to the Superman ("Of Manly Prudence," in *Thus Spoke Zarathustra* [p. 164]); Lampert, *Nietzsche's Teaching*, p. 190.

144. Or so Zarathustra thinks: he has yet to face his ultimate temptation, pity for the Higher Man. See Part Four, "The Cry of Distress," in *Thus Spoke Zarathustra* (p. 255). See also "Why I Am So Clever," § 4, in *Ecce Homo* (pp. 13–14).

145. "At Noontide," in *Thus Spoke Zarathustra* (p. 287).

146. "The Song of Melancholy," § 1, in *Thus Spoke Zarathustra* (p. 306).

147. "The Home-Coming," in *Thus Spoke Zarathustra* (p. 205).

148. Jung, *Nietzsche's "Zarathustra,"* 2:1422.

149. *Ibid.*

150. Compare Jung, "Archaic Man" (1931), in *Civilization in Transition*, § 141.

151. Jung, *Nietzsche's "Zarathustra,"* 2:1423.

152. Compare with the title and subtitle of a book by Anthony Storr originally entitled *The School of Genius,* as chosen for its French translation: *Solitude: Les Vertus du retour à soi-même* (Solitude: The Virtues of Returning to Oneself).

153. Jung, *Memories, Dreams, Reflections,* p. 392.

154. Jung, "Psychological Aspects of the Mother Archetype" (1938/1954), in *The Archetypes and the Collective Unconscious,* § 198.

The Wonder of Wandering: Archetype, Myth, and Metaphor in William Faulkner's "The Bear"

DENNIS PATRICK SLATTERY

> I am a wanderer and mountain-climber, he said to his heart, I love not the plains, and it seemeth I cannot long sit still.
> —Nietzche, *Thus Spake Zarathustra*[1]

I still remember an extended pilgrimage that held me wandering out on the road for three and a half months in the fall of 1998. I use that deeply disturbing and consciousness-expanding moment and its subsequent backwash to begin this essay on the power and gravity of wandering.

Dennis Patrick Slattery, Ph.D., is Core Faculty in Mythological Studies at Pacifica Graduate Institute, Carpinteria, California. He is the author, co-author, editor, and co-editor of fifteen books, including four volumes of poetry. Among his titles are *The Wounded Body: Remembering the Markings of Flesh* (SUNY Press, 2000) and *Grace in the Desert: Awakening to the Gifts of Monastic Life* (Jossey-Bass, 2004). He has co-edited two books with Lionel Corbett: *Depth Psychology: Meditations in the Field* (Daimon Verlag, 2000) and *Psychology at the Threshold* (Pacifica Graduate Institute, 2000). With Charles Asher he has written a novel, *Simon's Crossing* (iUniverse, 2010), as well as a meditation book, *Day-to-Day Dante: Exploring Personal Mythology through The Divine Comedy* (iUniverse, 2011). He offers writing workshops on the works of Joseph Campbell and exploring one's personal myth.

PERSONAL WANDERING

In a bookstore in San Antonio, Texas, many years ago, I was led by some impulse to the travel section, where I pulled down a book on Ireland, the origin of my family lineage, for I had dreams of returning to that ancient land. But with that book another one, seemingly stuck to it, came tumbling out to land on my left shoe. I remember the leftiness of that drop for reasons that became more apparent as I entered into the writings of popular mythologist Joseph Campbell. But at that moment, I picked up the book and read the black title set against a creamy yellow backdrop: *A Guide to Monasteries and Retreat Centers in the Western Half of the United States*. When I read it, I shifted my attention from the Emerald Isle to locales closer to home and decided on the spot that I would spend my first sabbatical wandering from monasteries to Zen Buddhist retreat centers to sacred sites of meditation and renewal in the States. My excitement made me giddy.

Life, however, had other plans. I left my teaching position in Texas and moved my family to Santa Barbara, California to begin a full-time position at Pacifica Graduate Institute. Then, after I had taught for four years in the Mythological Studies program, another sabbatical opportunity presented itself: to pursue sites listed and described in that initial foot-fall book. In August of 1998 I packed my Ford Ranger pickup truck with camping supplies, clothes, a used laptop, and more books than I could read in a decade and set the compass north, up the California coastline. From then until December I drifted from site to site, often camping in state or national parks in between sacred places that included monasteries and retreat centers operated by Benedictines, Carmelites, Franciscans, Dominicans, and other religious denominations as well as two Zen centers, all of which were spread throughout eight states in the western United States.

During my stays I experienced deep depressions, bouts of loneliness, feelings of complete estrangement from everything I loved, bewilderment over who I was, and mystical moments of profound spiritual growth. In the process, I shed twenty-five pounds in long walks through forest and desert landscapes while enjoying vegetarian meals. I pilgrimaged through these landscapes of uncertainty and more than one moment of deep confusion as to my place in the world. I was accompanied, however, by one sustained conviction that visited me early in the journey: Wherever I visited and stayed, I would meet people who had something important to relay to me. Moreover, I would be directed to tell the people I met something they needed. Not once was this untrue in the twelve or thirteen different locales I made home for several days or a week at a time. I kept a daily journal of my experiences and gathered my entries into a memoir that was subsequently published.[2] The experience of wandering alone for these months, along with the subsequent writing about its more poignant moments, renewed and redefined me at the deepest levels of my being.

Even earlier in my life, at the age of twenty, although I had a secure job as a deputy bailiff at a municipal court, a new car, and a part-time college career, I felt empty and restless. Soon, with a friend, I began pursuing avenues of escape. One time we found ourselves at the Cleveland docks on the shores of Lake Erie, signed on as hired mess boys on a German freighter, the SS *Transamerica,* which was owned by Poseidon Lines in Hamburg. We shipped out from Cleveland to Bremerhaven, Germany. We then meandered through Western Europe into Wales and the British Isles, resting finally with relatives in southern Ireland. Only the intensifying war in Vietnam in that year of 1965 and our revised status, which made us eligible for the draft, forced us home earlier than we had planned. From both of these experiences I learned that the soul has an innate impulse—a need—to wander out of familiar territory to renew and revive itself throughout one's life.

Wandering, I now recognize, has a hidden order, a unique flow of psychic energy, its own mythos, and when that experience is reflected upon, as I reflected a year after returning from my experience of being adrift for a time, it reveals a series of patterns impossible to discern when one is in the moment of experience. I therefore begin with the observation that wandering and the wanderer carry in their respective backpacks a paradox: wandering is another form of being guided, directed, toward a telos that feels in the process circumambient, tangential, slanted, and not infrequently disconnected. Only the act of imaginative reflection brings it to light with a clarity of presence that is nothing shy of miraculous. Memory is at the heart of this myth-making discovery. C. G. Jung understood the intrinsic force of such experiences when he wrote of a religious experience that "strives for expression and can be expressed only 'symbolically' because it transcends understanding. It *must* be expressed one way or another, for therein is revealed its immanent vital force."[3]

As I think about it now, wandering feels more akin to a spiral than a haphazard squiggle; it carries in it a circling, a moving around and through something not yet identifiable. One feels as if one's travels and travails are aimless, without shape or form. It also carries a bit of a strip-tease wherein so much of what one felt was essential is discarded, until what remains is only the clean bones needed for survival. One may feel deeply the aura of being cast adrift, left only with the substantial self that may seem diseased, afflicted, inflected, and infected, such that courage in a strong heart is the best baggage one can maintain through the experience; that, and a faith in whatever it is that supports one's emotional and moral order.

I have written in another context the following observation that bears directly on wandering and the wanderer's shifting presence in the world:

> To be wounded is to be opened to the world; it is to be pushed off the straight, fixed, and predictable path of certainty and thrown into ambiguity, or onto the circuitous path, and into the unseen and unforeseen. One begins to wobble, to wander, and perhaps even to wonder not only about one's present condition, but also about one's origins. Circling the edges of the wound, so to speak, one's vision may clear, one's perception sharpens, and one may grasp for the first time what James Hillman describes . . . as that "innate image" that lies at the heart of the acorn that is me, that defines my heritage and my destiny.[4]

In this context I found helpful a fine article by Jungian analyst Steven Joseph that explores the power of desert wanderings. Such journeys salve the shattered psyche in biblical narratives: "Dwelling imaginally in the desert, listening carefully to the midrashic antitheses that characterize desert living and journeying, we may gain insight in to the Real. We learn to see into the state of being always on the way, always betwixt-and-between, being a passer-over."[5] Perhaps we have made too much of "centeredness" and mandala-inspired wholeness and balance, sacrificing in these moments of goodwill the fragmentation and aimless, drifting qualities of the psyche along the margins and in the interstices of life that lead to where affliction offers its own form of blessed knowing.

It may also introduce us to an epistemology of uncertainty, which is akin to "incapacity," as Jung reveals in his own wandering outlined in *The Red Book,* which, like "negative capability," the oft-cited term from the poet John Keats, relies on not grasping after certainty and surety but on the ability to dwell instead in the circuitous circuits of being that wandering italicizes. Jung relates that "we cannot slay our incapacity and rise above it.... Incapacity will overcome us and demand its share of life.... The one who learns to live with his incapacity has learned a great deal. This will lead us to the valuation of the smallest things, and to wise limitation, which the greater height demands."[6]

Historical and Literary Wanderers

When we turn to the literary traditions, we notice no end of wanderers in some of the great classics. Homer's *Odyssey* may be the most popular and well-known story of the wandering soul. Odysseus is devastated by years of combat, disassembled, decentered, deconstructed, seeking home but inevitably forced to wander for years until every vestige of the Trojan War is stripped from him—all but his memories and narratives of that brutal encounter. Sophocles' Oedipus experiences a moment of slippage from his calculating mind and precise questioning about the slayer of the former king, his father Laius. When his wife/mother Jocasta attempts to eliminate all doubt from the king's mind about his own possible involvement in his father's death, a worry that is becoming an obsession for Oedipus, he starts suddenly: "Strange, / hearing you just now . . . my mind wandered, / my thoughts racing back and forth."[7] At the end of *Oedipus Rex,* after his own self-wounding, he wanders through the wilderness with his daughter Antigone for years before finally stumbling blindly into the sacred grove of Colonus, there to experience another journey, during which his pollutedness is transformed into blessedness.[8]

Just as an individual may wander, so too may a nation, as is the case with the Israelites seeking freedom from bondage; they wander in the Sinai Desert with an image of a land of bounty to guide them, yet wandering seems a necessary condition in their destiny before they are gifted a place, a site, in which to prosper. George Williams writes of the wilderness in pre-Christian and Christian thought: "The wilderness is not only geographical but psychological. It can be a state of mind as well as a state of nature. It can betoken alternatively either a state of bewilderment or a place of protective refuge . . . as well as literally the wilds."[9] Religious leaders and spiritual guides have themselves fulfilled part of their calling in wandering—Jesus, Mohammad, Buddha, Gandhi—as if to underscore that wandering is a mythic necessity in a life called forth and singled out for service. Bereft by loss, the Sumerian hero Gilgamesh, afflicted by the loss of his beloved Enkidu, wanders through threatening landscapes seeking an antidote to his mortality; his wandering reveals the inevitability of sacrifice and finite boundaries. Dante's *Commedia,* his magnificent poem on individuation, begins with his pilgrim-poet, as himself, waking in a dark wood at midlife, conscious that somehow he has strayed from the right path and now terrified and vulnerable in the obscure woods of uncertainty.[10] In his chapter on "Paracelsus as a Spiritual Phenomenon," Jung cites Conrad Gessner of Zurich, who wrote to Crato von Grafftheim, a physician, about Paracelsus. In that same letter Gessner denounces the forbidden arts still practiced in his day and references the rise of "the wandering scholars, as they were commonly called. The most famous of these was Faust, who died not so long ago."[11]

Faust had a powerful pull on Jung; he returned repeatedly to Goethe's masterpiece for further insights into the soul. In his chapter "The Origin of the Hero" in *Symbols of Transformation,* Jung again focuses on the heroic Faust and quotes a passage from the German play that bears on the wandering impulse of the soul. In a conversation with Mephistopheles, Faust is instructed to find the habitation of the Goddesses, powerful, threatening, and formidable forces "named indeed with dread among our kind. / To reach them you must plumb the earth's deepest vault." When Faust asks for directions, Mephistopheles snaps back: "There's none! To the untrodden, / Unreadable regions— the unforgotten. . . . / Through endless solitudes you shall be drifted. / Can you imagine Nothing everywhere?"[12]

A new form of research opens for Faust at such a terrifying revelation, as it does for any wanderer. One must be willing to risk landscapes that have not yet been imprinted by others, for there the treasure is to be found. When one does not have the courage or heart-will to enter the unfamiliar and live within it on its terms, the journey will not yield what is necessary for the soul. Where no path exists, that is the path assigned within the paradox of wandering. If the path is clear, the directions crisp and accurate, footprints already present, no wandering ensues. Moreover, as Joseph Campbell develops the theme of calling forth the heroic in us, he notes that "there are many ways in which the adventure can begin. A blunder—apparently the merest chance—reveals an unsuspected world, and the individual is drawn into a relationship with forces that are not rightly understood."[13] The blunder may be an archetypal short course in wandering. A blunder may initiate wandering when other forces deflect us from the narrow path we had so carefully planned and intended.

Jung criticized the Western psyche's propensity "to turn everything into methods and intentions," according to the editor of *The Red Book*.[14] Jung realizes in that text a quality of his soul's nature: "My soul leads me into the desert of my own self. I did not think my soul is a desert, a barren hot desert, dusty and without drink."[15] He senses the power of solitude when one enters the desert of the soul: "Solitude is true only when the self is a desert."[16]

Finally, another powerful influence on Jung was Nietzsche's Zarathustra, who, we learn in the prophet's Prologue, left home when he was thirty years old "and went into the mountains. There he enjoyed his spirit and his solitude, and for ten years did not weary of it. But at last his heart changed."[17]

Psychology of Wandering

In many of these references a tension emerges between the willingness to be guided and a powerful libidinal urge to wander off the path in search of something needed, something that is perhaps to be discovered only by stepping into virginal territory, blundering into what is unfamiliar, where a part of the soul needing to be redeemed carries the necessary energy for the project.

To wander may then be a psychological need to restore the soul, as Jung intimates in an essay on poetry in *Psychological Types*: "Loss of soul amounts to a tearing loose of part of one's nature; it is the disappearance and emancipation of a complex. . . . It throws him off course and drives him to actions whose blind one-sidedness inevitably leads to self-destruction."[18] Wandering may be the occasion for some dimension of the soul to expire, to be burned in the fire of uncertainty and ambiguity that attends the wandering person or the collective soul, for an entire people may lose their bearings and be cast adrift when the myth that has served them no longer contains the necessary psychic energy to congeal their collective identity in a cauldron of shared values and beliefs. Fragmented, the collective soul begins to wander and, to mix the metaphor, to lose heart.

A little later in *Psychological Types,* Jung meditates on the archetype of the wandering Jew, Ahasuerus, who is described as having been born as "a late Christian legend which cannot be traced back earlier than the thirteenth century." As a part of the soul, Jung suggests, Ahasuerus represents "an unredeemed element in the unconscious" that frustrates the work of the Redeemer and must be held in check by being chained and restricted. This element "is projected upon those who have never accepted Christianity. . . . The restlessness of the wandering Jew is a concretization of this unredeemed state." Jung was writing about Ahasuerus in the context of the belief system of the Christian Church, noting that this figure of the wandering Jew "could find no outlet in the Christian attitude to life and the world and was therefore repressed."[19]

It should be noted that Jung was not a stranger to the impulses of the wandering soul. In a section of *The Red Book* entitled "Soul and God" he observes: "I wandered for many years, so long that I forgot that I possessed a soul."[20] In an editorial note, Shamdasani completed Jung's quote: "I belonged to men and things; I did not belong to myself." Shamdasani continues: "In *Black Book* 2, Jung states that he wandered for eleven years (p. 19). He had stopped writing in this book in 1902, picking it up again in 1913."[21] Finally, the editor asserts that "in 1912 Jung argued that scholarliness was insufficient if one wanted to become a 'knower of the human soul'"[22] and then leads us to a paragraph in Jung's 1912 essay "New Paths in Psychology," which I quote here:

> Therefore, anyone who wants to know the human psyche will learn next to nothing from experimental psychology. He would be better advised to [abandon exact science,] put away his scholar's gown, bid farewell to his study, and wander with human heart through the world. There, in the horrors of prisons, lunatic asylums and hospitals . . . through love and hate, through the experience of passion in every form in his own body, he would reap richer stores of knowledge than text-books a foot thick could give him.[23]

Jung explores the relationship of the heroic with wandering in another context in "The Origin of the Hero," a source that likely was one of Joseph Campbell's inspirations for *The Hero with a Thousand Faces*. He conjectures that "the heroes are usually wanderers, and wandering is a symbol of longing, of the restless urge which never finds its object, of nostalgia for the lost mother. . . . The heroes are like the wandering sun."[24] He continues that the heroic in each of us "is first and foremost a self-representation of the longing of the unconscious, of its unquenched and unquenchable desire for the light of consciousness."[25]

Just before he quotes from Goethe's *Faust* in *Symbols of Transformation*, where he focuses on the power of the natural order in the heroes' wandering, Jung makes this observation: "But consciousness, continually in danger of being led astray by its own light and of becoming a rootless will o' the wisp, longs for the healing power of nature, for the deep wells of being and for unconscious communion with life in all its countless forms."[26] Jung's insight takes us into the heartbeat of this essay.

The wanderer is not always restless, but the wanderer seeks something missing in the soul, an archetypal figure, to redeem what has remained outside of redemption, to recycle a quality, attribute, or image that the soul needs to complete itself. As an archetypal action, wandering fills the same function. Wandering grows from a lack, from a test, an occasion for endurance, or situations that demand or evoke courage, where the heart has been suffering and seeks the completion or further addition of the narrative that contains, buried within it, a sustained mythos seeking emergence and recognition. We do not normally encounter a youth wandering these days. I have therefore chosen a young man, Isaac McCaslin in William Faulkner's chapter "The Bear," which comprises part of a larger epic narrative, *Go Down, Moses,* to explore the healing motion of the wandering journey into wilderness.

The Bear and Isaac McCaslin

Go Down, Moses and Other Stories was first published by Random House in 1942. It was republished in 1949 under the title *Go Down, Moses,* one that Faulkner much preferred. He claimed that "the unity of the work as a novel" was preserved with this title, according to Nicholas Fargnoli.[27] Faulkner, one of the richest mytho-poetic writers of the American South, crafted an entire cosmos in his fictional Yoknapatawpha County, in which all seven of the interconnected stories that comprise *Go Down, Moses* occur. "The Bear," one of Faulkner's masterpieces, is the fifth story in the series. Faulkner scholar James Early has written that it "brings in the tangled history of the McCaslin family and the South, relating a recognition of the evil of slavery to the death of the bear," Old Ben.[28]

Go Down, Moses is one of Faulkner's most mythic tales of the South in its continual struggle to negotiate both mythic time and historical time, especially in the dissolution of an old order and the concomitant encroachment of man and machine into the primeval order of nature. It also describes an initiation experienced by a sixteen-year-old boy, Ike McCaslin, who is educated in the ways of the wilderness by his mentor, now an old man, Sam Fathers, "son of a negro slave and a Chickasaw chief," who embodies the two worlds of indigenous people and an enslaved civilization.[29] A significant moment in his initiation into the wilderness is Ike's solitary wandering into the woods one morning in anticipation of seeing a particular bear, an indomitable animal who has been hunted for decades every November by a group of men in a ritual that connects them to primal qualities in themselves. That moment of Ike's decision to enter the woods alone is the focus of the remainder of this essay.

Of the story and its significance, we might listen to Faulkner himself when he was interviewed in Japan in 1955 about its impact. To a question about the "symbolized feature of truth" in the story, Faulkner responded:

> The story itself, I hope and intended, told the truth. "The Bear," as a story, was a truth of the bears and animals, was a natural force which represented not a deliberate evil, not a satanic evil, but the quality of evil in sample size and force, which exists, which man has got to face and not be afraid of, that force itself has certain rights which must be respected. That force must not be reduced by trickery, it must be reduced by a bravery comparably as strong as its power.[30]

Faulkner's response takes the reader to the heart of myth and into the archetypal vessel the natural world affords. He also outlines the place and value of the heroic heart in its refusal to shrink from the force of this presence, instead deciding to move toward it, scared but not afraid, as Sam Fathers instructs Ike as he contemplates his wandering into the wilderness.[31] It is also worth mentioning at the outset that Faulkner's observation reaches back to one of the core values that appears in his "Address upon Receiving the Nobel Prize for Literature" in Stockholm on 10 December 1950, a one-page speech that is as eloquent as any statement of a world view or a people's collective myth that ever has been uttered. In it, Faulkner shares the "verities" that sustained his life and writing. He is explicit about having as his audience young writers who share with him the anguish attendant upon the creative act, creating "out of the materials of the human spirit something which did not exist before."[32]

He laments the fact that writers have forgotten "the problems of the human heart in conflict with itself, which alone can make good writing."[33] For our purposes I call attention to one additional aspect of this magnificent document: the ability to remember what has been culturally forgotten and the writer's responsibility to help the rest of us remember: "He must learn them again. He must teach himself that the basest of all things is to be afraid, and, teaching himself that, forget it forever, leaving no room in his workshop for anything but the old verities and truths of the heart," which he names as "love and honor and pity and pride and compassion and sacrifice."[34] Without them, nothing else seems worth writing about.

"The Bear" is a poetic witness to the fears of the heart that are being conquered in the breast of one young man who finds within himself the ability and courage to go it alone and to enter a place of dissolution and revelation, what Campbell refers to as "the morphogenetic field into which the enraptured yogi lets dissolve his humanity and its world."[35] There Ike McCaslin confronts what has already loomed blur-edged and alone in his imagination: "It loomed and towered in his dreams before he even saw the unaxed woods where it left its crooked print, shaggy, tremendous, red-eyed, not malevolent but just big, too big for the dogs."[36] His imagination stirs with a reality that his longing for the journey promises to satisfy, or at least intensify in its urges, for the bear is connected with a larger reality, one that breeds fear in the hearts of men who struggle to subdue it through conquest. This reality takes us to the fearful center of the story: "It was as if the boy had already divined what his senses and intellect had not encompassed yet: that doomed wilderness whose edges were being constantly and punily gnawed at by men with plows and axes who feared it because it was wilderness."[37]

The courage of the human heart begins to loom like the phantom of the bear itself as a testing ground for a soul that must relinquish certainty, protection, and safety if it is to know on a deeper level the power of the numinous presence in the world and its fierce ability to ravage any who come within its fateful grasp. The way to such a presence is not by means of a linear trajectory but slantwise, circuitous, wandering in and through; then what one seeks will be offered, but on its own terms and, as the narrative makes clear, only for an instant and more like an apparition than a thing of substance. Such is the wonder that can often attend wandering. The wandering soul must conquer or integrate the fearful heart in order to be worthy of the vision. Its reward is a moment of wonder at the ineffable, that which cannot be described but can be experienced.

Old Ben is the reason the men gather for two weeks each November during the wet and dreary change of season. When the story opens, Ike is sixteen years old and has been accompanying the men each November for six years. But earlier, when he was only ten, he was invited one June to accompany the men on a special annual celebratory trip into the wilderness to acknowledge the birthdays of Major de Spain and General Compson. On this special festive two week trip, the young Ike steals alone into the wilderness in pursuit of a glimpse of Old Ben. Up to this time, he had never enjoyed even a glimpse of the old bear, only its ragged traces after the dogs had chased it without succeeding in cornering it. Only once before, in the previous fall's two-week hunt, had Ike witnessed the traces of the bear's fleeting presence. "In the great gloom of ancient woods and the winter's dying afternoon, he looked quietly down at the rotted log scored and gutted with claw-marks and, in the wet earth beside it, the print of the enormous warped two-toed foot."[38]

The bear has been in the human imagination from time immemorial as an archetype of an animal guide that embodies the numinous quality of the natural order that frightens those without courage or consciousness. Even the dogs suffer an initiation into courage when they return from their own confrontation with this animal force of nature. In the fall before the next summer's birthday celebration in the woods noted above, one of eleven dogs that hunts Old Ben returns quivering and torn up from its battle, and Sam "daub[s] her tattered ear and raked shoulder with turpentine and axlegrease"[39] as he muses out loud: "Just like a man. . . . Put off as long as she could having to be brave, knowing all the time that sooner or later she would have to be brave once so she could keep on calling herself a dog, and knowing beforehand what was going to happen when she done it."[40]

In June of the following year a few men return to the woods as they have repeatedly for the special two-week birthday hunt, but this time inviting ten-year-old Ike to join them. It is on this trip that the young boy wanders each morning for four consecutive days into the wilderness, and as events will reveal, he enjoys his own "birthing day" of sorts, more akin to a birth into a consciousness that will integrate the mythology of the bear into his being and allow the image to live within him for the rest of his life.[41] A call, a presentiment, an invitation coaxes Ike into the woods alone on three consecutive mornings, accompanied always by his new rifle, given to him as a Christmas gift, with the date 1878 engraved on it. All of the others present to celebrate the birthdays of DeSpain and Compson assume he is out early hunting squirrels. All but his mentor, Sam Fathers, who begins to suspect the young man is after larger game.

The moment of initiation into the soul of the wilderness in the form of Old Ben commences in a slow circumambulating motion that Ike follows when he enters the woods on the first of four mornings with his compass and rifle. With them he penetrates its interior, "green with gloom," to hunt the bear on his own terms.[42] He wanders farther into its embrace as it opens to allow him entrance, then closes immediately behind him, enveloping him fully. But his equipment actually retards his field of vision; he sees nothing.

Sam, now aware of Ike's motives, tells him on the third evening of Ike's return: "'You aint looked right yet.'"[43] According to Sam, what holds his vision back and makes his searching impotent is his rifle. "*The gun*, the boy thought. *The gun*. 'You will have to choose,' Sam said."[44] The gun is both his protection and his impediment; while he is carrying it, the bear is unlikely to present itself to him. He cannot have it both ways, so

> He had left the gun; by his own will and relinquishment he had accepted not a gambit, not a choice, but a condition in which not only the bear's heretofore inviolable anonymity but all the ancient rules and balances of hunter and hunted had been abrogated.[45]

Equipped still with his compass and his watch, Ike enters what is for him virgin territory, the "immemorial darkness of the woods."[46] He follows the directive of the compass for guidance in space but also with "the old heavy, biscuit-thick silver watch which had been his father's" to order him in time.[47] These technologies, however, prevent him from slipping over the abyss of complete unknowing, but they too will become more hindrances than helps in his pilgrimage into the sanctity of the natural order, ancient, mysterious and oblique, which demands more a meandering than a methodical ordering of the self in space and time. "He stood for a moment—a child, alien and lost in the green and soaring gloom of the markless wilderness. Then he relinquished completely to it. It was the watch and the compass. He was still tainted."[48]

What is fascinating in this moment of total abandon and unequivocal yielding is that Ike gives himself over to the soul of the wilderness, which has its own terms, autonomy, and measures of engagement. The wilderness has its own hermeneutic, its own laws that govern its revelation. What is free is the choice: whether to give up, in, or over or remain protected and limited in one's orbit of understanding. The wilderness will disclose its enduring and ancient mysteries in direct proportion to what one is willing to forego. What it demands of the young man, who is of an age to be initiated into a deeper dimension of his life, is total abandon, becoming completely lost, turning himself over without reservation to presences and energies that are both anonymous and autonomous. Ike enters the deep terror of becoming lost and vulnerable without the knowledge that brings certainty and security.

I briefly note here Barbara Hannah's recollection of something Jung observed:

> In his essay on the transcendent function Jung says that to go back to nature in the primitive sense would be a mere regression, but to strive to reach it through psychological development is something quite different, for this time it means doing

consciously what we previously did unconsciously, consciousness being continually widened through the confrontation with previously unconscious contents.[49]

For Ike, entering the bear's field constitutes the latter instance that Jung addressed. It is his initial initiation into the unconscious that will make it conscious through his vulnerable state. Vulnerable wandering appears to be able to or to invite a porousness that the normally walled partition between consciousness and the unconscious prohibits. For the men who come to the annual hunt, Old Ben's continued existence is cause for an annual ritual with the possibility of conquest; for Ike, wandering into the woods enables him to confront the archetype of the soul of wilderness and, in the process, one of the deepest places in his own interior forest. Jung observes that "archetypes are typical modes of apprehension, and wherever we meet with uniform and regularly recurring modes of apprehension we are dealing with an archetype, no matter whether its mythological character is recognized or not."[50]

Ike turns without hesitation and links the compass and watch together on a nearby bush. Then he "leaned the stick beside them and entered [the matchless wilderness]."[51] Soon, however, he realizes he is lost, so he calls on the coaching of Sam Fathers as his Virgilian guide in the thick woods. He slows, he deliberates, he goes inward rather than seeking the external technologies he has relinquished. From a psychological point of view, his movements are informative. He begins to move in small circles in one direction so he can recognize where he has been when he crosses that spot. When this strategy proves at first to be futile, he "made this next circle in the opposite direction and much larger so that the pattern of the two [circles] would bisect his track somewhere, but crossing no trace nor mark anywhere of his feet or any feet, and now he was going faster though still not panicked."[52]

In the moment, unfamiliar time and unknown space coalesce around the young man to place him in a terrain strange and alien; he has no analogies to pull from, no remembrances that will help make a connection to where the landscape is recognized. In fact, as he uses up the last of Sam Fathers's instructions on how to move in the wilderness with one's own wits and skills for tracking back and around, he inhabits a wilderness that completely bewilders him. His space is liminal and at the same time a temenos, for he is in the inner sanctum of the wilderness, a sacred place of refuge and danger, open now to the unexpected and the wished-for, a terrain of both terror and delicious anticipation.

Ike soon comes on a tree that could be one he had passed earlier, he thinks; but no, "because there was a down log beside it which he had never seen before and beyond the log a little swamp, a seepage of moisture somewhere between earth and water."[53] He has wandered into the unknown, but in the strange paradox that may be an essential element of all wandering, he has also been guided by forces unnamed and unknown, invisible, mythic, and eternally present. However, he cannot discern such a reality yet. That does not happen until it appears to him as powerfully as any hierophany.

Yet he has invited these presences to guide him by his act of humility and respect: his relinquishment of stick, rifle, compass, and watch. By doing so he bares himself to the eternal and the primeval presence of Old Ben, archetype and architect of the natural order as well as steward of the wilderness that men filled with fear continue to gnaw into fragments in order to domesticate its mystery.

Ike pauses now, as a last resort, for Sam Fathers's training has also been strained to its limits. I believe his mentor's training also needed to be shed, jettisoned, worn out and through before Ike could be completely free. Only then was he in a state of abandonment, isolated and alienated from all forms of the familiar scaffolding that had served him in the past. In the swamp, he is between water and earth. Yet the swamp maintains solidity in the stew of the earth he will steward for the next seventy years of his life. Ike sits down on the log and immediately is guided in perception,

> seeing . . . the crooked print, the *warped indentation* in the wet ground which while he looked at it continued to fill with water until it was level full and the water began to overflow and the sides of the print began to dissolve away.[54]

One might be inclined to say Ike has wandered into this moment that is so close to the pawprints of the animal's presence. But it would be more accurate to entertain the idea that he has been guided here, at this instant, where the presentness of the bear has been replaced by a trace, in its absence, of its consequences in nature: the weighty indention in a middle region between two elements and the mixing of those elements to complete fullness in the

THE WONDER OF WANDERING

"crooked print."[55] The condition of the print is also relevant to Ike's wandering, for its malformation imprints the identity of *this* bear in *this* region at *this* moment.

The crooked nature of the pawprint reminds me of the crooked lower jaw of the multi-scarred white whale, Moby Dick, that Ahab has wandered into the vicinity of, his own Old Ben in the watery wilderness of the world's seas.[56] Both white whale and brown bear convey as natural symbols the presence of the *anima mundi* that each person must meet on his/her journey, and both mark that presence through jagged and malformed imperfection. Their histories and the markings of their eternal presence are conveyed in the afflicted bodies that announce their identities to the world.

Neither this pawprint filling with water and already disappearing in another instant nor the next nor the next would have manifested if Ike had not abrogated his control of the journey and allowed the reins of his life to fall slack so another force could take them up: from his perspective, he is lost. From the perspective of the ancient other, he is about to be found: "Even as he looked up he saw the next one, and moving, the one beyond it; moving, not hurrying, running, but merely keeping pace with them as they appeared before him as though they were being shaped out of thin air just one constant pace short of where he would lose them forever and be lost forever himself."[57]

Then, from the wilderness, Ike finds he has been led into a little glade "and the wilderness coalesced. It rushed, soundless, and solidified—the tree, the bush, the compass and the watch glinting where a ray of sunlight touched them."[58] So in his wandering he has been led back to those instruments of time and space that situate him in the world of the familiar. He has, in the lexicon of psyche's voyage, come full circle to where home is easily retraced. Then he sees the bear, which carries qualities of the mystical union, a moment where one is in the presence of a god or goddess, a luminous force, a *mana* power beyond time, space, or causality. Such is the gift often received by one who yields to the presences that remain invisible until one steps into their field and allows their persuasive pattern to become part of one's being:

> Then he saw the bear. It did not emerge, appear: it was just there, immobile, fixed in the green and windless noon's hot dappling, not as big as he had dreamed it but as big as he had

expected, bigger, dimensionless against the dappled obscurity, looking at him."⁵⁹

I recall in this description something that Jung wrote in *The Red Book* that aids our understanding of what Ike has just become witness and disciple to. Jung discovers an essential truth early on in his quest in 1913, when he feels that he has lost his own soul: "If we possess the image of a thing, we possess half the thing. The image of the world is half the world. He who possesses the world but not its image possesses only half the world, since his soul is poor and has nothing. The wealth of the soul exists in images."⁶⁰

I believe his insight helps illuminate what happened to Ike in the bear's presence. When the story begins, Ike at sixteen has carried this image of the bear for at least six years, from even before the first time he is brought with the men in November to hunt Old Ben at the age of ten and the next summer, when he actually perceives Old Ben. At that young age, as he sits on the log and perceives the bear as a gift, his imagination coalesces two images of Old Ben: his physical appearance as well as his mythic presence. I believe he comes to possess the whole world by yoking the two halves, the world and its image, in a moment of symbolic comprehension. Writ large, the bear is the pulsating heart of the wilderness. As a symbol it can lead one to a fuller depth of participation in the world when one simultaneously yields and imagines. Ike's wandering is circular, mandala-like in design, and it completes the young man's search. Not a hunter of the bear but now one of its devotees, Ike's moment passes quickly: "Then it moved. It crossed the glade without haste, walking for an instant into the sun's full glare and out of it, and stopped again and looked back at him across one shoulder. Then it was gone."⁶¹

Old Ben assumes the tone and pressure of an apparition; it is a haunting presence that is neither fully flesh nor complete spirit but both in unison to reveal a full vision of the natural and supernatural realms in harmonic correspondence: "It faded, sank back into the wilderness without motion as he had watched a fish, a huge old bass, sink back into the dark depths of its pool and vanish without even any movement of its fins."⁶² Such is the motion of an apparition as it fades back into a timeless abyss the way dream images begin to dissolve as one wakens and lies for a moment in bed trying to remember and discern their still-disturbing traces. They are like liquid images, watery and solid, like the consistency of mercury, insisting on being both solid and liquid in the same moment.

Finally, there is an important correspondence between the freshly initiated Ike and the more seasoned Zarathustra. In his experience as "The Wanderer," the title of one of Nietzsche's chapters, Zarathustra laughs to himself on his solitary walks in the mountains where he wanders in his thoughts and on the landscape, confiding to himself: "Ever hast thou approached confidently all that is terrible. Every monster wouldst thou caress. A whiff of warm breath, a little soft tuft on its paw—: and immediately wert thou ready to love and to lure it."[63]

Ike too carries this profound archetype of the wanderer who comes to himself by confronting, within the "strong rapid little hammer of his heart"[64] the *mysterium tremendum* that Joseph Campbell believed contained "the energies of the deepest secret of our being."[65] Perhaps it is the most soulful moment of Ike's life, captured in the hunter-turned-aspirant, a vocation that Old Ben invites him into—the *sanctum sanctorum*—to realize through a vision captured within a glade brightly, one that allows one luminescent moment to illuminate his soul for the succeeding seven decades.

NOTES

1. Friedrich Nietzsche, *Thus Spake Zarathustra,* trans. Thomas Commons (Mineola, N.Y.: Dover Publications, 1999), p. 106.

2. Dennis Patrick Slattery, *Grace in the Desert: Awakening to the Gifts of Monastic Life,* foreword by Thomas Moore (San Francisco: Jossey-Bass, 2004).

3. Jung to Kurtt Plachte, 10 January 1929, in C. G. Jung, *Letters,* vol. 1, *1906–1950,* selected and edited by Gerhard Adler and Aniela Jaffé, translated by R. F. C. Hull (Princeton, N.J.: Princeton University Press, 1973), p. 59. Quoted in Murray Stein, "Symbol as Psychic Transformer," *Spring: A Journal of Archetype and Culture* 82 (Fall 2009): 12.

4. Dennis Patrick Slattery, *The Wounded Body: Remembering the Markings of Flesh* (New York: SUNY Press, 2000), p. 13.

5. Steven Joseph, "Desert Wanderings: Pathways for Whole, Broken and Shattered Psyches," *Journal of Analytical Psychology* 45 (2000): 397.

6. C. G. Jung, *The Red Book: Liber Novus,* edited by Sonu Shamdasani, translated by Mark Kyburz, John Peck, and Sonu Shamdasani (New York: W. W. Norton and Company, 2009), p. 240.

7. Sophocles, *Oedipus the King,* in *The Three Theban Plays,* translated by Robert Fagles (New York: Penguin Books, 1984), ll. 800–803, p. 201.

8. Sophocles, *Oedipus at Colonus,* in *The Three Theban Plays,* p. 284.

9. George H. Williams, "The Wilderness Theme," in Williams, *Wilderness and Paradise in Christian Thought: The Biblical Experience of the Desert in the History of Christianity* (New York: Harper and Brothers, 1962), p. 4.

10. "*Nel mezzo del cammin di nostra vita / mi ritrovai per una selva oscura, / che la diritta via era smarrita*" (When I had journeyed half of our life's way, / I found myself within a shadowed forest, / for I had lost the path that does not stray). Dante, *Inferno,* in *The Divine Comedy of Dante Alighieri,* translated by Allen Mandelbaum (New York: Bantam, 1982), ll. 1–3, pp. 2–3.

11. C. G. Jung, *Alchemical Studies,* vol. 13 of *The Collected Works of C. G. Jung,* edited and translated by G. Adler and R. F. C. Hull (Princeton, N.J.: Princeton University Press, 1968), § 154.

12. Quoted in C. G. Jung, *Symbols of Transformation,* vol. 5 of *The Collected Works of C. G. Jung,* edited and translated by G. Adler and R. F. C. Hull (Princeton, N.J.: Princeton University Press, 1967), § 299.

13. Joseph Campbell, *The Hero with a Thousand Faces* (Princeton, N.J.: Princeton University Press, 1973), p. 51.

14. Shamdasani made this remark on note 78 of page 237 of *The Red Book.*

15. *Ibid.*, p. 235.

16. *Ibid.,* p. 236.

17. Nietzsche, "Zarathustra's Prologue," in *Thus Spoke Zarathustra,* p. 1.

18. Jung, "The Type Problem in Poetry," in Jung, *Psychological Types,* vol. 6 of *The Collected Works of C. G. Jung,* edited and translated by G. Adler and R. F. C. Hull (Princeton, N.J.: Princeton University Press, 1971), § 384.

19. *Ibid.*, § 454.
20. Jung, *The Red Book*, p. 233.
21. *Ibid.*, p. 233n48.
22. *Ibid.*, p. 233n55.
23. Jung, "New Paths in Psychology," in *Two Essays in Analytical Psychology*, vol. 7 of *The Collected Works of C. G. Jung*, edited and translated by G. Adler and R. F. C. Hull (Princeton, N.J.: Princeton University Press, 1967), § 409.
24. Jung, *Symbols of Transformation*, § 299.
25. *Ibid.*
26. *Ibid.*
27. Nicholas Fargnoli, ed., *William Faulkner: A Literary Companion* (New York: Pegasus Books, 2008), p. 441.
28. James Early, *The Making of Go Down, Moses* (Dallas, Tex.: Southern Methodist University Press, 1972), p. 33.
29. William Faulkner, "The Bear," in *Go Down, Moses* (New York: Vintage Books, 1970), p. 197.
30. "Interviews in Japan, 1955," in *Lion in the Garden: Interviews with William Faulkner, 1926-1952*, edited by James B. Meriwether and Michael Millgate (Lincoln, Nebraska: University of Nebraska Press, 1964), p. 120.
31. Faulkner, "The Bear," p. 198.
32. Faulkner, "Address upon Receiving the Nobel Prize for Literature," Stockholm, 10 December 1950, in William Faulkner, *Essays, Speeches, & Public Letters,* edited by James Meriwether (New York: Random House, 1965), pp. 119–120.
33. *Ibid.*, p. 119.
34. *Ibid.*, p. 120.
35. Joseph Campbell, *The Inner Reaches of Outer Space: Metaphor as Myth and as Religion* (Novato, Calif.: New World Library, 2002), p. 80.
36. Faulkner, "The Bear," p. 185.
37. *Ibid.*
38. *Ibid.*, p. 192.
39. *Ibid.*, p. 190.
40. *Ibid.*, pp. 190–191.
41. *Ibid.*, p. 196.
42. *Ibid.*

43. *Ibid.*, p. 197.
44. *Ibid.*, p. 198.
45. *Ibid.*
46. *Ibid.*, p. 197.
47. *Ibid.*, p. 198.
48. *Ibid.*, p. 199.
49. Barbara Hannah, *The Archetypal Symbolism of Animals: Lectures Given at the C. G. Jung Institute, Zurich, 1954–1958,* edited by David Eldred (Wilmette, Ill.: Chiron Books, 2006), pp. 4–5.
50. *Ibid.*, p. 6.
51. Faulkner, "The Bear," p. 199.
52. *Ibid.*, pp. 199–200.
53. *Ibid.*, p. 200.
54. *Ibid.* My italics.
55. *Ibid.*
56. "Ahab . . . found himself hard by the very latitude and longitude where his tormenting wound had been inflicted"; Herman Melville, *Moby-Dick,* edited by Harrison Hayford and Hershel Parker (New York: W. W. Norton, 1967), p. 437.
57. Faulkner, "The Bear," p. 200.
58. *Ibid.*
59. *Ibid.*
60. Jung, "Refinding the Soul," in *The Red Book,* p. 232.
61. Faulkner, "The Bear," p. 200.
62. *Ibid.*, pp. 200–201.
63. Nietzsche, *Thus Spoke Zarathustra,* p. 105.
64. Faulkner, "The Bear," p. 200.
65. Joseph Campbell, "Renewal Myths and Rites," in *The Mythic Dimension: Selected Essays 1959–1987* (Novato, Calif.: New World Library, 2007), p. 82.

Cultural Tourism and Soul Care: Traveling to Recover the *Anima Mundi*

KAJ NOSCHIS

Introduction

My focus in this essay is leisure travel—travel to explore new places and to see and meet new people. Such travel is often done in the pursuit of two things, access to nature and access to culture: on the one hand, journeys to see beautiful natural environments (such as a white sandy beach in front of the infinite ocean, an incredible waterfall, or beautiful snow-covered mountains), and on the other hand, trips to see cities (Paris, Cairo, Vilnius). I will concentrate on the second category: leisure travel to see cities.

My questions will be about the psychological meaning and benefits of such travel: What does it promote in terms of personal balance or, in a more Jungian fashion, in terms of individuation? And how do we

---

Kaj Noschis, Ph.D., is a Jungian analyst in private practice in Lausanne, Switzerland. He is a member of the faculty at the C. G. Jung Institute in Zurich and a lecturer at the University of Lausanne (in Jungian psychology) and the Federal Institute of Technology Lausanne (in environmental psychology). His publications are mainly in French; his most recent book is *Monte Verità—Ascona et le génie du lieu* (Presses polytechniques et universitaires romandes, 2011).

**This essay is based on a paper presented at the First European Conference of Analytical Psychology in Vilnius, Lithuania, on 26 June 2009.

look at it as a collective phenomenon? Flocks of tourists spend hard-earned money on travel to a faraway city. Why? There is certainly a danger in trying to state something general about traveling, as everyone travels for his or her own reasons, but my point is that there is likely also a collective force at work. We could probably do without leisure travel, but it is a largely shared and pervasive need. I will suggest that in this sense travel can be viewed as preventive therapy, as prophylaxis, and perhaps even as direct therapy.

To look at this in more Jungian terms, I will suggest that the outside world, the new places and the people one meets in those places, might stir the traveler's unconscious or, to say it archetypally, reawaken his or her soul through contact with the *anima mundi*. Those who are familiar with the writings of James Hillman—or for that matter with the work of Plato or Marsilio Ficino—will be familiar with the concept of world as having a soul (anima).[1] I refer to not only the natural world—although that would be easily understood today, given the reappearance of Gaia in Western culture—but also the cultural world, mainly the cities and collective constructions of mankind. These are conscious constructions that have become depositories of the collective unconscious. Looking at cities as places where the collective unconscious is materially alive as an organism appears to be therapeutic. Thus, travel can be seen *as a way to recover the anima mundi*. Our participation in the collective unconscious demands our recognition, and we might consider this need the fundamental force that underlies travel.

The Desire for Travel

Most of leisure travel is motivated by curiosity about new places and the desire to get away from current life, to get out of a daily routine and the feeling of being stuck in a rut. We know this from our own experience: when we are stuck, we just want to get away. Many writers who have traveled felt that they just had to get away from home, from their current preoccupations, after an unhappy love affair, after a professional failure, after a family tragedy. They wanted to open up to or have their minds inspired by the new sights and concerns that would be offered to or imposed upon them in a journey. This is not always stated overtly in the works of literature such authors have produced; some of them stick to the voyage and write only about the adventures.

But their biographers have provided the personal details in many cases. As a result we have great literary works by such travelers/authors/writers/explorers as Goethe, Stendhal, D. H. Lawrence, and John Steinbeck, to name a few.[2] These authors have opened the minds of readers to new environments and encounters.

Literary accounts are extremely important in promoting travel, just as oral accounts have been through history. To hear or read about unknown places stimulates curiosity about them, and we think, "I would also like to go there." Such messengers include Herodotus and Marco Polo. Closer to our own time we have Paul Theroux and V. S. Naipaul.[3] Interestingly, travel writing again became very fashionable in the late 1980s with Bruce Chatwin, and its popularity continues to this day.[4] Modern technology has added pictures and movies as an integral part of the travel narrative. Such images stimulate the desire to go there oneself.

What is this desire? My contention is that *we project* atmospheres, events tinged with mystery, excitement, and adventure, on stories we have heard and on pictures we have seen. Such stories and pictures let us get away from our home environment. They activate our fantasy. Projection makes us relate personally with such events taking place elsewhere.

How does projection work here—or generally, for that matter? Projection allows us to recognize something (Latin, *re-cognosco*) that has to do with ourselves in what we see and hear. The part that resonates within us can come from a past experience or it can relate to future aspirations or it can relate to both. This inner part lies somewhere deep within us, but the projection brings it much closer to the surface. But how can we recognize something that we don't know or a place we have never been?

In a projection there is some indication of familiarity, otherwise projection would not happen: a bridge or a tower in Paris unites or expresses something in us. And then we want to get closer in reality. Such places are the products of our fantasy, evoked or put in motion by something we have seen, heard, or read about, often because a public event is associated with that place. These places have become symbols of other things: the place where that miracle happened, where that queen was murdered, where that painting is to be seen, where those two people fell in love.

Our projections probably serve some compensatory function for our daily lives, yet they also become a reason that we want to travel. We want to get closer to what we have recognized. When we use the word *recognize* about something we have seen or heard or read about, something of it is already there within us, hidden deep down under, but there. According to Jung, through projection we are putting it *out there*, onto someone or something. Could we say that by getting to the place in the outside world that triggered the recognition, we can continue to build upon a story that already exists or add our story to the one that made our projection come alive? And do we believe or feel that by reaching that place, by going there in the outside world, by getting closer in reality, we will also get closer to our inner self? It is interesting that Hillman is against the notion that projections should be returned to our interior.[5] About the term itself, he says: "What psychology has had to call 'projection' is simply animation, as this thing or that spontaneously comes alive, arrests our attention, draws us to it. . . . The soul of the thing corresponds or coalesces with ours."[6] Let projections live in the outside world!

The paradox is that the place is unknown to us in the outside world, in the real world, yet it is its *familiarity* that gets us moving—an inner recognition. This is where I believe that the collective enters into the picture. We travel in order to get to the symbol, the something shared by all of us, an expression of the *anima mundi,* of the collective unconscious. Traveling is fundamentally a need or a desire to confirm that *out there* I can find what has emerged from my own inner depths.

Traveling for leisure became fashionable in the eighteenth century. Yet even this fashion was often associated with travel for healing. A physician might suggest that a wealthy person should travel to a faraway place as a cure for melancholy, for example. Even as early as ancient Roman times, some authors referred to travel as a cure. From the eighteenth century, we also have the *Bildungsroman,* the story that frequently relates coming of age, or becoming an adult, with travel. So here we have explicit or implicit references to travel as therapy. In psychological terms, the assumption is that traveling to new places may give the traveler the ability to see things differently, to rescale his or her problems or view them from a new angle.

If we go somewhat deeper, travel carries the vestiges of the notion of pilgrimage—travel in order to seek pardon for one's sins or travel to wash the soul. So here is another association of travel with therapy, one that goes back to antiquity (Delphi, Jerusalem, Mecca). We know that almost all religions have a tradition of pilgrimage, of holy places where the believer is expected to go or might go to get closer to the gods and where the voyage itself is an essential component of spiritual life. The travel itself, the experience of being en route, is an essential aspect of progressing toward the goal.

For instance, I want to go to Santiago de Compostela, in Galicia, Spain, where I have never been, but I feel that there I will be closer to God (until Columbus, Compostela was the Western extreme of the known world for Europeans). If I believe my desire to travel there is because of what I have heard, that somehow also makes Compostela a place for my projections. Again, this entails/involves/includes some kind of recognition. And walking there, getting there slowly from far away, might be a condition of that meeting. (A Swiss colleague, Florence Bachetta, has written a very nice book about this particular pilgrimage.[7])

Meeting the *Anima Mundi*

Psyche lives and is nourished through such experiences. In archetypal terms, the personal anima dissolves and comes into contact with the *anima mundi* or eventually even dissolves into it. We reawaken to the mystery and otherness of the outside world and do not need to affirm our interiority and specificity anymore. These are views from James Hillman, who suggests that there is something immediately alive in such experiences, that in this way we can be in the world through the heart rather than through the head.[8]

In analytical psychology, we are accustomed to using the term "collective unconscious." But what does that mean? Put simply, it is the sense that we share something "in the background" or "deep down under." When our projections urge us to travel, we reach for a part of our own foundation that we recognize in a place that attracts us. It draws us because it is part of our "deep down under" yet is in the outside world and is alive. This is often what gets us moving.

My view is that all cultural artifacts are collectively built, whether they be cities and their architecture, monuments, and public spaces or the manners and ways of being of the inhabitants. These are collectively built through history and have in time also become depositories of the collective unconscious. Buildings and the spaces around them contain their history, the events that have taken place in and around them. In turn, these experiences become somehow part of the buildings and spaces, in the same way that we carry inside us a history that goes well beyond our own experienced life. This process entails a move from consciousness to unconsciousness in the constructed environment, and this is how the environment builds, contains, and expresses the collective unconscious. I suggest that what makes the experience of a new city intense is the presence of traces of the collective unconscious, symbols to connect to.

Once we get there, when we meet and mix with this new and unknown culture, we have an opportunity to open to the world soul, the *anima mundi*. When we travel, we want to join this collective world soul. Connecting with the collective is how travel can give us access to another view of ourselves.

Those who were just becoming adults in the late 1960s will remember the hippie and flower-power years, a time when American and British pop songs were invading most European radio programs. Among these was a song sung by Scott McKenzie called "San Francisco (Be Sure to Wear Some Flowers in Your Hair)." It is emblematic of that period and the lyrics are still familiar to all who remember this song from their youth:

> If you're going to San Francisco
> Be sure to wear some flowers in your hair
> If you're going to San Francisco
> You're gonna meet some gentle people there
>
> For those who come to San Francisco
> Summertime will be a love-in there
> In the streets of San Francisco
> Gentle people with flowers in their hair
>
> All across the nation such a strange vibration
> People in motion
> There's a whole generation with a new explanation
> People in motion people in motion
>
> For those who come to San Francisco
> Be sure to wear some flowers in your hair

> If you come to San Francisco
> Summertime will be a love-in there.[9]

The song represents San Francisco with the image of "gentle people with flowers in their hair." Very evocative. In the late 1960s, the West Coast of the United States was a center of the pacifist hippie and flower-power movements that opposed the Vietnam War—the war led by Washington on the East Coast. The pacifists said: Make love, not war. Dance with flowers on your head, wear flowing garments, be in the skies. For many, this song put San Francisco on the map as the center of the hippie movement. For Europeans (and probably also many Americans), the flower-power people were now clearly located *out there*. For many, San Francisco became a hoped-for destination and the symbol of a way to connect with the heart of the hippie in ourselves. The lyrics of this song are a good example of a *story*—like Marco Polo telling about exotic experiences in China. These lyrics told a story that many of us heard and took into ourselves. San Francisco became a reference for something more personal *in ourselves* and yet also *out there* in the world. By going to San Francisco we would re-cognize *out there* something that is *in here* and make it alive.

This process is somehow paradoxical in the sense that the assumption is that you will discover something unknown, a new place, yet that place is also familiar, something inside yourself. I would argue that the unknown is the unexpected that we encounter on the journey, but once we are there, we are part of the pulsating *anima mundi*. The "strange vibration" of the song is the *animation* that one can sense as it moves from the imagination to the heart.

During the last decades we have witnessed an enormous increase in mass tourism. In most historical cities you will find tour groups moving from monuments to museums and back to more monuments. To me this is a very impressive phenomenon. People will invest significant amounts of what they have earned through their labor and use their precious vacation days to travel to Paris, Prague, Rome, London, or any other city, where they are shuffled from one location to the next. The rhythm of such traveling, be it just sitting in a bus or walking through a museum, is often quite hectic and demands energy and effort.

However, even on packaged, guided tours, something unforeseen invariably happens. The discovery of an unexpected place or building is part of the excitement of travel. And this might change our plans, such that our journey becomes a discovery of places in the world that are altogether unknown to us. Often losing one's way or one's money adds to the complications of a journey, but these events also contribute to the challenge we have set ourselves. When these things happen, we begin to live an adventure. And it might even be that this unforeseen event becomes the most important part of the journey. In fact, the projections that initially set the journey in motion might be forgotten, as was the case with Ulysses. Like that ancient wanderer, we might also fall in love with something or someone we meet during our journey.

In fact, I would suggest that encountering the unexpected is the most important aspect of traveling, because when that happens the outside world takes over and we are nourished by its offerings and the experience of exploring something new. We feel how the *anima mundi* enters us. The guided tour leaves less place for this, which is where I see its limits, although it still responds to the need to travel.

Isabelle Eberhardt (1877–1904), a lonely woman who was nevertheless emancipated for her time, a Swiss traveler of Russian aristocratic origin, became an expert on the desert and Middle Eastern countries. When she was twenty-six (just before she drowned in a flood in Africa), she wrote in her journal a beautiful statement that illustrates what I am trying to say. She wrote, "So many times on the roads of my itinerant life I have asked myself where I was going and I finally understood, among the North African nomads, that I was going back toward the sources of life."[10] What better description of recovering the *anima mundi* and connecting with the collective unconscious?

The parallel between inner and outer traveling is an old and often investigated theme. Facing unknown places and dangers in the outside world is often referred to as an image of one's inner travel, one's journey to explore new facets of oneself and meet frightening aspects of oneself. In a similar vein, learning to overcome difficulties outside can be seen as looking for ways of making progress in the inner world: getting further, undergoing transformation, reaching individuation.

In our analytical practice we draw upon this principle often, particularly when we talk about a dream in which the story is about traveling to new places. We often discuss such a dream as an inner journey of discovering and becoming familiar with new aspects of the dreamer. Associations will easily bring the dreamer to talk about some of his or her voyages in the outer world, and such memories can then become clear to the dreamer as particularly expressive of the difficulties or challenges of his or her present inner situation.

GETTING BACK HOME

One of the founding stories, if not *the* founding story, of Western literature is the story of Ulysses traveling back home to Ithaca after the Trojan War. The journey itself is the essential story, replete with adventures and challenges, fascinations and dangers. The aim, however, is to get back home to Penelope. Twenty-five hundred years later, Henry of Ofterdingen, the hero of the 1802 novel by Novalis that is named after the protagonist, asks the suddenly appearing young lady, "Where are we going?" and she answers, "Home, all the time."[11] Novalis's hero travels to faraway places and times simply in order to get home, to find himself through travel. So do many other heroes of books. An example in modern literature, for instance, can be found in Paolo Coelho's books.[12]

The Christian journey on earth is a linear journey that hopefully ends in Heaven. In that world view, with the certitude that there is no way back, we must strive to get far enough. However, Novalis and other travel writers often focus on the motif of *getting back home*. And as might be inferred from Mircea Eliade, traveling to get back home is rejoining the center of the world.[13] In the Christian tradition, do we not often say that we hope to get to Paradise? And is Paradise not also often synonymous with the Garden of Eden, where it all started? The circular model keeps popping up.

Why is this so? My answer is that traveling exists to reconnect us with the collective unconscious. To make this connection, we have to get on the road, we have to get to where we have projected our recognition. Whether we are "en route" or in place, once we have recovered the *anima mundi*, we are on our way back home. Thus the cycle begins. First, when we feel that our home is a void, we project a journey. Then, by exploring new places out in the world, we create the conditions for getting deeper into ourselves via the collective, through meeting the *anima mundi*.

Poetry is certainly the most concise and expressive means for catching our imagination and our hearts, so let me end with a beautiful poem that makes this central point. The poem is about Ithaka, the place we all associate with Ulysses, who longed for his island home. In this poem, by Constantin Cavafy, one of the great twentieth-century Greek poets, we are all Ulysses.

Ithaka

As you set out for Ithaka
hope your road is a long one,
full of adventure, full of discovery.
Laistrygonians, Cyclops,
angry Poseidon—don't be afraid of them:
you'll never find things like that one on your way
as long as you keep your thoughts raised high,
as long as a rare excitement
stirs your spirit and your body.
Laistrygonians, Cyclops,
wild Poseidon—you won't encounter them
unless you bring them along inside your soul,
unless your soul sets them up in front of you.

Hope your road is a long one.
May there be many summer mornings when,
with what pleasure, what joy,
you enter harbours you're seeing for the first time;
may you stop at Phoenician trading stations
to buy fine things,
mother of pearl and coral, amber and ebony,
sensual perfumes of every kind—
as many sensual perfumes as you can;
and may you visit many Egyptian cities
to learn and go on learning from their scholars.
Keep Ithaka always in your mind.
Arriving there is what you're destined for.
But don't hurry the journey at all.
Better if it lasts for years,
so you're old by the time you reach the island,
wealthy with all you've gained on the way,
not expecting Ithaka to make you rich.
Ithaka gave you the marvellous journey.

> Without her you wouldn't have set out.
> She has nothing left to give you now.
> And if you find her poor, Ithaka won't have fooled you.
> Wise as you will have become, so full of experience,
> you'll have understood by then what these Ithakas mean.[14]

So I conclude and try to bring my point home, although in less evocative words, by suggesting that Ithaka gave birth to projections, got us moving, and thus eventually brought us into contact with the *anima mundi,* became the treasure that might give meaning to our travel on earth. So when we feel an urge to travel, we had better get on the road. It is the call of our soul.

NOTES

1. Plato, *Timaeus,* 34b–37c, in *Dialogues of Plato,* translated by Benjamin Jowett (New York: Boni & Liveright, 1927); Marsilio Ficino, *Book of Life,* translated by Charles Boer (Woodstock, Conn.: Spring Publications, 1994), pp. 87–88.

2. Examples of such writing include Johann Wolfgang von Goethe, *Italian Journey (1786–1788),* translated by W. H. Auden and Elisabeth Mayer (London: Penguin Classics, 1992); Stendhal, *Rome, Naples, Florence,* translated by Richard Coe (New York: Braziller, 1960); D. H. Lawrence, *Mornings in Mexico* (1927; repr., London: Tauris Parke Paperbacks, 2009); and John Steinbeck, *Travels with Charley: In Search of America* (1962; London: Penguin Classics, 1997).

3. See Paul Theroux, *The Great Railway Bazaar* (Boston: Houghton Mifflin, 1975); and V. S. Naipaul, *Among the Believers: An Islamic Journey* (New York: Alfred Knopf, 1981).

4. See Bruce Chatwin, *The Songlines* (New York: Viking, 1987); and the contributions of Chatwin and other travel writers to issues of *Granta* in the late twentieth century, collected in *The Best of Granta Travel* (London: Granta Books, 1994).

5. "The attempt to take back soul from life outside deprives the outside of its 'within,' stuffing the person with subjective soulfulness and leaving the world a slagheap from which all projections, personifications, and psyche have been extracted." James Hillman, *Anima: An Anatomy of a Personified Notion* (Dallas, Tex.: Spring, 1985), p. 81.

6. James Hillman, "Anima Mundi: The Return of the Soul to the World," *Spring: A Journal of Archetype and Culture* (1982): 78.

7. Florence Bachetta, *En marche vers Compostelle: Un chemin de transformation* (Geneva: Éditions du Tricorne, 1994).

8. Hillman, "Anima Mundi," pp. 78–79.

9. "San Francisco (Be Sure to Wear Some Flowers in Your Hair)," words by John Phillips. First recorded by Scott McKenzie on *The Voice of Scott McKenzie,* Ode Records, 1967.

10. *"Bien des fois sur les routes de ma vie errante, je me suis demandée où j'allais et j'ai fini par comprendre, parmi les gens du peuple et chez les nomades, que je remontais aux sources de la vie."* Isabelle Eberhardt, *Un voyage oriental* (1904; repr., Paris: Livre de poche, 1991), p. 139.

11. Novalis, *Henri d'Ofterdingen,* translated by Palmer Hilty (Long Grove, Ill.: Waveland Press, 1990), p. 159.

12. For example, Paulo Coelho, *The Alchemist,* translated by Alan R. Clarke (New York: HarperCollins, 1993); and Paulo Coelho, *The Pilgrimage,* translated by Alan R. Clarke (New York: HarperCollins, 1992).

13. Mircea Eliade discusses the notions of circularity, linearity, and the center of the world with respect to space and time in *The Sacred and the Profane: The Nature of Religion,* translated by Willard R. Trask (Harcourt: Harcourt, Brace, 1959). See especially Chapter 1, "Sacred Space and Making the World Sacred," and Chapter 2, "Sacred Time and Myth."

14. *C. P. Cavafy: Collected Poems,* translated by Edmund Keeley and Phillip Sherrard, revised edition edited by George Savadis (1975; rev. ed., Princeton, N.J.: Princeton University Press, 1996), pp. 36–37.

WHO AM I?
INDIA, JUNG, AND ME

JÖRG RASCHE

> What we find in the life and teachings of Sri Ramana is the purest of India; with its breath of world-liberated and liberating humanity, it is the chant of millenniums.
> —C. G. Jung, 1938[1]

> I had a chance, when I was in Madras, to see the Maharshi, but by that time I was so imbued with the overwhelming Indian atmosphere of irrelevant wisdom and with the obvious Maya of this world that I didn't care anymore if there had been twelve Maharshis on top of each other.
> —C. G. Jung, 1947[2]

The Maharshi died in 1950, Jung in 1961. Jung visited India in 1937–1938. I had the chance to spend three weeks in India in November 2010. The journey was a deeply moving and

---

Jörg Rasche, M.D., is a child psychiatrist, Jungian analyst, and sandplay therapist in Berlin where he teaches at the Berlin Jung Institute. He has served as President of the German Jungian Association (DGAP) and as Vice President of the International Association of Analytical Psychology. Dr. Rasche is also a trained musician (organ, harpsichord, piano). His publications include books on mythology (*Prometheus*, 1988), sandplay therapy (1992), and music and analytical psychology (*The Song of the Green Lion: Music as a Mirror of the Soul*). He has published many clinical papers and performed Jungian concert-lectures around the world.

enriching experience, but it was also disturbing. I visited Tiruvannamalai, the place where Sri Ramana Maharshi lived. Sri Ramana is regarded as one of the most authentic contemporary saints of Indian culture. This journey became a challenge to me.

I was invited to an international conference titled "Science and the Spiritual Heritage of India" in Hyderabad, the capital of Andhra Pradesh in southern India. I was to give a Jungian dream workshop there. I am especially interested in parallels or differences between European and Indian approaches to the interpretation of symbols and experiences in dreams. To prepare for my trip I reread Jung's writings about his journey to India in 1937: "The Dreamlike World of India," "What India Can Teach Us," and "The Holy Men of India."[3] I had some doubts about whether Jung found what he was expecting in India. He was obviously overwhelmed by what he experienced there. In addition, he became ill, and at the end of his journey he was exhausted. This is why he decided not to visit the Maharshi. When I began my trip to India, I had no idea who the Maharshi was, but I was curious.

I didn't know how close India would come to me. To tell the story I want to begin with a review of my experiences in 2010.

Steps Going Down

For me, 2010 was a very rich year. But it was also a year of farewell and a year of thresholds. I saw many countries: I was in sunny Italy for conferences, in Switzerland, in Canada, in Kazakhstan. In Paris, I played the piano at an international amateur competition. I had my 60th birthday in June. But everything had a special touch of melancholy for me. The year before I had fallen down a staircase in my country house on the Baltic Sea; fortunately I did not break any bones, but the shock went deep. I began to understand how quickly our self-confidence or self-assertion can lose its fundaments, and with that loss, the loss of what we call reality. I began to walk more consciously, both because of the pain and to avoid any further falls. And I started to reflect that it might make more sense for me to go down stairs consciously than to crash down unwillingly.

In early summer my wife Beate and I went to Kazakhstan to visit the Jungian Developing Group there, for whom I am the liaison for the International Association for Analytical Psychology (IAAP). It was a fine reencounter with those kind people, who are so open to Jungian psychology and so interested in cultural exchange. We spent a wonderful time in a *jurta* in the green meadows of the Tien-Shan Mountains, the northern part of the Himalayas located on the border of the great steppes. When we returned to Europe I organized a farewell. My engagement to train Polish analysts in the use of sandplay had come to an end after over five years. I loved the work in Krakow and Warsaw and hope that one day I will be invited again. The farewell was like going down steps. I was calm about this transition: it would give me more time to play Chopin.

The proof of the wisdom of this attitude toward retirement came in August at the international conference of the IAAP in Montreal. I was vice-president of this large organization, and I had decided to run for the position of president-elect, as my colleagues and friends expected me to do. I was not so convinced about this move, though, and I ran for office mostly to ensure that the election would be a democratic one. I was not elected, and my friend Tom Kelly will be the next president of IAAP. I felt disappointed but I also felt released and set free: I told myself that I gotten back six years of my life (three years as president-elect and three as president). I also thought that in view of my limited organizational capacities and my addiction to music and writing, I had other contributions to give to the world. So I descended step by step from the Montreal stage very consciously. After the conference Beate and I visited our friend Horta van Hoye, an artist and sculptor who lives an hour north of Montreal in the countryside. When Horta emigrated from Belgium to Canada, the first thing she built on her new property was a chapel for meditation. The house and atelier came later. Horta congratulated me on my new freedom.

I had to renew this view of endings as new freedom in Italy at the Cortona conference of Eidgenössische Technische Hochschule Zürich (ETH Zürich) in September. It was the twenty-fifth anniversary of this one-week residential conference, held in one of the finest places in Tuscany. Prof. Luigi Luisi created this unique project to explore questions about "science and the wholeness of life." After twenty-four years of participating—almost from the beginning—I had to step down to make room for younger spirits. Cortona was a kind of Eranos conference for me. The major difference from Jung's Eranos meetings might be that in Cortona many students participate. So the Cortona week is not only an academy-like inner circle of senior people but also a school for young people who will carry the message to the future, as well as a place for asking fearless questions. I have met many excellent thinkers there, gifted students, wise men and women—and very good friends. But now this period of my life had ended, too.

A New Beginning

But there was also a beginning. In November the first Cortona-India took place. "Science and the Spiritual Heritage of India" was the theme. The conference was organized by my friend Luigi Luisi. It took place in Hyderabad (Andhra Pradesh) and was financed by ETH for about eighty students from India and Switzerland and twenty speakers and workshop leaders. I ran a one-week Jungian dream seminar, together with Beate.

The aim of Cortona-India is to create bridges between science and the humanities and between different cultures and continents. It is a new beginning. Luigi wants to start a new level of questioning and searching for important issues, research topics, and viewpoints for the future. The list of the speakers Luigi brought together for the first conference was impressive, and the conference fulfilled his vision of bringing together the wisdom of the Upanishads and the oldest traditions and rituals, knowledge about the ecological collapse, reports of the newest scientific developments, the experience of scientists and spiritual practitioners, and the enthusiasm of a new generation of students. I must say that I was very impressed by the skills of the young Indian people I met and their ability to connect their traditions with the newest scientific projects. The conference really transcended borders. In one of the discussions in the plenary an Indian student sang a prayer in his language as a contribution to a panel with Prof. Michel Bitbol (Sorbonne), Prof. Sangeetha Menon (National Institute of Advanced Studies, Bangalore), Brother David Steindl-Rast (Mount Saviour Monastery in New York State), Prof. Clifford Saron (Center for Mind and Brain, UCLA), Prof. Joseph Prabhu (California State University, Los Angeles), and Luigi Luisi. The panel was about human dignity and the question "Who am I?"[4]

The former president of India, Abdul Kalam, a scientist by origin, opened the conference with an inspiring speech. Bitbol presented a paper on "Schrödinger and the Upanishads" and what Schrödinger called his Second Schrödinger Equation. Schrödinger, an eminent scientist in the early years of quantum physics, said that "Atman equals Brahman"; by this he meant that the individual soul and the principle of creation are the same. Biologist Pushpa Mittra Bhargava and writer and sculptor Shakti Maira spoke about beauty in nature, art, science, and the "relational world." Mathematician Chandra Kant Raju spoke about the Indian origins of basic mathematical techniques such as calculus.[5] Economist Bernard Lietaer explained the need for a green "Marshall Plan" for a sustainable world. I was deeply impressed by Mani Bhaumik (UCLA), who told me about his childhood in one of the poorest regions in India, the time he spent as fourteen-year-old boy in the camp of Mahatma Gandhi near Tamluk in Bengal, his scientific work in physics and laser technology, and his insights about the divinity of the cosmos. He still feels blessed by what he learned from Gandhi, but this eminent man is still on his quest. He gave me his book *Code Name God*, which I highly recommend.[6] I also met and became friends with Vithal Rajan from Hyderabad, a scientist and peace activist who gave me his latest book, *Holmes of the Raj*, a novel about the adventures of Sherlock Holmes in India during the time of British occupation—a book full of funny moments and deep insights into the dynamics of colonialism and the fight for freedom and independence.[7]

Indian Dreams

The dream seminar I conducted was well received by both Indian and European participants. The differences between Indian and European dreams were not as deep as I had expected, but participants from these two cultures interpreted the meaning of dreams differently. In the Indian tradition, the texts of dreams seem to be regarded as more "objective" than in European traditions, with their tendency to look for a psychological meaning. One example was a recurrent dream from the childhood of an adult Indian man. He was a six-year-old boy when the dream first came to him. The colors of the dream images are washed out, as in old photographs. The dreaming boy saw the morning sun rising over the ocean and a sandy beach, but he couldn't go for a swim in the water, because a great lion stood between the dreamer and the sea. The lion looked like a dark silhouette that was looking to the right.

This dream was repeated often in those years of early childhood, but then it disappeared.

The associations of the dreamer led us the interpretation that the dream presented symbols of the time when he discovered his Ego at the age of six. The rising sun symbolized the morning of his conscious life, the ending of a twilight in his consciousness. Something hindered the boy from going back into the waters of unconsciousness, the ocean of childlike dreaming and having no responsibilities. The dangerous lion looking to the right, standing like a silhouette against the sun, reminded the dreamer suddenly of an important figure in earlier generations of his family: he remembered that one of his grandfathers was a Brahman and a priest in a temple of Narasimha, the Man-Lion. The Man-Lion is an avatar of Lord Vishnu, a half-lion, half-man who killed his antagonist in the twilight, not night, not day, not indoors, not outdoors (at the threshold), neither on earth nor in the sky (while lifting him from the ground). In Hindu tradition, Narasimha is the god who appears at the threshold, a bit like the Sphinx in ancient Egypt. Here a connection to the paternal line of family tradition was found to give the boy an orientation for his growing up and later life. With this imagery, his discovery of his Ego was linked back to the basic question "Who am I?"

With this dream at the Hyderabad workshop, I was reminded of my connection with the symbol of the threshold. I recalled that my first Jungian paper, which I wrote in 1986, had been about the Sphinx. I called it "Symbol at the Threshold: Origin and Development of the Sphinx Symbol."[8] I was still a trainee then, at the beginning of my career as a Jungian analyst. Now in 2010, in my sixties, I am facing a threshold again. Who am I now?

Another dream led us into the field of cultural complexes. A young Indian scientist told us about a recurrent dream of his childhood. The dream came back again recently when he started postgraduate study in Europe. In this dream he went to school in his Indian village on his bicycle, proud and happy and full of energy. When he entered the school building he looked down at his feet. To his shock he saw that he had no shoes on, that he was barefooted. With a flush of shame and fear he woke up.

Naked feet do have some connotations with exposing the body and with shame, but the meaning we found in that dream went deeper.

The dreamer told us that shoes were and still are an important obligatory part of the school uniform that was introduced by the British in India. If anyone came to school without shoes, he was beaten and punished. But the worst was the feeling of shame, the sense of nearly being killed by that shame. One felt absolutely worthless for shame, and there was no remedy.

We then began to talk about guilt and shame, about humiliation and the different patterns in our cultures. Traditional Indians had no shoes. Schoolboys wore their shoes proudly as an expression of progress. Their parents had no shoes, and the new habit alienated the children from tradition. And as we noted, it also alienated them from the earth. Western education was accompanied by a deep sense of humiliation. This feeling came back when the successful student went to Europe for his postgraduate study!

Indian Realities

By the time the conference ended, I thought I was well prepared for my encounter with Indian reality outside the five-star resort where the conference took place. It was my first visit to this country and this continent. The experience was and still is much stronger than I expected it would be. My first excursions into the city of Hyderabad were shocking—to see so many people, so many poor people, beggars, all those cows quietly standing or lying in the midst of busy traffic in the narrow streets, the many tuk-tuks (three-wheel taxis), the women in their beautiful saris (even the poorest ones), the schoolchildren with their white teeth and optimistic eyes. It was a tropical world of heat, dust, colorful Hindu temples, and majestic mosques. In the middle of a traffic jam, a beggar knocked on the window of our taxi with his arm; he had no hands. How do you give something to a beggar who has no hands?

Back home in our five-star resort I began to realize that India was going to be a challenge. You can't escape the heat or the many people, the noise, the social contradictions, the hot spicy Indian food. In addition, the lectures at the conference were very intensive and challenging. At one point, I was standing at a little well in the hotel gardens where some water was dropping from an antique statue into a basin. It was a magic moment. The view touched me and I felt how much I was longing for stillness and silence. Somehow I was thinking of Greece, an old fountain under a tree. The words came to me: I am a European, and I felt how glad I was to be European. And I felt an unexpected touch of homesickness.

An old friend and workshop leader at the conference, Hans Peter Siebler, recommended that we see Tiruvannamalai. At the time I was not aware that this was the place of the Maharshi, the Indian wise man whom Jung had avoided seeing. After the conference ended, Beate and I went for a journey to see a bit of India. We flew to Chennai (the former Madras) and spent several days in Mahabalipuram in the Gulf of Bengal. We visited the remains of the ancient harbor and the famous temples from the seventh century AD and were impressed by the height of the ocean waves. We were told that six years earlier, the Christmas tsunami had killed some people here but had also uncovered an ancient temple that had been buried in the sand of centuries. I also saw the huge bas-relief of Arjuna's Penance, showing a saga from the Mahabharata about the descent of the heavenly waters of Ganga, the sacred river Ganges, with the help of Lord Shiva. Arjuna's meditation and intense penance overcame the gods (although some say that it was Bhagiratha, not Arjuna, who did this). It was very hot this day. In the evening the sky became black.

The onset of the monsoon season and a strong cyclone the next day showed us a new side of India. Sometimes the water fell so densely from the dark sky that one could see nothing. It rained much more than in other years, and this rain was very unusual for the season. The palm trees were shaken by the storm. The meadows were flooded; the restaurant pavilion of our hotel became an island. When the rain stopped for a while all the paths in the village were wet and muddy. The sacred cows looked even more depressed than usual, and drenched people sat on wet heaps of clay or stones.

The next day we went by car to Tiruvannamalai. We passed through the poorest villages I have ever seen. I tried to distract myself from paying attention to the traffic: our driver, like all Indian drivers, drove where he wanted, on the left or the right side of the road, avoiding the deepest holes, overtaking other vehicles whenever he could (on both sides), often escaping head-on collisions with buses or painted trucks only in the last second but never touching any of the cows, bulls, dogs, or monkeys. Many of the huts I saw consisted only of wet clay floors and woven palm leaves that were rotting, and often the space between the huts was flooded. Nevertheless, the women everywhere wore their colorful saris with dignity. Once we passed a little house with some musicians playing drums in front of it. I asked our driver, who understood a bit of English, whether there was a wedding. He said no, somebody had died. I asked if the Hindu burn or bury their dead, and he answered: Burn. Then I asked: But if all the firewood is wet? His answer was: Tires. They use old tires to burn their people.

The Site of the Maharshi

So we came to Tiruvannamalai, the holy site of Sri Ramana Maharshi. The village is situated on a plateau at the foot of a mountain called Arunachala. Here Lord Shiva is said to have appeared as a column of fire on top of the rock. Every year, this event is celebrated with a huge fire on the peak of Arunachala in the form of a wick made of thousands of liters of ghee (clarified butter). The fire can be seen for thirty kilometers. Many thousands of pilgrims from all of southern

Figure 1: The author in front of Ramana Maharshi's cave, overlooking the Hindu temple at Tiruvannamalai.

India come to this event every year. It had taken place just two weeks before our arrival.

When we arrived, though, Tiru (as they call it) was suffering from the heavy rain. The shit of the cows had transformed the roads into muddy, slippery runs. We had to find our way to the hotel and to a restaurant we could trust. In the afternoon we went by tuk-tuk to the great temple in the center of the village. It is said to be one of the biggest Hindu temples in India. In contrast to the muddy village outside, the temple is like a city unto itself, surrounded by high and thick walls and protected by high white towers decorated with thousands of figures of the Hindu pantheon. We had to leave our shoes outside and walk barefoot. The vast open spaces of the temple city had stone floors but stood under water. We waded through the wide spaces and climbed stairs to smaller temples with colored statues of Shiva, Vishnu, Ganesh, and all the other gods, or "energies." In one hall there was a large live elephant who for a coin would bless people with his trunk. He wore the Om symbol on his forehead. Many people were waiting for the *puja* (service) in the holiest center. Monkeys played in the rafters overhead and aggressively tried to take away the belongings of the pilgrims. We were the only non-Indians among thousands of pilgrims, and everybody studied us with curiosity. We asked if, as non-Hindus, we would be allowed to enter the sacred center with the golden Shiva Lingam, and we were told that we could. We joined the queue. Standing in the long labyrinth-like corridor in the inner halls was like traveling back in time. A thousand people in the dark, many many candles, golden statues in the shimmery light, and painted mandalas on the floor everywhere. Groups of nearly naked young men with the Shiva emblem on their foreheads wore only black fabric around their hips and seemed to have come from far away and to regard this sanctuary as their own. They were Shivaists. Their aggressive behavior was a bit troubling, but nothing happened. I had heard that there is a quasi-fascistic Hindu movement in India, supported by a nationalist party that is hostile to Muslims and Christians, but what we saw in Tiru was just a group of young men dedicated to the male energy of Shiva. In the center of this temple we finally saw the golden Lingam of Shiva, expressing both the phallic creativity and the destructive aspect of Shiva energy. It is a great mystery. There is no creation without destruction.

I was reminded of Sabina Spielrein, Jung's patient and the first Jungian psychoanalyst, who wrote in the 1920s about destruction as a precondition for becoming.[9] Later on, after her return to Russia, she lost her license and her freedom to work in the Stalinist years. She was killed in 1942 by German Nazis who were inflated by the destructive side.

I had heavy dreams the following night. I was thinking of Sabina, Jung, the sad story of her death, and the power of archetypal images and energies. The next day we wanted to see the ashram of Ramana Maharshi—the wise man Jung had not visited.

C. G. Jung's Visit to India, 1937–1938

In his important early study about unconscious processes, *Symbols of Transformation* (1912), Jung had shown how deeply influenced he was by Indian culture and philosophy.[10] He developed the concepts of the Self as the center of the individual and the wholeness of reality from ancient Indian patterns of thinking. So he says with the words of a Chandogya-Upanishad:

> This soul of mine within the Heart is smaller than a grain of rice or barley-corn, or a mustard-seed, or a grain of millet, or the kernel of a grain of millet; this is my Self within my heart, greater than the earth, greater than the atmosphere, greater than the sky, greater than all these worlds. All works, all desires, all scents, all tastes belong to it: it encompasses all this universe, does not speak and has no care. This my Self within the heart is that Brahman.[11]

As Jung wrote, this paradox is the result of thousands of years of the human experience of the reality and nonreality of the psyche and of the introverted Indian tradition of philosophy. The emphasis of Western traditions on the rational individual is much more extraverted, and many westerners have difficulty with introspection. As Jung was well aware, in Western culture, there is also a pattern of unconsciously projecting one's shadow side onto people from other cultures. India's ancient culture and philosophy became a field of projection for Europeans who wanted to find what was missing in Europe. This is still true today.

In the 1930s, Indian culture and philosophy became central issues in the psychoanalysis of C. G. Jung and his circle. In 1933, the year the Nazis came to power in Germany, Jung was invited to the first Eranos Conference in Ascona, Switzerland. At this conference Indologists Heinrich Zimmer (Heidelberg) and Mrs. Rhys Davids (London) gave the main lectures, about Indian tantra yoga and Pali texts on Jhana (Dhyana) traditions. Jung himself spoke about what he called the individuation process—how to become who you are and how to integrate the shadow in your own psyche. The central question was "Who am I?" In the following years he drew many mandalas as healing expressions of the processes, imagination, and integration of his own unconscious. Mandalas became a means of creating and balancing his psyche. When *The Red Book* was published in 2010, a book that Jung wrote and illustrated in the years 1913 to 1917, we learned that Jung made his first mandala in those early years.[12]

In December 1937, Jung began his first and only trip to India. He was invited by the British Indian government to participate in the twenty-fifth anniversary celebration of the University of Calcutta. On that occasion, he received honorary doctorates from the universities of Allahabad, Benares, and Calcutta. He wrote about his impressions in two papers: "The Dreamlike World of India" and "What India Can Teach Us."[13] He also wrote "The Holy Men of India," where he stated: "Maybe I should have visited the Maharshi."[14] The question still remains why Jung did not go to Tiru when he was in Madras (now Chennai); Tiruvannamalai is only about 200 kilometers from Madras.

My ideas went in the following directions: One can ask why Jung was again so interested in Indian thought and religious practice in the years just before World War II. I think there are two reasons: the first is that analytical psychology in some of its basic patterns is in fact close to the thought of ancient Buddhism or even the Upanishads. The other reason might be found in the Zeitgeist and the growing threat of Nazism and the German psychosis. In the years after the disaster of World War I in Europe (1914–1918) there was great traumatic confusion in Germany and elsewhere that manifested itself in depression and a longing for direction. Mythology of every kind was in vogue. Jung was aware of the dangers of an unprepared encounter with mythology and the dangers of inflation. Then came Hitler and the German psychosis. In his 1936 text "Wotan," Jung compared some archetypes of the collective unconscious to the dry bed of a river that after a rain can immediately become swollen with stormy waters that destroy everything in their way.[15] The following year Jung went to India.

In those years, Jung was very concerned about the future of Europe. The invitation to visit India came at the right moment. Maybe it was a kind of flight from an ominous reality, or maybe Jung was looking for lost traditions of living archetypes, for sustaining psychological structures, or for a humanized mythology in the other culture. He said he was looking for "what India could tell us."[16] Nevertheless I can also imagine that while he was in India Jung needed to protect himself from the deep impressions and influences of the ancient and powerful culture of India and the social contrasts he saw. Jung was a thin-skinned introvert, and he was a European. I was thinking of my own experience with the dropping water in Hyderabad. At the end of his Indian trip he sometimes preferred to stay aboard the ship he was traveling on and read his European alchemical texts instead of making yet another foray on the continent.[17] It may seem that Jung was avoiding or repressing something that was too much for (or too close to) him.

Why Didn't Jung Visit the Maharshi?

The next day we went to visit the ashram where the Maharshi had lived. From the age of sixteen the sage spent most of his time in caves on Arunachala Mountain, and we climbed uphill along the sacred path to one of those caves. We had to go barefoot because this was sacred ground. The Maharshi took this same path when he went down to his ashram, where in later years he used to teach and supervise the kitchen for his many followers, afterward returning up the mountain for meditation. Our European feet were not accustomed to the uneven, slippery, sharp stones, and we learned something about European footwear in these four kilometers. I tried to imagine C. G. Jung on this path. When we arrived at the cave a horde of monkeys and some Indian women selling bananas were waiting for us. The two groups were a team; of course the monkeys got some bananas from us. In the cave we sat in front of the saint's seat in the rocks.

Back at the ashram we were surprised to find an article in the library about Jung and his missed visit when he was in India in 1937; its title is "Cold Feet."[18] The author, obviously a British psychiatrist who is very attached to the ideas of the Maharshi, argues that the intellectual

Jung may have avoided the encounter because he feared it could be too much for him and might threaten his inner balance. He writes: "Jung's understanding of the Self was only from an intellectual stance, not from one of experiencing the *atman,* 'the self,' through existence-consciousness-bliss (Sat Chit Ananda)."[19] He says that Jung was writing about himself when he made the observation in *Memories, Dreams, Reflections* that given the choice between going to heaven and talking about it, most people would prefer to talk about it.[20]

The author quotes from Jung's letter to G. H. Mees of September 1947, ten years after his trip to India, in which he sarcastically wrote: "I didn't care anymore if there were twelve Maharshis on top of each other."[21] In a biographical note, the author refers to Paul Brunton, the American writer who had visited Jung in Küßnacht in 1936 and spoken with him about India.[22] "Brunton narcissistically claimed that he was particularly spiritually advanced,"[23] and he may well have had a strong influence on Jung's decision not to visit Sri Ramana; in the years just before Jung's trip, Brunton had fallen out with the ashram, as Nimenko points out.

I don't think that this explains everything. Jung went to India following an invitation of the British colonial government and because his friend Heinrich Zimmer warmly encouraged him to do so and to see the Maharshi. The life and teachings of the Maharshi were about the Self. This must have deeply interested Jung.

Jung's text "The Holy Men of India" was originally written at this time; it was used after Heinrich Zimmer's death as an introduction to Zimmer's book about Sri Maharshi, *Der Weg zum Selbst* (The Way to the Self). Zimmer had told Jung a lot about the Maharshi.

In India, accompanied by Fowler McCormick, Jung saw many things as he traveled by train from Bombay via Allahabad to Calcutta. He visited many ancient sites and met many interesting people. Among them was the guru of the Maharaja of Mysore, whom Paul Brunton claimed as his new guru after he broke with Maharshi's ashram. It must have been an exhausting voyage, first by ship to Bombay, then by train and car through the subcontinent.

In Calcutta, the 62-year-old Jung became ill and had to spend ten days at a military hospital. This was a crisis, and later he reported the heavy and significant dreams he had in those days and nights. He saw the Holy Grail on the other side of the ocean and felt a strong desire to go back to Europe and to his own concerns and responsibilities. On the return journey, the harbor of Madras was the first stop after Calcutta. But for a convalescing Jung, the 200-kilometer distance from Madras to Tiruvannamalai on bad country roads in the heat would have been too much. I can easily imagine that Jung had seen enough of India to make the decision not to meet the Maharshi in Tiru. The travelers stopped in Colombo for a short rest and then went back to Europe.

MEDITATION AND POLITICS

The picture would not be complete if the historical context was missing. What was happening in India in the 1930s around the time of Jung's visit?

I am not an Indologist—I have tried to bring together what I found through research in the work of others. In Jung's writings about his Indian experiences, he mentions another, older Indian sage, Ramakrishna (1836—1886), who had lived as a priest of Kali in Bengal. Ramakrishna is famous for his deep devotion to his goddess. He often lost consciousness when adoring the Great Mother and went into *samadhi*. His teachings attracted many followers, who also adored Kali as an incarnation of Durga.

Ramakrishna and Ramana Maharshi (who was born one generation later) both would spontaneously fall into trance states of happiness. Ramakrishna had this experience for the first time when he was seven, when he saw white birds flying against the dark sky one day. The Marharshi's first experience of the feeling of "bliss," as he called it, happened when he was sixteen, when he had a near death-experience. He realized that only his body had died but not his soul (the Atman, or the Self). During decades of meditation in the caves of Mount Arunachala, he longed for and experienced this feeling of blessing again. In the ashram, he taught about the difference between ego and Self, about Self-realization, about the question "Who am I?" and about the loss of ego consciousness in the all-embracing consciousness of Brahma. These, one can say, are Jungian topics.

There were other streams of spirituality alive in India that Jung didn't mention in his writings. They were more connected to the political and social movements of those years. It was the time of India's fight for independence. There was a more philosophical tone in the work of the great poet and novelist Rabindranath Tagore (1861–1941) and poet and nationalist Sri Aurobindo (1872–1950). And the teachings of Mahatma Gandhi (1869–1948) were definitely political. All three had visited or studied in Europe.

Aurobindo, who was born in Bengal, had studied in London. After his religious conversion, he practiced yoga and integrated other traditions. He was politically active in the cause of Indian independence. Finally, after solitary confinement in prison for a year, he was freed, and in 1910 he fled to Pondicherry, a French enclave on the southern Indian shore to protect himself from British persecution. Despite his previous anticolonial political activism, Aurobindo supported the British and the Allies during World War II. Jung could easily have visited him in 1938 in Pondicherry, which is just the next harbor south of Madras. But this was French territory, and Jung, as we have seen, was not in good health.

In 1937, when Jung came to India, Mahatma Gandhi was one of the nation's most famous men, both a spiritual teacher and politician, a lawyer and a fighter for freedom. Gandhi had already achieved great success with his spinning campaign, which promoted the idea that everybody should spin his own cloth instead of buying British fabric. He had also organized the famous salt campaign in 1930 as a symbolic way to break the British salt monopoly. The colonial government put him in prison again and again, but he succeeded with nonviolent activities (Ahimsa), with fasting and the idea of humiliating himself so far that no enemy could humiliate him more deeply. (This is what Mani Bhaumik told me in Hyderabad.) Unfortunately, he could not convince members of the Indian National Congress to join forces with the Muslim League, and the British government promoted divisions in the Indian Independence Movement between Hindus and Muslims. The last viceroy of India, Lord Mountbatten, finally promoted the division of India itself and the founding of Pakistan as an Islamic nation. In 1947 the British left behind a broken subcontinent, and independence was overshadowed by waves of violence. Between 1 to 3 million people were killed, and about 10 million people had to leave their homes. In Kashmir, armed conflicts are still going on that dates to this time. I can imagine that Jung, as a guest of the British government, either tried to avoid or had no opportunity to come into contact with the revolutionary movements in India. But he must at least have felt the tensions.

I find it remarkable that in the very same years there were such different streams of thought and important teachers in India. The wise men of India knew about each other. Gandhi is said to have sometimes sent overworked friends, members of the Indian National Congress, to the Maharshi to find some peace: "Go and stay at Ramanasramam for a time."[24] He was in Tiru only once, for a political speech in the 1930s, but he didn't visit the Maharshi. Gandhi's companion, a leading Congress politician, Rajagopalachari, told the driver not to enter the ashram. Ramana later said he knew the reason: "Gandhi would like to come here but Rajagopalachari was worried about the consequences. Because he knows that Gandhi is an advanced soul, he fears that he might go into *samadhi* here and forget all about politics. That is why he gestured to the driver to drive on."[25] The Maharshi emphasized that everything is the Self and Brahman. Any attempt to change something would be the actions of the "I want" or "I-thought." But "correcting oneself is correcting the whole world. The sun is simply bright. It does not correct anyone. Because it shines the whole world is full of light. Transforming yourself is a means of giving light to the whole world."[26]

Marharshi compared his work with Gandhi's work: "Our business is to keep quiet. If we enter into all these [political activities], people will naturally ask, and justifiably, 'Why is he interfering in all these instead of keeping quiet?' Similarly if Mahatma Gandhi keeps quiet leaving aside all his activities, they will ask, 'Why is he keeping quiet instead of engaging in all these activities?' He must do what he has come for. We must do what we have come for."[27]

Arvind Sharma describes these different goals as follows:

> Both Mahatma Gandhi and Ramana Maharshi emphasized the fact that one must change oneself in order to change the world. ... Gandhi ... would have endorsed Albert Schweitzer's remark that "example is not the main thing, it is the only thing." ... This convergence however conceals the fact that while Mahatma Gandhi's basis of advocating self-reform was moral, that of Ramana Maharshi was metaphysical. Mahatma Gandhi released forces for bettering the world by setting an example through dedicated observance of truth and nonviolence. His reason for prioritizing reform of self over reform of the world was moral.

> Although Ramana Maharshi would probably agree on this point, his reason for advocating self-reform before setting out to reform the world was metaphysical. He believed that one was not in the world, the world was within oneself and so it is bound to change if one did. His position may be philosophically hard to digest but there is little doubt that he stood by it.[28]

I think that Gandhi had a strong metaphysical side and believed that he would influence and change the world directly by his fasting, nonviolent actions, and penance—like the old sage Arjuna in Hindu tradition who could even master and overcome the gods. But Gandhi also had a European education and was strongly influenced by the Christian ideas of Tolstoy. Although Tagore was initially enthusiastic about Gandhi, he later criticized him when his Tolstoyanism became clear and the Indian National Congress, which had begun as a Western-oriented organization, gained strong political power through the support of Hindu peasants and people of the lower castes.

Aurobindo, who was more European oriented, lived in exile in French Pondicherry in southern India, where he retired from politics. Compared with Gandhi and Aurobindo the Maharshi looks conservative, if not reactionary. He was certainly not interested in the kind of politics that sought to broker an agreement with Muslims. His Tiruvannamalai ashram is a truly Hindu place.

Obviously a movement that is as deep and as widespread as the independence movement of such a large population in such a large culture can give birth to many different streams. Such a movement will awaken the best and most powerful traditions of a culture. Introverted meditation in Tiru has its place there as well as the intelligent integrative yoga of Aurobindo or the spiritual wisdom and clever political activity of Mahatma Gandhi.

Jung and Gandhi? Closing the Circle

Jung's fascination with the spiritual heritage of India is sometimes interpreted as evidence of his disinterest in the political realities of his time. I do not think this is true. Jung was certainly an introverted intuitive, and he believed that the most important task was to work through the problems in the individual's psyche. In his *Red Book,* he worked through World War I on this internal level. He saw the individual psyche and the collective psyche as linked and complementary.[29] But Jung's behavior was much more complex. In his role as president of the International Psychoanalytical Association in 1910, his actions were clearly political, as they were again in 1933, when he was president of the International Medical Society for Psychotherapy. He tried to make arrangements with the Nazi government of Germany and burned his fingers. His reference to "Jewish psychology" in 1933–34 demonstrates that he was not conscious of the deadly political meaning of that racist terminology under Hitler.[30] The political situation in the early 1930s in Europe was confused. Jung has often been criticized for not making overt political statements against the dictatorship in Germany and the persecution of Jews, Sinti and Roma, homosexuals, and mentally ill and handicapped people. I think that in 1933–34 what the Germans were capable of was beyond Jung's imagination. Also, and this is not well known, after the establishment of fascism under Franco in Spain in 1936, there was an informal censorship in Switzerland. In addition, important officials were openly in favor of Franco and Hitler. All Western governments hoped that Hitler would fight Stalin and protect capitalism. Churchill himself said that time would tell whether Hitler would be one of the greatest Germans or one of the worst.[31] When the war began, everyone feared that the Germans would occupy Switzerland—another reason not to provoke Hitler.

Many dangerous collective complexes were activated during these years. In 1931, Churchill scornfully spoke of Gandhi as a "fakir."[32] Some months after his return from India, Jung gave his famous Knickerbocker interview, published as "Diagnosing the Dictators"(1938), in which he described Hitler as somebody who was driven by whisperings and voices.[33] After that, Jung was put on the Nazi blacklist. From 1942 on, Jung was involved in the intelligence services of the Allies with Allan Dulles from the U.S. Office of Strategic Services (which later became the CIA). Dulles said after the war that "nobody will probably ever know how much Professor Jung contributed to the Allied cause during the war, by seeing people who were connected somehow with the other side."[34] Unfortunately the documents about Jung's collaboration with Allan Dulles and the U.S. intelligence service have not been published.

In 1946, after the war, Churchill visited Switzerland, and when the Swiss government asked him who he would like to see, he put Jung first on the list. The meeting took place in Zurich. It is significant that Churchill regarded Jung as an important potential adviser after the war.[35] All of this raises many questions. To return to the Indian topic: Jung's emphasis on the "European way" and his warning about adopting "eastern meditation" is in principle complementary to the position of the Maharshi. Each followed the path of his own culture or what he thought his cultural heritage was. The Maharshi practiced and spoke about "realiz[ing] oneself as the Self of the whole universe." He must have had an impressive look about him; one biographer wrote that "the truth the sage has realized shines in him like the sun, in the light of which one may see things properly and thereby free oneself from worldly entanglements."[36] Jung did meditation too, but he always emphasized that he was an empirical scientist of the unconscious. His idea was "to eat the world" and to realize one's existence, to integrate one's dark sides, which is quite different from giving up the "I" for the Self. For Jung, the "Holy Grail" was different from meditation on the identity of Atman and Brahman. The Grail can be achieved only through compassion and only if one asks the wounded Fisher King the right question. The Upanishads teach of fate and say that our existence is an illusion, and if you follow the Bhagavad Gita you even have to kill your brother if Lord Krishna gives you a good explanation of why it is necessary.

Neither of these belief systems are political. I think that Jung did what he could in the political realm. It is not fair to criticize Jung for not being more like Gandhi, who was more successful in integrating Western and Eastern belief systems. Nevertheless, the Maharshi and Mahatma Gandhi, the "great soul," have something in common with C. G. Jung. It is said that Jung never gave a seminar about active imagination without telling the story of the rainmaker:

> There was a drought in a village in China. They sent for a rainmaker from far away. When he arrived he found the village in a miserable state. The cattle were dying, the vegetation was dying, and the people were affected. The people crowded around him and were curious what he would do. He said: "Give me a hut and leave me alone for a few days." So he went into his hut, and the people were wondering. One, two days passed. On the third day it started pouring rain and he came out. "What did you do?" they asked. "Oh", he said, "this is very simple. I didn't

do anything. . . . I come into your area and find that it is chaotic. The rhythm of life is disturbed, so when I come into it I, too, am disturbed. The whole thing affects me and I am immediately out of order. So what can I do? I want a little hut to be by myself, to meditate, to set myself straight. And then, when I am able to get myself in order, everything around is set right. We are now in Tao, and since the rain was missing, now it rains."[37]

One of Gandhi's famous sayings was "Be the change you want to see in the world." This is exactly the idea that Jung wanted to emphasize.

Although Gandhi was successful in achieving India's independence in 1947, he was not successful in keeping the country together. He couldn't prevent the subcontinent from falling apart, and he witnessed horrible massacres caused by conflict between Hindus and Muslims. Gandhi was able to stop the civil war for a short time by fasting in Delhi to protest the aggression between the two factions. He was killed by a Hindu fanatic because he had consented to the split between India and Pakistan. In the photos taken late in his life, he looks sad. He was opposed to the industrialization of India. Like Tolstoy, his hope for the future of his country rested with villages and rural traditions. Nehru, his friend and India's first prime minister, supported the development of an Indian middle class. India became what it is now, with all its contradictions. Gandhi is still an icon, but his ideas have lost their enlightening power. Today economists such as Bernard Lietaer (at Cortona-India) and Manmohan Singh, India's current prime minister, say that a new international Marshall Plan is needed to feed the poor, to protect natural resources, and to equalize social structures.

Jung did not have a political project, as Gandhi did. He was a psychiatrist who was devoted to his psychology and the quest for his own myth and the myth of mankind in his time. He was very concerned about destructive archetypal powers, about the dangers humans posed to the world in the form of the atom bomb. He became frustrated about his loss of influence and felt that he was being falsely accused of anti-Semitism. After the war, Jung retreated from politics and entered an enormously creative period. He became more and more the wise old man in his Bollingen retreat, chopping firewood like Tolstoy and meditating like an Indian *sadhu*. Alchemy was his main interest, in addition to working with his patients and his circle. He died at home in 1961, aged 86. His warning about the dangers of cultural inflation as the result of unconnected archetypal powers in the collective unconscious is as appropriate today as it was in the 1930s.

The more urgent a situation becomes, the stronger is the longing for help and clarity and the inclination to project shadow aspects of ourselves onto others. Are we more conscious than Jung? The pendulum swung wide for Jung, from his deep insights into the archetypal dynamics of the psyche and wisdom to total political naiveté, from altruism to opportunism, from supporting Zionism to anti-Semitism and collaboration with the Germans or the British. It would be fine if Jung was simply a wise old man with no shadows. When he insisted on the need to connect the "I" with the unconscious and the need to integrate shadows, he knew what he was talking about. He wanted to learn to see in the dark. In the global political darkness of his time, finding one's bearings was obviously very difficult. He studied the darkness in his own unconscious to "regain his soul," as he stated in *The Red Book*. I am not sure if he ever found the bright sun shining in him as the Maharshi did. He never gave up his "I" for the Self.

But what, then, about our situation today?

Steps Down?

From Tiru we went to Bangalore, the capital of Karnataka, now called Bungaluru, as it was before the British arrived. We visited Kusum Dhar Prabhu, the Jungian analyst, and the Jungian Developing Group at the Jung Center Bangalore. Again I gave a dream seminar, and as in Hyderabad I was impressed by the level of insight into psychodynamics and archetypal images based on Indian traditions and identities. I learned something about Shivaists and Vishnuists—followers of the cosmic energies of transformation (Shiva) and preservation (Vishnu). Both energies are essential. We also had an inspiring exchange between Hindus and Muslims in the Developing Group. I felt at home in this atmosphere of mutual interest and understanding.

Bungaluru is a city in transformation. There you will see highly modernized districts (such as the city's "cyber town") near traditional market streets and bourgeois residential neighborhoods. You will see a great deal of traffic, and you will see many many people, including Hindus and Muslims in traditional garb. You will see colorful Hindu temples with Nandis in front as well as solemn mosques. You will see many cows. And you will also see many poor districts and slums.

This fascinating city is full of contrasts. And the archaic India is still alive there. In a newspaper I read about a mother who had sacrificed her tongue to the goddess Kali for the sake of her son's marriage. Of course she died. Her action reminded me of Zimmer's text "The Indian World Mother" about the bloodthirsty Kali.[38] On the front page of this newspaper was a story of how French president Nicolas Sarkozy had just visited Bungaluru and had persuaded India to sign a contract to buy four French nuclear power stations for southern India. His demagogic argument: a country as important as India should no longer be left behind. Obviously he was manipulating an Indian inferiority complex. I was thinking of the dream of the barefoot student and the humiliation of the Indian culture from the dream seminar I held in Hyderabad. Thanks to Sarkozy, I was immediately back in the here and now. They were selling and building nuclear reactors in southern India!

Hadn't I felt like a European when I was in Hyderabad watching the dropping water? But Europe was playing a dangerous game in selling that technology to India. What about Chernobyl? And Bhopal? What shall India do with the nuclear waste from these plants? Isn't pursuing nuclear power a one-way street with no chance of return? What about responsibility for the shadow sides of industrialization? How can old India survive? Was the heavy rain in Mahalipuram, which came at the wrong time, a symptom of global warming and alterations in global thermodynamics? I thought of the catastrophic flood that had recently happened in Pakistan, and one that had happened some years ago in Bangladesh. I had seen impoverished people in front of their wet huts on my way to Tiru. Nuclear industry is not the answer; it is a big business that uses the most poisonous and toxic substances we know of. Will the Western loss of responsibility, the growing immorality never stop? I felt very concerned about India. This cannot be the only future that we can invent.

The question of fundamentalism came into my mind—isn't it a reaction to humiliation and losing one's roots? In an impressive article about her city, Kusum Dhar Prabhu says that the rise of Hindu fundamentalism can be regarded as an "expression of the unvoiced longing of many modern Indians to reconnect with their religious roots. Under the spell of secularism—which is indeed an archetype—we lose the sense that religion is an instinct in the human being. And no instinct can be neglected for long without consequences. Unless we address this longing in depth we will swing between religious fundamentalism and secular rootlessness."³⁹

Everything came into my mind. Gandhi and Tolstoy, Churchill, the Maharshi under the trees, Jung in Bollingen, the optimistic schoolchildren I saw in Hyderabad, and my own age. It was somehow too much for me—and as I am writing these lines, I am still striving to bring order to my mind.

Also the students of Cortona-India came into my mind, with their open faces and their courage and spirit in asking questions. Questions are always better than answers. I was thinking of the new green Marshall Plan, the need for a renewed morality in economics and politics, and the optimistic project of Luigi's Cortona-India to bring people of different cultures together. It was so good to have the chance to listen to and speak to the Indian people with mutual respect. It was also good to remember the many shadows of my European culture and especially the history of my own country, without fixing such memories in projections.

Finally, I am thinking about my own future. What can I do? What shall I do? Who am I? How can self-realization and politically action be connected?

NOTES

1. C. G. Jung, "Die träumende Welt Indiens" ["The Dreamlike World of India"] (1939), in *Civilization in Transition,* vol. 10 of *The Collected Works of C. G. Jung,* edited and translated by G. Adler and R. F. C. Hull (Princeton, N.J.: Princeton University Press, 1970).

2. C. G. Jung to G. H. Mees, 15 September 1947, in *C. G. Jung: Letters,* vol. 1, *1906–1950,* edited by Gerhard Adler and Aniele Jaffé, translated by R. F. C. Hull (Princeton, N.J.: Princeton University Press, 1973), p. 477.

3. Jung, "What India Can Teach Us" (1939), in *Civilization in Transition*; Jung, "The Holy Men of India" (1944), in *Psychology and Religion: West and East,* vol. 11 of *The Collected Works of C. G. Jung,* edited and translated by G. Adler and R. F. C. Hull (Princeton, N.J.: Princeton University Press, 1970).

4. For detailed information, see the website of Cortona-India 2010 at www.cortona-india.org.

5. C. K. Raju, *Is Science Western in Origin?* Dissenting Knowledges Pamphlet Series No. 8 (Penang, Malaysia: Multiversity and Citizens International, 2009).

6. Mani Bhaumik, *Code Name God: The Spiritual Journey of a Man of Science* (New Delhi: Penguin Books India, 2005).

7. Vithal Rajan, *Holmes of the Raj* (Uttar Pradesh: Random House India, 2010).

8. Jörg Rasche, "Die Sphinx—Symbol am Anfang" (Symbol at the Threshold: Origin and Development of the Sphinx Symbol), *Analytische Psychologie* 17, no. 2 (1986): 97–124.

9. Sabina Spielrein, "Die Destruktion als Ursache des Werdens," *Jahrbuch für psychoanalytische und psychopathologische Forschungen* 4 (1912): 465–503; translated into English as "Destruction as the Cause of Coming into Being," *Journal of Analytical Psychology* 39, no. 2 (1994): 155–186.

10. C. G. Jung, *Wandlungen und Symbole der Libido: Beiträge zur Entwicklungsgeschichte des Denkens* (Leipzig: Deuticke, 1912); first translated into English as C. G. Jung, *Psychology of the Unconscious: A Study of the Transformations and Symbolisms of the Libido*, translated by Beatrice Moses Hinkle (New York: Moffat, Yard, and Co., 1916). Later titled *Symbols of Transformation* and published as vol. 5 of *The Collected Works of C. G. Jung*.

11. *Chandogya Upanishad* 3.14.2–3.

12. C. G. Jung, *Das Rote Buch* (*The Red Book*), edited by Sonu Shamdasani, translated by Christian Hermes (Düsseldorf: Patmos, 2009; New York: W. W. Norton, 2010).

13. C. G. Jung, "The Dreamlike World of India"; C. G. Jung, "What India Can Teach Us," *Asia* 39, nos. 1–2 (1939), reprinted in *Civilization in Transition*.

14. C. G. Jung, "Über den Indischen Heiligen" ("The Holy Men of India"), originally published in Heinrich Zimmer, *Der Weg zum Selbst: Lehre u. Leben d. Shri Ramana Maharishi* (The Way to the Self: Life and Teachings of Sri Ramana Maharishi) (Zürich: Rascher, 1944). The quote is from the English-language publication in *Psychology and Religion: West and East*, § 952.

15. Jung, "Wotan," in *Civilization in Transition,* § 395.
16. Jung, "What India Can Teach Us," in *Civilization in Transition,* §§ 1002–1013.
17. C. G. Jung, *Erinnerungen Träume Gedanken* (Olten: Walter, 1984), p. 288; English version *Memories, Dreams, Reflections,* edited by Aniela Jaffé, translated by Richard and Clara Winston (New York: Vintage, 1989).
18. Wasyl Nimenko, "Cold Feet," *The Mountain Path* 47, no. 3 (2010): 41–51; and 47, no. 4 (2010): 69–76.
19. Nimenko, "Cold Feet," *The Mountain Path* 47, no. 3, p. 51.
20. Nimenko, "Cold Feet," *The Mountain Path* 47, no. 4, p. 71.
21. Jung to G. H. Mees, 15 September 1947.
22. Paul Brunton, *A Search in Secret India* (New York: E. P. Dutton, 1935).
23. Anthony Storr, *Feet of Clay: A Study of Gurus* (London: HarperCollins Publishers, 1996), p. 163, quoted in Nimenko, "Cold Feet," *The Mountain Path* 47, no. 4, p. 72.
24. David Godman, "Bhagavan and the Politics of His Day," p. 10, unpublished essay, available at http://davidgodman.org/rteach/rteach.shtml.
25. *Ibid.,* p. 9.
26. *Ibid.,* p. 3.
27. *Ibid.,* p. 15.
28. Arvind Sharma, *Ramana Maharshi: The Sage of Arunachala* (New Delhi: Penguin 2005), pp. 81–82.
29. Jung, *Das Rote Buch,* p. 240n103.
30. See, for example, Jung, "Geleitwort" (Preface), *Zentralblatt für Psychotherapie* 6 (1933): 139–140.
31. Deirdre Bair, *Jung: A Biography* (Boston: Little, Brown and Co., 2003; Munich: Knaus Verlag, 2005), p. 643 and note 107 of chapter 6; Allan W. Dulles, *Germany's Underground* (New York: Da Capo Press, 2000), p. 16.
32. Churchill said: "It is alarming and also nauseating to see Mr. Gandhi, a seditious Middle Temple lawyer, now posing as a *fakir* of the type well known in the East, striding half-naked up the steps of the viceregal palace, while he is still organising and conducting a defiant campaign of civil disobedience, to parlay on equal terms with the representative of the King-Emperor." Quoted in Winston Spencer

Churchill, *Never Give In! The Best of Winston Churchill's Speeches* (New York: Hyperion, 2003), p. 97.

33. See H. R. Knickerbocker, "Diagnosing the Dictators," *Hearst's International-Cosmopolitan,* January 1939; reprinted in *C. G. Jung Speaking: Interviews and Encounters,* edited by William McGuire and R. F. C. Hull (Princeton, N.J.: Princeton University Press, 1977), pp. 115–135.

34. Bair, *Jung,* pp. 493–494.

35. *Ibid.,* p. 520. Adolf Guggenbühl-Craig, who was present, recalls that Churchill's daughter had a long conversation with Jung at a dinner after the war. Churchill had wanted to sit next to Jung, but both men were too tired to engage in meaningful conversation.

36. Aksharajna (G. R. Subbaramayya), *Sri Ramana, the Sage of Arunagiri* (Tiruvannamalai: Sri Ramanasramam, 2010), p. 32.

37. Zeller 1982, quoted in Joan Chodorow, "Introduction," in *Jung on Active Imagination,* edited by Joan Chodorow (London: Routledge, 1997), p. 19.

38. Heinrich Zimmer, "The Indian World Mother" (1938), in *The Mystic Vision: Papers from the Eranos Yearbooks,* vol. 6, edited by Joseph Campbell, translated by Ralph Mannheim (Princeton, N.J.: Princeton University Press, 1968), pp. 70–102. Originally published as "Die indische Weltmutter."

39. Kusum Dhar Prabhu, "Whispers in a Bull's Ear: The Natural Soul of Bangalore," in *Psyche and the City,* edited by Thomas Singer (New Orleans: Spring Journal Books, 2010), p. 368.

SACRED TRAVEL, DIVINE TRAVELER

JULIE A. SGARZI

Now and again the siren call of Hermes—god of travelers—infuses body and heart, rendering us powerless to decline his summons. Wary of the irresistible temptation, a truculent refrain often echoes in the mind—*waste of time; too expensive; possibly dangerous; more important things to do; why go there.* That recalcitrant chorus, however, inevitably succumbs to an amorphous intuition that some soul-altering, heart-delighting opportunity beckons. An impulse to pack a bag, muster our courage, and surrender to the mysterious adventures hidden in some unknown or long-forgotten place finally obliterates the fear and the ever-present obstacles. Hermes has called us to his journey, and if we are wise enough to follow, unimagined possibilities await the divinely bidden traveler.

What propels someone to travel to faraway places and into unfamiliar cultures? How might travel serve soul and psyche, and what archetypal urge lures us to such adventures? These questions feed the heart of a pilgrim. Such hermetic calls, seemingly spontaneous and

---

Julie A. Sgarzi, Ph.D., holds a doctorate in depth psychology and currently writes and lectures on cultural issues from a depth psychological perspective. She is a member of the board of directors of the Philemon Foundation.

surprising to our conscious minds, are often blessings that expand unconscious fissures in our defenses, frequently reflecting deeper spiritual and psychological imperatives. Undertaken in response to Hermes' invitation, an excursion becomes a sacred, soul-filled journey, and a tourist becomes a pilgrim. Shortly before leaving for India, a woman dreamed that a trickster figure asked if she knew the difference between a tourist and a pilgrim. When she struggled with the question, the dream figure replied: "A pilgrim returns from the journey as someone else."[1] When we travel as pilgrim or sacred wanderer, any outer adventure will inevitably catalyze a transforming inner journey. In what ways heart and soul will transform, however, remains the mystery embedded in every journey imagined by Hermes and undertaken with an open heart. When we are compelled to explore an unknown continent or are invited into alien cultures and traditions, a rare opportunity awaits, though such expeditions are not necessarily free from inner or outer peril and certainly are not for the faint of heart— or soul. The word *travel* itself hints at danger and peril, having evolved from the French *travail,* which long ago in its etymological lineage described a tool of medieval torture. Travelers, beware!

    The traveler is an archetypal character alive in everyone, enticing us into the larger world with an eye toward discovery, connection, and transformation. The ancients wisely understood this universal impulse and the attendant need for protection and guidance through the challenges inherent in our inevitable wanderings. Hermes guides, protects, and often tricks us onto the necessary paths of our lives. He invites us as a wanderer to shed our well-honed persona and to relinquish habitual encumbrances that inhibit us from meeting others and ourselves honestly with fully opened eyes. As the traveler's customary persona wanes, he or she is free to discover dormant passions or witness shadowy impulses appearing as unconscious prejudices or vicious judgments manifesting in a desperate attempt to gain control or maintain a feeling of superiority in alien surroundings. We vainly cling to the illusion that our habitual ways of navigating the world are superior, only to discover their complete inadequacy when facing the realities of the utterly foreign. A voice, perhaps rooted in fear or ignorance, may pontificate that unusual expressions of worship or social structure are inferior. Another bemoans the lack of Western comforts or the strangeness of smells and sounds. Confronting such judgmental reflexes rattles an ordinary sense of self, bringing us face to face with the depths of our personal and cultural shadow.

The idea of the Indian caste system, for example, was unquestionably abhorrent to me, yet while I was traveling in India, many Indians explained that the erosion of the traditional caste system left dangerous holes in the safety net of their society. Caste, for all of its limitations and atrocities, also serves as a kind of extended clan providing some semblance of protection during the hardest times, frequently functioning as labor union, community association, or absent family. As my reflexive judgments subsided, I glimpsed a different understanding witnessed from a wholly foreign vantage point—an alternate reality grounded in centuries that is slowly adapting to the shifting ground of a rapidly evolving society. One irony of the interaction among the traditional castes struck me as particularly curious. The untouchables, the lowest of the castes, are the traditional attendants at funeral pyres, maintaining the holy flame essential for the cremation ritual. At this inevitable and pivotal moment of death, even the highest-caste Brahmin must bow humbly to the "untouchable" attendant, requesting the sacred flame needed to initiate the cremation. There is some divine symmetry in such a system that is perhaps beyond our easy understanding.

Being physically present in alien cultures provokes experiences and emotions that we can easily avoid by remaining comfortably ensconced in the familiar. On a sacred journey, we are invited to confront our deepest feelings and reactions, to explore the roots of our assumptions and responses. Standing on a hilltop in a small village in northern India, I looked down on a gathering crowd of villagers. The scene was extremely animated: several people shouted while racing back and forth between what seemed like opposing camps. An elder navigated among the participants and spectators with the grace of a conductor leading a slightly unruly orchestra. I inquired about the scene and was told that it was a village process, perhaps resolving a quarrel among neighbors, between family members, or among differing village viewpoints. There was no judge or jury, no lengthy litigation; instead, they were engaged in a community practice for airing and resolving grievances that brought family, neighbors, and elders together to collectively craft an acceptable resolution. The process well suited the needs of this village. While a judgmental Western mind might condescendingly think it quaint or primitive, the process was extremely effective and brought immediate closure. I found myself envying the immediacy of the ritual and respecting a solution so clearly derived from the particularity and context of the issue, uncomplicated by needless formality or abstraction. Might the West learn something from this local tradition instead of habitually escalating issues into legal and even criminal proceedings? I read recently that a six-year-old in the States was arrested on a felony charge of assault. The little girl had had a tantrum in school; she had become disruptive and shouted and flailed at all who approached her until she was forcefully subdued and arrested by local police. A conclave of respected community elders and peers might have effectively explicated the problem and resolved the issue more compassionately than handcuffing and criminally charging a distraught child. Perhaps our "superior" system of justice needs to regain a bit of its humanity as modeled in the village wisdom of other cultures.

Pico Iyer, renowned traveler and author, once remarked in conversation that travel is an exercise in vulnerability.[2] How true, and how fortunate to experience our vulnerability, escaping for a moment the habitual bonds and protective coverings we instinctively hide behind. As travelers, we encounter an imperative to escape familiar definitions of self, experiencing in its place openness, warmth, compassion, and discovery of every kind. While it is not always easy, the vulnerable posture of the traveler facilitates awakening in its own peculiar way. When lost or disoriented while traveling, we have a chance to investigate what arises from that particular vulnerability. While caution is prudent, we also have an occasion to welcome assistance that might surprise and delight. Sometimes a pilgrim encounters Baucis, the character in Greek myth who extends extraordinary generosity to travelers and strangers. On a path in Thimphu, the capital city of Bhutan, I was startled by a young voice behind me reciting her refrain in proper English: "Good morning madam. It is a very lovely day." I turned and met the radiant eyes of a beautiful little girl—Baucis as a child, perhaps—eager to greet a westerner with her newly learned phrases. We spoke for a bit and I asked if she would direct me to the local marketplace. Not only could she direct me, she eagerly escorted me. Interested in my clothes and my camera, filled with curiosity and questions, she nestled close by my side, with her giggling companions trailing behind us on the path. As we approached the market, the young girl offered to bargain on my behalf, explaining that I would receive a fair price only if she assisted me. She was undoubtedly absolutely correct. We shared an exquisite and memorable afternoon together as a result of her few words of English and my willingness to surrender to the innocence and excitement of a child. Such gestures of hospitality are precious gifts that soothe the vulnerable wanderer, warm the heart, and open the mind. My affection for the Bhutanese people lives on in memories embodied in the image of that young girl.

Travel, especially sacred travel, offers rewards unequaled by any other form of inquiry or investigation. While we can appreciate images on television or research a place on the Internet, the map is never the territory and the Web is hardly the experience. The map and the Web offer tools that must be employed skillfully to enhance but not interfere with actual experience. We risk fixing expectations too rigidly or delineating our path too literally, leaving little opportunity for the mystery inherent in the foreign to lead us forward. Particularly now, when sound bites and 30-second visual glimpses form our impressions of other peoples and cultures, the hermetic call to visit old and new places in person—as an embodied witness—is essential for awakening an authentic relationship with the unknown other. Travel is not a decadent privilege but a worthy mission, particularly if we depart, explore, and return as one on a sacred assignment. We convey a more individual experience of being American and in turn bring back a human and storied understanding of places, cultures, and traditions far different from our own. Such encounters are essential in this time of global interdependence, shared planetary challenges, and the tendency toward sweeping collective judgments about cultures we do not understand. American students (and many adults) know little geography, demonstrating only modest awareness of the 192 independent countries that exist outside the United States. When we arrive in any of these places with the heart of a pilgrim and the soul of a vulnerable traveler, our impressions and interactions create living relationships. The place and its people awaken something in consciousness and a natural curiosity ensues, expanding the traveler's world and enlivening our shared human interconnections. After visiting the Himalayas, Indonesia, Argentina, Turkey, China, and India, for example, I am decidedly more attentive to the political, environmental, and social reports emanating from those regions. Each transformed from an abstract shape on a globe, reanimating as living, storied experiences that are now part of me and for which I must hold some accountability. They are no longer wholly other but are entwined in cellular memory, experience, and imagination.

The impact of travel rests, in part, in the inherent opportunity to remain present and engaged in each unfolding moment; in fact, it is necessary. In the ordinary routines of life, we function easily in a sort of disengaged momentum on automatic pilot, oblivious to the preciousness and sensory richness of each individual moment. The scent of orange blossoms is lost among the daily duties of work and family. An intuition that lingers in the background of experience is drowned out by the actions and decisions demanded of us. The familiarity of our habitual life offers solace, but it masks treasures that live within the ordinary and leap out as bas-relief when experienced in the slightly altered state of the wanderer. Travel's power to unsettle and transform derives in part from its constant reminder that we are always both present and visible. When we are in our familiar routines and persona, we slip into invisibility, but when we wander in foreign cultures, we are conspicuously visible all of the time. Our presence is mirrored in every stare and curious interaction. We seem taller, louder, and more awkward in unaccustomed surroundings. People stand too close or smells are more intense. Familiar rules of engagement do not apply in India, China, Bhutan, Turkey, or Tibet or the inner cities of our own countries. Attempting to impose a familiar order in India or Nepal inevitably causes suffering; Western logic fails and some more mysterious pattern emerges that is perfectly suited to the immediate surroundings. One morning, a group of traveling companions and I arrived at the main station in Delhi to catch a train for the far northern Indian state of Himachal Pradesh. Western logic had us searching for a cart to haul our bags and the proper queue for boarding the train. In minutes, however, we realized that such expectations were futile amid the dense sea of people rushing in every direction. Finding the right train felt impossible; signs were confusing and sometimes contradictory. Few people—and certainly fewer westerners—shuttled their own bags on carts. A small group of men suddenly appeared unbidden, immediately stacking our suitcases on their shoulders and heads, rushing off with us trailing behind like baby geese trying to keep up with the flock. The maze of signs would never have led an unfamiliar westerner to the proper platform, but these strong young and old men parted an ocean of travelers so that we could follow relatively unimpeded, and we eventually arrived at the correct departure platform. Only later did we recognize their colorful head wraps as identifying the trustworthy porters who could safely snatch your bags, disappear, and reappear at the proper spot without incident. Their bodies morphed into extraordinary machines as we marveled at the acrobatic moves and strength of these hard-working men who each carried six and seven huge bags at one time. We safely arrived at a dark departure platform just before dawn, gratefully paid the meager fee for their service, and waited among the meandering cows and departing passengers until our train finally arrived out of the dark morning mist. The simple task of boarding a train had become a true cultural indoctrination. No guidebook could explain the logic of a Delhi train station at dawn or the economic need for people to perform chores we expect to do for ourselves. No Internet photo could convey the density of people and the symphony of sounds possible in a predawn Delhi morning or capture the surprising realization that you shared a platform with a drowsy cow emerging from the darkness. This persistent interaction with the unfamiliar generates vitality in being seen and in seeing, in being heard and hearing in surprisingly new ways. All the senses awaken, shedding new light on everything in our path. The reciprocity of connection with the place itself and the interconnection with strangers emerges more easily when we surrender as a pilgrim to the innate power of the journey and the mystery of place.

I spent a month wandering the villages of Bhutan in late 1983 with a small group of westerners, studying Buddhist traditions and meditation along the way, marveling at the timeless dimension of life in the Himalayas. There were few Americans or Europeans in Bhutan at that time, making us as intriguing to the Bhutanese as they were to us. Together we meandered centuries-old mountain trails newly transformed into a national road, although barely able to accommodate a single Jeep or truck. Our journey into the interior ended where the road stopped. Today the road penetrates a bit further, but in that year long ago, I felt as though we were test pilots for an extravagant undertaking—modern access into the mystical interior of a timeless kingdom. We slept in tents, creating makeshift communities each night. Our dinner was fished from a stream or bartered for in whatever village we came upon. Our guides were comfortable among the fields and forests that remained magical mysteries to me. However, they were far less confident about the automobiles and roads we took for granted. We were a great curiosity to the Bhutanese, laden as we were with cameras, clothes, and stories that were so unfamiliar to them. Our conversations and inquiries of one another brought laughs and great joy as we explored our differences and commonalities. When a vehicle in our caravan failed to arrive at the evening's campsite, we inquired about the missing crew and were reluctantly told that their Jeep had gone off the road, falling into one of the steep ravines that lined the serpentine roadway. They assured us that all aboard were fine, awaiting rescue by another truck being sent from the capital city many hours away. Our Bhutanese companions were not uncaring but rather lived every day in the precarious proximity of life and death, birth and rebirth. I still wonder about the fate of those young guides on that perilous mountain road, but life pushed on, with us in tow.

Yaks grazed unfazed. Monks chanted as ceremonial long horns sounded the beginning of rituals honored in enduring tradition. Men carried huge planks strapped across their backs appearing like walking crucifixes en route to a construction project at the *dzong,* or monastery, nearby. Spectacular carvings adorned old buildings and the spiritual aura of their Buddhist lineage wove seamlessly throughout daily life. Magnificent birds flew overhead, and I imagined that one carried a silk scarf as in the old Buddhist story, gently wearing away the world's highest mountains as it flew past. As legend explains, when at last the mountain was worn away after innumerable flights and caresses of the silk across the summit, then one *kulpa,* or "immeasurable," would have passed. This is a spiritual measure of time, an eternity of the soul and a dimension of time long forgotten by the modern world but remembered in these places and by the earth herself. Today, Bhutan is a nation that measures its well-being not by gross national product but by "gross national happiness," the nation's attempt to meet the changing needs of their world with a collective recollection of its origins as a deeply spiritual community. As Bhutan slowly modernizes its economy and government, I pray that the nation will not abandon the essential qualities that were so palpable to me twenty-five years ago. I was deeply touched by the lives of the people I encountered there, who so joyfully entwined soul and spirit, heart and mind in a sacred dance of place and person, even amid the harshest demands of physical labor and daily survival.

Sometimes we discover a magical connection with a place or culture that strikes as wildly as love at first sight or as sweetly as the familiar sense of homecoming. I was startled during this first visit to Bhutan to realize that this utterly foreign place felt extraordinarily familiar, as though I had found my soul's home in the most unknown place I had ever imagined. Food tasted familiar and the red chilies drying on the rooftops felt like home. Dark monasteries filled with yak-butter lamps and sounds of pious chanting all felt a part of me. Sometimes tears filled my eyes for no apparent reason, save a sense of reverence. Notions of a past life arose as a way to contain the pervasive sense of already "knowing" this land and culture. How else could it be explained? Perhaps more simply, I felt the experience of true connection recognized in both body and psyche. Leaving Bhutan was difficult, as though I were leaving home, uncertain as to when—or if—I would return.

It is said that Martin Buber once remarked, "Every journey has a secret destination of which the traveler is unaware." Our intended destination lies only on the surface of the journey, and the pilgrim must plumb the depths to discover the journey's secret destination. Bhutan was my conscious destination, but my discovery of an ethereal ancestral homecoming was the secret revealed in an immediate, deep, and transforming connection with a tradition and culture that was an unexpected gift. I had no inkling that this visit and the experiences of these people and places would shape the foundation of my life and initiate a lifelong Buddhist practice. Those surprises were never anticipated and never intended, but they emerged as one of the transforming sacred realities of the journey.

Leaving Bhutan, I continued on to Nepal, trekking the foothills of the Himalayas, where still other mysteries awaited. An extended family of sherpas, from a village high in the Everest region that was three days' walk from our starting point, lovingly guided and supported our group of five trekkers. The crew of men, women, and young boys had already walked a distance nearly equal to our anticipated trek, arriving to work our eleven-day trip because each would earn enough to support their family for that entire winter. Each of these wonderful individuals became like family to us as we walked, cooked, ate, slept, and wandered together through villages and across mountain passes. Language mattered little as smiles, eyes, and songs became the currency of conversation. One freezing night, high on a Hindu pilgrimage trail in Nepal's Gosainkunda Lakes region, my fragility and vulnerability enabled me to receive a truly mystical gift. It was bitter cold with air so thin that breathing was difficult. I could sleep or breathe but not both at the same time, it seemed. Late at night, cold and a bit frightened by the altitude, I wandered from my tent to the small hut where the crew spent their nights. I was reluctant to intrude upon their privacy, but the warmth of their fire was irresistible. I tentatively approached the gathering of women sherpas seated on the dirt floor of the hut, aware of the curious stares of the men sitting nearby at their own fire. Perhaps they wondered why I had left the privacy of my tent and the warmth of my sleeping bag to come into their small communal compound with no doors and only thin blankets to protect them from the night's bitter cold. Without hesitation, the women eagerly drew me into their circle and nestled me among them, shoulder to shoulder and thigh to thigh, as they continued chattering in sounds that were unintelligible to me, yet somehow viscerally understood. Their eyes sang and the cadence of their words revealed stories and questions. One young woman took my hands in hers, smiling as she felt the softness of my skin in contrast to her own rugged, hard-working hands. I felt the earth in her fingers and inklings of experience vastly different from my own. Maybe she wondered where my hands grew up, so pampered and protected from the elements, able to remain soft for one as old as I. She also felt the frigid, icy flesh that I tried unsuccessfully to warm with my breath. As she looked deeply into my eyes, she spoke to her sisters around the fire. Without missing a beat of conversation, they each took turns thrusting their own hands into the flames of their fire and then cradling my wrists in their hot palms. This generous gesture sent warm currents throughout my body with every pulse. I was thawing in their midst as they took me into their hearts without pause or question. I was cold in a place where being that cold was dangerous. Without judgment, each responded with wisdom and unselfconscious generosity. I was among them now, feeling the warmth of their lives mingle with the pulsing flow of my own blood. It was a mysterious gift that initiated me into my place among these magnificent women of the mountains. I felt totally embraced—a part of something eternal, wise, and feminine as blessings passed from flame to hand to heart. Tears filled my eyes and we met one another fully, oblivious to any need for words.

In the morning, a wandering *sadhu,* or Indian holy man, came to speak with us. He was curious about who we were, just as we were eager to understand how this bearded traveler had come to rest at the pristine mountain lakes. He was young, well-educated, and fluent in English and he welcomed conversation. He asked what had brought us to this place and why we intended to cross the high, snow-covered mountain pass ahead of us. We spoke of curiosity and a desire to see the mountains of Nepal, explaining how we had come to be on a Hindu pilgrimage trail where we admired the impromptu creations of small rock stupas and the remains of sacred puja offerings along the way. We were passing through on our way to other villages, eventually planning to return to Katmandu and then to homes in the West. He, on the other hand, was simply walking. He had no particular destination and no timetable. No one awaited his arrival or celebrated his departure. He had been at these holy lakes for several weeks and would remain until a spirit called him forth to resume walking, whenever that might be. He had grown up in an Indian city but had long ago abandoned his privileged urban life to become a spiritual pilgrim. I admired his choice to relinquish his world to undertake the uncertain path of seeker. In some curious way, I realized that I too had undertaken something similar when I departed for Bhutan and Nepal. I was ignorant about both countries, yet something compelled me to join a small group of strangers to explore places and cultures that were utterly foreign and had only recently opened to Western travelers. I didn't understand exactly what had prompted my actions or what unseen force had guided me to this place, but I recognized that Bhutan and its people had changed my life forever. It had become a pilgrimage of the heart, truly a sacred journey.

Sadly, many travelers shun the mystery and archetypal significance of departure, exploration, and return that structures a true journey. If we travel only as an anonymous salesman or an American tourist, we likely avoid the promise and peril of pilgrimage, rife with its internal and external risks. Traveling as a pilgrim or seeker is a far richer experience. Whether consciously structured as pilgrimage or not, travel is most rewarding when undertaken with the attitude of a pilgrim rather than that of a tourist. Jung warned about traveling as a tourist, which he believed stole the soul from the places and people one visited. In contrast, when we travel as a pilgrim, our intention is to receive places and their people without perpetrating a theft, instead meeting them with humility and generosity. The attitude of pilgrimage recognizes a sacred domain where the heart and mind open as if in prayerful dialogue with all that arises and constellates as our experience. When travel becomes sacred, something magical transpires.

How we understand two related themes—*intention* and *attention*—also informs a pilgrimage or sacred journey. Our intention reflects the plans and purpose we imagine when we embark on an expedition. Intention establishes the ground of our relationship to an activity or thought, carrying within it much of the meaning of experience. Intention also provides the basis of karmic patterning, deeply imprinting the quality of our experience. If our intention is to explore with the eyes and heart of a pilgrim, then even a visit to a favorite park can open in unexpected ways. Yosemite National Park has always been a beloved escape for me. One time I returned to the park with the expressed intention of meeting the natural surroundings in a new way, as if seeing them for the first time. I went alone, hiking in the early morning and stopping often to sit among the fields and trees. The deer in the valley meadows came alive in an exceptional way on that visit. I listened more carefully and tried to see more deeply into the eyes of the doe that grazed just feet from me. She and I stared at each other for a long, quiet time and I recognized an understanding revealed in the soft auburn eyes that fearlessly met mine. We were curious about and accepting of each other. Later, when a rockslide trapped a group of us on a trail, I discovered a different relationship to that familiar mountain and was humbled by its sheer power and unpredictability. Had my intention been solely that of tourist, I might have been annoyed by the delays in returning from that hike up Yosemite Falls or might have simply snapped a photo of the deer in the meadow without stopping to look eye to eye for many minutes. The experiences on this particular visit were palpable and transforming. I remember it more clearly than many of the innumerable visits that preceded it. Something in me shifted, and my relationship to Yosemite changed in ways that enriched and enlivened the complexity of my connection to that place.

Intention, however, is not merely the province of ego consciousness. Psyche and the unconscious also express intentions that appear in the shadows, sometimes shocking us awake with unexpected emotions and responses. Paying attention to when and how these unbidden forces appear helps maintain the spirit of pilgrimage. Whether a great fear arises at some unexpected moment or a deeply felt intuition leads you around a corner to meet the unknown in a café or a bookstore, attend the messages or understandings inherent in these surprising moments. They too are sacred gifts. While in Katmandu preparing to depart for the Gosainkunda trek, I was suddenly overcome by a tremendous fear and a feeling that I was very ill. I went to bed for two days, yet somehow I realized that what had befallen me was not a physical illness but a terror that anticipated something very important and totally beyond my control. I felt that I might die yet knew that I must undertake the trek. After many hours lying in bed gripped by my own fears, I felt a sense of ease return, a kind of resignation that while something might truly die on the coming trek, I was safe nonetheless. It was imperative that I make the trip. The fear was not a premonition of personal danger but an intuition of the transformative power of the journey ahead. Something would in fact die off—a nagging sense of defeat or insufficiency—replaced by a tremendous sense of accomplishment and an ability to embrace a part of my own nature that I had never fully engaged. A momentous psychic shift emerged during that trek that both strengthened and softened my heart simultaneously.

Attention, which is different from intention, connotes the mental focus or concentration that allows us to notice and attend to what arises. It is impossible to maintain complete attention when our minds wander. When we pay attention, we selectively chose from the innumerable perceptions flying around all the time. Jung noted that consciousness by its very nature is limited:

> The world of consciousness is inevitably a world full of restrictions, of walls blocking the way.... No consciousness can harbour more than a very small number of simultaneous perceptions. All else must lie in shadow, withdrawn from sight.... We owe our general orientation simply and solely to the fact that through attention we are able to register a fairly rapid succession of images. But attention is an effort of which

> we are not capable all the time. We have to make do, so to speak, with a minimum of simultaneous perceptions and succession of images.³

Jung further explains that in the unconscious lies the potential of "total vision"; this is where all perceptions of consciousness and the unconscious coexist *in potentia*.

When we are on a journey guided by the eyes and heart of a pilgrim, the hope is that we will broaden our attention to notice and ingest as many perceptions and impressions as possible. I believe this requires us to cultivate a particular type of attention that we do not usually use in our habitual ways of seeing. Jung appropriated French psychologist Pierre Janet's term for this mode of attention, *abaissement du nuveau mental,* or the relaxation of the ego's focus, allowing a softer, more creative eye to emerge. The *abaissement* is like the twilight time just before we drift off to sleep, when we are neither wholly conscious nor unconscious. It is a rich space of mind where we are present and yet also receptive to other dimensions of perception. This mode of focus resembles a waking dream, a liminal space of awareness where attention is diffused and alive. Psyche is permeable, offering insights from beyond the narrow range of ego, while ego consciousness is simultaneously participating fully though not fully in control. Attention or awareness held in this manner invites the unknown, using unconscious tools of perception to contribute to our understanding of experience. If we attempt to rationally order the incongruous elements experienced in an alien environment, we will be battered, in constant conflict with the surroundings. If, on the other hand, we can drift in a participatory state as in a waking dream, accepting the inexplicable happenings without worrying about their logic, a truer, more meaningful understanding emerges. Later, as with a dream, the images and elements can be digested and appreciated with reflection and awe.

Traveling in India offered me a perfect illustration of the need to broaden our field of perception, opening the attention to innumerable images and details that would ordinarily be overwhelming and chaotic. But like in a dream, it is possible to meet these chaotic happenings without judgment or censorship. The pilgrim's goal is to simply receive with open attention and gratitude all that arises. Slowly the hidden patterns and meanings will emerge from the kaleidoscope of images and sense impressions. Traveling through Bihar state in northern India was a disorienting excursion into timelessness. With my attention broadened and an open state of *abaissement,* however, it was possible to drift in and out of the twenty-first century through a constant play of events and characters. An elephant ambled along a dirt road escorted by two men in brightly colored garments. Thatched huts clustered at the edges of green fields. Women in vibrant saris bent low over dark green plants, tending some unfamiliar crop. Men pounded huge boulders with small hammers until mounds of tiny granules remained, creating gravel for pathways and building materials. Children played with sticks and balls while carrying younger siblings on their backs. A man walked along a road at twilight leading a large brown bear on a leash. This could be the 1900s or the 1700s or perhaps the days of the Buddha. All this, in fact, occurred along the route the Buddha traveled some 2,500 years earlier on his way to the place of his eventual enlightenment. It seemed that the Buddha might be the next to pass by. Then a motorbike screeched and the sounds of a generator and a nearby radio rattled the quiet afternoon. I dropped back into the twenty-first century. A truck rushed past, too large for the narrow road. A bus approached filled with people and crowned with dozens more huddled on the roof as dust clouds rose in its wake. It was hard to establish the time of this place; it felt ancient with a tinge of modernity. The trip continued as we moved from village to village among the wandering *sadhus,* precocious monkeys, and ever-present cows that meander the streets, drinking in the feast of color and sound that is India. It is a blessing to meet each of these experiences nonjudgmentally, as we meet a dream upon waking. To do otherwise invites only frustration, disorientation, and distance from the truth of the experience.

Once, when I was in Turkey, I entered an ancient Roman amphitheater. I had been to many beautiful ruins, but something was palpably different in this place. I was awed by the magnificence of the structure and the majesty of its construction. I climbed the steep marble steps into the highest rows to admire the extraordinary space. As I sat on the worn slabs of stone, something happened that is difficult to recount. The space came alive, full of the sounds and shadows of its life in Roman times. It was no longer a ruin but a living repository of the events and images held so vividly by the structure itself. The great stones remembered and somehow shared a glimpse into the events that had transpired within its walls—performances and spectacles alike. The worn steps and benches reawakened in the presence of my open, imaginative perception, offering a whispered invitation into the life that had inhabited the amphitheater centuries earlier. Mine was a visceral experience, disorienting and fleeting but definitely present. It was a gift from place to person, a sort of blessing, or *darshan,* that transcends time. For just a few miraculous moments, I had a felt sense of being part of this Roman theater and its crowds in a way that no book or imagination could construct.

Sadly, our contemporary sense of pilgrimage is too often limited to formal religious practices such as the journey to Mecca, a visit to Jerusalem's holiest shrines, or travel to Lourdes. If we are able to recognize ourselves as pilgrims and our movement throughout this sacred planet as pilgrimage, we can rediscover the essential inspiration underlying our wanderings. Houston Smith, noted scholar of world religions, wrote that

> travel brings a special kind of wisdom.... Attentive travel helps us to see this, because the continually changing outward scene helps us to see through the world's pretensions.... We can understand how perpetual wandering can be a spiritual vocation.[4]

The journey itself is the path that opens our hearts, that helps us appreciate the complexity of interconnection among the peoples, cultures, and places that are so very essential to our survival and well-being in the twenty-first century. Scholar and teacher Joan Halifax wrote:

> Everybody has a geography itself that can be used for change. That is why we travel to far-off places. Whether we know it or not, we need to renew ourselves in territories that are fresh and wild. We need to come home through the body of alien lands. For some, these are journeys of change that are taken intentionally and mindfully. They are pilgrimages, occasions when Earth heals us directly. Pilgrimage has been for me, and many others, a form of inquiry in action.[5]

Living in a time of air travel permits us to traverse innumerable cultures in a lifetime, affording an opportunity to sample the riches of many places. With this gift comes a corresponding responsibility to use this privilege for awakening rather than voyeurism. Writing about his travels in India, Jung noted that

> a first impression of a country is very often like meeting a person for the first time: your impression may be quite inaccurate, even definitely wrong in many respects, yet you are likely to perceive certain qualities or certain shadows which would very probably be blurred by the more accurate impressions of a second or third visit. My reader would make a great mistake if he were to take any statements I make about India for gospel truth.[6]

The point is not to claim absolute knowledge but rather to stimulate the heart and mind to gather perceptions and pursue the questions that inevitably arise. Sacred travel expands consciousness, enlarging our understanding of self and world because we are activated into dialogue with our surroundings and with our cherished beliefs. Life becomes more textured and our understanding of issues more refined. It is increasingly difficult to remain removed and distant from events in places around the globe when you have shared a meal or laughed together with inhabitants from those places.

When at last he or she returns home, the pilgrim discovers that the adventure has not yet concluded. As Pico Iyer has observed, the last destination isn't the final place on the itinerary; rather, it is what happens when we get home and try to make sense of the journey.[7] The concluding phase of the pilgrimage entails reentry and integration of experience and insight. Often these understandings emerge slowly. Sometimes they appear as we try to recount our most meaningful experiences to family and friends. Other times, we recognize a changed response, recalling an image or perception that altered our sense of self. When I first returned from Bhutan, I couldn't watch television or be among friends for a period of time. Everything seemed superficial and insignificant after returning from a culture where the spiritual dimension of life was so deeply entwined with daily events. I was suddenly stunned by the wealth and material richness of American society in contrast to the countries I had visited. Our carelessness with the earth and frivolous use of material goods seemed decadent and ostentatious. I remained steeped in hundreds of images, trying to sort out my impressions and feelings. In the inevitable period of inquiry that follows the return, we slowly discover how our attitudes and understandings of self and other have shifted. As the dream figure mentioned earlier foretold, the pilgrim returns as someone else.

I became quite sick shortly after returning from India, perhaps in part because both body and soul needed a time to stop, a time to let the soul catch up to the body, as one friend suggested. The fourteen-hour flight home was too fast for the worlds of East and West to transition smoothly. My daily life had fewer interactions than the days on pilgrimage. The secular world of responsibilities paled in comparison to the richly sensuous and spiritual images that accompanied me every day in India. People walking along Indian roads wore marks of spiritual devotion, reminding others of the divine presence in that moment. Bells and chanting announced the passing of a funeral en route to a cremation pyre, and the proximity of life and death remained palpable. Each of my senses had been alert and awake, but once I returned home, the pull of daily chores and endless responsibilities dulled my senses and I felt myself falling out of the *abaissement* back into the harsher light of ego consciousness. The protective persona slowly reemerged, though a little different now.

The challenge at the end of every spiritual journey is how best to ingest the wisdom glimpsed and the insights touched. Reflection on and amplification of the experiences and impressions of the journey slowly reveal the points of lasting impact. Perhaps we release a stereotype, broaden our appreciation for the unfamiliar, or feel touched by something that will change our orientation to the world. Whether we take up study of a new language, bring images into our home, or simply allow the experiences to percolate, we have been touched by the world in a new way. Pilgrimage is not a process of collecting countries like trophies but rather an opportunity to enlarge the psychological, intellectual, and emotional field from which our life emerges. It may even be possible to retain the heart and eyes of a pilgrim in the everyday and familiar routines of our life. T. S. Eliot explained the task of homecoming most beautifully:

> We shall not cease from exploration
> And the end of all our exploring
> Will be to arrive where we started
> And know the place for the first time.[8]

NOTES

1. Dream of 2001 recorded by Rebecca Armstrong, who at the time was the International OutReach Director of the Joseph Campbell Foundation, recorded on the Joseph Campbell Foundation website, http://www.jcf.org/, accessed March 2006.

2. Pico Iyer, personal conversation with me, ca. 2005.

3. C. G. Jung, "Introduction to Zen Buddhism," in C. G. Jung, *Psychology and Religion: West and East*, vol. 11 of *The Collected Works of C. G. Jung*, edited and translated by G. Adler and R. F. C. Hull (Princeton, N.J.: Princeton University Press, 1970), p. 538.

4. Houston Smith, "Foreword," in Philip Cousineau, *The Art of Pilgrimage: The Seeker's Guide to Making Travel Sacred* (Berkeley, Calif.: Conari Press, 1998), p. xi.

5. Joan Halifax, *A Fruitful Darkness* (1994), quoted in Cousineau, *The Art of Pilgrimage*, p. 104.

6. C. G. Jung, "The Dreamlike World of India" (1939), in *Civilization in Transition*, vol. 10 of *The Collected Works of C. G. Jung*, edited and translated by G. Adler and R. F. C. Hull (Princeton, N.J.: Princeton University Press, 1970), p. 515.

7. Thanks to Shantum Seth for bringing this observation to my attention. Personal communication, 18 March 2005.

8. Thomas Stearns Eliot, "Little Gidding," in *Four Quartets* (1943; repr., New York: Harcourt, Brace, 1971), p. 59.

THE BAYNES FILM OF JUNG'S 1925-26 EXPEDITION TO EAST AFRICA

BLAKE BURLESON

FOREWORD BY DIANA BAYNES JANSEN

My father, H. G. (Peter) Baynes (1882-1943), had traveled the world widely before his association with C. G. Jung began in 1920. In both a personal and intellectual sense, he saw himself as an explorer. As an undergraduate at the University of Cambridge he was a larger than life, charismatic figure; a fine athlete competing for his university in both rowing and swimming. He was also a central figure among the group of writers and intellectuals surrounding the poet Rupert Brooke. (Brooke, along with Paul Gauguin, Robert Louis Stevenson, Andre Gide, D. H. Lawrence, Georgia O'Keeffe, Michel Leiris, and Antonin Artaud were all wanderers to exotic and "primitive" places.) After qualifying as a physician, my father went to Turkey during the Balkan War and then

---

Blake Burleson is Associate Dean for Undergraduate Studies in the College of Arts and Sciences and Senior Lecturer in World Religions at Baylor University where he formerly directed the African Studies Program. He is the author of *Jung in Africa* (2005) and *Pathways to Integrity* (2000).

Diana Baynes Jansen is a Jungian-trained analytical psychotherapist with a practice in the North of England. She is the youngest of H. G. Baynes's six children and the author of *Jung's Apprentice: A Biography of Helton Godwin Baynes* (2003).

to France and Mesopotamia during World War I. He was wounded at the Battle of the Somme. He returned home in 1919 to find that his wife had left him for another man. It was during this difficult time, while working in the Maudelsy Hospital in London, that he met Jung.

After his own wanderings, the encounter with Jung was a true homecoming. He wrote:

> He did not try to teach, to illuminate, or to impress. In fact he made no effort of any kind. But what he said had for me the character of a rare natural experience, as though for a moment I had stood on the rim of the known world and looked over the edge into the source from which all living forms had sprung. I entered a door that seemed like many from which I had emerged unscathed. But this one was the last; I could not leave it. I had been gripped by a view which went to the roots of mental life, and this experience changed the course of my life.[1]

My father devoted the rest of his life to working as a Jungian analyst and to spreading Jung's ideas through his writings, lectures, teaching, and practice. He became Jung's first assistant in Zurich and began translating many of Jung's early works into English. By 1922, he had set up his own practice as the first Jungian analyst in London.

When Jung, at fifty, proposed a trip to East Africa in 1925, my father became the trip's principle organizer with responsibilities for all of the practical aspects of the expedition: obtaining permission from the British Colonial Office for the "Bugishu Psychological Expedition" which enabled the research team to conduct interviews among indigenous peoples; securing the safari equipment, weapons, and food stuffs for camping and survival in the bush; hiring African help for the safari and negotiating the logistical details with district commissioners in Kenya, Uganda, and the Sudan. The tragic death of his new wife, Hilda, on the eve of the expedition, however, put the whole enterprise in jeopardy. Remarkably, he arranged for the care of his one-year-old son and left for Africa on the afternoon of Hilda's cremation. Without his participation, the trip would likely have been cancelled.

Perhaps my father's most lasting contribution to the expedition was his record of the entire journey with a 16 mm camera. Though he had no experience as a camera man, the many scenes of Jung's encounters with Africa and Africans provide an indispensible historical record of Jung's most extensive foreign trip. Like so many other Westerners in their time, Jung and Baynes sought out in an almost nostalgic and spiritual way the secrets of indigenous peoples in the vast expanses of wilderness. The three reels of film titled "Jung's African Journey, 1925" are held at the British National Museum in London; copies may be found at the C. G. Jung Analytical Psychology Club of London and the C. G. Jung Institute of San Francisco. I was recently given a DVD copy from Daniel Bauman, Jung's great grandson, although the order of scenes is scrambled.

I had the opportunity in 2009 to retrace the steps of the Ugandan part of my father's journey. I visited Jinja, Lake Victoria and the source of the Nile, the place where the Ripon Falls had been (it has now been replaced by a hydro-electric plant), and ended with a memorable trip down the Nile. We enjoyed seeing the many exotic birds, also the elephants and hippos playing in the water, which must have been the daily experience of Jung and company as they made their return trip towards Egypt and home.

In the essay which follows, Blake Burleson, author of *Jung in Africa* (2005), provides a definitive historical explication of the film's contents including its chronology, subjects, settings, and actions.

Introduction

The forty-eight scenes filmed by Peter Baynes during C. G. Jung's 1925-26 five-month expedition through Kenya, Uganda, the Sudan, and Egypt are identified and contextualized in this article.[2] In addition to published sources from both Jung and Baynes, this work relies upon Baynes's formerly unpublished notes of the film's contents provided to me by Diana Baynes Jansen (Appendix I); Ruth Bailey's unpublished interviews (including her commentary on the Baynes film as she watched it for the first time in 1970); Jung's unpublished "Protocols"; numerous colonial maps, reports, and newspaper articles held at the Kenya National Archives; and interviews I conducted with Elgonyi[3] elders at Mt. Elgon. I have divided the three reels of the film into ten major episodes which follow the elliptical route of the "Bugishu Psychological Expedition."

Map 1: Map detailing Jung's travel (southern half).

THE BAYNES FILM

Map 2: Map detailing Jung's travel (northern half).

First Reel

(1) Arrival at Kilindini Harbor, Mombasa, Kenya

The November 9, 1925 edition of the *East African Standard* gives a list of sixty-four passengers "arriving [on November 12] at Kilindini [the Mombasa harbor] from Europe per S. S. *Wangoni*."[4] These were settlers, government officials, tourists, professional hunters, scientists, missionaries, and military personnel from the United Kingdom, Germany, Switzerland, America, Spain, France, and Italy. Among them were the three members of the "Bugishu Psychological Expedition": C. G. Jung, H. G. Baynes, and George Beckwith (Jung and Baynes's American analysand). Jung had boarded the German steamer from Southampton on October 15 while Baynes and Beckwith had taken a train on October 24 from London to Genoa where they boarded. Baynes was delayed in departing due to the tragic death of his wife, Hilda, on October 21. Her suicide weighed heavily on Baynes during the entire five-month expedition.[5]

Also listed among the passengers was "Miss R. Bailey." "Ruth Bailey, a twenty-eight year old nurse, was accompanying her younger sister, Bertha, who was engaged to a railroad engineer in Kenya named Richard Gowthorpe."[6] Though destined to become the fourth member of the "psychological expedition," Bailey did not meet Jung, Baynes, or Beckwith during the voyage to Kenya.

As the *Wangoni* enters the brilliant blue-green waters of the Mombasa channel, Baynes begins using his camera apparently for the first time, filming the shoreline of green undergrowth framed by enormous, leafless baobab trees. A motor car on the mainland, keeping pace with the *Wangoni*, skirts a dirt road on which walk Africans dressed in white. Dhows, "lighters," barges, and a steam ship can be seen in the harbor.

Bailey indicates that Bertha's fiancée was able to get them off the ship first which allowed them to proceed through customs and board the train to Nairobi on that same day.[7] Bertha and Richard were married on November 14 in Nairobi.[8] Jung, Baynes, and Beckwith remained in Mombasa for "two days" before departing for the interior.[9]

(2) Central Highlands, Kenya

The Athi Plains

The team spent approximately ten days in the Nairobi vicinity of the central highlands preparing for their expedition to Mt. Elgon in western Kenya. Most of the organization fell to Baynes who had brought with him "letters of introduction to the East African governors from the Under Secretary of State for the Colonies [Hon. W.G.A. Ormsby-Gore MP] who [wa]s interested in their research."[10] According to the *East African Standard*, Baynes met with His Excellency Sir William Gowers, the Governor of Uganda who was at that time visiting Nairobi.[11] In the "Protocols", Jung indicated that they were entertained by the Governor at an evening meal.[12] While in Nairobi, Jung befriended Ruth Bailey and invited her to join their safari.

One day Jung, Baynes, and Beckwith rented a small Ford to visit the Athi Plains which was just to the south of town. Jung writes that they saw "gigantic herds of animals."[13] While watching this mesmerizing scene, Jung reached a pivotal moment in his life. On these plains, he would later write that he had found his "myth": namely, that the purpose of human life is the creation of consciousness.

Figure 1: Jung on Athi Plains with wildebeests and zebras.

In the film, wildebeests and zebras gallop across the rolling savanna. Finally, a European (possibly Jung) in safari suit and pith helmet sets up a tripod, looks through a camera lens, and then walks on into the distance.

Kikuyu dance at Kikuyu

During their stay in the central highlands, Baynes traveled fifteen miles to the northwest of Nairobi where he attempted to film a Kikuyu dance in the village of Kikuyu.[14] The Kikuyu, a Bantu people, were the largest ethnic population in Kenya. The excursion was likely organized at Baynes's request by colonial officials so that he could film a "native" dance.

Jung and Baynes were interested in African dance as an expression of the "primitive" psyche. Baynes wrote about this phenomenon:

> Tribes living in or near the primitive level are readily subject to mass excitements. The savage war dances, and the famous spring dances, preceding the work of the agricultural season, are by no means a mere outlet for superfluous energy. The intoxication of the dance is the means by which energy is pumped up from a latent, inert condition in the unconscious to the active state in which it can be harnessed to the necessary seasonal tasks. It is doubtful if any savage people could be induced to fight unless they had first lashed themselves into war-frenzy with the dance. In the same way the conversion of energy from the primordial level of the *libido sexualis* to the relatively higher potential needed for agricultural work in spring-time must be regarded as an indispensable cultural process. The magnificent and grotesque painting of the body, the technique of ornamentation, the feathers, the masks, and the whole impressive crescendo of the dance, are all effective in arousing the inert *libido* into action. Thus the dance is really the power-station of the primitive community.[15]

So the trip to Kikuyu provided Baynes with the opportunity to observe the "primitive power-station." Of course, one of the most well-known events of the expedition would occur during the caravan march through southern Sudan when they encountered a dance troupe. After having been "infected by the primitive," Jung and Baynes joined in this "tribal" romp only to become alarmed at its frenzy which, to their minds,

THE BAYNES FILM

required the abrupt dispersal of their indigenous guests. Jung was later chastised by a district commissioner (DC) for illegally "working up the natives." By 1926, *ngomas* (dances) were highly regulated or forbidden in Kenya.

In the Baynes film, there are two dance circles in these brief scenes at Kikuyu; the first is of men in traditional *shukas* (loincloths), carrying *rungus* (knobbed sticks), and moving rhythmically in a clockwise direction, the second is of women, also traditionally clothed in *kitangas* (colorful wraps), stomping and swaying. Baynes is largely unsuccessful in filming these circles since Kikuyu youth crowd in around him to watch him film and, thus, prevent him from being able to see the entire dance circles. An *askari* (soldier), who has perhaps been employed as an official escort for Baynes, attempts to manage the youth by hitting them with his baton.[16] The youth are much more interested in watching a European film the dance than they are in the dance; the commotion prevents Baynes, despite his tall height, from getting good shots. In the end, most of his footage is of the curious faces of dozens of boys and young men watching him, some making faces at the camera! While aggressive management of the crowd by an *askari* and by a Kikuyu elder temporarily clears space, Baynes apparently gives up without having succeeded.

Figure 2: Kikuyu youth at dance

(3) Kakamega, North Kavirondo District, Kenya

Market

Around November 24, Jung, Baynes, and Beckwith departed from Nairobi on the Uganda Railroad to begin their "scientific" work among the Bugishu in eastern Uganda. Accompanying them and all of their safari equipment were five Africans who served as guides and help. After crossing the Great Rift Valley during the evening, the team arrived the next day at Eldoret where they loaded their equipment into two automobiles. They traveled for the rest of that day through field and forest to Kakamega, the district headquarters of the North Kavirondo where they were hosted by A. C. Chamier, the DC. While at Kakamega the ethnic group for their research is apparently changed from the Bugishu to the Elgonyi.[17]

While Jung convalesces due to a fever, Baynes films the market at Kakamega. The Kakamega township with a population of 321 consisted of some 200 *bandas* (huts). The vibrancy of the local commerce can be seen as the indigenous population of Nandi walk briskly to and from market on a dirt road lined with blue gum trees. The women, often shirtless and in *kitangas*, carry loads of firewood or clay pots on their heads. Men in *shukas* walk with *rungus* in hand; children run down

Figure 3: Kakamega Market.

the road. The day is cloudy and windy; November was the season of the short rains, particularly heavy in 1925. Beneath a wooden pavilion with a thatched roof, Nandi women sit on mats displaying their vegetables, fruits, and wares. One woman reaches into a large sisal basket and scoops out cups of grain, perhaps millet.

Tent-Pitching exercise

While at Kakamega, Jung "supervises" a tent-pitching exercise in order to make sure their equipment is in good working order. In this scene, Jung strolls around the area smoking his pipe and closely observing three of the African assistants driving stakes into the ground with a large wooden mallet and, then, pulling taunt the ropes. The sides of the tents flap vigorously and the blue gum trees in the background sway in the strong wind. One of the assistants, Ibrahim, converses with Jung as Jung sets up a camera on a pole. Ibrahim was Jung's personal assistant and "safari headman," "a long thin Somali" who always wore a stocking cap. A Sufi Muslim,[18] he served the British in the First World War as "an officier de liaison."[19]

The expedition took three tents, one for each *mzungu* (European). These were ten by eight, double-roof ridge tents, the typical fare for safaris. Bailey noted that the tents were very fine with thick canvas

Figure 4: Ibrahim and Jung—tent-pitching exercise.

flooring which came up the sides of the tent and fastened so that snakes and small creatures could not enter.[20]

(4) Caravan from Kakamega to Mt. Elgon, North Kavirondo District

Mwanza rest house, Kabras location

Around November 29, Jung, Baynes, and Beckwith began a five-day walk from Kakamega to Mt. Elgon, some sixty miles away. They were supported by forty-eight Elgonyi porters,[21] three *askaris* (who were likely drawn from the King's African Rifles stationed nearby), a cook, and four personal assistants; a total of fifty-eight men. Each porter carried a maximum of sixty pounds up to eight hours per day.

Their trek took them through the sparsely populated open grasslands of North Kavirondo with occasional pockets of pristine rain forests. "They passed . . . Nandi homesteads, with low, circular mud walls and thatched roofs fenced by thorn-bush or euphorbia hedges, and *shambas* (cultivated fields) growing maize and sorghum."[22] Each evening the caravan stopped at rest houses (safari camps) which were supported by the indigenous population. Rest houses consisted "generally of a square building of hard mud and wattles with a thatched roof and a verandah."[23] There were four rest houses located on the dirt road leading to Mt. Elgon: Mwanza, Mulubi, Murumbu, and Kimilili.[24]

Baynes films the "first *boma* of safari"[25] at Mwanza. A dozen Nandi children sit outside the rest house while seven women, dressed in *kitangas*, carry clay jars of water on their heads into the rest house. Having emptied their loads into a basin for the cook, they exit and stand near the children. Ibrahim and Jung make brief appearances in front of the Nandi entourage.

Later, Jung sits on the verandah of the rest house smoking his pipe and talking to the caravan's cook. Baynes identifies the cook as "Ephlaim" (a Kikuyu corruption of Ephraim).[26] Ephraim holds a tea cup in one hand and a tin in the other. Jung opens the chop box next to him and searches its contents for the appropriate canned goods for the evening meal which Ephraim is preparing. Chop boxes, prepared by Lawn and Adler of London, were wooden crates with lock and key which weighed sixty pounds each. The crates contained various canned meats, milk products in tins, tinned fruits and vegetables, condiments, beverages, and sweets. Ephraim supplemented these processed goods with fresh meat and vegetables purchased from the locals near the rest house.

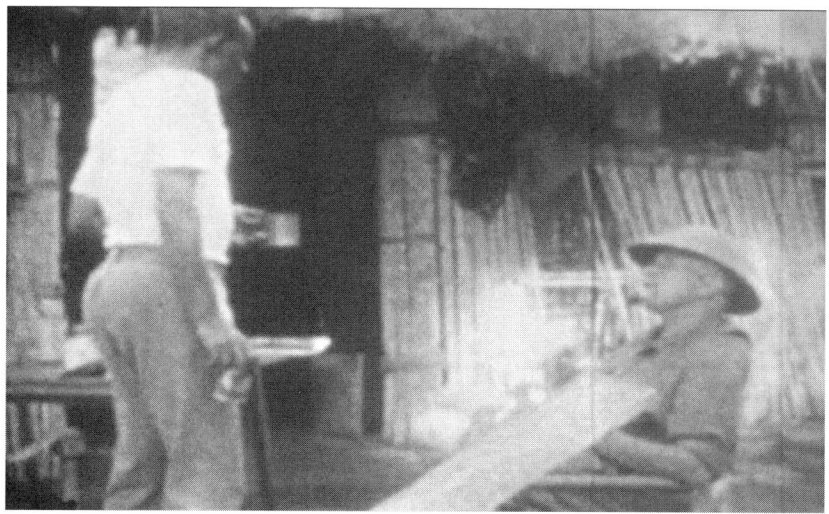

Figure 5: Jung and Ephraim at rest house.

Safari up to Broderick Falls[27]

The second rest house on the march was at Mulubi. At this location, the caravan's rest following an evening meal of mutton was disturbed by a pack of hyenas, one of which entered Ephraim's cooking hut, an event which caused a great deal of excitement.

On the third day the caravan headed towards the Nzoia River at Broderick Falls. Baynes films an apparent mid-day break before crossing the river. While sitting on their loads, the porters are entertained by a local Nandi playing a homemade stringed instrument. An armed *askari* hands one of the sitting porters a cigarette; he takes a long drag. Beckwith dressed in a white pith helmet and white socks reclines next to Jung. As they eat their lunch, Jung gestures energetically with his fork.

Following their break, the porters with loads on their heads continue the march at a brisk pace. An *askari* waits on Jung to join the line. Beckwith strides into view crossing the motor road in his bright whites followed by his African assistant.

Figure 6: Caravan at rest.

Figure 7: Nandi entertainment.

Bridge over Nzoia River at Broderick Falls

The caravan crossed a wooden bridge used by motor cars over the Nzoia, a fast-moving, clear, boulder-lined river fed by streams from the Nzoia basin. In this staged scene, Jung and Beckwith lead the way across like explorers into the great unknown. Just beyond the bridge but unseen there was a large "railway camp" with conscripted Luo workers who were building the Uasin Gishu Line which would open rail service to Uganda in 1928; one of the world's remote "outplaces" was being eliminated. After crossing the river, the caravan stopped at the nearby Murumba rest house.

Figure 8: Jung and Beckwith lead caravan over Nzoia.

Paying the porters, Murumba rest house

This episode is one of the most descriptive of the colonial context in which the expedition occurs.[28] Jung, sitting at a folding table under the verandah of the rest house, distributes money to the porters with assistance from two *askaris* identified in Baynes's notes as "Sabei and Corporal."[29] Beckwith sits behind Jung during the exercise. Bailey confirms that this is the line for receiving payments such as East African money, cigarettes, and things.[30]

After Jung lights his pipe and arranges his purse, the *askaris* move the porters through the line to the waiting Bwana. In the distribution of payments, Jung appears to give one coin to two porters, which they will apparently share. In 1925 the typical payment to a porter was seventeen cents per day.[31] Most of the Elgonyi porters in this line are dressed in *shukas*, two wear shorts. As the distribution begins, Jung calls in an animated way for his personal assistant; Ibrahim appears and is sent away on an assignment. Forty-four porters proceed through the line. Corporal and Sabei, who loom much larger than the porters, handle each set as they move to the table, sometimes shoving them forward. At one point, one of the porters lags behind after his partner has received payment, apparently trying to get an extra coin. Corporal notices this, yells at the porter, and forcefully pushes him on his way. The *askaris* are noticeably more judicious after this incident. Following the exercise there is general congratulations all around at the completion of the task.

Figure 9: Jung, Corporal, and Sabei paying porters.

RE-ENACTMENT OF THE HYENA ATTACK, MURUMBA REST HOUSE

On the same day, Baynes films a staged re-enactment of the hyena attack on the cook Ephraim which had taken place at the previous rest house. He labels this the "nfigi play", a misspelling of the Swahili *fisi* (hyena). Jung acts as theatre director, placing Corporal and Sabei in their roles as sleeping cook and sneaky hyena. The lanky *askari* playing the role of hyena creeps slowly on all fours to the *askari* curled up "asleep" on the ground, then jumps on him in feigned attack. The frightened cook runs away with hyena chasing him. Jung wrote that there were "roars of laughter" from the "boys' quarters" as they relived the excitement of the previous evening.[32] Ephraim was subsequently nicknamed "*Fisi*."

Re-enactments of encounters involving wild animals were part and parcel of nineteen and twentieth century African hunting expeditions. Adventure and travel books written by ex-patriots (such as Karen Blixen and J. H. Patterson) include accounts of African mimicry.

Figure 10: Jung directing Corporal and Sabei in re-enactment.

Kimilili

The final rest house before reaching Mt. Elgon was at Kimilili. Rest houses on the southern flanks of the mountain were operated by Chief Murunga,[33] a member of a prestigious clan of chiefs from the Wanga people, a subgroup of the Bantu Kavirondo.[34] The Wanga's

Bantu cousins, the Bugishu,[35] had recently migrated into the North Kavirondo area from Uganda. The Bugishu migration along with the British gazetting of ancestral forest regions forced the smaller Nilotic population of Elgonyi, who numbered only about 5,000 in 1925, to move either higher up the mountain or lower down into and around trading centers like Kimilili.[36]

Baynes documents the caravan's presence in the Kimilili area in several scenes. In the first, the safari marches in group (rather than single file) down a dirt motor road. One of the uniformed *askaris* strides into view with rifle on shoulder. In the second scene, a dignified, handsome Elgonyi elder with shaved head stands in traditional dress in front of a herd of cattle. The Elgonyi, sometimes referred to as the Elgon Masai, were pastoralists.

In the third scene, one of the safari's assistants approaches some local women who carry their loads; their children following behind. The women move away shyly.

The fourth scene is that of the Kimilili centre lined with blue gum trees. It appears that the caravan has arrived on a day in which headmen from North Kavirondo have gathered for a meeting, perhaps called by Chief Murunga. Baynes identifies a group of approximately thirty "headmen" dressed in white *kanzus* (robes) who pose for his camera.[37]

Figure 11: Elgonyi elder with cattle.

THE BAYNES FILM 265

The Kimilili grounds are filled with Bugishu men, many dressed sharply in *kanzus*; some have arrived by riding bicycles. The Bugishu are contrasted with the shabbily dressed Elgonyi porters. One of the *askaris* shouts orders to the lowly porters.

(5) Mt. Elgon

Elgonyi Women Bearing Water

In early December, the caravan established camp at 6,900 feet on the Kibuuk stream beneath the Kamutiang' escarpment, approximately twelve kilometers north of Kimilili.[38] They remained at this site for three weeks as Jung and Baynes attempted to study the Elgonyi who lived in nearby *manyattas* (traditional homesteads).

In this scene, seven young Elgonyi women pose for the camera after hauling water from the stream. Some of them appear to be girls of twelve or thirteen. On their heads they wear rings which assist in balancing their clay jars. Jung describes these women as:

> ...chocolate-brown and strikingly pretty, with fine slim figures and an aristocratic leisureliness about their movements. It was a pleasure for me each morning to hear the soft cling-clang of their

Figure 12: Elgonyi women bearing water.

iron rings, brass bracelets and necklaces, earrings of cooper or wood in the shape of small spools. Their lower lips were pierced with either a bone or iron nail. They had very good manners, and always greeted us with shy, charming smiles.[39]

After setting up camp, Jung sent a letter by a runner to Ruth Bailey who was staying with her sister in the town of Turbo, near Broderick Falls, inviting her to join the men at camp. She would arrive shortly thereafter.

THE VISIT OF TENDEET

Jung indicated that upon their arrival at Elgon they "were greeted by the local chief, who was the son of the laibon, the medicine man."[40] Although Jung never identified the "chief" by name, the colonial records and Baynes's notes indicate that this was Tendeet, the "headman" for the Elgonyi of the North Kitosh location.[41] Jung's use of the term "chief" was inaccurate since leadership in Elgonyi society was decentralized and charismatic; indigenous titles such as judge, military commander, or prophet "rested largely on personal qualities."[42] The office of headman was a recent colonial imposition. Tendeet, whose *manyatta* was about two miles northwest of Kimilili,[43] had been made headman by Chief Murunga, an action approved by Chamier, the DC. Tendeet's visit to the campsite was a formal courtesy and insured that the party would be well received during their stay. Jung recorded that Tendeet appeared riding on a horse.[44] I interviewed an Elgonyi elder born in 1908 who had seen Tendeet riding on this horse which the British had given him; the elder recalled that the horse was white.[45]

In this scene, Tendeet poses with an *askari* on his left (perhaps Sabei) and a younger Elgonyi on his right (perhaps Gibroat). Gibroat[46], the "son of a chief", was Jung's principle Elgonyi informant during his stay on Elgon.[47] The distinguished Tendeet wears a European style hat, coat, and scarf over a traditional white *kanzu*. Standing behind the men are several Elgonyi women who Baynes identifies as Tendeet's wives.[48]

Baynes continues filming as they organize for a palaver with Tendeet. A palaver was "a parley between European explorers and representatives of local populations."[49] Jung and Beckwith prepare for the palaver by reviewing their notes at their camp table. Beckwith was the "secretary"[50] of the expedition though there is scant evidence that he did much work in this capacity. Sabei and Tendeet discuss matters as the preparation continues. Finally, the palaver commences with Jung

Figure 13: Tendeet (center).

and Tendeet facing each other. Ibrahim sits to Tendeet's left, Sabei to his right. As many as twenty African men are gathered in a circle for the palaver. Tendeet's "wives" can be seen standing in the distance. There is no record as to what was discussed at this palaver.

Figure 14: Palaver with Tendeet.

Palaver with Cheebteek

Jung wrote that at one of the palavers, the "*laibon*, the old medicine man" appeared. While Jung never identified this individual by name, Baynes titles this scene in the film as "Palaver with Gaptek and others." This is a variant spelling of Cheebteek, the father of Tendeet and the reigning *warkonteet* of the Elgonyi in 1925.[51] A *warkonteet* (prophet) held enormous political and spiritual powers as one who gave advice on major events in the life of the people, such as war, famine, hunting expeditions, epidemics, droughts, etc. The *warkonteet's* powers were principally derived from his ability to interpret "big" dreams.[52] Jung wrote:

> When I was doing fieldwork with a primitive tribe in East Africa, I discovered to my amazement that [ordinary people] denied having dreams at all. But by patient indirect talk I soon found that they had dreams all right, like everybody else, but were convinced that their dreams meant nothing. "Dreams of ordinary men mean nothing," they said. The only dreams that mattered were those of the chief and the medicine man, which concerned the welfare of the tribe. Such dreams were highly appreciated.[53]

Jung's insight into Elgonyi oneirology was accurate and corresponded with the ethnographies on pre-literate societies worldwide. Jackson Lincoln's *The Dream in Primitive Cultures* (1935), the first comprehensive study of dreaming among pre-literate peoples, referenced Jung's interpretation of Elgonyi "big" dreams. As is well known, Jung wrote about "big" dreams on many occasions and incorporated this Elgonyi perspective into his analytic practice.

In the film, Jung, Ibrahim, and Sabei sit with approximately twenty Elgonyi men. Ibrahim is to Jung's right. A large, impressive-looking Elgonyi covered only in an animal skin sits directly in front of Jung. This is Cheebteek who was said to have worn "a splendid cloak made from the skins of blue monkeys—a valuable article of display."[54] In 2003, I interviewed Cheebteek's ninety-seven-year-old great nephew, Samuel Naibei Kimukung'. Kimukung', a *warkonteet* himself, recalled that this prophetic cloak was "made from Colobos monkey skins." Sitting to the right of Cheebteek is an Elgonyi in a European-style coat and hat. During the palaver, Jung and Cheebteek can be seen gesturing as they speak. Near the end of the scene, Sabei gets up and departs having been given an assignment by Jung. Women in the distance haul water from the Kibuuk stream.

If Jung's primary objective in the palavers was to record dreams from the Elgonyi, he failed. Jung admitted that he "discovered nothing"[55] in the palavers. During the entire three weeks on Elgon, he only received one dream from his informants. Cheebteek's explanation of this silence was that the dreams had ceased when the British had taken control of the country:

> His father had still had "big" dreams, he told me, and had known where the herds strayed, where the cows took their calves, and when there was going to be a war or a pestilence. It was now the District Commissioner who knew everything, and they knew nothing... God now speaks... to the British, and not to the medicine-man of the Elgonyi, he told me, because it is the British who have the power.[56]

Did Jung realize that for Cheebteek, whose son—Tendeet—was an appointed official of the colonial government, to admit that he had "big" dreams could result in arrest? In the late 1920s, a *warkonteet* on the northeastern side of Elgon was arrested and deported when he announced that his dreams had foretold "the imminent departure of the Europeans."[57]

Figure 15: Palaver with Cheebteek.

Acacias of Kamutiang' escarpment

Baynes, who had an interest in natural history, spent much of his time on Elgon studying the various plants and trees. Bailey commented that he had a great interest in trees, especially the "fever trees" (acacia) and that that is why he took so many pictures of them. He also collected many species of African butterflies "which became a part of his vast . . . collection."[58] In this scene, Baynes films nine different acacias in the valley beneath the Kamutiang' escarpment.

The forest caves of Elgon

Jung, Baynes, Beckwith, and Bailey (who had now joined the men) were guided by *askaris* and locals to caves further up the mountain. Throughout much of Elgonyi history, these caves—located in volcanic ash bands between 6,000 and 9,000 feet in altitude—provided shelter and protection for the people. In 1925 there were still a few Elgonyi living in caves and Baynes was able to film one of these families: a mother, father, and two small boys. Perhaps unbeknownst to Baynes was the fact that this forest area was being gazetted and occupation of these traditional homes of the Elgonyi declared illegal.[59] It is no surprise that the Elgonyi were highly suspicious of armed Europeans setting up camp near their *manyattas* and trying to learn about their traditional ways.

Baynes and Jung must have felt that they had found specimens of the most "primitive" layer of the human psyche in these cave dwellers living underground with their cattle, goats, and chickens in one of the most remote places on the entire African continent. Jung chose Mt. Elgon as his laboratory for "psychic observations" for numerous reasons but, in part, the destination was inspired by the novel *She* by H. Rider Haggard. Only months before the African excursion, Jung had conducted a seminar in Zurich which examined this psychological novel. The settings for the novel were caves in the African interior. Haggard's novel itself was inspired by British explorer Joseph Thomson's report of the Elgon caves, the first ever written. Thomson explored Elgon in 1883, describing a number of large caves occupied by the Elgonyi.

Baynes films the family standing outside the cave, the team's entrance into the cave, and brief exploration within. Of particular interest is Jung's coaxing the two boys from their mud domicile within cave's dark recess. The unclothed shy children are teased playfully by the fatherly Jung until they retreat into their lean-to shelter. Before leaving, Jung traded his steel axe for the cave man's stone axe.[60] This he brought home, along with some spears and a chair, and displayed them on his wall at Kusnacht.[61]

Figure 16: Elgonyi cave dwellers.

Trees on the edge of the montane forest

Elgon, one of the planet's great natural cathedrals of the twentieth century, was a vast rainforest of giant timbers—camphors, teaks, cedars, olives, and podocarpus. In this scene, Baynes films the trees above the Kamutiang' escarpment where the nearly impenetrable montane forest began. In the last segment, the ledge of the escarpment can be seen as one views the southern horizon. Bailey remarks that from that spot one looks out from Mt. Elgon.

Trip to dead man's cave

Baynes films an entourage marching single file into the forest and titles it: "trip to dead man's cave." An Elgonyi man leads the way followed by Beckwith, Jung, Bailey, two *askaris*, and another Elgonyi.

Beckwith and the two *askaris* are armed with rifles. Bailey remarks that for protection against venomous snakes, the "doctors" wore canvas gaiters while she wore long boots. Beckwith, who was happy-go-lucky, wore no protection.

Bailey explains that that they went up the mountain very far one day in order to find a cave which they had been told had a "devil" in it.[62] According to Jung, the cave was located at "almost eight thousand feet" and that "if anyone entered it, he was instantly killed" by "devils."[63] Bailey notes that neither Ibrahim nor the other Swahili assistants would accompany them on this trek because of their fear of the "devil."

Upon reaching the cave, an Elgonyi man living nearby in the forest volunteered to lead them into the cave. He assured the entourage that there was no "devil" in it.[64] They proceeded through a tunnel and stepped into a foot of bat guano dust. With great caution the team "descended in spirals about three hundred feet into the bowels of the earth" where they found "deep crevasses filled with water."[65] At one of these crevasses, Bailey spotted the body of a man who had apparently become disoriented in the darkness after his torch had been accidently extinguished.[66]

Figure 17: Trekking to dead man's cave.

THE BAYNES FILM

Afternoon rainstorm

This scene is brief and nearly indecipherable. It appears that Baynes films a violent rainstorm from within his tent. These storms were common in the afternoon and were often accompanied by wind, lightening, and hail. While viewing the film, Bailey remarks that during one terrible thunderstorm a tree fell down near their camp. Jung told them not to worry since if lightening struck them, they wouldn't feel a thing. Bailey was not amused.[67]

Mt. Elgon campsite

These scenes of the campsite are framed by three safari tents in a row with a fourth tent in the distance. Baynes films the morning camp chores: an assistant cleans a gun; Beckwith emerges from his tent in what appears to be bright, clean clothes; the cook and assistants are washing dishes and setting them to dry on a rack made of sticks; and Jung emerges from the distant tent.

Figure 18: Beckwith in camp.

Elgonyi Village in the Moorlands

Next, Baynes's notes indicate "scenes and groups in village." These shots are taken of an isolated Elgonyi village in the moorlands of high-altitude grasses and groundsels above the timberline of 9,600 feet. An *askari* and Ibrahim accompany Jung, Baynes, and Bailey to the site. Bailey remarks that this was a very poor village in which the people were "emaciated." She described them as "queer people."[68]

Figure 19: Elgonyi elders of moorland village.

The fourteen scenes of the episode depict the hiking party at rest, an encounter with four elders of the village (who Bailey calls the "chiefs"), groups of women and adolescent girls posing for the camera, a frail elder walking unsteadily, and an inspection of the village by the hiking party. The homes of the villagers are made of wooden poles and thatching. Bailey notes the granary bins of the village. She also reported that the "chiefs" asked Jung if he would trade her for four cows! Beckwith would kid her unmercifully about this for the rest of the trip.

Trek to Bamboo Belt

A bamboo belt encircled the mountain between 8,000 and 9,000 feet. One day Corporeal, Sabei,[69] and two locals led Baynes and Jung

Figure 20: Bailey and Jung in moorland village.

into this zone. Baynes wrote that in these groves, "the spirits lurk, and ran up one's spine."[70] He and Jung believed that the bamboo belt was the home of the ancestral spirits of the Elgonyi, an assumption that turned out to be inaccurate.[71]

The film depicts the party's march through this dense mountain forest. One of the locals, perhaps "Gibroat," carries a basket. In one scene Jung holds up a plant which he has harvested. In another Jung points his staff into the undergrowth to the "spoor of rhino" which has been found.[72] The fact that there were rhino, buffalo, lions, leopards, and venomous snakes in these jungles made these hikes particularly intense.

While they were in the bamboo, Jung reported that a "thunderstorm" raged above them and he noticed that Corporeal and Sabei became alarmed:

> One of the soldiers of a particularly courageous tribe was trembling all over and quite ashen in the face, and when I asked him if he was cold, he admitted that he was afraid. I said, "But it is awfully nice here. What are you afraid of? Are there perhaps some ghosts?" And then he whispered into my ear, "Yes, thousands and thousands."[73]

This episode ends with a fire in the bamboo. There is no information as to why the hiking party started this large fire which Bailey calls a "bush fire."[74] Were they wet or cold? Afraid of rhinos or ghosts?

Figure 21: Trek through bamboo.

STRIKING CAMP

A few days before Christmas, Jung asked Bailey if she would accompany the men through Uganda and down the Nile to Egypt and home. She agreed and left camp in order to retrieve her belongings in Nairobi. She would meet the men in Jinja in early January.

Soon after Bailey departed, the men broke camp in order to begin their march to Uganda. This episode depicts Jung, the *askaris*, and assistants saying goodbye to their Elgonyi hosts. The porters pick up their loads and begin the march in single file to the west.

THE BAYNES FILM

Figure 22: Striking camp.

Second Reel

(6) Caravan from Mt. Elgon, Kenya to Mbale, Uganda

Caravan to Malikisi

As in their first march, the caravan used rest houses along the route to Mbale, a distance of approximately sixty miles, about one week's walk. Baynes's notes indicate that from their Elgon campsite they march twenty-five miles southwest to the town of Malikisi on the southern flanks of the mountain. They likely made one camp at either the Arizigo rest house or the Anicrula rest house before arriving at Malikisi. Somewhere along the way, Baynes films the "porters crossing a difficult bridge" made of logs.[75]

Bugishu dance performance at Bunambale rest house, Uganda

The first rest house in Uganda was located at Bunambale, some seventeen miles from Malikisi. Jung wrote that they had entered "the territory of the Bugishu."[76] They "stayed some time", including New Year's Day, at Bunambale where there was "a splendid view of the broad Nile valley."[77]

Figure 23: Porter's crossing difficult bridge.

Baynes labels this scene: "first day in Uganda celebrated by *ngoma*. Buganda dancing."[78] From their chairs on the verandah of the rest house, Jung, Beckwith, and an *askari* watch a Bukusu man playing a stringed musical instrument and stomping in rhythm with jingles

Figure 24: Bugishu dance (with Beckwith handing coins to Jung).

strapped to both legs. He is immediately joined by two boys and one girl. Jung enters the scene with pipe in mouth and instructs the dancers to turn to face the camera. Bailey narrates that Jung is encouraging the dancing. Soon other Bukusu, young and old, join in the dance performance. After several minutes, the performers begin watching the *wazungu* on the porch while they continue dancing. Beckwith goes inside the rest house and returns with a handful of coins; he hands some of the coins to the sitting Jung. Hopeful of receiving money, other Bukusu by-standers join the dancers. Coins from Jung and Beckwith are thrown onto the ground; the dancers scramble to pick them up and the scene ends.

Headmen at Bunambale

Baynes titles this scene: "groups of local chiefs with Dr. Jung." Approximately ten Bukusu headmen in white *kanzus*, the traditional dress of men in Uganda, pose with Jung and Beckwith. Those on the front row sit on chop boxes and those on the back row stand. There are approximately twenty-five men in the photo including Ibrahim (who Bailey identifies in his wool hat). Relaxed and laughing, Beckwith is smoking a cigarette and wearing a bandana on his head.

Figure 25: Jung and Beckwith with headmen.

Figure 26: Ibrahim (center).

Caravan through Bugishu District

From Bunambale, the caravan treks seven miles to the rest house at Bubulo, the district headquarters of the Bugishu District. Bailey indicates that Jung spent the evening there with the DC.[79] Baynes records the hilly landscape where there were numerous banana plantations. Then, in the final caravan scene of the film, the porters stop to rest on a hillside before picking up their loads and proceeding. After the caravan leaves, we see several Bukusu men in *kanzus* standing on the hillside talking.

Banana plantation

Baynes continues filming the Ugandan hills, some of which were terraced and with thatched homes. Somewhere along the way, he and Jung walk through a "banana plantation"[80] collecting bananas. In one scene, a reposing Jung removes his pith helmet and wipes his forehead with a bandana.

Excursion to "Slippery Ridge"

This scene begins with a shot of a tall crater with a steep escarpment on its right side. Baynes labels this section: "Dr Jung and Ibrahim on way up to Slippery Ridge." "Slippery Ridge" is likely the volcanic Mt. Nkokonjeru located three miles to the east of Mbale. It appears that Baynes, Jung, Ibrahim, and, perhaps, Beckwith make an excursion up the volcano which is noted for its beautiful views and spectacular waterfalls. In many of these scenes the mist from the waterfalls floats across the lush jungle.

Figure 27: Ibrahim and Jung climbing "Slippery Ridge".

(7) JINJA AREA, UGANDA

JINJA AERODROME

After completing the march from Mt. Elgon to Mbale, the Elgonyi porters of the caravan were dismissed. Jung and party traveled the rest of the way through Uganda by automobile, boat, and train. From Mbale they rode in two Ford trucks to Jinja where they stayed in a hotel for approximately one week. Bailey rejoined the men there.

On January 8, 1926, the world-famous adventurer Sir Alan Cobham landed his "aeroplane" at the Jinja aerodrome. This was the first trans-African airplane flight ever attempted. This historic flight, which was being followed by Reuters with daily updates worldwide, would be successfully completed when Cobham landed in Cape Town,

South Africa several weeks later. Upon his return to London, he was knighted by King George V.

Baynes films several minutes of this event which attracted a large and diverse crowd of Ugandans, Indians, British colonial officials and settlers, and European tourists. In these first clips, before the plane arrives, one can see colonial officials, dressed in white safari suits and pith helmets, stationed along the runway to mark the boundary beyond which the spectators could not proceed. People and cars are lined up along the boundary for hundreds of yards. Cobham would later write that the "natives" ran in front of the plane as it landed and nearly caused an accident.[81] After the plane lands, Baynes captures, from a raised platform, the energy and excitement of the crowd. A throng of hundreds in animated conversation press in around the plane and the triumphant Cobham.

Bailey indicates that she and the men were able to converse with Cobham upon his arrival. When they told him about their plans to walk through the Sudan on foot, he remarked that they were "crazy." Nonetheless, Cobham entrusted Bailey with a bundle of letters which she posted once they arrived in Khartoum.[82]

Figure 28: Cobham's aeroplane.

Ripon Falls

Jinja is located on Lake Victoria near Ripon Falls which John Hanning Speke identified as the source of the Nile in 1862. Baynes films an excursion to the falls which he and the others took during their stay at Jinja. The camera pans across the cataracts, twelve feet high and 700 yards across, then down to the immediate bank at the foot of the viewer where it focuses on a plague. This marker identified the spot where Speke had once stood. It read: "Speke Discovered This Source Of The Nile On 28 July 1862."

Baynes, enthralled by the beauty, power, and the historical significance of the rapids, takes fifty-two different shots of Ripon Falls. In one shot an elegant Ugandan woman with a parasol stands at the water's edge; Baynes labels the scene: "Black Venus at Ripon Falls." Bailey remarks that they encountered a beautiful woman from Ugandan aristocracy.

Figure 29: Woman at Ripon Falls.

(8) Nile Route, through Uganda

Train depot at Jinja

It was Jung's desire to follow the Nile from its source all the way to Cairo. From Ripon Falls, the Victoria Nile flows some sixty miles to Lake Kioga. On January 13, the team departed from Jinja on the 10 am train to Namasagali on Lake Kioga.[83] Baynes films the train's arrival at the Jinja depot. Bailey recalls with embarrassment that the Provincial Commissioner, the Bishop, the owners of the Uganda hotel, and two young cotton farmers came to the train station to see her off while "invidiously" ignoring the world-famous Jung.[84]

Namasagali, Lake Kioga

At the port of Namasagali, dozens of porters await the arrival of a paddle-wheel steamer. This steamer, like the rail-link to the port, ran fortnightly.[85] Once it arrives, the porters load boxes onto the boat. Jung wrote that the "paddle-wheel steamer whose boiler was fired by wood picked us up and after a number of incidents brought us to Masindi Port."[86] Baynes notes that the "[j]ourney down the Nile begins."

Figure 30: Porters loading steamer.

Arrival at Port Masindi, Lake Kioga

The steamer arrives at the westernmost port of the lake and the passengers disembark. Baynes films a chaotic unloading scene at Port Masindi where the "[p]orters [are] seething out of wrong lighter."[87] Bailey reports that their luggage was lost here and that Baynes and Beckwith must return to the port to retrieve it.[88]

The team traveled from Lake Kioga to Lake Albert by automobile. Halfway to Lake Albert, there was a hotel at Masindi Town where they stayed for several days.

Figure 31: Porters unloading steamer.

Butiaba, Lake Albert

At "Butiaba", the team "embark[s] on the Samuel Baker"[89] paddle wheel steamer for a 171-mile trip down the Albert Nile to Nimule at the Uganda-Sudan border. The Samuel Baker was named for the British explorer and naturalist credited with discovering Lake Albert. Baynes films *askaris* and porters watching the steamer as it departs from the Lake Albert Marine. In the background are the trucks which apparently took the team to Butiaba. The camera rests on a group of "[l]abourers returning home."[90]

Figure 32: Lake Albert Marine.

THE ALBERT NILE

Baynes shoots panoramic views of the lush vegetation on the banks of the Albert Nile with distant mountains in the background. When asked what they did on the steamer, Bailey answered that they just sat and watched the villages passing by.

(9) NILE ROUTE, THROUGH THE SUDAN

ARRIVAL AT NIMULE

When the Samuel Baker arrived at the southern Sudanese outpost of Nimule, the steamer was met by dozens of porters who scramble into position in order to assist the passengers with their luggage. A chaotic scene ensues as *askaris* attempt to organize the porters lining up for work. Everything on the steamer had to be unloaded since the Nile was not navigable from Nimule to Rejaf, a distance of 100 miles.

The team stayed briefly with the *mamur* of Nimule, an administrative assistant to the British DC. In 1926, the Sudan was a condominium administered jointly by the British and Egyptian governments. With the *mamur's* help, a team of fifteen porters and three *askaris* were assembled to walk with Jung, Baynes, Beckwith, and Bailey across the Mongalla Province, an arid, flat plain with extreme day time temperatures. As is well-documented, this walk nearly proved disastrous as the team ran out of water only halfway across. Fortuitously, they encountered a lorry approaching from the south and Jung commandeered the driver to take them and their luggage to Rejaf.

Figure 33: Docking at Nimule.

Night fire

The night before their rescue by the lorry, one of the most memorable events of the entire five-month trip occurred. Exhausted and reclining at a rest house, halfway between Nimule and Rejaf, the safari was greeted by a troupe of dancers from the Bari people, the extremely dark-skinned and tall Nilotes living along the banks of the White Nile in southern Sudan.[91] Their Bari visitors built a large fire and entertained the caravan with dancing for hours. At one point, both Jung and Baynes joined in the *boma* which increased its zeal. Around eleven o'clock, somewhat exhausted and anxious about the increasing frenzy of the dance, Jung dismissed the dance troupe.

In this brief scene, we see a large fire at night with people moving rhythmically around it. Perhaps Baynes has filmed the dance with the Bari. Baynes did not, however, label this scene or the next scene in his notes.[92]

Bush fire near Rejaf

Following this nearly-disastrous march through the Mongalla district, the team stayed for approximately one week at Rejaf awaiting a paddle-wheel steamer to take them through the Sudd.[93] The waters of the Nile were low in late January and the boat had difficulty docking. Rejaf consisted of "a few cement block homes, and many straw ones."[94] According to Bailey, Jung started a bush fire near Rejaf which was "terrifying" and "fearsome." Indeed, once they embarked from Rejaf on the paddle-wheel steamer, Baynes films an enormous plumb of smoke rising thousands of feet into the Sudanese sky. Fleeing this bellowing black cloud is a Hitchcock-like scene of hundreds of egrets, herons, ducks, ibis, cranes, and storks. Except for Bailey's commentary there is no documentation of this eerie scene.

Passing Dinka Villages[95] in the Sudd

From Rejaf, the paddle-wheel steamer navigated the enormous Sudd swamp through the Bahr-el-Jebel channel of the White Nile.

Figure 34: Dinka village.

They passed the stations of Juba, Lado, Mongalla (where Jung dreamed of having his hair kinked by a black barber),[96] and Tombe. Baynes films these Dinka villages of round mud and thatched huts along the banks where children can be seen running along the village path keeping pace with the slow-moving steamer.

DOCKING AT MALAKAL IN BAHR-EL-JEBEL

The final station in the Sudd is Malakal. In viewing this segment of the film, Bailey indicates that she was sent into the market at Malakal to buy a watermelon. Baynes films one of the European passengers standing on the upper deck of the boat looking at the rows of tables at the busy market below. There is a lively mix of people: Muslim men wearing long white *jalabiya* (loose-fitting dresses) stand in conversation, European travelers in safari suits and pith helmets wander through the rows of goods, armed *askaris* in shorts escort scantily-clad porters with their loads to the boat, Sudanese women with scarves hawk their wares, and children play. Flying above the scene are the flags of Great Britain and Egypt. The Kingdom of Egypt flag was adopted in 1923 after Britain recognized Egyptian independence in 1922; the flag consisted of a white crescent moon with three white stars on a green background.

Figure 35: Malakal market.

A large pile of fire wood is stacked near the dock; fuel to power the steamer. The scene ends with Jung walking slowly through the market shooing flies with a goat tail.

The Sudd

Before the steamer leaves the Bahr-el-Jebel, Baynes provides images of the great papyrus swamp. The Sudd, the world's largest wetlands, extends from Mongalla in the south to just beyond Malakal in the north. The camera captures the seemingly endless expanse of lagoons, channels, and floating papyrus and reed fields. Beckwith stands on the top deck peering out with his binoculars. Enormous flocks of birds explode in front of the steamer, as Beckwith searches the waters for ever-present hippopotami and crocodile.

The steamer then docks at a tiny outpost. Eleven Dinka stand waiting as the boat maneuvers to the shore where, perhaps, they will buy wood to fuel the vessel. Near this same location, Baynes films a dike along the channel and yet another bush fire.

Figure 36: Outpost in the Sudd.

Third Reel

The Khartoum Zoo

After approximately eleven days on the steamer, the team arrived in Khartoum, the Sudanese capital with a population of 50,000. They stayed in Khartoum for one week as Jung lectured at Gordon Memorial College. Both Beckwith and Bailey were stricken with severe cases of malaria and bedridden for several days. After recovering, Bailey was accompanied by Jung and Baynes to the Zoological Gardens where there was an open-air zoo with no cages except for the big cats. In this scene, they are given a tour of the zoo by Major H. C. Brocklehurst, the decorated British Game Warden in the Sudan, now retired and overseeing the zoo.[97]

Brocklehurst entices several animals to perform stage tricks for his guests. In these comical and endearing but mostly pitiful scenes we see a representation of Sudanese wildlife: lions, chimpanzees, giraffes, deer, antelope, sheep, gazelles, baboons, leopards, secretary birds, ostriches, vultures, shoebills, cranes, ibises, pelicans, and storks. In one segment, Jung and Bailey play affectionately with a chimp. Bailey comments that she and the chimp became good friends.

Figure 37: Jung and Bailey with chimp.

(10) Nile Route, through Egypt

Nile between Wadi Halfa and Aswan

At Khartoum, the White Nile and the Blue Nile meet to form the Nile proper. Because of the cataracts, Jung and company took a train from Khartoum to the Egyptian border town of Wadi Halfa. It was mid-February. From Wadi Halfa, they reentered the Nile on one of the Sudan government express steamers for a thirty-seven-hour, 300-mile trip to Aswan.[98] There, where the Nile becomes Lake Nasser, Baynes films the romantic shore line of palms and sand. *Dahabeahs* (house boats with sails) appear as the lake widens; distant mountains come into view.

Figure 38: Nile in Egypt.

Aswan

In 1926, Aswan was a tourist resort with 16,000 residents. There were numerous tourist attractions including the Aswan Dam which was completed by the British in 1912, creating Lake Nasser. Baynes films the enormous, mile-thick dam wall in two separate sittings.

THE BAYNES FILM

Between the dam scenes, Baynes films a camel ride into the desert which Bailey describes in the Nameche interviews.[99] She indicates that a sheik provided the camels and a dragoman (guide) took them out onto the sands. Bailey, Jung, and Beckwith rest in the shade of a rock outcrop, then mount the camels and ride off into the hot desert. Bailey indicates that on the ride back they stop and enter a Coptic monastery. This is likely the Monastery at St. Simeon, one of the major tourist attractions of Aswan.[100]

Figure 39: Jung, Bailey, and Beckwith resting during camel ride.

SNAKE CHARMER AT LUXOR

From Aswan, the team took a train to Luxor, the principal tourist center in Upper Egypt with 19,000 residents. The discovery of Tutankhamen's tomb at Luxor in 1922 drew world attention to this once sleepy town which was built on the ruins of the ancient city of Thebes and was now one of the world's great tourist designations.

At Luxor, Jung and Baynes are fascinated with the snake charmers who perform for the tourists. Baynes films one of the snake charmers and his cobra. Bailey comments that the man was a fake because he had removed the cobra's venom.[101]

Figure 40: Snake charmer holding cobra.

Dahabeahs on Nile at Luxor

This final Nile scene is taken from the river bank at Luxor. From Luxor, they continue by train to Cairo.

Wheel Well

The last scene, filmed at an unknown location, is a wheel well powered by an ox. A nymph-like boy riding on this ancient invention to draw water gazes at the camera. The water drawn from the well has completed its long journey from Ripon Falls in Uganda to this village in Lower Egypt.

Conclusion: Coming Home

The team's stay in Cairo lasted approximately one week. From there, they traveled by train to Port Said where they waited four days for a ship to take them to Genoa, Italy. Baynes suffered with a terrible toothache at Port Said which incapacitated him.[102] After sailing to Italy, Jung's son, Franz, met them and accompanied Jung and Baynes by train to Zurich while Beckwith and Bailey sailed on to Marseilles, France. Jung and Baynes arrived in Zurich on March 14. Baynes remained Jung's

Figure 41: Boy on wheel well.

first assistant until 1931 when he returned to London on a full-time basis as the unquestioned leader of analytical psychology in the United Kingdom. After a short illness from a brain tumor, he died in 1943 at the age of sixty-one.

NOTES

1. Diana Baynes Jansen, *Jung's Apprentice: A Biography of Helton Godwin Baynes* (Einsiedeln: Diamon Verlag, 2003), p. 121.

2. Jim Hare, Academic Consultant Senior in the Technology Center of the College of Arts and Sciences at Baylor University, assisted with the extraction of still photos published in this article from a DVD copy of the film.

3. The term "Elgonyi" is no longer in use today; the people are known today as the Sabaoot.

3. *East African Standard*, November 9, 1925, p. 3. Some of the sixty-four names were listed as "with family."

4. I explain the details of this journey in *Jung in Africa* (London: Continuum, 2005).

5. Burleson, *Jung in Africa*, p. 38.

6. Ruth Bailey, Unpublished oral interview with Miss Ruth Bailey. Interviewed by Gene F. Nameche (Boston: Countway Library of Medicine at Harvard University, 1970), p. 1.

7. *East African Standard*, November 15, 1925, p. 4.

8. C. G. Jung, *Memories, Dreams, Reflections* (New York: Vintage Books, 1963), p. 254. (Subsequently *MDR*.)

9. *East African Standard*, November 19, 1925, p. 5.

10. *Ibid.*

11. C. G. Jung, *Protocols* (the unpublished German Urtext of *Memories, Dreams, Reflections* assembled by Aniela Jaffe and held in the "Papers of C. G. Jung" container at the Manuscript Division of the Library of Congress, Washington, DC), box 1, folder 13, p. 373.

12. *MDR*, p. 255.

13. H. G. Baynes, unpublished notes on his film of C. G. Jung's Expedition to E. Africa. He writes, "Kikuyu dance at Kikuru." "Kikuru" is a Kikuyu corruption of "Kikuyu."

14. H. G. Baynes, *Germany Possessed* (London: Cape, 1941), p. 127.

15. For an explanation of the cultural complexes behind this scene and others in the film, see: Blake Burleson, "Jung in Africa: The Historical Record," *Journal of Analytical Psychology* 53 (2008): 209-223.

16. See Burleson, *Jung in Africa*, pp. 108-109 for an explanation of this change in destination.

17. C. G. Jung, *Collected Works,* Vol. 18 (Princeton: Princeton University Press), §1288.

18. C. G. Jung, *Visions: Notes of the Seminar given in 1930-1934 by C. G. Jung*, Vol. 2, edited by Claire Douglas (Princeton: Princeton University Press, 1997), p. 472.

19. Bailey, 1970, p. 7.

20. *Collected Works*, Vol. 10, §126 and §143.

21. Burleson, *Jung in Africa*, p. 115.

22. Patrick M. Synge, *Mountains of the Moon: An Expedition to the Equatorial Mountains of Africa* (London: Lindsay Drummond, 1979), p. 59.

23. "A map of North Kavirondo drawn in 1924," Kenya National Archives.
24. Baynes, unpublished notes.
25. Ibid.
26. Baynes indicates "Roderick Falls," a misspelling.
27. See Burleson, "Jung in Africa: The Historical Record," pp. 214-215.
28. The Sabei were one of four clusters of the Elgonyi people located on Mt. Elgon. The *askari* named "Sabei" was likely an Elgonyi.
29. Bailey, 1970, p. 10.
30. Carl Akeley and Mary Akeley, *Adventures in the African Jungle* (New York: Junior Literary Guild, 1931), p. 146.
31. *MDR*, p. 259.
32. Phillip Kiborom, Interview by Blake Burleson, July 20, 2003, Kapsokowny, Kenya. Kiborom was one of my Elgonyi (Sabawoot) informants from Mt. Elgon.
33. Baynes labels this scene "arrival at Murungas' in his notes. Murunga was the name of the chief of the Wanga and also the name of a village. It would not seem likely that the caravan stopped at Murunga, the village, since it is to the west of the assumed route of the caravan to Elgon. Baynes may have confused Kimilili which had a rest house operated by Chief Murunga, with Murunga, the village.
34. The Kenyan branch of the Bugishu is known today as the Bukusu.
35. R. W. Hemsted, "Annual Report: Nyanza Province Kisumu, 1925," Kenya National Archives, p. 8.
36. Baynes, unpublished notes.
37. I was able to establish the location of the campsite by tracing the Kibuuk stream from Kimilili. Jung wrote in a letter home that the campsite was twelve kilometers north of Kimilili. See C. G. Jung, *Letters*, Vol. 1 (Princeton: Princeton University Press, 1973), p. 43.
38. *MDR*, p. 261.
39. *Ibid.*, p. 260.
40. A. E. Chamier, "Annual Report: North Kavirondo District: Kakamega," Kenya National Archives, p. 7 and Baynes, unpublished notes. Note: Baynes labels this scene "Tendete and his wives."

41. Walter Goldschmidt, *Culture and Behavior of the Sabei: A Study in Continuity and Adaptation* (Los Angeles: University of California Press, 1976), p. 55.
42. "A map of North Kavirondo drawn in 1924."
43. *MDR*, p. 260.
44. Yakobo Siikiiryo, Interview by Blake Burleson, July 22, 2003, Kapsokwony, Kenya. Kiikiiryo was one of my Elgonyi (Sabawoot) informants from Mt. Elgon.
45. "Gibroat" is probably a mispronunciation of the Elgonyi name Kiprotich.
46. *MDR*, p. 262.
47. Baynes, unpublished notes.
48. *American Heritage Dictionary.*
49. Francis Daniel Hislop, "Doctor Jung, I presume," *Corona: The Journal of Her Majesty's Colonial Service* (June, 1960), p. 237.
50. Francis Kiboi, personal communication, February 2, 2004. Kiboi was one of my Elgonyi (Sabawoot) informants from Mt. Elgon.
51. Goldschmidt, p. 311.
52. *Collected Works*, Vol. 18, §436.
53. *MDR*, p. 265.
54. *Collected Works*, Vol. 10, §144.
55. *Ibid.*, §128.
56. Goldschmidt, p. 59.
57. Jansen, p. 173.
58. Hemsted, p. 8
59. Vincent Brome, *Jung* (New York: Atheneum, 1978), p. 205.
60. Bailey, 1969, p. 11.
61. Bailey, 1969, p. 10.
62. Jung, *Visions,* p. 740.
63. *Ibid.*
64. *Ibid.*
65. Bailey, 1969, p. 10.
66. Bailey, 1970, p. 10.
67. Bailey, 1969, p. 13.
68. Baynes's unpublished notes.
69. H. G. Baynes, *Mythology of the Soul: A Research into the Unconscious from Schizophrenic Dreams and Drawings* (London: Bailliere, Tindell & Cox, 1940), p. 194.

70. For a full explanation, see Burleson, *Jung in Africa*, pp. 153-155.
71. Baynes's unpublished notes.
72. Jung, *Visions*, p. 742.
73. Bailey, 1970, p. 15.
74. Baynes's unpublished notes.
75. *MDR*, p. 270.
76. Jung, *Letters*, Vol. 1, p. 44.
77. Baynes labels this "Buganda Dancing." This is inaccurate since the Buganda people were located in Central Uganda.
78. Bailey, 1970, p. 22.
79. Baynes's unpublished notes.
80. Alan J. Cobham, *My Flight to the Cape and Back* (London: A. & C. Black, 1926), p. 29.
81. Bailey, 1969, p. 31.
82. *Ibid.*, p. 19.
83. *Ibid.*
84. Karl Baedeker, *Egypt and the Sudan: Handbook for Travelers* (Leipzig: Karl Baedeker, 1929), p. 567.
85. *MDR*, p. 270.
86. The title of this scene is apparently out of order in Baynes's notes.
87. Bailey, 1969, p. 37.
88. Baynes's unpublished notes.
89. *Ibid.*
90. Burleson, *Jung in Africa*, p. 191f.
91. Baynes might have been reluctant to identify this scene in his notes since dances by "natives" were illegal and Jung had encouraged and participated in the illegal dance.
92. Hannah, p. 176.
93. Nettie Dietz, *A White Woman in a Black Man's Country: Three Thousands Miles Up the Nile to Rejaf* (Omaha, NE: private printing, 1926), p. 192.
94. Baynes's unpublished notes.
95. Burleson, *Jung in Africa*, p. 199f.
96. Bailey, 1970, p. 25.

97. Baedeker, p. 409.

98. Bailey says that the camel ride occurred in the Valley of the Kings at Luxor. Perhaps there were two camel rides and Baynes only films this first one at Aswan or, perhaps, Bailey is mistaken in the location of the camel ride.

99. There is no Coptic monastery in the Valley of the Kings.

100. Bailey, 1970, p. 27.

101. Bailey, 1969, p. 52.

APPENDIX I: PREVIOUSLY UNPUBLISHED NOTES OF H. G. BAYNES
ON THE CONTENTS OF HIS FILM OF THE
BUGISHU PSYCHOLOGICAL EXPEDITION TO EAST AFRICA

DR. C.G. JUNG'S EXPEDITION TO E.AFRICA, 1925 - 1926
(TO STUDY THE TRIBES OF BUGISHUS & ELGONYIS, MT. ELGON, KENYA)

CONTENTS

Kikuyu dance at Kikuru. Scenes at Kakamegas.
Tent-pitching exercise supervised by Dr Jung.
First Boma of safari. Dr Jung & Ephlaim.
Safari up to Roderick Falls.
Dr Jung paying porters. Sabei & Corporal. Nfigi play.
Arrival at Marungas. Headmen.
Elgon Camp. Group of women. Tendete & his wives.
Palaver with Gaptek & others.
Trek to cave-dwellers.
Cave, with goats, mtotos & Dr Jung.
Trip to 'dead-man' cave. Scenes & groups in village.
Trek up Elgon to bamboo-belt.
Dr. Jung, Corporal & Sabei.
Spoor of rhino.
Departure from Elgon. Striking camp.

* * *

Safari to Malakisi.
Porters crossing difficult bridge.
First day in Uganda celebrated by Ngoma. Buganda dancing.
Way up to Bunambali. Groups of local chiefs with Dr. Jung.
Banana plantation, Dr. Jung & Ibrahim.
On the way up to Slippery Ridge.
Scenes at Jinja. Crowds waiting for Sir Alan Cobham.
Ripon Falls. Beginning of the Nile.
Black Venus at Ripon Falls.
Journey down Nile begins. Butiaba.
Embarking on 'Samuel Baker'.
Groups of labourers returning home.
Porters seething out of wrong lighter.

Dinka villages along the banks of the Nile.
Desert & camels.
Dr. Jung & Miss Ruth Bailey at Khartoum Zoo.
Assuan Dam.
Snake Charmer.
Egyptian Water-Mill.

(Filmed by Dr. H.G. Baynes)

Appendix II
The 48 scenes of the Baynes film
Blake Burleson

First Reel
(1) Arrival at Kilindini harbor, Mombasa, Kenya
(2) Central Highlands, Kenya
   (a) The Athi Plains
   (b) Kikuyu dance at Kikuyu
(3) Kakamega
   (a) Market
   (b) Tent-pitching exercise
(4) Caravan from Kakamega to Mt. Elgon, North Kavirondo District
   (a) Mwanza rest house, Kabras location
   (b) Safari up to Broderick Falls.
   (c) Bridge over Nzoia River at Broderick Falls.
   (d) Paying the Porters, Murumba rest house
   (e) Re-enactment of hyena attack, Murumba rest house
   (f) Kimilili
(5) Mt. Elgon
   (a) Elgonyi women bearing water
   (b) Visit of Tendeet
   (c) Palaver with Cheebteek
   (d) Acacias of the Kamutiang' escarpment
   (e) The forest caves of Elgon
   (f) Trees on the edge of the montane forest
   (g) Trip to dead man's cave
   (h) Afternoon rainstorm
   (i) Mt. Elgon campsite

(j) Elgonyi village in moorlands
(k) Trek to bamboo belt
(l) Striking camp

Second Reel
(6) Caravan from Mt. Elgon, Kenya to Mbale, Uganda
   (a) Caravan to Malikisi
   (b) Bugishu dance performance at Bunambale rest house, Uganda
   (c) Headmen at Bunambale
   (d) Caravan through Bugishu District
   (e) Banana plantation
   (f) Excursion to "Slippery Ridge"
(7) Jinja area, Uganda
   (a) Jinja Aerodrome
   (b) Ripon Falls
(8) Nile Route, through Uganda.
   (a) Train Depot at Jinja.
   (b) Namasagali, Lake Kioga.
   (c) Arrival at Port Masindi, Lake Kioga
   (d) Butiaba, Lake Albert
   (e) The Albert Nile
(9) Nile Route, through the Sudan.
   (a) Arrival at Nimule
   (b) Night fire
   (c) Bush fire near Rejaf
   (d) Passing Dinka villages in the Sudd
   (e) Docking at Malakal in Bahr-el-Jebel
   (f) The Sudd

Third Reel
   (g) The Khartoum Zoo
(10) Nile Route, through Egypt.
   (a) Nile between Wadi Halfa and Aswan.
   (b) Aswan
   (c) Snake Charmer at Luxor
   (d) Dahabeahs on Nile at Luxor
   (e) Wheel well

Continuing Responses to the Giegerich/Romanyshyn Debate

The next 3 articles, by John Hoedl, Linda Buzzell, and Craig Chalquist, are responses to previously published *Spring* articles by Wolfgang Giegerich and Robert Romanyshyn and rejoinders to them. Below is a chronological listing of these prior articles:

1. *Spring*, Vol. 80 (Fall 2008): *Spring* published "The Melting of the Polar Ice: Revisiting *Technology as Symptom and Dream*" by Robert Romanyshyn.

2. *Spring*, Vol. 82 (Fall 2009): Wolfgang Giegerich wrote a critique of Romanyshyn's article called "The Psychologist as Repentence Preacher and Revivalist/Robert Romanyshyn on the Melting Polar Ice."

3. Spring, Vol. 84 (Fall 2010): This issue, called *God Must Not Die! Or Must He?: Jung and Christianity,* contained a new article by Giegerich on the Jung and Christianity theme, followed by responses to it.
   This issue also contained four rejoinders to Giegerich's critique of Romanyshyn's Polar Ice article: Robert Romanyshyn's ("Who is Wolfgang Giegerich?"), Susan Rowland's ("Robert Romanyshyn and Wolfgang Giegerich: Poles Apart"), Joel Weishaus's ("Response to Wolfgang Giegerich's 'The Psychologist as Repentence Preacher and Revivalist: Robert Romanyshyn on the Melting of the Polar Ice'), and David Rosen's "Response to Wolfgang Giegerich's 'The Psychologist as Repentence Preacher and Revivalist: Robert Romanyshyn on the Melting of the Polar Ice').

John Hoedl responds to the Giegerich/Romanyshyn debate as well as to Giegerich's work, more generally. Linda Buzzell and Craig Chalquist engage specifically with the issues raised in the Giegerich/Romanyshyn controversy.

WOLFGANG GIEGERICH: THE SEARCH FOR PSYCHOLOGICAL "SOUL"

JOHN HOEDL

It was with much interest that I read the last issue of *Spring* entitled *God Must Not Die! (Or Must He?)*, making my way through Wolfgang Giegerich's provocative article, "God Must Not Die! C. G. Jung's Thesis of the One-Sidedness of Christianity" and the thoughtful, varied, and even polarized comments to it, and then going on to read the four rejoinders to Giegerich's earlier article, "The Psychologist as Repentence Preacher and Revivalist/Robert Romanyshyn on the Melting Polar Ice," which had been published in the fall 2009 issue of *Spring*. It is heartening to see the editor pushing beyond concerns and criticisms to give this material a central place in the journal's focus. Indeed, I haven't waited so impatiently for the delivery of my copy for quite some time. The debate between Robert Romanyshyn and Giegerich, for example, is concerned with a question that is central to our field: what exactly should be the focus

---

John Hoedl is a Jungian psychoanalyst with a private practice in Edmonton, Alberta, Canada. He trained at the C. G. Jung Institute in Zurich, is the current president of the Western Canadian Association of Jungian Analysts, and is an executive member of the International Society for Psychology as the Discipline of Interiority. He is also the current president of and regular presenter at the Edmonton Jung Forum Association. He has lectured in a number of Canadian cities on various topics, including alchemy and Jungian psychology.

of the psychologist? The patient, the environment, melting icebergs, or the "soul"?

Of note was the fact that all four rejoinders to Giegerich (by Romanyshyn, Susan Rowland, Joel Weishaus, and David H. Rosen) were very critical of his critique of Romanyshyn's article "The Melting Polar Ice: Revisiting Technology as Symptom and Dream."[1] For the record, although Giegerich's language was strong and the tone at times surprisingly pointed, I found his article to be a breath of fresh air in the often-stale room of predictable Jungian discourse. The critique may have been focused on Romanyshyn's article, but I read it as a Leviathan-sized reaction to an outdated, undisciplined, one-sided approach to psychology, "soul", and Jung.

Giegerich is heralding an animus-oriented psychology, and if you haven't noticed, there will be no taking of prisoners. This neglected but indispensable animus compensates for an anima-only attitude and challenges us to embrace a new understanding of psychological *thought*. It takes absolutely seriously Jung's notion of the objective psyche and his admonition to not let anything from outside into the alchemical vessel of psychological analysis. It takes off the rose-colored glasses in order to *think* through what "soul" might possibly mean for us today.

For me, and a growing number of people, this understanding of psychology has been relegated to the back of the Jungian classroom for too long. It's puzzling that even though Giegerich has been writing and publishing in this vein for over three decades, we still have to ask the question "Who Is Wolfgang Giegerich?"[2] Has his psychological perspective been ignored for so long that when it is finally heard, as Glen Slater disapprovingly writes, it "bears no resemblance to that which Jung or Jungians of any ilk hold at the core of their work"?[3] But of course this is not true; even in the selfsame journal, four Jungians responding to the article were inspired to write penetrating amplifications and critiques. And the momentum seems to be growing. Giegerich's outstanding four-volume *Collected English Papers* has recently been published;[4] groups are forming around the world to study and discuss his works; candidates in training eagerly anticipate his lectures; and the International Society for Psychology as the Discipline of Interiority (ISPDI) has been recently formed to continue his work. Even those who had earlier, for whatever reason, found Jungian psychology lacking are, through Giegerich's work, looking at it again with fresh and open eyes.

Far from thinking that Giegerich has "snapped a few links with reality"[5] or that his arguments are "beside the point,"[6] as authors in this journal have written, these indications are proof to me that early hunches about Giegerich's work were correct: that this profound thinker's ideas need to be engaged, reflected upon, *entered into,* and critiqued—one would hope with the same care that he brings to his critique of Jung's work. For example, Giegerich writes, "[in critiquing a body of work] we have to table our own conviction and, leaving it behind for the moment, move into the center of our object of study, *giving ourselves over to it*, in order to view its peripheral statements from 'behind,' as it were (*immanent reflection*) . . . A real understanding presupposes a kind of love, one's abandon of one's own subjectivity; not love as a sentiment or emotion, but logical love. If we have not succeeded in (at least experimentally) *giving ourselves over* to the inspiring core of the work we are examining, we will not even be able to criticize it. The criticism would simply pass it by. It would be the criticism of our own opposite, our own rejected counterpart."[7]

What perhaps does not come through in the rejoinders or critiques in *Spring Journal*—but does when one reads through Giegerich's work—is his deep respect and honoring of Jung's psychology. It is obvious, however, that this does not keep him from clearly pointing out what parts he sees as unpsychological and in need of revision. The revision he calls for is ultimately based on a desire to keep this psychology relevant and to continue to work at comprehending the groundbreaking, singular insights of Jung so that when necessary we will move, as Giegerich writes, "*with* Jung *beyond* Jung."[8] One may or may not agree with Giegerich's critique, but taken seriously, it cannot help but engender a more penetrating and comprehensive reading of Jung's work as well as continually clarify what we mean when we use the word "psychology." This should always be welcome.

NOTES

1. *Spring: A Journal of Archetype and Culture* 80 (Fall 2008): 79–116.

2. See Robert D. Romanyshyn, "Who Is Wolfgang Giegerich?" *Spring: A Journal of Archetype and Culture* 84 (Fall 2010): 273–310.

3. Glen Slater, "No As If, No Between: The Giegerich Inversion of Mind and Soul," *Spring: A Journal of Archetype and Culture* 84 (Fall 2010): 185.

4. *The Neurosis of Psychology: Primary Papers towards a Critical Psychology* (New Orleans, La.: Spring Journal Books, 2006); *Technology and the Soul: From the Nuclear Bomb to the Worldwide Web* (New Orleans, La.: Spring Journal Books, 2007); *Soul-Violence* (New Orleans, La.: Spring Journal Books, 2008); and *The Soul Always Thinks* (New Orleans, La.: Spring Journal Books, 2010).

5. Joel Weishaus, "Response to Wolfgang Giegerich's 'The Psychologist as Repentance Preacher and Revivalist: Robert Romanyshyn on the Melting of the Polar Ice,'" *Spring: A Journal of Archetype and Culture* 84 (Fall 2010): 324.

6. Slater, "No As If, No Between," p. 185.

7. Wolfgang Giegerich, *The Soul's Logical Life: Towards a Rigorous Notion of Psychology*, 3rd rev. ed. (Frankfurt am Main: Peter Lang, 2008), p. 89.

8. Wolfgang Giegerich, "Psychology—the Study of the Soul's Logical Life," in *Who Owns Jung?* edited by Ann Casement (London: Karnac, 2007), p. 247.

THE GIEGERICH/ROMANYSHYN DEBATE ABOUT DEPTH PSYCHOLOGY AND CLIMATE CHANGE: NO SOUL IN NATURE?

LINDA BUZZELL

As a psychotherapist and ecotherapist, I found some of Wolfgang Giegerich's statements in "The Psychologist as Repentance Preacher and Revivalist" deeply disturbing.[1] He bemoans "a growing tendency in the Jungian field to advocate what has been called eco-psychology" and finds that field to be "incompatible with what I would consider psychology proper, a 'psychology with soul' in the tradition of C.G. Jung."[2]

Here I believe we encounter one of the logical fallacies underlying the current disastrous state of the human-nature relationship: the assumption that psyche and soul are to be found in humans but not

---

Linda Buzzell, M.A., M.F.T., is co-editor with Craig Chalquist of *Ecotherapy: Healing with Nature in Mind* (Sierra Club Books 2009) and the founder of the International Association for Ecotherapy. She has been a practicing psychotherapist for over thirty years and an ecotherapist since 2000. From 2006 to 2010 she was Adjunct Faculty at Pacifica Graduate Institute, supervising the community and ecological fieldwork of first-year students in the Depth Psychology Ph.D. program. She is on the board of the OPUS Archives and Research Center in Santa Barbara, California, which holds the works of Joseph Campbell, Maria Gimbutas, James Hillman, Marion Woodman, Jane Hollister Wheelwright, Joseph Wheelwright, Adolf Guggenbühl-Craig, Christine Downing, and Katie Sanford.

in the rest of nature. According to this way of thinking, the animals, the plants, the planet, and the cosmos have no soul or voice—so we have no need to consider them as relevant to our field of psychology.

Giegerich also doesn't trust human emotions as a source of valid information about the world. "Emotions in general inevitably make us unfree to the extent that we are under their spell."[3] Apparently he remains unaware that emotions are not only a useful and practical mode of knowing but also play a critical role in human health and any soul-centered healing practice. His writing is also curiously silent about the third critical member of the body-mind-soul trilogy—the flesh that is such an undeniable and inseparable part of larger nature. It is a basic tenet of ecopsychology that a healthy human being cannot exist in the absence of a healthy natural context. We are embedded in the earth as long as we are alive on this planet. Denying the scientific fact that our bodies are a part of wider nature is a form of truly destructive madness—an abnormal psychological condition that is now in the process of destroying the nature on which we and other living beings depend for life on this planet.

But not to worry. According to Giegerich, apparently the soul doesn't depend on the health of the body or the rest of nature for its continued existence. "The soul is 'un-natural' from the outset," he says. "If it were not 'un-natural,' if it were itself a piece of nature, there would not be soul at all."[4] Really? This sounds like religious belief rather than modern psychology. Perhaps Giegerich, like the radical Christian rapturists, looks forward to his soul being beamed up if conditions become too tough here on Earth to support him or his descendants.

Geigerich also seems to be unaware of the severity of the jeopardies currently facing the human body-mind-soul (and the living substance of many other sentient beings as well) on a planet reeling from climate disruption (yes, Romanyshyn's melting glaciers are a visible symptom); energy, food, and water shortages; toxic contamination of life-sustaining soil, water, and air—all leading to historically unprecedented economic and social breakdown affecting billions around the world.

But perhaps Giegerich just doesn't care? "What's so special about the coming doom?" he asks. "We all know that we will have to die. Is this a reason to make . . . a huge fuss and bother about it? Let's keep both feet on the ground."[5] What an incredibly callous and *un*grounded remark from a supposedly compassionate Jungian analyst! Perhaps he feels safe and unconcerned about the state of the rest of the world as he sits in his insulated consulting room while the very ground under his feet is poisoned, degraded, flooded by rising seas, or shaken apart by an earthquake.

According to Giegerich, psychologists and psychotherapists have no role to play in addressing the currently disastrous state of the human-nature relationship. "What is it to a psychologist . . . whether the world is getting worse or better?"[6] Ecopsychologists and ecotherapists—whether their orientation is analytical, behavioral, cognitive, interpersonal, or neurochemical—beg to differ: who better to analyze and treat our currently suicidal, matricidal, and fratricidal relationship with the rest of nature than those with deep knowledge of the human psyche and all its gifts and shadows? The fact that the human species is in the process of destroying its own life support systems is a giant elephant in *every* consulting room. How can we in good conscience closet ourselves away in our ivory-towered offices (the ivory presumably coming from dying elephants or walruses we don't mention) at this unique time in history, oblivious to all that is happening around us that directly affects our clients' moods, dreams, anxiety levels, and physical and economic well-being?

One may or may not argue with the particulars of Robert Romanyshyn's presentation but surely we must acknowledge his courage in addressing the fact that Rome and the planet are indeed burning while we sit in our pleasant, well-decorated offices, comfortably "attending to" our clients.

Our whole profession would do well to attend to Romanyshyn's admonition that "as psychologists in service to soul we have an obligation to stay in touch with the experience of anxiety [at the state of the world], examine it, and *not* benumb ourselves to it, particularly and specifically when the response of denial is so widespread in the cultural circumstances of our time. Anxiety and its denial over the melting polar ice in particular and climate changes in general is a pervasive cultural experience and as such a legitimate issue for psychology in general, and, I believe for depth psychology in particular."[7]

In my view, Romanyshyn offers a much more "grounded" response than Geigerich's ostrich-like delusion of separateness from what is really going on in our world and the rest of nature at this uniquely challenging point in human history.

Ecotherapist Sarah Anne Edwards and I wrote an essay on "The Waking Up Syndrome" that outlines the stages of awareness people may go through as they begin to grasp the true nature and enormity of those challenges, based on Elisabeth Kübler-Ross's stages of dealing with death and dying.[8] The first of these stages is denial. This is where I would place Wolfgang Giegerich's remarks. Robert Romanyshyn seems to be in the often-painful stage of awakening to what's happening, and I find his bravery in sharing that emotionally messy state with his colleagues quite moving. All of us are in various stages of this process—therapist and client alike—and hopefully we will find our way through shock and despair to acceptance and empowerment.

NOTES

1. Wolfgang Giegerich, "The Psychologist as Repentance Preacher and Revivalist: Robert Romanyshyn on the Melting of the Polar Ice," *Spring: A Journal of Archetype and Culture* 82 (Fall 2009): 193–221.

2. *Ibid.*, p. 194.

3. *Ibid.*, p. 195.

4. *Ibid.*, p. 208.

5. *Ibid.*, p. 197.

6. *Ibid.*, p. 210.

7. Robert D. Romanyshyn, "Who Is Wolfgang Giegerich?" *Spring: A Journal of Archetype and Culture* 84 (Fall 2010): 277.

8. Sarah Anne Edwards and Linda Buzzell, "The Waking Up Syndrome," in *Ecotherapy: Healing with Nature in Mind,* edited by Linda Buzzell and Craig Chalquist (San Francisco: Sierra Club Books, 2009), pp. 123–130.

GIEGERICH, ROMANYSHYN, AND THE ECO-APOCALYPSE WITNESSES-ONLY CLUB

CRAIG CHALQUIST

The debate began in the Fall 2008 issue of *Spring Journal* with Robert Romanyshyn's thoughtful and moving article reflecting on the decline of polar ice.[1] Wolfgang Giegerich responded by calling Romanyshyn a preacher,[2] prompting Romanyshyn to define his position in contrast to ecopsychology, a field he sees as largely self-righteous and activist.[3] Jung was invoked, and Rilke. Latin phrases were resorted to. That kind of debate.

Both men agreed at least on this, though: that being an ecopsychologist and activist precludes deep psychological work. For Giegerich, eco-oriented activism of the type he accuses Romanyshyn

---

Craig Chalquist is a core faculty member in East-West Psychology at the California Institute of Integral Studies, where he teaches depth psychology and ecopsychology, and adjunct faculty at John F. Kennedy University and Pacifica Graduate Institute. He is the author of *Terrapsychology: Reengaging the Soul of Place* (Spring Journal Books, 2007), co-editor with Linda Buzzell of *Ecotherapy: Healing the Nature with Mind* (Sierra Club Books, 2009), and editor of *Rebearths: Conversations with a World Ensouled* (World Soul Books, 2010). He lives in California's Bay Area, a highly productive ecological, cultural, and spirirtual estuary. His website is Chalquist.com.

of indulging in is not only "incompatible with what I would consider psychology proper,"[4] it is also moralistic,[5] an imposition of subjective value judgments,[6] an ego trip,[7] an example of playing world-rescuer,[8] being "a politician, a technician . . . a social engineer . . . a healer or savior, educator, or reformer . . . do-gooder,"[9] and other presumably bad things. "Ecological psychology," he announces without realizing that the field bearing that name is completely different in aims and methods from ecopsychology, is "an oxymoron or even a down-right contradiction in terms,"[10] evidently because it takes the external world seriously enough to do more than think about it. As for Romanyshyn, he "would not label my work eco-psychology" [sic] without extensive qualifications,[11] presumably because it represents "a psychology that often seems to lack a proper humility in the face of the Anima Mundi"[12] and "serves our own narcissism."[13] He gives no examples of these faults, but in spite of them he approvingly cites ecopsychologist Andy Fisher for his lack of inner/outer self/world dualism.[14]

If either academic ever had an earnest conversation with real activists or real ecopsychologists, it didn't show. Neither acknowledges any of the significant psychological differences between activism as narcissistic rescue and activism as legitimate soul work. Both accept without question the entrenched, institutionalized split between psychological/ intellectual speechifying and getting one's hands dirty in the real world, although Romanyshyn does wonder briefly, if only about Giegerich, why depth psychology "too often seems irrelevant today and perhaps even dangerous in its disregard of the world."[15] My activist students would have much to say about that!

This relatively recent split between psychological work and activism is puzzling given the activist history of depth psychology. Jung, who began scribbling mandalas while on active military duty at the end of World War I, drew up psychological portraits of leading Nazis for the American Office of Strategic Services during World War II. Alfred Adler, a socialist, helped build and promote child guidance clinics. Wilhelm Reich worked as an advocate for women's rights, and Harry Stack Sullivan worked for UNESCO (the United Nations Educational, Scientific and Cultural Organization). Otto Fenichel was an active socialist. Nancy Caro Hollander has written movingly of psychoanalysts working under conditions of extreme political oppression in South America.[16] Ignacio Martin-Baro, the founder of liberation psychology, was shot to death in El Salvador while conducting psychodynamic research on the inner consequences of state terrorism. His last words were, "This is an injustice!" Karl Abraham treated wounded soldiers.

More recently, Mary Watkins and Helene Lorenz have conducted depth-psychological cultural work in South America.[17] James Hillman has a long record of showing up for civic events. Analyst Andrew Samuels is a political consultant; in 1995 he co-founded Psychotherapists and Counselors for Social Responsibility.

Are we seriously to believe that all these foundational depth psychologists stopped being depth psychologists every time they worked for a just cause? Would they have seen their activities in this pale, intellectually filtered light? And not only them, but the feminists, the deep ecologists, the environmentalists, the protesters who speak out so eloquently against sexism, racism, and totalistic control: all to be diagnosed as self-absorbed narcissists, saviors, and do-gooders unworthy of carrying the official Soul ID card issued by the Department of Homeland Psychology?

It seems to me that Giegerich and Romanyshyn are trying to write a one-size-fits-all prescription for what should be a matter of temperament, talent, and personal passion: namely, how much activism a depth practitioner feels called to undertake. A basic strength of depth psychology remains its capacity for tending psychic diversity and polycentricity, actively welcoming silenced voices that inhabit the margins of culture and consciousness. Likewise, in ecopsychology we delight in how the natural world avoids monolithic absolutes in its ongoing abundance and organic experimentation.

Both fields teach us that the more diversity we welcome and the less "othering" we indulge in, the more productive will be the ecosystem to which we belong. Neither field seems to favor a Witnesses-Only Club of those who prefer to write at each other from across the ivory ramparts while the hard work of cultural transformation goes on elsewhere, carried forward by those who fight the wholesale dismantling of education and academia every day and struggle to preserve what's left of democracy.

Nevertheless, if eco-activists and their colleagues don't get to be credited with doing "real" psychological work out in the field where it counts, perhaps it doesn't matter in the long run. They will struggle on as usual, rising seas or no, until the academic theorists finally catch up or float away.

NOTES

1. Robert D. Romanyshyn, "The Melting Polar Ice: Revisiting Technology as Symptom and Dream," *Spring: A Journal of Archetype and Culture* 80 (Fall 2008): 79–116.
2. Wolfgang Giegerich, "The Psychologist as Repentance Preacher and Revivalist: Robert Romanyshyn on the Melting of the Polar Ice," *Spring: A Journal of Archetype and Culture* 82 (Fall 2009): 193–221.
3. Robert D. Romanyshyn, "Who Is Wolfgang Giegerich?" *Spring: A Journal of Archetype and Culture* 84 (Fall 2010): 273–310.
4. Giegerich, "The Psychologist as Repentance Preacher and Revivalist," p. 194.
5. *Ibid.*, p. 200.
6. *Ibid.*, p. 201.
7. *Ibid.*, p. 206.
8. *Ibid.*, p. 210.
9. *Ibid.*, p. 211.
10. *Ibid.*, p. 215.
11. Romanyshyn, "Who Is Wolfgang Giegerich?" p. 275.
12. *Ibid.*, p. 278.
13. *Ibid.*, p. 296.
14. *Ibid.*, p. 298.
15. *Ibid.*, p. 298.
16. Nancy Caro Hollander, *Love in a Time of Hate: Liberation Psychology in Latin America* (New Brunswick, N.J.: Rutgers University Press, 1997).
17. See Mary Watkins and Helene Shulman, *Toward Psychologies of Liberation* (New York: Palgrave MacMillan, 2010).

BOOK REVIEWS

Andreas Jung, Regula Michel, Arthur Rüegg, Judith Rohrer, and Daniel Ganz, *The House of C. G. Jung: The History and Restoration of the Residence of Emma and Carl Gustav Jung-Rauschenbach*. Foreword by Irene Gerber. Küsnacht, Switzerland: Stiftung C. G. Jung, 2009; Wilmette, Ill.: Chiron Publications, 2009.

John Hill, *At Home in the World: Sounds and Symmetries of Belonging*. New Orleans, La.: Spring Journal, 2010.

REVIEWED BY LEONARD CRUZ

House and Home

> Exile is a dream of a glorious return.
> —Salmon Rushdie

Early hominids seeking shelter under a verdant canopy appreciated a certain primordial dimension of home—shelter from the storm. Later, nomadic tribes began carrying their shelter and belongings with

---

Leonard Cruz, M.D., is a Cuban-American, Jungian-oriented psychiatrist in practice in Asheville, North Carolina. With Dr. Steven Buser, he co-founded the Asheville Jung Center. He is a consultant to small and medium-sized businesses on leadership issues, new venture creation, and strategic planning. He is interested in the application of analytical psychology, especially the principle of the transcendent function, to clinical practice and business consulting.

them and a more permanent sense of home appeared. Following the Neolithic Revolution, sedentary people gave rise to villages, then cities and states. This simultaneously expanded the interior experience of home into a collective polis and fostered a personal dimension to home that distinguished it from the community and further delimited the interior experience of home. Now our postmodern, pluralistic, globalized, and highly mobile society is exerting new influences on our psychological experience of home.

Two recently published books, *The House of C. G. Jung: The History and Restoration of the Residence of Emma and Carl Gustav Jung-Rauschenbach* and *At Home in the World: Sounds and Symmetries of Belonging,* provide distinctly different surveys of the landscape we call home. Together they offer counterpoint perspectives on the subject. *The House of C. G. Jung* illustrates the importance of maintaining a physical sanctuary as one plumbs the depths of the inner landscape of the psyche. For C. G. Jung, home served as an anchor. From the security and familiarity of his home on Lake Zürich, Jung embarked on daring explorations of the farthest reaches of the unconscious. In contrast, in *At Home in the World,* John Hill reminds us of the transitory, impermanent nature of home in an exploration that is especially relevant for our time.

Home Port

The publication of *The Red Book* in late 2009 created a rich, fascinating window into the life of C. G. Jung. It broadened Jung's earlier disclosures in *Memories, Dreams, Reflections* while revealing the toolkit of a cartographer of the soul. *The House of C. G. Jung,* co-edited by architect and preservationist Andreas Jung, the grandson of Carl and Emma Jung, grounds the other two works about Jung in the material reality of his home life.

Shortly after Emma Jung inherited a small fortune as a result of her father's early demise in 1905, Carl Jung wrote to his cousin, an architect, "We have in mind to build a house someday, in the country, near Zürich, on the lake."[1] Years later, after Emma's death, Jung carved a stone with her name and an inscription, "She was the foundation of my house." The tone of *The House of C. G. Jung* is reminiscent of the opening lines of W. H. Auden's poem "Herman Melville":

> Towards the end he sailed into an extraordinary mildness,
> And anchored in his home and reached his wife
> And rode within the harbour of her hand,
> And went across each morning to an office
> As though his occupation were another island.[2]

The House of C. G. Jung is a biography of a house that animates the inanimate by interweaving biographical information and architectural history. The illustrations and explanatory text offer insight into Jung and his wife and demonstrate how the house was a symbol of the dynamism of its inhabitants. The ontogeny of the house, where Jung lived for three-quarters of his life, is a testament to the intentional, conscious involvement Jung had with his home and later with Bollingen Tower.

Jung was deeply interested in architecture, both in the real world and in the world of the soul. Andreas Jung points out that in *Memories, Dreams, Reflections,* Jung described his childhood fascination with building "castles and artfully fortified emplacements out of small stones" instead of daydreaming.[3] And in *Memories, Dreams, Reflections,* Jung recounted his famous "house dream," which he had after the house on Seestrasse had been built. In the dream, he descended two levels below an ancient ground floor to "a low cave cut into the rock," where he came upon "scattered bones and broken pottery, like remains of a primitive culture."[4] This is the dream that suggested the realm of the collective unconscious to Jung. Andreas Jung notes that the building of the house on Seestrasse "as it was realized would only reflect the conventional—that is, 'conscious'—layers of the image of the human psyche outlined in the dream."[5] But it was the very conventionality of the house that helped ground Jung, a point he once alluded to:

> The unconscious contents could have driven me out of my wits. But my family, and the knowledge: I have a medical diploma from a Swiss university, I must help my patients, I have a wife and five children, *I live at 228 Seestrasse in Kusnacht*—these were the actualities which made demands upon me and proved to me again and again that I really existed, that I was not a blank page whirling about in the winds of the spirit.[6]

The chapter titled "Between Palatial Villa and Home on Lake Zurich" details various significant architectural features of the house while noting how difficult it is to categorize it. The house, like its creator, does not submit to a simple architectural rendering. The chapter titled "Living in a Museum?" chronicles the renovations done to the house from 2005 to 2007. Preservationists will delight in the photographic plates and explanatory text illustrating how the house's unique features were preserved.

Another chapter of the book presents "C. G. Jung's Garden Realm." The gardens were mature elaborations of C. G. Jung's original vision. The earth excavated from the sunken garden enabled the Jungs to build up the terrace around their veranda while producing "an exciting topography that directed views toward the vase at the central intersection of the paths in the heart of the sunken garden."[7] The photograph of this vase in the garden conjures images of a chalice located at the heart of a cross.

The House of C. G. Jung conveys the importance of 228 Seestrasse as a place of return, a home port to which Jung the ambitious explorer could always return. A ship's home port is often the one best suited for making repairs. This appears to have been true with Jung's home. The house has a quality of permanence and substance that the Jung family and the Stiftung C. G. Jung Küsnacht have honored.[8]

If *The House of C. G. Jung* depicts a home port for the consummate explorer of the interior realms, John Hill's *At Home in the World: Sounds and Symmetries of Belonging* is a thoughtful, multilayered examination of the home port for the wanderer in the world, perhaps most especially for one who is a member of a diaspora. It is a valuable companion to *The House of C. G. Jung* and will enrich the ideas considered in this issue of *Spring Journal*. Hill announces his goal:

> One purpose of this book is to encourage reflection on the affinity between two words with very different meanings: "home" and "world." The former implies a local, safe dwelling place, the latter an extension of space and time, as their etymology suggests.[9]

Hill accomplishes this with a lyricism that leaves one to wonder if he is channeling Irish poets.

According to Hill, many people today tend to interpret the world in ways that no longer encompass the complexity of human nature. Signs replace symbols in an endless procession that elevates facts over ritual and functionality over the sustaining power of nature's beauty.

Hill observes that when we experience moments of deep bonding with the unified world, we form a foundation for relating to the world and others. Examples of such moments include the attunement between mother and child that is so critical to the bonding process and to the child's ability to gain control of affects and form a sense of self. William Blake hinted at the expansiveness from which so many flee.

> If the doors of perception were cleansed, every thing
> would appear to man as it is, infinite
> For man has closed himself up, till he sees all things
> thro' narrow chinks in his cavern.[10]

Hill writes that symbols are "the housing of the self in the universe." When one maintains a connection to the symbolic level, the personalizing of one's space takes on sacramental qualities. The global reach of retailers such as IKEA testifies to the inclination to make a home unique through elements that are in fact standardized. Such a home, according to Hill, "is without a soul." He cautions against relying on the pseudo-historical constructs that are readily available in home decor stores, since they "can express a grandiose idea of the past that is unrelated to one's actual life situation."[11] Hill attends to the "creative capacity of the human being to invest dwelling places with symbolic meaning."[12] He also explores the mythological aspects of home. Building on Ernst Cassier's writings, he observes that myth-making involves distilling something that is essential to the whole and then elevating it above "the exigencies of the moment."

The House of C. G. Jung illustrates how a house functions as an anchor for explorers of the unchartered waters of the unconscious; *At Home in the World* illustrates how home also functions as a psychological anchor for all of us who are wanderers in the world.

IN THE WORLD VERSUS OF THE WORLD

Identity involves a separation between self and the world. Aboriginal people do not differentiate between home and the outer world or between self and world. Listen to the words from a poem by the poet David Wagoner as he fashions a Native American's reply to the question, "What do I do when I'm lost in the forest?"

"Lost"

Stand Still. The trees ahead and bushes beside you
Are not lost. Wherever you are is called Here.
And you must treat it as a powerful stranger.
Must ask permission to know it and be known.
The forest breathes. Listen. It answers.
I have made this place around you.
If you leave it you may come back again, saying Here.
No two trees are the same to Raven.
No two branches are the same to Wren.
If what a tree or a bush does is lost on you.
You art surely lost. Stand still.
The forest knows
Where you are. You must let it find you.[13]

The poem invites the listener to bridge the divide between self and the world.

Home frames the experience of both the denizen and the exile. We speak of homeland, of being homeward bound, of missing home. This idea of home throws exile, wandering, and migration into relief. C. G. Jung lived his entire life in Switzerland and did not know exile from his homeland. John Hill, as are so many today, is a member of a huge diaspora. Thus, these two books are infused with the by-products of very different experiences of home. *At Home in the World* is a perfect complement to *The House of C. G. Jung* and is, as its author had hoped it would be, an "an object of delight and contemplation . . . for all who have crossed its threshold."[14]

NOTES

1. Jung to Ernst Fiechter, 10 June 1907, quoted in Jung et al., *The House of C. G. Jung*, p. 17.

2. W. H. Auden, "Herman Melville," in *W. H. Auden: Collected Poems*, edited by Edward Mendelson (New York: Vintage International, 1991), p. 249.

3. C. G. Jung, *Memories, Dreams, Reflections*, edited by Aniela Jaffé, translated by Richard and Clara Winston (New York: Vintage Books, 1989), p. 82.

4. *Ibid.*, p. 159.

5. Jung et al., *The House of C. G. Jung*, p. 25.
6. *Ibid.*, p. 189, my italics.
7. *Ibid.*, p. 116.
8. The Stiftung C. G. Jung Küsnacht was instituted to preserve the memory of C. G. Jung and Emma Jung-Rauschenbach. It acquires property and other items associated with the Jungs and makes them accessible to researchers.
9. Hill, *At Home in the World*, p. 42.
10. Blake, "The Marriage of Heaven and Hell," in *The Portable Blake: Selected and Arranged with an Introduction,* edited by Alfred Kazan (New York: Penguin Books, 1985), p. 258.
11. Hill, *At Home in the World*, p. 55.
12. *Ibid.*, p. 70.
13. David Wagoner, "Lost," in *The Poetry Anthology, 1912–2002: Ninety Years of America's Most Distinguished Verse Magazine,* edited by Joseph Parsi and Stephen Young (Chicago: Ivan R. Dee, 2002), p. 234, quoted in David Whyte, *The Heart Aroused: Poetry and the Preservation of the Soul in Corporate America* (New York: Doubleday, 1994), p. 249.
14. Hill, *At Home in the World*, p. 263.

BOOK REVIEWS

Gail Thomas, *Healing Pandora: The Restoration of Hope and Abundance*. Benson, N.C.: Goldenstone Press; Berkeley, Calif.: North Atlantic Books, 2009.

REVIEWED BY DENNIS PATRICK SLATTERY

CHTHONIC GODDESS AS GROUND OF CULTURE

Not unlike a vital and vibrant myth, the title of Gail Thomas's new exploration takes us in at least two directions simultaneously: it suggests first that Pandora needs healing and that the book is a witness to this salvific action; and second that Pandora heals, which the author will reveal as a valid re-reading of the myth

---

Dennis Patrick Slattery, Ph.D., is Core Faculty in Mythological Studies at Pacifica Graduate Institute, Carpinteria, California. He is the author, co-author, editor, and co-editor of fifteen books, including four volumes of poetry. Among his titles are *The Wounded Body: Remembering the Markings of Flesh* (SUNY Press, 2000) and *Grace in the Desert: Awakening to the Gifts of Monastic Life* (Jossey-Bass, 2004). He has co-edited two books with Lionel Corbett: *Depth Psychology: Meditations in the Field* (Daimon Verlag, 2000) and *Psychology at the Threshold* (Pacifica Graduate Institute, 2000). With Charles Asher he has written a novel, *Simon's Crossing* (iUniverse, 2010), as well as a meditation book, *Day-to-Day Dante: Exploring Personal Mythology through The Divine Comedy* (iUniverse, 2011). He offers writing workshops on the works of Joseph Campbell and exploring one's personal myth.

as well as an illustration of the myriad ways that Pandora might accomplish this beneficent enterprise.

While reading this exciting psychological study, I was also enjoying my copy of Jung's newly released *Red Book*. There I discovered this provocative insight that I suggest is also part of Thomas's *modus operandi*. Well into *The Red Book*, Jung observes a quality of the psyche in its relation to image:

> If we possess the image of a thing, we possess half the thing. The image of the world is half the world. He who possesses the world but not its image possesses only half the world, since the soul is poor and has nothing. The wealth of the soul exists in images.[1]

Healing Pandora is, in part, a case study that illustrates the truth of Jung's observation. Moreover, while the image the reader can "possess" is the mythical image of this feminine presence, the heartbeat of *Healing Pandora* is the figure of culture itself and its grounding in vital, even juicy and nourishing mythic images. *Healing Pandora* is a succinct and provocative short course on how myths converse with culture and, in some historical instances, change the values of cultures. Myths persuade but do not dictate; they open a dialectic between themselves and cultures and invite cultures to respond with the voice of their own values. For me, that is the great achievement of Thomas's study: her revelation of the dialogue between myth and culture. Her co-edited volume with Joanne Stroud, *Images of the Untouched: Virginity in Psyche, Myth and Community* (1982), announced her deep concern with the status of the feminine in the complex web of culture.[2] Her co-edited volume with Robert Sardello, *Stirrings of Culture: Essays from the Dallas Institute* (1986), also revealed her sustained and deepening grasp of culture's centrality in the mythic imagination of its citizens.[3] This was also revealed in her co-founding of the Dallas Institute of Humanities and Culture in the early 1980s as well as her current work with the city of Dallas on the Trinity River Project. In her devotion to the imagination of the city as vessel of culture, it is not a stretch to suggest that Thomas is herself a Pandora for the city of Dallas as well as a voice for the necessity of culture. *Healing Pandora* reveals the place and role of the feminine as an active agent in culture whereby her presence can influence and guide the renewal of that culture's mythology.

Robert Sardello's very helpful foreword to the book sets out what Thomas's study is *not*: it is not priming us to seek out "our inner Pandora" (p. xiii). Quite the opposite: "We are being asked to reside deeply within the activities of the world. There we will experience desire and longing" (p. xiii), qualities that are present in Pandora's absence. Depth psychology, Thomas's mythodology, if you will, is a devotional act of remembering, retrieving, and revisioning the place of this one feminine figure in the vast population of mythic images that may reside in a people's imagination.

The book is divided into two large sections. Part 1 is titled "Pandora: Her Myths and Her Making"; Part 2, "The Making of Culture." A sampling of chapter titles includes "Pandora: Divine Benefactress or the Beautiful Evil?," "Prometheus: The Formulation of a New Order," "Psychological Wordplay: Myth or Fact?," "Healing the Denial of Death: Demeter and Persephone," and "Healing Our 'Dis-ease': Bulimia." I chose these titles to reveal that while Pandora is the centerpiece of the study, Thomas uses her to expand the orbit of her concerns. Her suggestion is that no god or goddess is a stand-alone reality. Imagining into the place and performance of a mythical figure is like touching a spider web: touch any strand and the entire historical and cultural filament shivers. Such is the powerful and ubiquitous presence of myth. Joseph Campbell reminded us that "the life of a mythology springs from and depends on the metaphoric vigor of its symbols."[4] Thomas takes his observation seriously. Her new and fresh study reveals the metaphoric outback that exploring one mythic figure as metaphor has the capacity to expose us to.

Moreover, her exploration into history, earlier cultures, other readings of Pandora (such as Hesiod's *Theogony,* a central text in Thomas's study), and contemporary readings of Pandora's influence and force in current culture allowed me to see that Thomas's central concern is not so much "Who is Pandora?" as it is "Whose Pandora?" Who makes the image of Pandora, and once this image is set in the hardening concrete of historical belief, can it be undone? Thomas also frees Pandora from millennia of maligning as the source of evil. According to the sustained mythos that was promoted most effectively by Hesiod (p. 22), Pandora unleashes all the evils that afflict humanity on the world, finally covering her malignant box of suffering just before

Hope escapes. Thomas asks the important question: Whose Pandora do we see through?

This question is crucial to Thomas's method: mythic figures are forms of psychological and imaginal perception. They are mytho-historical, embedded in culture and time, and at the same time they offer some quality of soul that is expressed as metaphor and symbol. Mythic figures are ways of reading and carry within themselves patterns of understanding. This insight, for me, is one of the study's strongest attributes. Here is another example of this methodology. It concerns the tendency of Prometheus to steal fire from the gods while offering Zeus an inferior sacrifice. At the same time, it reveals how Prometheus's brother, Epimetheus, is given Pandora as his wife, a gift from Olympus. As an image of afterthought, or reflection, Pandora carries wisdom that "Prometheus, because of his foresight, did not and could not see" (p. 29). Thomas steps back to consider the epistemology that stirs in the Pandora figure that I suggest may be present in every mythology:

> If the myth is read with a purely Promethean eye, it cannot make sense to take in a woman who will bring disease and discomfort into one's life. But take an Epimethean posture for a moment. Something new and incredible is at the door. We don't know what is there, but we are compelled to open it. (pp. 28–29).

Now while I am careful not to diminish the figure of Pandora in this review, I do detect something bigger, something more profound at work in Thomas's study than Pandora or, better, *because of* Pandora. As a mythic presence that needs to be rescued from a constricted interpretation in history, Pandora serves Thomas as a model for imagining. Myths imagine; they are not literal, but they are no less real and true. Moreover, leaders who shape and determine which cultural qualities will be allowed in and which will be denied but have no mythic imagination are not only naive, they are dangerous to the population. Dangerous because they lose or dismiss mythic memory, something a figure such as Pandora is anxious to restore: "Crafted, the way culture is crafted, containing the mystery of mortality, Pandora reflects the splendor of the divine in the world. . . . She reminds us of our own mortality. She becomes the image of the tension we experience in attempting to live in the midst of both the real and the ideal" (p. 57).

Pandora's vessel, either as earthen jar (*pithos*) or a box (*pyxis*) (p. 74), is revealed through a container in the same multiple ways Pandora has been translated in culture. But the shift of one word, from *pithos* to *pyxis,* in Thomas's citing of Jane Helen Harrison's *Prolegomena to the Study of Greek Religion* is not incidental. The shift from earthen jar to box rearranges the entire cosmology of the myth. Pandora is no longer related to a funeral jar, as Harrison describes it, but to a box.[5] Only by extensive archeological and linguistic digging is Thomas able to uncover the origin of Pandora's "evil nature" in order to revive her culturally as a benevolent presence. One has to wonder, as I did, how many other myths we have accepted as authentic origins when the stories have in fact been misaligned by prejudice, politics, or personal error. How many of the mythic forces we believe in are inaccurate, slanted, and wrong? What Thomas uncovers about the nature and impulses of Pandora may be the beginning of a reassessment of mythic stories that we assume are accurate historically and psychologically. Perhaps a wholesale revisioning will begin with her reclamation of Pandora.

Well into her study, Thomas shifts to a direct exploration of culture's development within a Pandoric presence: "Her jar contained the Keres—bacilli or sprites that bring life-giving fermentation and growth. It is as if her role were to invite the gods to be present within mortal life" (p. 92). *Healing Pandora* reveals that Pandora's earlier connection to disease, decay, and death and to her new tasks argues that there is something true about the older readings of the myth, although not in quite as absolute a package as its originators may have hoped. That is, as with any seed, its gestation is a death; only when the seed decays does it push through the soil of the underground to promote new life. Pandora is, as Thomas imagines her, a seedling whose cultivation within the soil becomes a cultural presence in the soul. Soul and soil are not antithetical but in fact participate in the same germination of individual and collective imagination. Such is the paradox of Pandora's nature and her multivalenced presence in culture.

Finally, I found Thomas's recurrent reveries on the nature of myth to be as interesting and provocative as any of her observations about the figure of Pandora; in fact, they spring from the jar that Pandora offers. Here is one of many that she offers, this time as she explores the myth of Medusa: "If we imagine all mythic happenings as a permanent realm of the collective psyche, we are able to understand the power the Medusa holds for us culturally. What does it mean for our most creative and fecund feminine energy to be frozen, stuck, stopped?" (p. 130). Note how the question personalizes and brings closer to home the larger mythic referent. The question universalizes the myth's particularity while particularizing its universality. I find this mythodology to be provocative and appreciate its avoidance of prescriptive colonizing.

The question is concrete and particular: the myth opens us psychologically and emotionally to a multiple set of options. Such is Thomas's developing hermeneutic: she remains close to the particularities of the myth and then allows reverie to assist her in seeing what possible directions the work can lead her into. This methodology is egoless, open, porous, persistent, and pervasive throughout her study. As I said earlier, her study offers a succinct short course in how myths function as well as a series of illustrations to reveal how myths transform over time as historical circumstances and shifting beliefs revamp earlier versions of mythic figures.

Her conclusion includes a few instructions that I found both useful and challenging. As she assesses the current mania for multitasking as a cultural symptom, Thomas invites another way of being in the everyday world: "Another way would be to allow ourselves to slip into a place of meditation, a place of not knowing, giving over to something unknown that can be sparked in some deep dark inner place and reveal itself though us. In this way the invisible can become visible" (p. 172). We have, as readers, just traveled through a landscape that embodies such a devotion to the unknown and the unknowing soul.

Perhaps we see through a myth darkly in her conclusion that cultures are shaped and blueprinted as much by what is yet to be known as they are by what we know about and plan into and for culture. If this is so, then Pandora may have two husbands, the foreknowing Prometheus and his more reflective brother, Epimetheus. Pandora brings their gifts together in a symmetry that the soul may delight in.

NOTES

1. C. G. Jung, *The Red Book: Liber Novus,* edited by Sonu Shamdasani, translated by Mark Kyburz, John Peck, and Sonu Shamdasani (New York: W. W. Norton and Company, 2009), p. 232.

2. Gail Thomas and Joanne Stroud, eds., *Images of the Untouched: Virginity in Psyche, Myth and Community* (Dallas, Tex.: The Dallas Institute Publications, 1982).

3. Robert Sardello and Gail Thomas, eds., *Stirrings of Culture: Essays from the Dallas Institute* (Dallas, Tex.: The Dallas Institute Publications, 1986).

4. Joseph Campbell, *Thou Art That: Transforming Religious Metaphor* (Novato, Calif.: New World Library, 2001), p. 6.

5. See Jane Helen Harrison, *Prolegomena to the Study of Greek Religion* (New York: Arno, 1975), pp. 43–44.

BOOK REVIEWS

Georg Nicolaus, *C. G. Jung and Nikolai Berdyaev: Individuation and the Person: A Critical Comparison*. East Sussex: Routledge, 2011.

REVIEWED BY GERT SAUER

In *C. G. Jung and Nikolai Berdyaev,* Georg Nicolaus presents a critical comparison of Jung and Berdyaev. To undertake this is somewhat hazardous work, since the two men come from very different traditions and cultures. But it is the merit of Nicolaus's book that it provides a way for Western-educated people to have a greater understanding of the complexity and common fundament of European thinking. Philosophical and psychological work in Russia was forgotten for many years during the Soviet era.

> Gert Sauer was born in 1942 in Germany to a Russian mother and a German father. He initially studied theology, but since 1976 he has been a psychoanalyst. He is a graduate of the C. G. Jung Institute in Zurich and has had an analytical practice in Freiburg, Germany, for many years. He is a teaching analyst at the Institute for Analytical Psychology in Stuttgart and a member of the International Association for Analytical Psychology and the German Association for Analytical Psychology. In 1991, he and his wife, Rodtraud Sauer, founded a network to support colleagues studying analytical psychology in Eastern Europe. He has written many articles on analytical theory and practice, especially about applying principles of analytical psychology to social issues in Eastern Europe. He also works in Eastern Europe as a psychoanalyst and a supervisor.

The book leads us into the depths of the philosophical concepts of Berdyaev and emphasizes their similarity to the psychological concepts of Jung. Nicolaus demonstrates the common intellectual ground of Berdyaev and Jung by showing how both participated in and studied the collective development of the human spirit. The discussion moves through well-crafted chapters: "Berdyaev's Life"; "Introduction to Berdyaev's Philosophy"; "Personality in Jung and Berdyaev"; "*Esse in anima* and Epistemology of the Heart"; "Person and God-Image"; "Individuation and the Ethics of Creativity"; and "Moving beyond the Pre/Trans Fallacy."

Nicolaus discusses his subjects in a delicate and admirable way. His knowledge of the philosophical material is immense, and he does not lose the focus of his purpose. As a result, the working psychoanalyst has an opportunity to become familiar with the ways that ideas that sound the same are used in philosophical and psychological discourse and to appreciate the differences in how these two fields use these ideas.

Nicolaus describes how Russian religious and political philosopher Berdyaev inspected his life history with sharp eyes and combined his inner departure point of his personal experiences, religious and otherwise, with brilliant formulations from Russian Orthodoxy, thus creating new orientations for the whole of Christianity and especially for Western faith by pointing to the presence of God in mankind. Jung also looked at his life critically and theorized about his own inner experiences and the experiences of his clients using terms drawn from philosophy to describe collective and individual psychic processes. Nicolaus makes it clear that the difference between Berdyaev and Jung lies in each man's hermeneutic and the language of his consciousness. Although each was touched by the deepest power of life, which Berdyaev described as "God" and Jung as "Self" or sometimes "God," and used that as the basis for his intellectual thought, as Nicolaus shows so clearly, Berdyaev's concept of the spirit as absolute and Jung's concept of the spirit as a complex of the psyche are radically different.

Perhaps because of his focus on the thinking function, Nicolaus could not show how these two protagonists were embedded in the history of their time and the fate of their respective cultures. Nor does he discuss the cultural connections between these two intellectual giants. It is known, for instance, that Jung had important encounters with Russian symbolism, but Nicolaus has largely overlooked this. Perhaps it could be the topic of his next work.

Now just a note for those who might not know who Berdyaev was. Nikolai Alexandrovich Berdyaev (1874–1948) was born in Kiev and died near Paris. He lived through the end of the Russian Tsarist period and the Russian Revolution in 1917, then witnessed the upsurge of national socialism in Germany and the occupation of France by Hitler's troops. All of these world historical events shocked him, and he was overwhelmed by immense anger, fear, and disgust at the human behavior he saw played out before him. Nevertheless, he was also inspired and carried forward by a vision of deep freedom and human potential.

Berdyaev was a Russian aristocrat, but he was linked on his mother's side to French culture and through his studies and convictions to German philosophy. Exiled by the communists in 1922, he arrived in Berlin but soon moved to Paris, where he lived and wrote for the rest of his life. The center of his work involved asking questions and questioning people. He was never content with previously given answers. In Russia, he was never reactionary, despite the traditions of his class. If he was a socialist, then he was an aristocratic socialist; if an aristocrat, then a socialistic aristocrat; if a Christian and an orthodox Christian, then a boisterous one like a child who is full of the plenitude of truth and disgusted by the lies of adults. Wherever he was, he could not be contained within the frames of any organization. The very air in which he lived was a spirit of his own inspiration, his way the analytical intellect based on inner experiences that were grounded in Dostoyevsky and the tradition of Russian mystics. But always he was engaged and full of passion.

He loved his wife his whole life but never spoke about it. They had no children, only the many books he wrote. He also loved his friends, who took part in the philosophical work he was doing in France. (Jacques Maritain was close to him.) Berdyaev was totally absorbed by the spirit living in him, and he fought for freedom throughout his life. Westerners may be surprised to learn that during World War II he strongly supported the role of the Soviet Union as a liberator of Europeans from the horrors of National Socialism. Because of his roots in Russia, he could see the difference between the National Socialists who were exterminating and annihilating people and the Soviet Empire, which had enlisted the help of the entirety of Russian culture in the battle against the German juggernaut of horror and death.

During his twenty-five years in Paris, Berdyaev wrote fifteen philosophical texts, some of which were published posthumously. His titles include *The Meaning of History* (1936), *Slavery and Freedom* (1939), *Spirit and Reality* (1946), *The Meaning of the Creative Act* (1955), *The Destiny of Man* (1960), and *Freedom and the Spirit* (1972). His work focused on the realm of the spirit, the union between human beings and the divine. One of his last books was a study of Dostoevsky. He died while writing at his desk, holding his feather pen in his hand.

If you do not have the time to read Berdyaev, take the time to read Nicolaus. He will possibly open a new path in your own exploration of the movement of the spirit, the ways that our consciousness can witness how our spirit is speaking and how the absolute is addressing us through our psyches.

FILM REVIEW

Black Swan. 2010. Directed by Darren Aronofsky. Written by Mark Heyman, Andres Heinz, and John J. McLaughlin. Natalie Portman, Mila Kunis, Vincent Cassel.

REVIEWED BY TERRIE WADDELL

"Must See the Bones"

*B*lack Swan, directed by Darren Aronofsky and released in 2010, comes across as a modern fusion of the Roman Polanski's 1965 film *Repulsion* and/or Gelsey Kirkland's autobiography *Dancing on My Grave* (1986), or perhaps "homage" is a kinder way to describe it. The two lead characters of *Black Swan* and *Repulsion*—Aronofsky's ballerina Nina Sayers (Natalie Portman) and Polanski's apprentice beautician Carole Ledoux (Catherine Deneuve)—are both tainted by the fantasy of what a woman-child really wants or needs: highly charged sex. The clichés of a psychologically and sexually troubled *puella* near to self-

---

Terrie Waddell, Ph.D., is a Senior Lecturer in Media and Cinema Studies at La Trobe University (Australia). Her most recent writing focuses on the relationships between screen media, myth, gender, popular culture, and analytical psychology. She is the author of *Wild/Lives: Trickster, Place and Liminality on Screen* (Routledge, 2010) and *Mis/takes: Archetype, Myth and Identity in Screen Fiction* (Routledge, 2006); the editor of *Cultural Expressions of Evil and Wickedness: Wrath, Sex, Crime* (Rodopi, 2003); and co-editor (with Annabel Rattigan) of *Lounge Critic: The Couch Theorist's Companion* (ACMI, 2004).

destruction in the earlier film carry over into *Black Swan*: the childhood toys/ornaments closely held with a trauma-teddy-like dependency; the absent, morally suspect father; the girlish voice; the deer-in-headlights close-ups of bewilderment; the stereotypical (era-appropriate) "beauty" of each female lead; and the predators allowed sexual access only in the highly charged erotic fantasies of each character. Kirkland's story, though, connects us to *Black Swan* through her account of life in the New York City Ballet under the directorship of George Balanchine. In lurid detail, we are told of the imposed soft-torture that led to her physical and emotional decline. But *Black Swan* isn't just a *Repulsion*/Kirkland retake. It's more nuanced than that. What struck me most, in what is ostensibly another Persephone myth, was Aronofsky's concentration on the *project of bodily perfection* as metaphor for the *project of the individuated state*: a continual desiring that keeps one tied to *want* over *being*.

Having landed the coveted role of principle dancer in a daring new production of Tchaikovsky's *Swan Lake,* Nina, the 28-year-old ballerina of a fictitious New York dance company, descends further into perfectionism. Not only is she bullied by artistic director Thomas Leroy (Vincent Cassel) to free up her exacting technique, but her dual roles of white swan (the enchanted Odette desired by prince Siegfried) and black swan (the evil sorcerer's daughter Odile disguised as Odette in order to win the prince) require her to source a dark psycho-eroticism that she finds overwhelming. Although we can superficially read the themes of shadow integration and child becoming woman via sexual awakening in the film, we can also go further into Nina's bigger-picture quest to control both her psyche and physique. Getting the *body* right gradually parallels getting the *self* right.

In an exploitation of the clichés surrounding the world of ballet, Aronofsky suggests that the very mechanics and ideologies of this particular practice inhibit genuine displays of self-expression, particularly for women. One might read the necessary physical contortions of *en pointe* work as a throwback to the seductive nineteenth-century "presenting of the ankle" from beneath lifted skirts or, more bluntly, foot-binding: it is an acrobatic skill designed to render the female body as unnaturally weightless, crippled, and therefore symbolically ungrounded, giving the impression of a waifish, aesthetically appealing fairy. It's an interesting irony given the muscular strength and years of dedicated training required for *pointe* work. A colleague who once managed to book seats close to the stage found the unexpected "noise" of ballet quite bizarre—the force of bodies hitting the floor, *pointe* shoes battering the boards, and audible gasps of breath from the dancers. All this of course is diminished with distance and music. In its most classical form, ballet encapsulates the hard slog and artifice of ethereal beauty. As the framing artistic device for the film, and Nina's raison d'être, it is the also the very thing that inhibits her emotional growth.

For the black swan to emerge, she is forced to challenge years of rigorously enforced rules, bodily manipulation, and adherence to/fear of authority. What surfaces, though, is a warping of self-perception that is again (now predictably) paralleled within her athletically warped little body—a site of pain without much pleasure. The camera works to show bones: the stunted development of the breasts, seemingly sacrificed for the exposure of sternum and frontal rib cage; the pounded feet/toes crunched into alignment every morning; the slow-motion force of toe bones as they impact on the hard toe box of the *pointe* shoe saturated with burlap, paper, and glue; hip sockets flexible enough for splayed legs to form a vertical line; and the linkages of muscle, scapulae, spine, and rear rib cage anorexically visible through paper-thin skin so that when the arms are in motion, a swan's flapping wings are more than hinted at.

Kirkland, who was a gifted baby ballerina in the 1960s, writes of Balanchine:

> With his knuckles, he thumped my sternum and down my rib cage, clucking his tongue and remarking, "Must see the bones." I was less than a hundred pounds even then. . . . He did not merely say, "Eat less." He said repeatedly, "Eat nothing."[1]

This unflattering portrait seems to be the inspiration for Nina's artistic director and choreographer Leroy. Both are intent on fashioning their dancing women into caricatures of perfection and so exemplify the inequity and barbarity of all power/love contracts where one partner, in effect, gives themselves up to be desired by the other.

A dinosaur of the contemporary ballet world, Leroy cajoles Nina into adopting his concept of the black swan by testing her physical prowess and probing her sexual history. In his opinion piece on *Black*

Swan's clichés, the artistic director of the Australian Ballet, David McAllister, writes that men in his position who harass dancers are treated no differently than any other sexually menacing CEO. Of the necessary body sculpting, he argues: "Fitness is encouraged, thinness is not. . . . Fuelling the body with healthy food is as important as the warm-up positions and *plies*" and yet "there are sometimes blisters and bleeding toes."[2] Perhaps this is the reality today, but in the 1990s when I interviewed Natalia Bessmertnova, then in her fifties and on tour in Australia with the Bolshoi, I was taken aback by the disproportionate thinness and bony protrusions of the younger female dancers mingling in the hotel's foyer.

Portman's much-publicized physical regime in preparing for her role as a convincing dancer struggling with the demands of an illusive flawlessness reinforces ballet's goal of positioning the body as a spectacle of disciple and creative sacrifice. In self-sculpting *the* ballerina body, her already slight frame becomes a display of skin worn as a fine sheath over exaggerated bone and muscle. Coupled with prematurely (makeup-enhanced) hollow facial features, indicative of the underfed, overworked, and highly stressed, she emerges as the personification of surrender in the service of unobtainable perfection. And as Marion Woodman, the influential Jungian analyst on female eating disorders, warns: "To move toward perfection is to move out of life, or what is worse, never to enter it."[3]

This body-centric campaign to sell *Black Swan* and promote Portman's best actress Oscar bid reminded me of the American surgical makeover program *The Swan,* brain child of producer Nely Galán. In this example of self-improvement gone berserk, women who believe they fall short of the beauty ideal are encouraged to proactively better themselves by undergoing a regime of enhancement at the hands of plastic surgeons, makeup artists, and fashionistas. The "improved" self is then presented to the contestants as they gaze (supposedly for the first time) into a large mirror. After this shock of the new, as if the drastic change is still not enough to meet the intangible benchmarks of femininity, the contestants compete in a beauty contest to see who will become *the swan.* They are then encouraged to pursue the project of bodily maintenance in their off-screen lives . . . for the rest of their lives. In her article "Media-Bodies and Screen-Births: Cosmetic Surgery Reality Television," Meredith Jones makes a link between the horror film and cosmetic surgery reality television (CSRTV), particularly *The Swan*'s reveal scene, which she sees as " the quintessential example of a rebirthing metaphor that permeates all CSRTV."[4] Both genres, she argues, express "the same cultural concerns about birth, technology, bodies and identity."[5] Like *The Swan*'s rebirthing mirror, a true marker of one's worth, mirrors and reflective glass feature strongly in *Black Swan* as windows to the soul. As *Repulsion*'s Carol gazes at her distorted reflection in mirrors and household objects, Nina obsessively appraises herself through reflections that become increasingly warped. Polanski and Aronofsky use this technique well to amplify a connection between outer and inner twisting, and in keeping with Jones's analysis, this uncomfortable reframing of identity and flesh also allows them to play on key elements of horror cinema.

The message of Nina seems clear—no matter how diligently you apply yourself to the unending project of self-betterment, it will never be enough. Then of course we need to add physical maturity into the mix. *Black Swan* ensures that we're in no doubt as to the relationship between *worth* and *aging* in the ballet world by incorporating characters that reflect this discomfort: Nina's controlling, protective, and slightly unbalanced mother Erica (Barbara Hershey), who gave up a dancing career to raise her daughter; and former prima ballerina Beth (Winona Ryder), an earlier production's white/black swan and Leroy's previous muse/lover. Both women, their careers over, are developed as figures of pity. Without anyone to champion their desirability and therefore their use, Erica and Beth wither away as aging has-beens.

Early in the film Leroy tells his *corps de ballet* the story of *Swan Lake*. We learn how the white swan's death is the only thing that facilitates her freedom. This, coupled with the relentless quest for female perfection, reminded me not only of Elizabeth Bonfren's psychoanalytic critique of Western culture's attraction to female invalidism and death, *Over Her Dead Body* (1992),[6] but also of Edgar Allan Poe and Gustave Flaubert's suspect thoughts on the issue. For Poe, "the death, then, of a beautiful woman, is, unquestionably the most poetical topic in the world,"[7] while, as Linda Kauffman writes, "Flaubert confessed that he could never look at a beautiful woman without visualizing her corpse."[8] Tchaikovsky, it seems, is somewhere in the same camp of snap-freezing women via death while they still have the ability to visually intoxicate.

Aronofsky, on the other hand, brings a refreshing sense of conscience to these still-dominant narrative themes.

The obsessive search for wholeness, as perfection or the individuated state, potentially leads to the antithesis of this goal. We are too necessarily unique, complex, and fragmented to ever realistically imagine ourselves as complete. Life is a relentlessly messy process. If *mindfully* living in self-appreciation carries with it a feeling of sufficiency, then I'm all for that, but striving for an illusive state of perfect inner/outer alignment implies that we lack, we are inadequate, we will never be enough. That we are often socially coerced into perpetual *want* is unfortunate. That certain artistic (and dare I add educational) institutions thrive on this message is destructive. Unable to loosen control over her exacting technique, Nina is even more incapable of disciplining the archetypal challenges that arise to shift her into the next gear of maturity. Reaching out to others as if they can provide a more adequate identity—and by extension a sense of wholeness—exacts a damaging toll. And here's what I found to be the thrust of *Black Swan*. There is no illusive someone or something out there that needs to be grasped in order to feel unbroken. Nothing is really missing. It is already here for us to find in the confusion of *being*.

NOTES

1. Gelsey Kirkland with Greg Lawrence, *Dancing on My Grave* (New York: Berkley Books, 1986), p. 56.

2. David McAllister, "Good Performances, but Swan Misses the Pointe," *National Times* (Sydney, Australia), 23 January 2011, http://www.theage.com.au/opinion/good-performances-but-swan-misses-the-pointe-20110122-1a0np.html, accessed 3 April 2011.

3. Marion Woodman, *Addiction to Perfection: The Still Unravished Bride* (Toronto: Inner City Books, 1982), p. 52.

4. Meredith Jones, "Media-Bodies and Screen-Births: Cosmetic Surgery Reality Television," *Continuum: Journal of Media and & Cultural Studies* 22, no. 4 (2008): 516.

5. *Ibid.*, p. 521.

6. Elisabeth Bronfen, *Over Her Dead Body: Death, Femininity and the Aesthetic* (London: Routledge, 1992).

7. Edgar Allen Poe, *Poe's Poems and Essays* (London: J. M. Dent and Sons, 1964), p. 170.

8. Linda Kauffman, *Bad Girls and Sick Boys: Fantasies in Contemporary Art and Culture* (London: University of California Press, 1998), p. 50.

FILM REVIEW

The King's Speech. Directed by Tom Hooper. Written by David Seidler. Colin Firth, Geoffrey Rush, Helena Bonham Carter, Guy Pearce.

REVIEWED BY GLEN SLATER

The King's Speech is the story of how a stuttering monarch-in-the-making faces his fear and ascends to the British throne to rally the empire at the start of World War II. Based on actual events, the film begins and ends with the royal protagonist, Prince Albert, who will become King George VI, locked in desperate battle with his speech impediment—on live radio, before worldwide audiences.

Within this frame a vivid cinematic canvas presents a courageous and highly sensitive man attempting to overcome the legacy of his father, King George V, and the waywardness of his older brother, the Prince of Wales—who will abdicate and hand the crown to Albert. Known to his family as "Bertie," Prince Albert takes his stutter to an unorthodox

---

Glen Slater, Ph.D., teaches Jungian and archetypal psychology at Pacifica Graduate Institute in California and Antioch University in Seattle. He edited and introduced the third volume of James Hillman's Uniform Edition, *Senex and Puer* (Spring, 2005), and co-edited (with Daniel Patrick Slattery) a volume of essays by Pacifica faculty, *Varieties of Mythic Experience: Essays on Religion, Psyche and Culture* (Daimon Verlag, 2008). He has contributed a number of essays to *Spring*.

Australian speech therapist, Lionel Logue, in whose London consulting room wounds are exposed and authenticity is uncovered. Together, Albert (Colin Firth) and Logue (Geoffrey Rush)—Bertie and Lionel—find the character of a man and the voice of a king.

Whether or not Albert's stammer was caused by his particularly harsh and punitive childhood at the palace, the problem becomes the centerpiece of a deeply etched sense of inadequacy, a feeling that he unsuccessfully masks with a brittle yet ultimately shallow persona of royalty. Albert is not a bore; his endearing traits are on full show with wife Elizabeth (Helena Bonham Carter) and daughters Elizabeth and Margaret. Rather, his personality is suspended somewhere between his painful upbringing and the seemingly insurmountable task of fulfilling his duty. Speech therapist Logue, a larrikin amateur actor and son of a brewer, provides the fitting antidote for this state of suspension. Armed with gritty insight and a Shakespearean-sized map of human topography, Logue guides Albert through the underworld of ordinary human failings and everyday foibles. When Albert reveals that he really has no friends and that Logue is the first common man with whom he'd ever really conversed, the full outline of the alchemical vessel is revealed. But much has to occur before the king can speak effectively to the common man. The prince must undergo a reluctant descent before he can assume the throne and fulfill his calling. And Logue must find an approach to Albert's problem that reflects the prince's inner terrain. The king's speech must be loosened right alongside his suspended, stuck psyche. Indeed, the speech must drop down into the gutter before it will be ready to raise a nation, just as Albert himself must stare down his demons before he can oversee his kingdom.

Overtly, this film glides along like a royal carriage, delighting us with its attention to detail, whip-smart dialogue, perfect pace, and superbly drawn characters. The real horsepower, though, is beneath the surface, moving us in unanticipated ways. Almost every scene reveals internal as well as external events. From a psychological and screenwriting perspective, this is achieved through a precise orchestration of the story's key metaphors, which amplify the soul movement taking place and build to a climax and resolution that is a pitch-perfect match for both the personal quest and the historic events that form the narrative. Among these metaphors, the movement between above and below, ascent and descent is most primary.

When the film opens, for example, Prince Albert is standing with his wife Elizabeth at the bottom of a staircase via which he must step up to the microphone set high in the stands of Wembley Stadium. Before launching into his first impossibly stunted utterance, he must look down the steep incline into a sea of common folk, who've turned out to take in the prince's every word. Vertigo sets in. That he's delivering a message on behalf of his overbearing father only reinforces the effect. Like the opening moments of a dream, it's all right there. To find his voice and a head that will support the crown, he must figure out how to stand on his own two feet, in his own shoes.

After a comical interlude of attempted treatment involving a mouth full of marbles and a physician right out of the Middle Ages, Elizabeth, anguished at the spectacle of her husband's disability, ventures into London to interview Logue. On arrival she must enter a narrow elevator and descend below street level to the therapist's quarters. Here Logue lives with his wife and three sons, conducting his work in a room where the peeling paint has turned the walls into something of an abstract fresco. Aptly, when the future Queen Mother enters, Logue is "in the loo" and first greets her from *this* throne. He's expecting a "Mrs. Johnson," having as yet no idea about the identity of his future client. What ensues is a witty exchange that soon reveals Logue's steadfast sense of his own ground, even when it comes to such an exceptional prospective client: "My game, my turf, my rules," he says.

When Prince Albert himself turns up for his first appointment with Logue, the direct assault on the royal persona begins. The question of how each should address the other starts with Albert rattling off the standard protocol. Logue responds with "How about Bertie?" and "You can call me Lionel." His Royal Highness is forced from his perch— though he won't go beyond using the therapist's surname. By the time Bertie pulls out his cigarettes, Logue is again asserting his ground— "My castle, my rules"—a line that simultaneously establishes the therapeutic container while suggesting an inversion of authority that becomes a key element in their chemical reaction. Eventually, each must come to inhabit the other's place; however, it's clear that this will take some time. When Logue begins to point to the psychological encasement surrounding the "mechanical" difficulty with Bertie's speech, the prince resists. Realizing the door to the royal closet is about to open, he storms out. Things must get worse—more heat is required.

Eventually the shadow side of palace life begins to leak out. Bertie comes to reveal his childhood isolation, which is distilled into accounts of a nanny who withheld food and pinched the infant to make him cry at the "daily viewings," being placed in splints to correct "knock knees," and being forced out of his natural left-handedness. Yet it is his father, the king, who seems to reflect the entire spectrum of these early torments. We learn that when the child prince stuttered, his father encouraged the teasing, and when we get to witness the king admonishing an adult Bertie to simply will his way through his speech problem—stiff upper lip and all—we glimpse the tyrannical thread running through the whole situation.

Whereas Bertie seems crushed by his father, his brother David, the Prince of Wales (Guy Pearce), has gone the way of *puer* escapism, eventually taking up with Wallace Simpson, the scandalously twice-divorced American socialite. David's own version of high and low, ascent and descent, consists of either flying his biplane or raiding the wine cellar for his frequent parties. His "work" focuses on introducing Wallace to his social circle. When the king dies and David assumes the throne, his first act as sovereign is to collapse into his mother's arms. As the film portrays the situation, David would never *be* a king. He may be drawn to living the high life, but his world seems destined for a lesser *coniunctio*. And while Bertie sees the instability of the situation quite clearly, actually coming to terms with its implications proves to be another matter. Before he can take over from his errant sibling, the archetypal king must be summoned from below—one word at a time.

Fittingly, back in his basement, Logue spends a lot of time "mucking around with his kids," including playing guessing games based on acting out scenes from *The Tempest*. The warmth and imaginative flourish evident here seems to be everything royal privilege didn't offer Bertie. So the perfect connective tissue occurs when he turns up early for his appointment and spots an unfinished model airplane on the coffee table. The young prince had always wanted such a hobby, but his father had directed his sons into stamp collecting instead. Still involved in digesting his father's death, Bertie has trouble articulating the emotionally laden events, so Logue bribes him into using popular songs, getting him to sing out the details by allowing the prince to complete the model plane. Singing lets the feelings and the words tumble forth. As the two share some whiskey, the pieces seem to be coming together.

Bertie and Logue endure several ruptures as they make their way to the king's crowning moments. The most pivotal of these occurs exactly halfway through the film. In a session that follows a confrontation between Bertie and his brother, now the king, Logue notices that Bertie's words become more fluid when he starts cursing about the situation. The therapist pushes him deeper: "Do you know the f-word?" Soon the expletives are flowing from the prince like storm runoff—stammer free! Logue notes wryly, "That's a side of you we don't see too often." But when the pair leaves the consulting room for some fresh air in the park it appears the lid's come off too quickly and the apparent breakthrough turns into another of Bertie's retreats. He walks off again, this time with a regressive restoration of the royal persona and an equally harsh put-down of Logue, whom he calls "a nobody," noting that he, by contrast, is "the son of a king" as well as "the brother of a king." Yet the subtext is resounding: Eclipsed by both father and brother, it is he himself who feels like nobody, a feeling no outer change in circumstance will be able to budge. His complex is finally emerging from the dungeons. But for now, the light is too bright.

Logue comes to realize that he has pushed too hard. But Bertie must fail again, this time right after his brother's abdication, standing before the Accession Council at St. James's Palace attempting yet another public address, with portraits of his ancestral predecessors—including Queen Victoria—looking on, this time his first speech as the new monarch. The ensuing breakdown involves confronting his own psychological reality, which is finally peeled away from the pomp and circumstance: "I am not a king. . . . I am not a king." The sober actuality of the new role is too much: a Christmas speech, a coronation, and a perceived future of endless humiliating public addresses. Now the inner man and the outer role must be cleanly separated. Here he hits bottom, but it is the only place from which he might truly rise.

With his defenses shredded and his wound fully exposed, a new humility kicks in. Albert returns to speech therapy by apologizing and presenting Logue with the shilling he owed him from an earlier bet. As his father's head is on the back of the coin, it's as if he's finally allowing the parental complex to fall into Logue's care. The therapist quips: "You're very much your own man, Bertie." With Elizabeth along, the couple has been welcomed into the family apartment. And what unfolds is one of the most gratifying scenes of the film: Logue's wife, Myrtle, to this point unaware of her husband's client, returns unexpectedly to find royalty sipping tea at her dining table. In a finely wrought moment of psychic inversion, Logue becomes anxious and at a loss for words while Albert seems in his element. Logue says gingerly to a startled Myrtle: "I don't think you know . . . King George VI." With the head of the British Empire standing alongside the commoners from the colonies, the dignity and stature of all seems to congeal. Once the king willingly surrenders his psyche to Logue, he begins to find himself.

Events work their way to the inevitable moment when the fledgling king must address the realm at the outbreak of war. The threads now come together in a riveting manner. Logue sets up a room for the two of them, with the microphone in between, telling the monarch to "forget everything else and just say it to me. Say it to me as a friend." Suddenly the two worlds that have unfolded in parallel—this contentiously forged, unlikely bond between two men and the vast ocean of humanity steadily turning their attention to war—meet in a way that allows the king to speak directly and authentically to his people. To this point we have little idea how the king will actually do. For the words to flow, "Bertie and Logue" will need to pull all of the tricks out of their mercurial bag. Astonishingly, as the speech proceeds, the pauses provide openings for all the past moments of their work to enter: the uplifting phrases bond with a glue of expletives, popular songs, and jokes mouthed under every breath. In the gaps where a stammer had torn apart the simplest of sentences what we hear is the resounding echo of soul-making.

Upper and lower find their place and produce a king. The resulting union is punctuated before the film concludes: Logue finally addresses the king as "Your Majesty," Elizabeth concedes and calls Logue "Lionel," and the king acknowledges the man whom history records as present for all of George VI's wartime speeches as "my friend."

Imaginal Objects

to see to touch
to make to buy

ANIMA figures

carved driftwood bark
from the Hudson River

Daniel Mack
objects + workshops

danielmack.com
845.986.7293

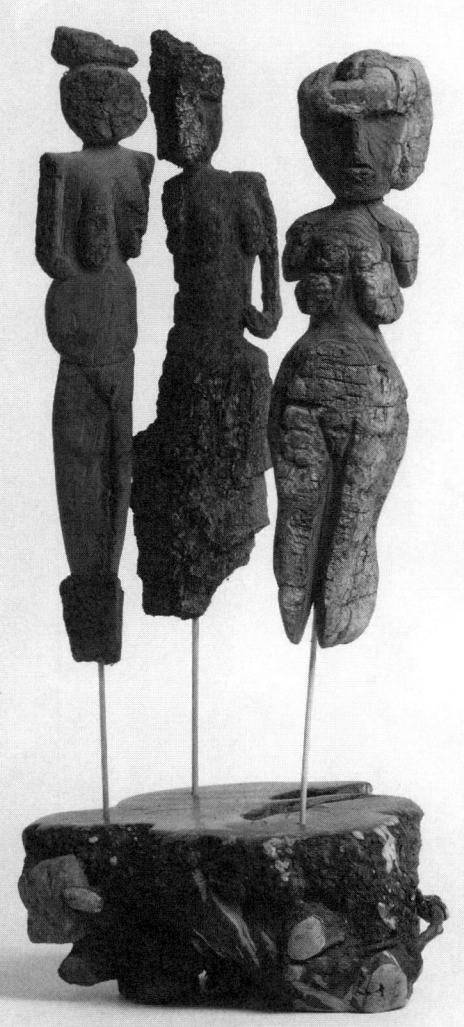

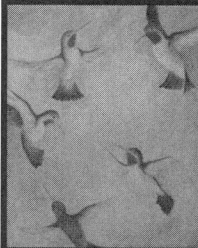

ARCHETYPAL DREAMWORK

WE OFFER:
One-on-One Therapy, Retreats, Workshops, Books, Online Classes

PRESENTATIONS AND WORKSHOPS
CHRISTA LANCASTER AND MARC BREGMAN

St. Ferriol, France, Sept. 2011
Weeklong Retreat

London, UK, Sept. 2011
Evening Presentation

Barcelona, Spain, Sept. 2011
Evening Presentation

New Orleans, LA, Oct. 2011
Presentation with Rodger Kamenetz

Bermuda, Nov. 2011
Evening Presentation & Weekend Workshop

Esalen, Big Sur, CA, Spring 2012
Weeklong Retreat

SUSAN MARIE SCAVO & BILL ST.CYR

One World Festival
Tuscany, Italy, August/September
Week of Presenting

www.northofeden.com • For more information call
Susan Marie Scavo or Bill St.Cyr at 802-229-4785

North of Eden

The Premiere Graduate School for Depth Psychology & Jungian Studies

M.A. & Ph.D. Programs in Depth Psychology, the Humanities, and Mythological Studies

Pacifica Graduate Institute is an accredited graduate school with two campuses in the coastal California foothills south of Santa Barbara. Both campuses offer ideal settings for contemplation and study.

For more information call ☒

☒ **or visit** ☒

Pacifica is accredited by the Western Association of Schools and Colleges (WASC).

- Degree programs informed by the work of C.G. Jung and other noted scholars in the tradition of depth psychology
- An interdisciplinary curriculum
- Monthly three or four-day residential class sessions or a hybrid low-residency/online educational format
- Small, interactive classes that are led by a dedicated faculty

PACIFICA
GRADUATE INSTITUTE
249 Lambert Rd. Carpinteria, CA 93013

NOW ACCEPTING APPLICATIONS FOR FALL 2011

THE 6TH JUNGIAN ODYSSEY

ANNUAL CONFERENCE & RETREAT

VALLEYS OF DESPAIR, MOUNTAINS OF BLISS

Measuring the Forces of Destiny

June 9-16, 2012
Hotel Pax Montana
Flüeli Ranft,
Switzerland

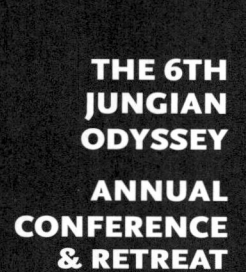

With
Ann Ulanov, PhD
James Hollis, PhD
and Faculty
of ISAPZURICH

INTERNATIONAL SCHOOL OF
ANALYTICAL PSYCHOLOGY ZURICH
AGAP POSTGRADUATE
JUNGIAN TRAINING

www.isapzurich.com
info@jungianodyssey.ch

Spring
A Journal of Archetype and Culture

Spring: A Journal of Archetype and Culture, founded in 1942, is the oldest Jungian psychology journal in the world. Published twice a year, each issue explores from the perspective of depth psychology a theme of contemporary relevance and contains articles as well as book and film reviews. Contributors include Jungian analysts, scholars from a wide variety of disciplines, and cultural commentators.

Upcoming Issues of Spring Journal

VOLUME 86 — FALL 2011
Swiss Culture and Depth Psychology
Guest Editors: Stacy Wirth and Isabelle Meier, Jungian analysts, ISAPZURICH

VOLUME 87 — SPRING 2012
Native American Culture and the Western Psyche
A Bridge Between
Guest Editor: Jerome Bernstein, author of *Living in the Borderland*

VOLUME 88 — FALL 2012
Environmental Disasters and Collective Trauma
Guest Co-Editor: Stephen J. Foster, Ph.D., Jungian analyst and environmental scientist, author of *Risky Business: A Jungian View of Environmental Disasters and the Nature Archetype*

VOLUME 89 — SPRING 2013
Buddhism and Depth Psychology
Refining the Encounter
Guest Editor: Polly Young Eisendrath, Ph.D., Jungian analyst, author, and editor (with Shoji Muramoto) of *Awakening and Insight: Zen Buddhism and Psychotherapy*

Subscribe to Spring Journal!

2 issues (1 year) *within United States* ($35.00)
2 issues (1 year) *foreign airmail* ($54.00)
4 issues (2 years) *within United States* ($60.00)
4 issues (2 years) *foreign airmail* ($100.00)

To order, please visit our online store at:
www.springjournalandbooks.com

Spring Journal, Inc.
627 Ursulines Street, #7 New Orleans, LA 70116 Tel: (504) 524-5117